ETERNAL VIGILANCE

Mathew D. Staver

ETERNAL VIGILANCE

Knowing and Protecting Your Religious Freedom

BROADMAN
&HOLMAN
PUBLISHERS

NASHVILLE, TENNESSEE

Ten-digit ISBN: 0-8054-4000-3
Thirteen-digit ISBN: 978-0-8054-4000-3

Published by Broadman & Holman Publishers,
Nashville, Tennessee

Dewey Decimal Classification: 261.72
Subject Heading: FREEDOM OF RELIGION \
CHRISTIANITY AND POLITICS \ FAITH

Scripture quotations are taken from the New King James
Version (NKJV), copyright © 1979, 1980, 1982, Thomas
Nelson, Inc., Publishers as well as the New American
Standard Bible (NASB), © the Lockman Foundation, 1960,
1962, 1963, 1968, 1971, 1972, 1973, 1975, 1977, 1985;
used by permission.

1 2 3 4 5 6 7 8 9 10   10 09 08 07 06 05

CONTENTS

Contents

ACKNOWLEDGMENTS

A BOOK OF THIS KIND doesn't materialize overnight. Countless hours of research have been spent on this project. However, this book contains much more than mere research; it is born out of real–life experiences. Since founding Liberty Counsel in 1989, I have advanced religious freedom through litigation in numerous courtrooms throughout America. The pages that follow are a result of those experiences.

There are many people I wish to thank for assisting me. I am grateful to the dedicated staff at Liberty Counsel, all of whom are highly talented, sincere Christians who live out their calling with passion each day. Candy McGuire, who for many years has remained faithfully by my side working nearly every position at Liberty Counsel, patiently and meticulously proofread the text and made valuable grammatical suggestions. Annette Stanley spent many hours mastering two different word–processing programs and did a wonderful job editing the footnotes.

Finally, I wish to thank my wife, Anita. As an attorney herself who works by my side every day, she has provided incredible support and inspiration. Our lives and our calling are joined as one. She is a wonderful wife, a respected colleague, and my best friend.

PREFACE

PRIOR TO ENTERING LAW SCHOOL, I was in the pastoral ministry. During my days as a pastor, I was continually confronted with the interaction between church and state. My life began to change when I was invited to a pastors' meeting where a film on abortion was shown. I had no position on the issue but presumed that I favored abortion. After viewing this video about the development of the unborn child, I changed my views and became pro-life. Thereupon I began reading the United States Supreme Court opinion of *Roe v. Wade*,[1] and the more I learned about the abortion, the more I was led to legal issues.

While pastoring, I also became frustrated every year during the Christmas season when one nativity scene after another was challenged in court. These events, among others, formed the background to my law school education. After entering law school and studying constitutional law, I began to realize that there is a great deal of misinformation regarding religious liberty.

---

[1] 410 U.S. 113 (1973).

In 1989, I founded Liberty Counsel in order to provide education and legal defense on religious liberty matters. I have learned that we lose our religious liberties for three primary reasons: (1) ignorance of the law, (2) hostility toward religion, and (3) apathy. Most of the cases in which Liberty Counsel is involved resolve through education. A minority of cases involve someone who is actually hostile toward religion. In this battle over religious liberty, I frequently encounter a great deal of apathy among Christians and people of faith. Most people would rather run than fight and lose their rights rather than struggle for them. Religious liberty is not simply a legal right; it is the ability to continue to spread the gospel in a free nation.

The intent of this book is to provide education in areas of free speech and religious liberty. Education is the best weapon against tyranny. The Constitution did not create civil rights. Our civil liberties predate the Constitution. As the signers of the Declaration of Independence would say, our civil liberties are God-given, "self-evident," "unalienable" rights. The government's sole duty is to protect these rights. It is my hope that this book will play a small part in protecting our precious liberties.

1

RELIGION: AN ENDANGERED SPECIES

AN OBJECTIVE OBSERVER cannot escape the conclusion that America was founded upon Judeo-Christian principles. During his travels in the 1830s, Alexis de Tocqueville stated, "On my arrival in the United States, the religious aspect of the country was the first thing that struck my attention."[1] The early founders of America came here not so much to flee religious persecution but to evangelize a new continent. The first colonial grant from Queen Elizabeth to Sir Walter Raleigh in 1584 was to enact laws provided "they be not against the true Christian faith."[2] The first charter of Virginia by King James in 1606 was to propagate the "Christian religion to such people, [who] as yet live in darkness."[3] One

---

[1]Alexis de Tocqueville, 1 DEMOCRACY IN AMERICA 319 (J. P. Mayer, ed., George Lawrence, trans., Doubleday 1975).
[2]*The Church of the Holy Trinity v. United States,* 143 U.S. 457, 466 (1892).
[3]*Id.*

1

purpose of the Mayflower Compact of 1620 was for the "advancement of the Christian Faith."[4]

The signers of the Declaration of Independence in 1776 clearly acknowledged that they were "endowed by their Creator with certain unalienable Rights." In the same year the Delaware Constitution required the following oath from all officers: "[I] profess faith in God the Father, and in Jesus Christ His only Son, and in the Holy Ghost, one God, blessed forevermore: and I do acknowledge the Holy Scriptures of the Old and New Testament to be given by divine inspiration."[5] The Massachusetts Constitution of 1780 spoke of the "right" and "duty" of all citizens to "worship the Supreme Being."[6] The Maryland Constitution of 1807 spoke of the "duty of every man to worship God," noting that no person could be a witness unless he or she "believes in the existence of God."[7] Likewise, the Mississippi Constitution of 1832 stated that one could not hold state office and deny the "being of God, or a future state of rewards and punishment."[8] Indeed, John Adams once said, "Our Constitution was made only for a moral and religious people. It is wholly inadequate for the government of any other."[9]

Reviewing this history, the United States Supreme Court stated in1892 that "this is a religious nation . . . we are a Christian people," and concluded that "this is a Christian

---

[4] *Id.*

[5] *Id.* at 469.

[6] *Id.*

[7] *Id.*

[8] *Id.*

[9] John Adams (1789), *quoted in* J. HOWE, THE CHANGING POLITICAL THOUGHT OF JOHN ADAMS 189 (1966), *and in* OUR SACRED HONOR 370 (William J. Bennett, ed., Simon & Schuster 1997).

nation."[10] When the Constitutional Convention was about to fall apart, Benjamin Franklin stood up and uttered his famous words: "If a sparrow cannot fall without [God's] notice, is it probable that an empire can rise without His aid?"[11]

George Washington distinguished himself as a great general, representative of Virginia, and the first President of the United States. He did not mince words with his convictions regarding religion when he stated: "Of all the disposition and habits which lead to political prosperity, religion and morality are indispensable supports."[12] Washington also observed: "Whatever may be conceded to the influence of refined education on minds or peculiar structure, reason and experience both forbid us to expect that the national morality can prevail in exclusion of religious principles."[13] He warned: "Let us with caution indulge the supposition, that morality can be maintained without religion."[14] George Washington acknowledged God's intervention during his Inaugural Address on April 30, 1789:

> It would be peculiarly improper to omit, in this first official act, my fervent supplications to that Almighty Being who rules over the universe, who presides in the councils of the nations and whose providential aids can supply every human defect, . . .

---

[10]*The Church of the Holy Trinity,* 143 U.S. at 470–71.

[11]Benjamin Franklin (June 28, 1787), 1 THE RECORDS OF THE FEDERAL CONVENTION OF 1787 451 (Max Farrand ed., revised ed. 1966), *also quoted in* 9 WRITINGS OF BENJAMIN FRANKLIN, 600 (Albert H. Smyth, ed., 1906).

[12]George Washington, Farewell Address (September 17, 1796), *quoted in* Bennett, OUR SACRED HONOR 368 (1997).

[13]*Id. See also* George Washington, Farewell Address (September 17, 1796), *quoted in* William Johnson, GEORGE WASHINGTON THE CHRISTIAN 217–18 (1917).

[14]*Id.*

★ ★ ★

No people can be bound to acknowledge and adore the Invisible Hand which conducts the affairs of men more than the people of the United States.

Every step by which they have advanced to their character of an independent nation seems to have been distinguished by some token of providential agency.[15]

John Quincy Adams, son of John Adams and the sixth U.S. President, once declared that the "highest glory of the American Revolution was this: It connected in one indissoluble bond, the principles of civil government with the principles of Christianity."[16] Interestingly, a House Judiciary report of March 27, 1854, issued the following statement in response to a petition to separate Christian principles from government:

If the people, during the Revolution, had a suspicion of any attempt to war against Christianity, that Revolution would have been strangled in its cradle.

At the time of the adoption of the Constitution and the amendments, the universal sentiment was that Christianity should be encouraged, not any one sect. Any attempt to level and discard all religion would

---

[15]George Washington, Inaugural Address (April 30, 1789), *quoted in* James D. Richardson, 1 A COMPILATION OF THE MESSAGES AND PAPERS OF THE PRESIDENTS, 1789–1897, at 52–53 (1910).

[16]John Quincy Adams (July 4, 1821), *quoted in* THE PULPIT OF THE AMERICAN REVOLUTION XXIX (John Wingate Thornton, ed., Boston, Gould & Lincoln 1860) (Burt Franklin 1970), *also quoted in* William J. Federer, AMERICA'S GOD AND COUNTRY ENCYCLOPEDIA OF QUOTATIONS 18 (1996).

have been viewed with universal indignation. The object was not to substitute Judaism or Mohammedanism, or infidelity, but to prevent rivalry among the Christian sects to the exclusion of others.

[Christianity] must be considered as the foundation on which the whole structure rests. Laws will not have preeminence or power without the sanction of religious sentiment,—without a firm belief that there is a Power above us that will reward our virtues and punish our vices.

In this age there can be no substitute for Christianity: that, in its general principles, is the great conservative element on which we must rely for the purity and permanence of free institutions. That was the religion of the founders of the republic, and they expected it to remain the religion of their descendants.[17]

In May 1854, the Congress of the United States passed a resolution in the House which declared: "A great vital and conservative element in our system is the belief of our people in the pure doctrines and divine truths of the gospel of Jesus Christ."[18] On July 13, 1787, the Continental Congress enacted the Northwest Ordinance which stated: "Religion, morality, and knowledge, being necessary to good government and the happiness of mankind, schools and the means

---

[17]Mr. Meacham's report to the House Committee on the Judiciary (March 27, 1854), *quoted in* B. F. Morris, THE CHRISTIAN LIFE AND CHARACTER OF THE CIVIL INSTITUTIONS OF THE UNITED STATES 320–327 (1864).
[18]*Id.* at 328.

of education shall be forever encouraged."[19] On August 7, 1789, after the final agreement on the wording of the Bill of Rights (which contains the First Amendment), the newly formed Congress reenacted the Northwest Ordinance.[20] On September 25, 1789, Congress unanimously approved a resolution asking President George Washington to proclaim a National Day of Thanksgiving,[21] and then on October 3, 1789, President Washington proclaimed a National Day of Thanksgiving.[22] On June 14, 1954, Congress approved a Joint Resolution which added "under God" to the *Pledge of Allegiance*.[23] Then, on July 30, 1956, Congress, by Joint Resolution, adopted "In God We Trust" as the official national motto.[24]

The Declaration of Independence, unanimously adopted on July 4, 1776, probably contains one of the best outlines for the purpose and place of government. The signers of the Declaration wrote the following:

> When in the Course of human events, it becomes necessary for one people to dissolve the political

---

[19]ORD. OF 1787, art. 3 (July 13, 1787), *reprinted in* DOCUMENTS ILLUSTRATIVE OF THE FORMATION OF THE UNION OF AMERICAN STATES 52 (Charles C. Tansell ed., 1927).

[20]AN ACT TO PROVIDE FOR THE GOVERNMENT OF THE TERRITORY NORTHWEST OF THE RIVER OHIO (NORTHWEST ORDINANCE), ch. 8, 1 Stat. 50–51 (Peter's ed., 1845).

[21]September 25, 1789, Congress recommended a National Day of Thanksgiving, *quoted in* 1 ANNALS OF CONG. 914 (Joseph Gales, ed., 1789).

[22]George Washington, Proclamation (Oct. 3, 1789), *reprinted in* 1 A COMPILATION OF THE MESSAGES AND PAPERS OF THE PRESIDENTS 1789–1907 64 (James D. Richardson, ed., 1908).

[23]H.R.J. Res. 243, 68 Stat. 249 (1954) (codified as amended at 4 U.S.C. § 4 [2002]).

[24]Joint Resolution to Establish a National Motto of the United States, 70 Stat. 732 (1957) (codified in 36 U.S.C. § 302).

bands which have connected them with another, and to assume among the powers of the earth, the separate and equal station of which the Laws of Nature and of Nature's God entitle them, a decent respect to the opinions of mankind requires that they should declare the causes which impel them to the separation.

We hold these truths to be self-evident, that all men are created equal, that they are endowed by their Creator with certain unalienable Rights, that among these are Life, Liberty and the pursuit of Happiness.

That to secure these rights, Governments are instituted among Men, deriving their just powers from the consent of the governed.

That whenever any Form of Government becomes destructive of these ends, it is the Right of the People to alter or to abolish it, and to institute new Government, laying its foundation on such principles and organizing its powers in such form, as to them shall seem most likely to effect their Safety and Happiness. Prudence, indeed, will dictate that Governments long established should not be changed for light and transient causes; and accordingly all experience hath shewn, that mankind are most disposed to suffer, while evils are sufferable, than to right themselves by abolishing the forms to which they are accustomed. But when a long train of abuses and usurpations, pursuing invariably the same Object evinces a design to reduce them under absolute Despotism, it is their right, it is their duty, to throw off such Government, and to provide new Guards for their future security.[25]

---

[25]THE DECLARATION OF INDEPENDENCE para. 1–4 (U.S. 1776).

The signers of the Declaration of Independence understood that there are certain God-given, inalienable rights among which are life, liberty, and the pursuit of happiness. Government does not establish these rights, cannot modify them, and must not infringe upon these liberties. The Constitution did not create these rights. Like the Declaration of Independence, the Constitution recognizes that these liberties predate our country and supersede any form of government. The *sole* purpose of government is to protect these God-given liberties. When any form of government fails to protect these rights, and more particularly, limits these liberties, it is the right of the people, it is their duty, to alter or even abolish that form of government and create a new government which protects these preexisting liberties. Put into perspective, the sole purpose of government is to protect God-given, God-ordained, preexisting liberties. Since these rights come from God, and since the role of government is to protect them, the governmental structure must not disavow God and exclude Him from public life. Politics may not be separated from religion, since politics should protect religion, and religion should stabilize politics.

The Founders did not separate their political lives from their religious beliefs. Indeed, this country was based upon Judeo-Christian principles that permeated society. A burning desire of many early pioneers was to develop a society in which religious freedom could flourish. Many sacrificed everything they accumulated, and some even forfeited their lives. Once the pioneers arrived on the shores of this continent, they staked out crosses and penned in their original charters the conviction that God had led them to a new world to spread the gospel of Jesus Christ.

Society has changed since those early days. After becoming comfortable with their new freedom, many mainline religions became infected by liberal theology. Some religious leaders forsook the gospel and searched for a historical Jesus whom they could not find. Some churches became socially oriented and neglected the very heart of the gospel. They lost the gospel through their liberal interpretation of the Bible—no longer believing in the resurrection of Jesus Christ, in miracles, or in the changing power of the gospel other than through psychology. However, some Christians became repulsed by the liberal trends brewing within the American church. These people shied away from the culture and began to focus on personal piety. This backlash resulted in the age of pietism, wherein the individual relationship with God was emphasized to the neglect of society. The pendulum thus swung to the opposite end of extremism.

During the era of pietism, many Christians, fed up with liberal denominations, withdrew from society and public influence, believing association with any social agenda was evil. As these Christians abandoned society, what remained were secularists in places of public influence, or so-called religionists who forgot their religious roots. The pietistic Christians and the liberal secularists were content to stuff God in a box. God had His own corner reserved within the church; he was hidden within the communion chalice.

This country is moving toward secularism at its peril. We have already begun to accept the idea that where government increases, religion must decrease. Some people adopt the presumption that government and religion mix like oil and water—that where government treads, religion must flee.

Paul Blanshard, a secular humanist writing in *The Humanist* magazine, once noted that the first seventy-five years of the twentieth century have been "a good seventy-five years, full of rebellion against religious superstition, inspired by developing science, and increasingly open to religious realism."[26] He also stated, "I doubt that any span in human history has carried the world farther along the road to honest doubt."[27] Mr. Blanshard noted that his "primary hero" in moving this nation to a secular society was the United States Supreme Court.

Reviewing the first seventy-five years of the twentieth century and the United States Supreme Court's impact on public education, Mr. Blanshard concluded:

> I think the most important factor moving us toward a secular society has been the educational factor. *Our schools may not teach Johnny to read properly, but the fact that Johnny is in school until he is sixteen tends to lead toward the elimination of religious superstition.* The average American child now acquires a high school education, and this militates against Adam and Eve and all other myths of alleged history. . . . I am convinced that religious belief of millions of Americans is only nominal. It is warm-hearted service religion, not creedal religion. When I was one of the editors of *The Nation* in the twenties, I wrote an editorial explaining that golf and intelligence were the

---

[26]Paul Blanshard, *Three Cheers for Our Secular State*, THE HUMANIST, Mar.–Apr. 1976, at 17.
[27]*Id.*

two primary reasons that men did not attend church. Perhaps I would now say golf and a high school diploma.[28]

Mr. Blanshard continued to describe the engine driving this country toward secularism:

> Indeed, *one of the factors moving this country toward a secularist society is the combination of the United States Supreme Court and public schools.* Originally the United States Supreme Court had no jurisdiction over First Amendment issues because the First Amendment only applied to restrict the activities of the federal government. The First Amendment was not applicable to the individual states until the 1940s when the Supreme Court said it was applicable to the states.[29]

In the early 1960s, the Supreme Court, using the First Amendment, struck down school-sponsored prayer[30] and Bible readings[31] in public school. The High Court pointed to testimony at trial which suggested that Bible reading could be "psychologically harmful" to children.[32] In 1980, the Supreme Court ripped the Ten Commandments from a

---

[28]*Id.* (emphasis added).

[29]*Id.* (emphasis added). The First Amendment Free Exercise Clause was first applied to the states in 1940 and the Establishment Clause was first applied to the states in 1947. *See Cantwell v. Connecticut,* 310 U.S. 296 (1940) (Free Exercise Clause); *Everson v. Board of Educ.,* 330 U.S. 1 (1947) (Establishment Clause); *Illinois ex rel. McCollum v. Board of Educ.,* 333 U.S. 203 (1948) (same).

[30]*Engel v. Vitale,* 370 U.S. 421 (1962).

[31]*School Dist. of Abington Township v. Schempp,* 374 U.S. 203 (1963).

[32]*Id.*

classroom bulletin board in the state of Kentucky.[33] One state court addressing the issue of prayers in public schools lamented:

> An unacceptably high number of citizens who are undergoing difficult times in this country are children and young people. School-sponsored prayer might provide hope to sustain them and principles to guide them in the difficult choices they confront today. But the Constitution as the Supreme Court views it does not permit it. Choices are made in order to protect the interest of all citizens. Unfortunately, in this instance there is no satisfactory middle ground. . . . Those who are anti-prayer thus have been deemed the victors. This is the difficult but obligatory choice this court makes today.[34]

The Supreme Court's "separationist" interpretation of the First Amendment tends to wax and wane from generation to generation. The Supreme Court will probably never return to its pre-1940 interpretation when the First Amendment restricted *only* the federal government from establishing a national church and from prohibiting the free exercise of religion within the sovereign states. The problem in moving away from the original intent of the First Amendment is that there has been no consistent jurisprudential approach to interpreting the Constitution. This is due, in part, to the Court treating the Constitution as a piece of clay which is molded by majority vote. However, within the myriad, ever-changing Supreme

---

[33]*Stone v. Graham,* 449 U.S. 39 (1980).
[34]*Bennett v. Livermore Unified Sch. Dist.,* 238 Cal. Rptr. 819 (1987).

Court interpretations, many religious liberty rights still remain. This book is intended to be a guide to those liberties.

This country must continue to remain free and must recognize the importance of protecting religious freedom. Once religion is suffocated or stuffed in a box, this country will certainly fail. The history of the former Soviet Union should teach the United States a lesson. For many years, religion was found mostly in churches turned into museums. However, religious belief and practice continued to operate underground. When the Soviet Communist government failed, the faithful rebounded and now religion flourishes within Russia. At one time Madalyn Murray O'Hair, the atheist who removed Bible readings from school, wanted to defect to the Soviet Union so that she could live in a country run by atheistic principles. She lost her desire to defect after some of the decisions by the United States Supreme Court in the 1960s began to secularize America. We must never take religious liberty for granted. Freedom was bought by sacrifice, and it's about time we defend our God-given liberty.

2
GENERAL CONSTITUTIONAL PRINCIPLES

RELIGION IN THE PUBLIC SQUARE is becoming an endangered species. I am not an alarmist or an extremist, but I am alarmed by attempts to cleanse religion from the public square.

Something needs to be done to protect people of faith from insidious discrimination. We are appalled by the human rights violations in China and elsewhere. Indeed we should be. Yet in this country public school students are reprimanded every day for expressing their faith. Students are made to feel that their faith is something to be avoided like the plague, something that must be left at home, and something that is inherently evil. The public must be better informed regarding religious liberty. The courts need to be more hospitable to people of faith.

Christians and people of faith are not asking for special privileges. However, religious expression must at least be afforded an equal playing field. Currently, the playing field is not level. Religious expression and practices are often treated as second-class speech and singled out for discrimination. I am not asking for a Christianized America, but people of faith should have an opportunity to express their religious beliefs equal to those who express nontheistic views.

The History of the First Amendment

To understand the present, we must first consider the past. Justice Oliver Wendell Holmes' statement is apropos: "A page of history is worth a volume of logic."[1] "The line we must draw between the permissible and impermissible is one which accords with history and faithfully reflects the understanding of the Founding Fathers."[2] "Government policies of accommodation, acknowledgment, and support for religion are an accepted part of our political and cultural heritage."[3] The best interpretation of the First Amendment is one that is "illuminated by history."[4] The United States Supreme Court has noted the following in this respect:

> In applying the First Amendment to the states through the Fourteenth Amendment . . . it would be incongruous to interpret that clause as imposing more stringent First Amendment limits on the states

---

[1]*New York Trust Co. v. Eisner,* 256 U.S. 345, 349 (1921).
[2]*School Dist. of Abington Township of Pa. v. Schempp,* 374 U.S. 203, 294 (1963) (Brennan, J., concurring).
[3]*County of Allegheny v. American Civil Liberties Union,* 492 U.S. 573, 657 (1989) (Kennedy. J., concurring in part and dissenting in part).
[4]*Lynch v. Donnelly,* 465 U.S. 668, 678 (1984) (citing *Walz v. Tax Comm'n,* 397 U.S. 664, 671 (1970)).

than the draftsmen imposed upon the Federal Government.[5]

The historical setting of the First Amendment should often be reviewed to ensure that court interpretations "comport with what history reveals was the contemporaneous understanding of its guarantees."[6] The Supreme Court recognizes "that religion has been closely identified with our history and our government."[7] The history of this country "is inseparable from the history of religion."[8] When adopted, the First Amendment prohibited the federal government from coercively intruding into religion. Interpreting the First Amendment consistent with history would certainly do a great deal to bring uniformity and reason back to constitutional jurisprudence. On occasion, the courts use history as part of their interpretation, and on other occasions, the courts simply ignore history. Despite these inconsistencies, there still remain clear constitutional decisions by which to guide religious liberty.

Although it may come as a surprise to some, history reveals that Christopher Columbus came to this continent not to flee persecution or for mere exploration, but because he believed God led him to our shores to spread the gospel.[9] Later the Puritans left England because they too were impressed that God was leading them to carry the gospel to foreign territories. Consistent with this history, public schools

---

[5]*Marsh v. Chambers,* 463 U.S. 783, 790–91 (1983).
[6]*Lynch,* 465 U.S. at 673; *see also Committee for Public Educ. and Religious Liberty v. Nyquist,* 413 U.S. 756 (1973); *Walz v. Tax Comm'n,* 397 U.S. 664 (1970); *Marsh,* 463 U.S. at 783.
[7]*Abington Township,* 374 U.S. at 212.
[8]*Engel v. Vitale,* 370 U.S. 421, 434 (1962).
[9]Peter Marshall & David Manual, THE LIGHT AND THE GLORY 29–48 (1977).

taught the principles of Christianity and were established in order to teach children how to read the Bible.[10]

After the original thirteen colonies declared independence from Great Britain in 1776, they considered forming a limited federal government for the primary purpose of national security. In order to "secure the blessings of liberty" for future generations, the colonies adopted the Constitution of the United States in 1787. The Constitution established a federal government with very limited and prescribed authority. It set forth three branches of government: the executive (to carry out the laws), the legislative (to enact the laws and be accountable to the people), and the judicial (to interpret the laws). At that time the Judicial was the weakest of the three branches.

The thirteen colonies were concerned that the new federal government would infringe upon the authority of the individual states by imposing federal bureaucracy into the state system. The colonies wanted to create a limited federal power that would serve the will of the individual sovereign states. They did not want to lose their identity to a national government. To accomplish this goal, in 1789 the first ten amendments (the Bill of Rights) were drafted and later adopted by the colonies on December 15, 1791. The First Amendment, which pertains to religious liberty, states, "Congress shall make no law respecting an establishment of religion, or prohibiting the free exercise thereof." These amendments were written for the

---

[10]The first compulsory education law was adopted by the Massachusetts colony in 1647. Commonly referred to as "The Old Deluder Satan Act," the law mandated universal education in order to teach people how to read the Scriptures ("It being one chief project of that old deluder, Satan, to keep men from the knowledge of the Scriptures.") See COLONIAL ORIGINS OF THE AMERICAN CONSTITUTION: A DOCUMENTARY HISTORY 129 (Donald S. Lutz, ed., Liberty Fund, 1998).

express purpose of limiting the authority of the federal government. The Tenth Amendment reaffirms this limitation when it states that any authority not specifically granted to the federal government was reserved solely for the individual states.

The First Amendment explicitly prohibited the federal government from establishing a national church and from prohibiting the free exercise of religion within the states.[11] The federal government had absolutely no jurisdiction over religious matters within the states. If a state established a state-sponsored church or religion, the federal government had no authority to promote or inhibit the practice of religion within the state. Indeed, as late as the Revolutionary War, there were established churches in at least eight of the thirteen colonies and established religions in at least four of the other five.[12] The individual states were regulated by their own constitutions or legislative actions, not by the federal government, and certainly not by the United States Supreme Court.

As the first act of the Continental Congress in 1774, the Reverend Mister Duche's opened with prayer and read from Psalm 31.[13] From its inception Congress has begun its

---

[11]John Eidsmoe, The Christian Legal Advisor 97–164 (1984).

[12]*Engel v. Vitale,* 370 U.S. 421, 427–48 (1962).

[13]Mr. Duche's prayer was as follows:

Be Thou present O God of Wisdom and direct the council of this honorable assembly; enable them to settle all things on the best and surest foundations; that the scene of blood may be speedily closed; that order, harmony, and peace may be effectually restored, and truth and justice, religion and piety, prevail and flourish among the people. Preserve the health of their bodies, and the vigor of their minds, shower down on them, and the millions they represent, such temporal blessings as Thou seest expedient for them in this world, and crown them with everlasting glory in the world to come. All this we ask in the name and through the merits of Jesus Christ Thy Son and our Saviour. Amen.

sessions with an invocation by a paid chaplain.[14] Courts have historically opened their daily proceedings with the invocation, "God save the United States and this Honorable Court."[15] Even the United States Supreme Court has Moses and the Ten Commandments inscribed above the bench, recognizing the biblical foundations of our legal heritage.[16]

George Washington began the tradition of taking the presidential oath of office upon the Bible. When he assumed office in 1789, he stated: "It would be peculiarly improper to omit in this first official act my fervent supplications to that Almighty Being who rules over the Universe."[17] Indeed, Washington added the phrase at the end of the presidential oath, "So help me God." After Washington, every president has invoked the protection and help of Almighty God.[18]

James Madison, was a member of the congressional committee that recommended the chaplaincy system.[19] Madison voted for the bill authorizing payment of chaplains.[20] Rev. William Lynn was elected chaplain of the House of Representatives and paid $500 from the federal treasury.

On September 25, 1789, the day the final agreement was made on the Bill of Rights, the House requested that President

---

[14]*Marsh,* 463 U.S. at 787–89. *See Lynch,* 465 U.S. at 673–74.

[15]*Marsh,* 463 U.S. at 786.

[16]*See Lynch,* 465 U.S. at 677.

[17]*Engel,* 370 U.S. at 446 (Stewart, J., dissenting).

[18]*Id.* at 446–49. *See generally* William J. Federer, A TREASURY OF PRESIDENTIAL QUOTATIONS (1996) (containing quotations referencing God from every American President beginning with George Washington).

[19]H. R. Rep. No. 124, 33rd Cong., 1st Sess. (1789), *reprinted in* 2 No. 2 REPORTS OF COMMITTEES OF THE HOUSE OF REPRESENTATIVES 4 (1854). *See also Buckley v. Valeo,* 424 U.S. 1, 686 n.165 (1976) (House rule on electing chaplain dates to 1789).

[20]1 ANNALS OF CONG. 891 (J. Gales ed., 1834).

Washington proclaim a day of Thanksgiving to acknowledge "the many signal favors of Almighty God."[21] He proclaimed November 26, 1789, a day of Thanksgiving to offer "our prayers and supplications to the great Lord and ruler of nations, and beseech Him to pardon our national and other transgressions."[22] Later President Madison issued four Thanksgiving Day proclamations on July 9, 1812; July 23, 1813; November 16, 1814; and March 4, 1815.[23] Successive presidents have continued this tradition.

In 1892 the United States Supreme Court considered the case of *The Church of the Holy Trinity v. United States.*[24] In that case, the Supreme Court unanimously held that a congressional statute forbidding the immigration of persons under contract to perform labor did not apply to an English minister who entered this country under a contract to preach at a New York church. After reviewing extensive legislative history, the Court concluded:

> But beyond all these matters no purpose of action against religion can be imputed against any legislation, state or national, because this is a religious people. This is historically true. From the discovery of this continent to the present hour, there is a single voice making this affirmation. . . . If we pass beyond these matters to a view of American life as expressed by its laws, its business, its customs and its society, we find everywhere a clear recognition of the same

---

[21]H. R. JOUR., 1st Cong., 1st Sess. 123 (1826 ed.); S. JOUR., 1st Cong., 1st Sess. 88 (1820 ed.); *Lynch,* 465 U.S. at 675 n.2.
[22]*Lynch,* 465 U.S. at 675 n.2.
[23]R. Cord, SEPARATION OF CHURCH & STATE 31 (1982).
[24]143 U.S. 457 (1892).

truth. . . . These, and many other matters which might be noticed, add a volume of unofficial declarations to the mass of organic utterances that this is a Christian nation.[25]

In 1875 Senator James Blaine, later a Republican candidate for president in 1884, introduced a resolution for a constitutional amendment that read:

No State shall make any law respecting an establishment of religion or prohibiting the free exercise thereof; and no money raised by taxation in any state for the support of public school or derived from any public fund therefor, nor any public land devoted thereto, shall ever be under the control of any religious sect or denomination; nor shall any money so raised or lands so devoted be divided between religious sects or denominations.[26]

This amendment was never added to the Constitution because it did not receive two-thirds majority vote of the Senate.

The first part of the Blaine Amendment is identical to the present First Amendment except that it replaces the word *Congress* with *State*. The debates indicate that this amendment would, for the first time, limit the authority of the states in religious matters; whereas previously, only the federal government had been prohibited from acting in state religious matters. During these debates Senator Stevenson stated:

---

[25]*Id.* at 465–71.
[26]Alfred W. Meyer, *The Blaine Amendment and the Bill of Rights,* 64 HARV. L. REV. 939 (1951).

Friend as he was of religious freedom, [Thomas Jefferson] would never have consented that the states, which brought the Constitution into existence, upon whose sovereignty this instrument rests, which keep it within its expressly limited powers, could be degraded in that the government of the United States, a government of limited authority, the mere agent of the state with prescribed powers, should undertake to take possession of their schools and of their religion.[27]

The issue did not die with the failure of the Blaine Amendment. In 1937 Senator Borah attempted a similar amendment which also failed for lack of two-thirds vote.[28] However, what the legislature failed to do for lack of support, and what the thirteen colonies specifically feared, eventually came to pass in 1940. The year 1940 marks a drastic departure from the intent and purpose of the First Amendment and begins a totally new era in our legal history. The First Amendment was specifically designed, and until 1940 was properly interpreted, to keep the federal government out of religious issues within the states. In other words, since the federal government only had authority to act where the colonies so granted, and the First Amendment specifically stated that the federal government had no authority in matters of religion, the federal government had no jurisdiction to act on religious matters within the states.

---

[27]4 CONG. REC. 5589 (1876). *See also* William K. Lietzau, *Rediscovering the Establishment Clause: Federalism and the Rollback of Incorporation*, DePaul L. Rev., Summer 1990, at 1234 n.103 (quoting Senator Stevenson during the Blaine Amendment debate).
[28]S.J. Res. 92, 75th Cong., 1st Sess. (1937).

In 1940 the United States Supreme Court ignored the historical context of the First Amendment and applied the First Amendment Free Exercise Clause to the states in the case of *Cantwell v. Connecticut.*[29] Then, in 1947, the Supreme Court applied the First Amendment Establishment Clause to the states in *Everson v. Board of Education.*[30] In my view, the Court has incorrectly applied the First Amendment to the states by application of the Fourteenth Amendment.[31] Now, instead of the First Amendment erecting a barrier against the federal government at the state border, it has been interpreted to create a bridge to allow the federal government to intrude on state matters pertaining to religion. Tossing aside the original understanding of the First Amendment and the volumes of history which document the religious liberty concerns of our founders, the Supreme Court, in the 1989 case of *County of Allegheny v. American Civil Liberties Union,*[32] stated that the purpose of the First Amendment was to mandate that the government remain secular. Over the years, the Supreme Court's understanding of the Constitution has moved from encouragement, to neutrality, to mandating secularism.

Even more amazing than the United States Supreme Court misinterpreting the First Amendment is the fact that there was very little public outcry denouncing its action. Since 1940, the Supreme Court has prohibited schools from composing a prayer

---

[29]310 U.S. 296 (1940).
[30]330 U.S. 1 (1947).
[31]The Fourteenth Amendment was adopted in 1868. Congressional debates on the Blaine Amendment in 1875 reveal that the intent of the Fourteenth Amendment was not to incorporate application of the First Amendment to the individual states.
[32]492 U.S. 573 (1989).

to recite before class,[33] prohibited the use of the Lord's Prayer in public schools,[34] and stripped the Ten Commandments from the classroom bulletin board.[35] The Court has also struck down an Arkansas statute that restricted the teaching of evolution by reasoning that the statute had a religious purpose.[36]

Since the Court ignored the clear meaning of the First Amendment and failed to appreciate the Judeo-Christian foundation of the Constitution, the Court has been forced to invent minute distinctions in order to rationalize its unpredictable rulings. For example, in 1989 the Court ruled that a nativity scene was unconstitutional but a Jewish menorah was constitutional.[37] Though the Court has upheld the constitutionality of other nativity scenes, the Court reasoned in the *County of Allegheny* case that the nativity scene there violated the First Amendment because it was at the dominant entrance to the county courthouse. The menorah was held constitutional because it was at a different location on the city property and was closer to the other secular symbols of Christmas such as a Christmas tree. The Court suggested that if the nativity scene had been closer in proximity to the Christmas tree, then it would have been constitutional. This nit-picking has no legal basis in the Constitution. The Court has created its own authority and its own quagmire; unfortunately, religious freedom suffers as a result.

The Constitution that was intended to secure religious freedom, in the hands of decision makers devoid of absolutes,

---

[33]*Engel,* 370 U.S. at 421.
[34]*Abington Township* 374 U.S. at 203.
[35]*Stone v. Graham,* 449 U.S. 39 (1980).
[36]*Epperson v. Arkansas,* 393 U.S. 97 (1968).
[37]*County of Allegheny,* 492 U.S. at 573.

has become the document that often restricts religious freedom. Although history clearly indicates that the First Amendment was never meant to apply to the states, the Supreme Court is unlikely to change its interpretation of the First Amendment, which has remained constant since 1940. A federal judge in Alabama ruled that he was unable to decide a First Amendment case because federal courts had no jurisdiction over state religious matters in that the First Amendment was never meant to be applicable to the states.[38] According to Judge Hand, since the First Amendment did not apply to the individual states, the states were free to establish their own religion, and the federal government could not prevent this practice.[39] Judge Hand's decision was quickly and succinctly overruled by the court of appeals, which held that it did not matter how the judge viewed the history of the First Amendment—the First Amendment was applicable to the states because the Supreme Court said it was, and federal courts must follow court precedent.[40] The federal appeals court indicated that federal "district courts and circuit courts are bound to adhere to the controlling decisions of the Supreme Court."[41] The appeals court also noted that if the federal courts did not follow the precedent of the United States Supreme Court, anarchy would occur, and therefore, the United States Supreme Court's decisions "must be followed by the lower federal courts no matter how misguided

---

[38]*Jaffree v. Board of Sch. Comm'rs*, 554 F. Supp. 1104, 1128 (S.D. Ala. 1983), *rev'd*, 705 F.2d 1526 (11th Cir. 1983), *aff'd sub nom.*, *Wallace v. Jaffree*, 472 U.S. 38 (1985).
[39]*Id.*
[40]*Jaffree*, 705 F.2d at 1535–36.
[41]*Id.* at 1532 (citing *Hutto v. Davis*, 454 U.S. 370, 375 (1982)).

the judges of those courts may think it to be."[42] Once the case made its way to the United States Supreme Court, the Court ruled that the states "have no greater power to restrain the individual freedoms protected by the First Amendment than does the Congress of the United States."[43] The Supreme Court then reiterated that it believed the First Amendment became applicable to the individual states after the adoption of the Fourteenth Amendment to the United States Constitution in 1868.[44] It is now assumed, without critical analysis, that the First Amendment is applicable to the individual states through the Fourteenth Amendment.

We have in many ways moved from the First Amendment's intent to create religious prosperity and freedom to the allegation that the First Amendment is designated to mandate "that the government remain secular."[45] History certainly does not confirm the idea that the First Amendment was intended to make government secular but instead supports the proposition that the First Amendment was meant to create religious prosperity—prohibiting government from intruding into religious matters but allowing religion to flourish in the public square. Indeed, Justice Joseph Story, who served on the Supreme Court from 1811 to 1845, noted the following about the First Amendment:

> Probably, at the time of the adoption of the Constitution, and of the amendment to it, now under consideration, the general, if not the universal, sentiment

---

[42]*Id.* at 1532 (citing *Davis,* 454 U.S. at 375).
[43]*Wallace v. Jaffree,* 472 U.S. 38, 48–49 (1985).
[44]*Id.* at 48–56.
[45]*Id.* at 610.

in America was, that Christianity ought to receive encouragement from the State, so far as such encouragement was not incompatible with the private rights of conscience, and the freedom of religious worship.[46]

The often-quoted expression of Thomas Jefferson regarding the "wall of separation between church and state"[47] has become so popular that many people believe these words are in the Constitution. However, this phrase is not in the Constitution. In fact, Thomas Jefferson was in France at the time the First Amendment was drafted. Jefferson rejected the notion that there should be no interaction between church and state. On three occasions President Jefferson signed into law federal land grants specifically to promote proselytizing among native American Indians.[48] In 1803 President Jefferson proposed to the United States Senate a treaty with the Kaskaskia Indians in which the federal government was to "give annually for seven years one hundred dollars towards the support of a priest" and "further give the sum of three hundred dollars to assist the said tribe in the erection of a church."[49] The treaty was ratified on December 23, 1803, and at Jefferson's request, it included an appropriation for a Catholic Mission.

---

[46]Joseph Story, 2 COMMENTARIES ON THE CONSTITUTION OF THE UNITED STATES 593 (1833).

[47]8 WORKS OF THOMAS JEFFERSON 113 (Paul Leicester Ford ed., G.P. Putnam, 1904).

[48]R. Cord, SEPARATION OF CHURCH & STATE, 41–46 (1982).

[49]A Treaty between the United States of America in the Kaskaskia Tribe of Indians, Aug. 13, 1803, art. III, 7 Stat. 78–79. *See also* J. Clifford Wallace, *The Framers' Establishment Clause: How High the Wall?*, 2001 B.Y.U. L. REV. 755, 766 n.98–101 (discussing the religious purpose of various treaties).

Moreover, Thomas Jefferson was the first president of the District of Columbia School Board. There the Bible and the Watts Hymnal were used as primary textbooks.[50] As the founder of the University of Virginia, Jefferson believed that religious instruction was important to a proper education. In fact, he stated: "The want of instruction in the various creeds of religious faith existing among our citizens presents, therefore, a chasm in the general institution of the useful sciences."[51]

On July 13, 1787, the Continental Congress enacted the Northwest Ordinance which provided: "Religion, morality, and knowledge being essential to good government and the happiness of mankind, schools and the means of education shall be forever encouraged."[52] On August 7, 1789, after the final agreement on the wording of the Bill of Rights, the newly formed Congress reenacted the Northwest Ordinance.[53]

History is a good teacher in determining the intent of the First Amendment. The amendment was not intended to erect an impregnable wall between church and state. Indeed, our national motto declares, "In God We Trust."[54] Not only our currency but also our national anthem contains the national

---

[50] J. Wilson, *Public Schools of Washington, in* 1 RECORDS OF THE COLUMBIA HISTORICAL SOCIETY 4 (1897).

[51] *Illinois ex rel. McCollum v. Board of Educ.*, 333 U.S. 203, 245–46 (1948) (Reed, J., dissenting) (citing 19 THE WRITINGS OF THOMAS JEFFERSON 414–17 (Memorial ed. 1904)).

[52] ORD. OF 1787, art. III (July 13, 1787), *reprinted in* DOCUMENTS ILLUSTRATIVE OF THE FORMATION OF THE UNION OF AMERICAN STATES at 52 (Charles C. Tansell ed., 1927).

[53] AN ACT TO PROVIDE FOR THE GOVERNMENT OF THE TERRITORY NORTHWEST OF THE RIVER OHIO (NORTHWEST ORDINANCE), ch. 8, 1 Stat. 50–51 (Peter's ed. 1845).

[54] Joint Resolution to Establish a National Motto of the United States, 70 Stat. 732 (1957) (codified in 36 U.S.C. § 302).

motto.[55] Since 1954 the Pledge of Allegiance has contained the words "One nation *under God*."[56] An objective observer "cannot look at even this brief resume without finding that our history is pervaded by expressions of religious beliefs."[57] As the United States Supreme Court has recognized, the "real object" of the First Amendment was "to prevent any national ecclesiastical establishment, which should give to an hierarchy the exclusive patronage of the national government."[58]

Governmental Action

When determining whether an individual has a constitutional right under the First Amendment, or any other provision in the Bill of Rights, it is important to note how these constitutional provisions are applied. In reference to the First Amendment, it is important to note that this Amendment has two Religion Clauses. The first clause is known as the Establishment Clause, which states: "Congress shall make no law respecting the Establishment of religion." The second clause, known as the Free Exercise Clause, completes the Religion Clauses by stating: "or prohibit the free exercise thereof." The entire First Amendment states as follows:

> Congress shall make no law respecting an establishment of religion, or prohibiting the free exercise thereof, or abridging the freedom of speech, or of the

---

[55]*Engel,* 370 U.S. at 440, 449.

[56]H.R.J. Res. 243, 68 Stat. 249 (1954) (codified as amended at 4 U.S.C. § 4 (2002)).

[57]*Lynch,* 465 U.S. at 677.

[58]*Id.* at 678 (quoting 3 Joseph Story, COMMENTARIES ON THE CONSTITUTION OF THE UNITED STATES 728 (1833)).

press, or the right of the people peacefully to assemble, and to petition the Government for a redress of grievances.[59]

The First Amendment is meant to protect individuals from government intrusion. Therefore, it provides liberty to individuals and restraint on the government. In order for the First Amendment to be applicable to any situation, two factors must be involved: (1) a person[60] and (2) some form of governmental action.[61] Only a governmental entity is prohibited from establishing a religion, and only a governmental entity is prohibited from restricting the free exercise of religion.

A classic example of how the Constitution works is illustrated by the difference between a public and a private school. A public school is a governmental entity and, therefore, is prohibited by the Establishment Clause from establishing a religion. As a governmental entity, the public school is also prohibited from restricting the free exercise of religion. On the other hand, a private school can promote or proselytize in religious matters without any governmental interference, and no matter how offensive the promotion or establishment of a religion may be to an individual, the First Amendment has no application to a private school. A private Christian school can require mandatory chapel every day and may also prohibit the distribution of religious literature. However, a public school would violate the Establishment Clause by requiring

---

[59]U.S. CONST. amend. I.
[60]Since corporations are considered legal persons, they can bring First Amendment claims.
[61]Governmental actors include federal and state government, as well as political subdivisions such as cities, counties, and public school boards.

mandatory chapel every day and would violate the Free Exercise and Free Speech Clauses by prohibiting the distribution of religious literature.[62] A public school could not compel a Jehovah's Witness to salute the flag because to do so would violate the student's free exercise of religion.[63] A private Christian school could compel a student to salute the flag.

In summary, there must be some governmental action for the Establishment Clause, the Free Speech Clause, or the Free Exercise Clause to apply in any given situation. Without governmental action, there is no application of the First Amendment.

Public Forum Doctrine

Throughout this book you will be confronted by the terms "traditional public forum," "limited or designated public forum," and "nonpublic forum." These terms are important in order to determine First Amendment free speech rights. In order to ascertain what limits, if any, may be imposed on free speech rights, the United States Supreme Court has "often focused on the place of that speech, considering the nature of the forum the speaker seeks to employ."[64] The United States Supreme Court has stated:

Public places are of necessity the locus for discussion of public issues, as well as protest against

---

[62]*See* John F. Nowak et al., CONSTITUTIONAL LAW 421–48 (3d ed. 1986).
[63]*West Virginia Bd. of Educ. v. Barnette,* 319 U.S. 624 (1943) (invalidating compulsory flag salute statute challenged by religious objectors).
[64]*Frisby v. Schultz,* 487 U.S. 474, 479 (1988); *see also Heffron v. ISKCON,* 452 U.S. 640 (1981).

arbitrary government action. At the heart of our jurisprudence lies the principle that in a free nation citizens must have the right to gather and speak with other persons in public places. The recognition that certain government-owned property is a public forum provides open notice to citizens that their freedoms may be exercised there without fear of a censorial government, adding tangible reinforcement to the idea that we are a free people.[65]

The "public forum doctrine is [designed] to give effect to the broad command of the First Amendment to protect speech from governmental interference."[66] There are three categories of public forums best described as follows: (1) traditional— defined as parks, streets, or sidewalks that have been held in trust for the use of the public and for purposes of assembly, communicating thoughts between citizens, and discussing public questions; (2) designated or limited—which is created when the government intentionally opens public property for use by the public for assembly, speech, or other expressive activities; and (3) nonpublic—which exists when the government does not designate public property for indiscriminate expression by the public at large, by certain speakers, or by certain subjects. Generally the standard of review for a traditional, limited, or designated public forum is a strict or intermediate scrutiny test; whereas, in a nonpublic forum the rational basis or reasonable nexus test is used. For the government to limit the *content* of speech in a traditional, limited, or designated

---

[65]*ISKCON v. Lee*, 505 U.S. 672, 696 (1992).
[66]*Id.* at 697.

public forum, it must show a *compelling* interest, and any restriction must be *narrowly* tailored to achieve that interest; while in a nonpublic forum the government must show a *reasonable* basis for the restriction. Time, place, and manner restrictions must be *content-neutral,* narrowly tailored to serve a significant government interest, and must leave open ample alternative channels of expression.[67] Content-neutral regulations are those that are "justified without reference to the content of the regulated speech."[68] A classic example of a content-neutral restriction is a time limit placed on parades. A governmental entity may limit parades to a certain time in order to avoid rush-hour traffic. This time restriction would be permissible so long as it was content-neutral and, therefore, applicable to all parades without exception. However, time, place, and manner restrictions may not be so stringent so as to effectively preclude use of the forum. For example, it would be impermissible to require a parade to be held only at midnight.

Traditional public forums consist only of public parks, streets, and sidewalks. These types of public property have immemorially been left open for expressive activity allowing citizens to assemble and communicate. The property by nature is considered a traditional public forum and cannot be closed to public use. A designated or limited public forum is one where the government intentionally opens up the public facility for use by the community. Examples include a public library where outside organizations can meet in various

---

[67] *See, e.g., Perry Educ. Ass'n v. Perry Local Educators' Ass'n,* 460 U.S. 37 (1983).
[68] *Virginia State Bd. of Pharmacy v. Virginia Citizens Consumer Council,* 425 U.S. 748, 771 (1976).

rooms, public school facilities used after hours by outside community organizations, and any other facility open to the public for expressive activity. Once the designated or limited public forum is open to the public, the same strict scrutiny standard used for the traditional public forum is applied. The main difference between this classification and a traditional public forum is that a traditional public forum, by the nature of the property, is always open to the public. A designated public forum need not be open and at any time can be closed so long as the closure of the property is done on a nondiscriminatory basis. For example, a public school could close its facilities to all groups in the community. A public library could prohibit all outsiders from using the facilities other than for checking out and reading books. However, a public school or public library cannot close its facilities only to religious but not secular speech, because to do so would discriminate on the content or viewpoint of the speech and would violate the First Amendment. Finally, an example of a nonpublic forum is an airport, but even in a public airport, all First Amendment activity cannot be prohibited.

Commenting on the traditional and designated or limited public forums, the Supreme Court stated:

> In these quintessential public [forums], the government may not prohibit all communicative activity. For the State to enforce a content-based exclusion it must show that its regulation is necessary to serve a compelling state interest and that it is narrowly drawn to achieve that end. . . . The State may also enforce regulations of the time, place, and manner of expression which are content neutral, and are narrowly tailored to

serve a significant government interest, and leave open ample alternative channels of communication.[69]

The Supreme Court has expressed its disdain for content-based restrictions on free speech. "The First Amendment generally prevents government from proscribing speech, or even expressive conduct because of disapproval of the ideas expressed. Content-based regulations are presumptively invalid."[70] Undoubtedly, the "First Amendment does not permit [government] to impose special prohibitions on those speakers who express views on disfavored subjects."[71]

Moreover, within a public forum, the government cannot prohibit expressive activity on the basis that the speaker is associated with some radical or disruptive group. The First Amendment protects freedom of speech *and* freedom of association. The Supreme Court has noted:

> Among the rights protected by the First Amendment is the right of individuals to associate to further their personal beliefs. While the freedom of association is not explicitly set out in the Amendment, it has long been held to be implicit in the freedoms of speech, assembly, and petition.[72]

The interrelationship between free speech and group activity was reaffirmed by the Supreme Court when it stated:

---

[69]*Frisby,* 487 U.S. at 481 (quoting *Perry,* 460 U.S. at 45).
[70]*R.A.V. v. City of St. Paul,* 505 U.S. 377, 382 (1992).
[71]*Id.* at 391.
[72]*Healy v. James,* 408 U.S. 169, 181 (1972).

It should be obvious that the exclusion of any person or group—all-Negro, all-Oriental, or all-white—from public facilities infringes upon the freedom of the individual to associate as he chooses. . . . "The associational rights which our system honors permit all white, all black, all brown, and all yellow clubs to be formed. They also permit all Catholic, all Jewish, or all agnostic clubs to be established. Government may not tell a man or woman who his or her associates must be." . . . The freedom to associate applies to the beliefs we share, and to those we consider reprehensible. It tends to produce the diversity of opinion that oils the machinery of democratic government and insures peaceful, orderly change.[73]

In one case the Supreme Court found that a public university violated the First Amendment when it banned a student club from campus solely because the club's national parent had a disruptive and violent history.[74] The government cannot prohibit speech within a public forum on the basis that another individual or group with which the speaker is affiliated has been violent or disruptive.[75] An "individual's freedom to speak, to worship, and to petition the government for the redresses of grievances could not be vigorously protected from interference by the state [if] our correlative freedom to engage in group effort toward those ends were not also guaranteed."[76]

---

[73]*Gilmore v. City of Montgomery,* 417 U.S. 556, 575 (1974).
[74]*Healy,* 408 U.S. at 169.
[75]*NAACP v. Claiborne Hardware Co.,* 458 U.S. 886 (1982).
[76]*Roberts v. United States Jaycees,* 468 U.S. 609, 622 (1984).

Although the Supreme Court may be tending to move away from the public forum doctrine to some extent,[77] the public forum doctrine is still well embedded in constitutional interpretation. It is important to know the difference between a traditional public forum, a designated or limited public forum, and a nonpublic forum. In summary, traditional public forums are public parks, streets, and sidewalks. Such public forums are always open to the public. Designated or limited public forums are those public facilities intentionally open to public use by the government. A nonpublic forum is neither a traditional public forum, nor has it been intentionally opened to outside use. However, not all free speech activities can be excluded from a nonpublic forum.

Application of the First Amendment

The three clauses of the First Amendment particularly important for religious liberty include the Establishment Clause, the Free Exercise Clause, and the Free Speech Clause. Applying the First Amendment to any given situation can be simplified by identifying: (1) the parties, (2) the forum, (3) the restriction, and (4) the test.[78]

THE PARTIES

In any constitutional case there must be a governmental party and a private party. The First Amendment restrains

---

[77]*R.A.V.,* 505 U.S. at 377 (not using the public forum analysis in a free speech case); *Lee,* 505 U.S. at 672 (not using a public forum analysis in a free speech case involving an international airport and discussing whether international airports are traditional public forums because of the similarity of the airport to such forums).

[78]*See* the Appendix entitled "First Amendment Outline."

government on the one hand and protects the private liberty of the individual on the other hand. There is no First Amendment application if the adversarial parties are private. One of the adversarial parties must be a governmental actor, and one must be a private actor.

THE FORUM

The three forums include a traditional public forum, a limited or designated public forum, or a nonpublic forum.[79] A traditional public forum includes a street, a sidewalk, or a park. A limited or designated public forum is any public facility intentionally opened to the public by the government for expressive activity. An example of such a forum is a public school which is used by private groups after school hours. A nonpublic forum is public property which the government has not intentionally opened for expressive activity. An example is a utility pole or a public airport.

THE RESTRICTION

The third step in applying the First Amendment is to identify the type of restraint. With respect to the First Amendment Free Speech Clause, the various kinds of restraint include a content-neutral restraint, a content-based restraint, a viewpoint restraint, or a prior restraint. A content-neutral restraint is a governmental restriction on speech that does not attempt to restrict the content of the message. An example of a content-neutral restriction is a parade permit which requires *all* applicants to specify the designated time and route of the parade. Such a requirement must be applicable to all speech

---

[79]*Perry,* 460 U.S. at 37.

regardless of the content. A content-based restraint is a restriction on a specific category of speech. An example is the government permitting political speech but restricting religious speech. An example of a viewpoint restriction is when the government allows political speech only from the Democratic as opposed to the Republican viewpoint. A prior restraint is some type of restriction on speech before it occurs. An example of a prior restraint is the government requiring the speaker to obtain prior permission to speak.

The above analysis of the parties, the forum, and the restriction can be outlined as follows:

I. Identify the Parties
  A. Governmental actor
  B. Private actor
II. Identify the Forum
  A. Traditional public forum
    1. Streets
    2. Sidewalks
    3. Parks
  B. Limited or Designated Public Forum
    1. Any facility which the government intentionally opens for expressive activity
    2. Government may open any facility for expressive activity but may also close the facility to preserve the facility for its intended purpose
  C. Nonpublic Forum
    1. Any government facility which is not intentionally opened for expressive activity
    2. Examples: airports, transportation facilities, utility poles

III. Identify the Restriction
   A. Content-neutral
   B. Content-based
   C. Viewpoint-based
   D. Prior restraint

THE TEST

Once the actors, the forum, and the restriction are identified, the applicable test can also be identified and then applied. The following analysis can be used when applying the First Amendment.

1. Establishment Clause

The Establishment Clause test has gone through several variations. Many members of the Supreme Court for the past several years have criticized the most widely used three-part *Lemon* test.[80] The Court does not always use the *Lemon* test.[81] Once during a graduation prayer case, the Court used a so-called coercion test,[82] but in a different case regarding

---

[80]*Lemon v. Kurtzman,* 403 U.S. 602 (1971); *see also Lee v. Weisman,* 505 U.S. 577 (1992) (Scalia, J., joined by White, J., and Thomas, J., dissenting); *County of Allegheny,* 492 U.S. at 655–57 (Kennedy, J., concurring in judgment in part and dissenting in part); *Corporation of the Presiding Bishop of the Church of Jesus Christ of Latter-Day Saints v. Amos,* 483 U.S. 327, 346–49 (1987) (O'Connor, J., concurring); *Wallace,* 472 U.S. at 107–13 (Rehnquist, J., dissenting); *Id.* at 90–91 (White, J., dissenting); *School Dist. of Grand Rapids v. Ball,* 473 U.S. 373, 400 (1985) (White, J., dissenting); *Widmar v. Vincent,* 454 U.S. 263, 282 (1981) (White, J., dissenting); *New York v. Cathedral Academy,* 434 U.S. 125, 134–35 (1977) (White, J., dissenting); *Roemer v. Maryland Bd. of Pub. Works,* 426 U.S. 736, 768 (1976) (White, J., concurring in judgment); *Committee for Pub. Educ. and Religious Liberty v. Nyquist,* 413 U.S. 756, 820 (1973) (White, J., dissenting).
[81]*Lamb's Chapel,* 508 U.S. at 398.
[82]*Lee,* 505 U.S. at 577.

legislative prayers, the Court used no test but instead relied on the original intent and the history surrounding the First Amendment.[83] The various Establishment Clause tests are outlined as follows:

I. The *Lemon* Test[84]
   A. Must have a secular purpose.
   B. The governmental action must not primarily promote, endorse, or inhibit religion.
   C. The governmental action must not foster excessive governmental entanglement with religion.
II. Coercion Test
   A. Governmental action must not coerce religious beliefs.
   B. Coercion may be direct or indirect.
III. The Historical Test
   A. Review history surrounding the First Amendment.
   B. Determine the original intent of the First Amendment.

As noted above, the primary test used by the Supreme Court is the so-called *Lemon* test. Despite repeated criticism of this unworkable test, it is still applied in some church-state cases. Justices Scalia and Thomas soundly criticized the *Lemon* test in their stinging critique of the Court as follows:

---

[83]*Marsh,* 463 U.S. at 783.

[84]The *Lemon* test has been somewhat modified by recent Supreme Court opinions. This modified version is referred to as the "Endorsement" test. This test considers (1) whether the government has a secular purpose for the action, and (2) whether the primary effect of the action endorses religion. The second prong of the test considers whether a "reasonable observer," informed by history and context, would consider the governmental action to endorse religion. *County of Allegheny,* 492 U.S. at 593–94.

Like some ghoul in a late-night horror movie that repeatedly sits up in its grave and shuffles abroad, after being repeatedly killed and buried, *Lemon* stalks our Establishment Clause jurisprudence once again by frightening the little children and school attorneys. . . . Its most recent burial, only last Term [in *Lee v. Weisman*] was, to be sure, not fully six-feet under. . . . Over the years, however, no fewer than five of the currently sitting Justices have, in their own opinion, personally driven pencils through the creature's heart. . . .

The secret of the *Lemon* test's survival, I think, is that it is so easy to kill. It is there to scare us (and our audience) when we wish to do so, but we can demand it to return to the tomb at will. . . . When we wish to strike down a practice it forbids, we evoke it. . . . Sometimes we take a middle course, calling its three prongs "no more than helpful signposts." Such a docile and useful monster is worth keeping around, at least in a somnolent state; one never knows when one might need him.[85]

Using the convoluted *Lemon* test, the Supreme Court has mandated that in order to pass constitutional muster, religion must be diluted with secular influences. Under the first prong there need only be a secular purpose although there may also be a religious purpose. The key here is to have some secular purpose along with the religious purpose. Under the second prong the primary purpose of the governmental action may not endorse, promote, or inhibit religion. Finally, the government

---

[85]*Lamb's Chapel v. Center Moriches Union Free Sch. Dist.*, 508 U.S. 384, 398 (1993) (Slalia, J., concurring).

may not become excessively entangled with religion. Thus, a nativity scene standing by itself is unconstitutional, but it magically becomes constitutional when secular symbols of the holiday are placed within its context. Christmas carols at public schools wherein children sing "Silent Night" are unconstitutional but magically become constitutional if the same children, during the same presentation, add to their repertoire a secular song such as "Rudolph, the Red-Nosed Reindeer." While some songs might endorse or promote religion, the entire pageant does not primarily endorse or promote religion because of the secular songs. Finally, there is little governmental entanglement since the government is acting neutrally by celebrating both secular and sacred aspects of the holiday.

If the government fails any one of the three prongs of the test, then the governmental action will be considered unconstitutional. The *Lemon* test has created havoc, misunderstanding, and hostility toward religion.

2. Free Exercise Clause

The Supreme Court has changed its interpretation with regard to the application of the Free Exercise Clause. Prior to 1990 the applicable test for violations of religious free exercise required: (1) a sincerely held religious belief negatively impacted or burdened by some government rule or regulation; (2) a compelling governmental interest for the restriction; and (3) that the government achieve its interest in the least restrictive means available.[86] After 1990 the Supreme

---

[86]*See Wisconsin v. Yoder,* 406 U.S. 205 (1972); *Sherbert v. Verner,* 374 U.S. 398 (1963).

Court changed the test so that a generally applicable and neutral law or regulation will be upheld.[87] The stricter standard that applied prior to 1990 will be used only if the law specifically targets religion,[88] or if the First Amendment Free Exercise Clause can be combined with some other constitutional violation.

The basic tests are outlined as follows.

I. Pre-1990 Test
   A. Sincerely held religious belief negatively impacted or burdened by some governmental rule or regulation.
   B. A compelling governmental interest.
   C. Government must use the least restrictive means.
II. Post-1990 Test
   A. General law of neutral applicability will be upheld.
   B. Pre-1990 test will be used when
      1. The government targets religion for discriminatory treatment; or
      2. The Free Exercise right is combined with another constitutional right.

The interpretation of the Free Exercise Clause remained fairly stable until 1990, when the United States Supreme Court, in *Employment Division v. Smith*,[89] severely limited free exercise rights. In 1993, Congress reacted to this dramatic shift in constitutional interpretation by passing the Religious Freedom Restoration Act (hereinafter "RFRA")

---

[87]*Employment Div. v. Smith*, 494 U.S. 872 (1990).
[88]*Church of the Lukumi Babalu Aye, Inc. v. City of Hialeah*, 508 U.S. 520 (1993).
[89]494 U.S. 872 (1990).

(pronounced "rifra").[90] RFRA restored free exercise rights to their pre-Smith status. On June 25, 1997, the Supreme Court declared RFRA unconstitutional as applied to the states.[91] RFRA still remains good law as applied to the federal government.[92]

The next section of this chapter discusses: (a) free exercise rights prior to the 1990 Smith decision, (b) free exercise rights during the Smith era, from 1990 to 1993, (c) free exercise rights under RFRA from 1993 to 1997, and (d) free exercise rights since 1997, when RFRA was declared invalid as applied to the states.

a. The Pre-Smith Era: Before 1990

Prior to 1990, the Free Exercise Clause reached its apex in two cases decided by the United States Supreme Court. The first was a 1963 case known as Sherbert v. Verner,[93] which dealt with unemployment compensation, and the second was Wisconsin v. Yoder,[94] which involved compulsory education laws.

In Sherbert, the South Carolina Employment Security Commission denied unemployment benefits to a Seventh-day Adventist because the claimant refused to perform a job

---

[90]42 U.S.C. § 2000bb. Visit www.lc.org/Resources/rfra.htm for the complete text. Following the passage of the federal RFRA, a majority of states passed RFRAs, which apply only to the respective states and their subdivisions.

[91]City of Boerne v. Flores, 521 U.S. 507 (1997).

[92]The individual state RFRAs also remain good law as applied to the respective states.

[93]374 U.S. 398 (1963).

[94]406 U.S. 205 (1972).

search on Saturday. Seventh-day Adventists have sincerely held religious beliefs that the Sabbath is to be observed on the seventh day of the week, beginning Friday evening at sundown and concluding Saturday evening at sundown. Because of this sincerely held religious belief, Adell Sherbert refused to work on Saturday and, therefore, was denied unemployment benefits on the grounds that her refusal to work on Saturday precluded her from obtaining suitable employment. The Supreme Court ruled that denying benefits for this reason violated her free exercise rights. First, the Court ruled that Ms. Sherbert had a sincerely held religious belief not to do any work on the Sabbath. Second, the state's action burdened her sincerely held religious belief by causing her to choose between the receipt of unemployment benefits or violating her religious convictions. Third, because of this conflict, the Court ruled that the state must have a compelling governmental interest in order to succeed. The Court found that there was no compelling governmental interest. The interest at stake was to preserve the unemployment compensation fund from dilution by false claims, but the state could clearly achieve that interest in a less restrictive manner. Consequently, to deny unemployment benefits to a claimant who refused to work on the Sabbath was a violation of the Free Exercise Clause.[95]

In *Yoder,* the Supreme Court ruled that the Wisconsin compulsory attendance law requiring children to attend school until age sixteen violated the free exercise rights of the

---

[95]*See also Thomas v. Review Bd., Indiana Employment Sec. Div.,* 450 U.S. 707 (1981); *Hobbie v. Unemployment Appeals Comm'n of Florida,* 480 U.S. 136 (1987) (a state cannot withhold unemployment benefits from a Seventh-day Adventist who refuses to work on the seventh-day Sabbath).

Old Order Amish faith. Wisconsin, like all fifty states, had a compulsory education law that required students to attend school until age sixteen. However, the religious tenets of the Old Order Amish conflicted with this compulsory attendance law. The Old Order Amish believed that by sending their children to high school, they would not only expose themselves to the danger of censorship by the church community, but they would also endanger their own salvation and the salvation of their children. According to the Old Order Amish heritage, salvation requires life in a church community separate and apart from the world and worldly influence.[96] The Supreme Court observed the following:

> Formal high school education beyond the eighth grade is contrary to Amish beliefs, not only because it places Amish children in an environment hostile to Amish beliefs with increasing emphasis on competition in classwork and sports and with pressure to conform to the styles, manners, and ways of the peer group, but also because it takes them away from their community, physically and emotionally, during the crucial and formative adolescent period of life.[97]

The Court ruled that (1) the Amish had a sincerely held religious belief which was contrary to compulsory education past the eighth grade, (2) the compulsory state education law placed a significant burden on this religious belief, and (3) there was no compelling governmental interest strong enough to violate this religious belief. Indeed, "a State's

---

[96]*Yoder,* 406 U.S. at 210.
[97]*Id.* at 211.

interest in universal education, however highly we rank it, is not totally free from a balancing process when it impinges on the fundamental rights and interests, such as those specifically protected by the Free Exercise Clause of the First Amendment."[98] In reaching its conclusion, the Court reviewed the history of the Amish religion and noted that one or two years of formal high school education for an Amish student would do little in view of the informal vocational education long practiced by the Amish community. The Amish formed a self-sufficient community with no evidence that one or two years of education would result in the students becoming burdensome to society. Consequently, this compulsory education law was unconstitutional as applied to the Amish religion.

Although not every claim was successful under the Free Exercise Clause,[99] prior to 1990, challenging a governmental regulation on religious grounds was less difficult. Any free

---

[98]*Id.* at 214.

[99]*Reynolds v. United States,* 98 U.S. 145 (1878) (rejecting a claim that criminal laws were unconstitutional as applied against the religious practice of polygamy); *Gillette v. United States,* 401 U.S. 437 (1971) (rejecting a claim that the military selective service system violated the free exercise of religion by conscripting persons who oppose a particular war on religious grounds); *United States v. Lee,* 455 U.S. 252 (1982) (rejecting a claim that the payment of social security tax violated the free exercise rights of the Amish religion); *Bowen v. Roy,* 476 U.S. 693 (1986) (rejecting a claim that obtaining a social security number for the benefit of the applicant's daughter violated free exercise rights); *Lyng v. Northwest Indian Cemetery Protective Ass'n,* 485 U.S. 439 (1988) (government's logging and road construction activities took precedence over traditional Indian religious practices); *Goldman v. Weinberger,* 475 U.S. 503 (1986) (rejecting a claim that the prohibition of wearing a yarmulke pursuant to a military dress regulation violated free exercise rights); *O'Lone v. Estate of Shabazz,* 482 U.S. 342 (1987) (sustaining a prison's refusal to excuse inmates from work

exercise challenge was analyzed using a four-step process. After the individual demonstrated that (1) sincerely held religious belief (2) was burdened by some governmental action, then the government was required to show (3) a compelling reason it must burden the religious belief and (4) that the regulation was the least restrictive means of achieving its governmental interest. The government could not rely on *any* asserted interest for restricting religious beliefs. The purported interest must be a *compelling* one. Moreover, the means the government chose to implement its interest could not be one selection of several alternatives; it must have been the *least restrictive* alternative available. The Supreme Court observed: "Many laws will not meet the test."[100]

b. The Smith Era: 1990—1993

On April 17, 1990, the United States Supreme Court drastically altered its interpretation of the Free Exercise Clause. In *Employment Division v. Smith,*[101] the Court essentially abolished the compelling governmental interest test in free exercise cases. In its place the Court fashioned a new test. In the *Smith* era, if a religious practice was burdened by a *general law of neutral applicability,* the religious claim failed, and the governmental action was upheld.

In *Smith,* the Court stated: "We cannot afford the luxury of deeming presumptively invalid as applied to the religious

---

requirements to attend religious worship services); *Hernandez v. Commissioner,* 490 U.S. 680 (1989) (rejecting a free exercise challenge to payment of income taxes alleged to make religious activities more difficult). In *Lyng, Goldman,* and *O'Lone,* the Court did not apply the *Sherbert* free exercise test.

[100]*Smith,* 494 U.S. at 888.

[101]*Id.* at 872.

objector, every regulation of conduct that does not protect an interest of the highest order."[102] Evidently, the Supreme Court felt that the past quarter of a century of free exercise rights was a "luxury" the country could no longer afford. Under the *Smith* test, a law that substantially burdens but does not single out religion as its object of regulation could still be valid. So long as the law applies to both religious and nonreligious activities, the law may prevail over religious objections. Ironically, in 1972 the United States Supreme Court came to the opposite conclusion: "A regulation neutral on its face may, in its application, nonetheless offend the constitutional requirement for governmental neutrality if it unduly burdens the free exercise of religion."[103] In other words, the Supreme Court in 1972 stated that a neutral law might still violate free exercise rights, but in 1990, the Supreme Court made a completely contradictory ruling.

A Minnesota Supreme Court ruled that an Amish person's refusal to place an orange triangle on the back of a buggy violated free exercise rights, but the United States Supreme Court vacated this decision in light of *Smith*.[104] After *Smith*, many religious rights were lost in cases involving immigration,[105] landmarking,[106] religious clothing,[107] workers' compensation,[108]

---

[102]*Id.*
[103]*Yoder*, 406 U.S. at 220.
[104]*Minnesota v. Hershberger*, 462 N.W.2d 393 (Minn. 1990).
[105]*Intercommunity Ctr. for Justice and Peace v. INS*, 910 F.2d 42 (2d Cir. 1990).
[106]*St. Bartholomew's Church v. City of N.Y.*, 914 F.2d 348 (2d Cir. 1990).
[107]*United States v. Board of Educ. for the Sch. Dist. of Phila.*, 911 F.2d 882 (3d Cir. 1990).
[108]*South Ridge Baptist Church v. Industrial Comm'n of Ohio*, 911 F.2d 1203 (6th Cir. 1990).

home education,[109] zoning,[110] jurisdiction of the National Labor Relations Board over religious schools,[111] the applicability of the Age Discrimination and Employment Act over religious organizations,[112] and religious objections to autopsies.[113]

According to one court, the Supreme Court's decision in *Smith* "cut back, possibly to minute dimensions, the doctrine that requires government to accommodate, at some cost, minority religious preferences."[114] Although the term "free exercise" appears in the First Amendment, the Supreme Court stated that in order to obtain the protection of free exercise rights that existed prior to 1990, a person must show one of the following: (1) the law impacting the religious practice is not neutral and generally applicable,[115] or (2) the free

---

[109]*Vandiver v. Hardin County Bd. of Educ.*, 925 F.2d 927 (6th Cir. 1991).

[110]*Cornerstone Bible Church v. City of Hastings*, 948 F.2d 464 (8th Cir. 1991).

[111]*NLRB v. Hanna Boys Ctr.*, 940 F.2d 1295 (9th Cir. 1991).

[112]*Lukaszewski v. Nazareth Hosp.*, 764 F. Supp. 57 (E.D. Pa. 1991).

[113]*Montgomery v. County of Clinton*, 743 F. Supp. 1253 (W.D. Mich. 1990); *You Vang Yang v. Sturner*, 728 F. Supp. 845 (D.R.I. 1990).

[114]*Hunafa v. Murphy*, 907 F.2d 46, 48 (7th Cir. 1990).

[115]*Lukumi*, 508 U.S. at 520 (a law specifically enacted against the Santeria religion violated free exercise rights because it did not meet the compelling interest test since the law was not neutral and generally applicable). Cases involving "individualized exemptions" also raise the free exercise right to the pre-1990 status. In *Fraternal Order of Police Newark Lodge No. 12 v. City of Newark*, 170 F.3d 359 (3d Cir.), *cert denied*, 525 U.S. 817 (1999), the court applied the pre-1990 free exercise standard to a city policy that prohibited police officers from wearing beards. Those who had a skin condition that prevented shaving were exempted from the policy for medical reasons. The court found if the government permits an exemption for secular reasons, then the First Amendment required an exemption for religious reasons. Unemployment and zoning cases are other examples of "individualized exemptions." In September 2000 the Religious Land Use and Institutionalized Persons Act became law. *See* 42 U.S.C. § 2000cc. This law grants broad protections to houses of worship affected by zoning or land

exercise right must be combined with some other constitutional right. In other words, in order for the compelling interest test to apply after *Smith,* the law must specifically target or discriminate against religion, or the free exercise right must be combined with some other constitutional right.[116] Under either scenario, the standard used by the Court prior to 1990 would still apply. Reacting to the Court's reinterpretation of free exercise rights, Congress took action in 1993 by passing the Religious Freedom Restoration Act.

c. The Post-Smith Era under RFRA: 1993–1997

Because the *Smith* decision in 1990, Congress passed the Religious Freedom Restoration Act in 1993.[117] RFRA states that government may not substantially burden free exercise rights without showing a compelling reason and without further showing that the governmental action is the least restrictive means available to achieve the purported interest.[118]

RFRA recreated the constitutional standard that existed prior to the *Smith* decision. Thus, all of the Supreme Court's

---

marking laws. *See* Chapter 13 entitled "Breaking Down the Zoning Barrier" for more information.

[116]Pursuant to *Smith,* combining a free exercise of religion with some other federally recognized right such as free speech brings the standard of protection to its highest level. *Smith,* 494 U.S. at 881. *Thomas,* 450 U.S. at 707 (unemployment benefits); *Yoder,* 406 U.S. 205, (1972) (invalidating compulsory school attendance laws as applied to Amish parents who refused on religious grounds to send their children to school); *Follett v. McCormick,* 321 U.S. 573 (1944) (same); *Barnette,* 319 U.S. at 624 (invalidating compulsory flag salute statute challenged by religious objectors); *Pierce v. Society of Sisters,* 268 U.S. 510 (1925) (directing the education of children).

[117]42 U.S.C. § 2000bb.

[118]42 U.S.C. § 2000bb–1.

decisions noted above involving free exercise rights prior to the *Smith* decision were revived by RFRA.[119]

d. The Post-RFRA Era: After 1997

On June 25, 1997, the United States Supreme Court found RFRA unconstitutional as applied to the states.[120] The battle originated in the city of Boerne, Texas, some twenty-eight miles northwest of San Antonio. Situated in this hilly city is Saint Peter Catholic Church built in 1923. The church's structure replicates the mission style of the region's earlier history. The sanctuary was designed to accommodate approximately 230 worshippers, but the congregation outgrew the church so that each Sunday 40 or 60 parishioners were turned away from the Sunday masses. In order to accommodate its growing congregation, the archbishop of San Antonio gave permission to enlarge the sanctuary.

A few months later, the Boerne city council passed an ordinance which authorized the city's Historic Landmark Commission to prepare a preservation plan with proposed historic landmarks and districts. Under this ordinance, the Commission was required to preapprove construction affecting any historical landmark. The archbishop applied for a building

---

[119]The National Right to Life Committee opposed RFRA because it did not contain an abortion-neutral amendment, arguing that the amendment would be used to justify abortion. Although some courts were requested to grant an abortion in the face of governmental restrictions to the contrary based on a free exercise right (*McCrae v. Califano*, 491 F. Supp. 630 (E.D.N.Y. 1980)), the United States Supreme Court previously rejected such a claim under the Free Exercise Clause of the Constitution. *See Harris v. McCrae*, 448 U.S. 297 (1980). *See* James Bopp, *Will There Be a Constitutional Right to Abortion after the Reconsideration of Roe v. Wade?*, 15 J. CONTEMPORARY L. 131 (1989).

[120]*City of Boerne*, 521 U.S. at 507.

permit to enlarge the church sanctuary. Relying on the city ordinance and the fact that the church was located in a designated historical district, city authorities denied the application.
The archbishop then filed suit claiming that the church's religious free exercise was violated under RFRA. When the case
finally made its way to the Supreme Court, the city argued that
RFRA was unconstitutional because it exceeded Congress's authority to pass substantive legislation affecting the states regarding the free exercise of religion.

When Congress passed RFRA, it relied upon the power
given it by Section 5 of the Fourteenth Amendment to the
United States Constitution. Section 1 of the Fourteenth
Amendment provides the following:

> No State shall make or enforce any law which
> shall abridge the privileges or immunities of citizens
> of the United States; nor shall any State deprive any
> person of life, liberty, or property, without due
> process of law; nor deny to any person within its ju-
> risdiction equal protection of the laws.[121]

Section 5 of the Fourteenth Amendment states: "The
Congress shall have power to enforce, by appropriate legislation, the provisions of this article."[122] The Fourteenth
Amendment was enacted after the Civil War to ensure equal
protection of all citizens. The genre of the amendment was to
provide protection among the individual states to all citizens,
regardless of race. However, the amendment was not limited
solely to race but applied to all privileges or immunities and

---

[121]U.S. CONST. amend. XIV, § 1.
[122]U.S. CONST. amend. XIV § 5.

prohibited states from depriving any person of life, liberty, or property without due process of law, and also provided equal protection to the laws to be applied to all citizens. Section 5 of the Fourteenth Amendment empowered Congress to enact appropriate legislation that would be remedial in nature. In simple terms, Congress could pass legislation that would put in practice the actual dictates of the Fourteenth Amendment. Therefore, Section 5 was a "positive grant of legislative power"[123] to Congress to enact legislation which would put in practice the specific dictates of the Fourteenth Amendment. In fact, the Supreme Court stated the following about Section 5 of the Fourteenth Amendment:

> Whatever legislation is appropriate, that is, adapted to carry out the objects the amendments have in view, whatever tends to enforce submission to the prohibitions they contain, and to secure to all persons the enjoyment of perfect equality of civil rights and the equal protection of the laws against State denial or invasion, if not prohibited, is brought within the domain of congressional power.[124]

However, the Supreme Court also noted that "as broad as the congressional enforcement power is, it is not unlimited."[125] The Supreme Court agreed that Congress has the authority to enforce the Free Exercise Clause through the Fourteenth Amendment but defined this power as remedial

---

[123] *Katzenbach v. Morgan,* 384 U.S. 641, 651 (1966).
[124] *Ex Parte Virginia,* 100 U.S. 339, 345–46 (1880).
[125] *Oregon v. Mitchell,* 400 U.S. 112, 128 (1970).

in nature, not substantive. The Supreme Court went on to state:

> Legislation which alters the meaning of the Free Exercise Clause cannot be said to be enforcing the Clause. Congress does not enforce a constitutional right by changing what the right is. It has been given the power "to enforce," not the power to determine what constitutes a constitutional violation. Were it not so, what Congress would be enforcing would no longer be, in any meaningful sense, the "provisions of [the Fourteenth Amendment]."[126]

To determine whether RFRA was remedial or substantive, the Court used circular reasoning by harkening back to its 1990 *Smith* decision. Congress obviously passed RFRA to overcome the 1990 *Smith* decision. The Supreme Court concluded that RFRA was attempting to enact substantive legislation regarding religious liberty and was, therefore, contrary to *Smith*, which weakened religious liberty. Additionally, the Court stated:

> Our national experience teaches that the Constitution is preserved best when each part of the government respects both the Constitution and the proper actions and determinations of the other branches. When the Court has interpreted the Constitution, it has acted within the province of the Judicial Branch, which embraces the duty to say what the law is. When the political branches of the

---

[126]*City of Boerne*, 521 U.S. at 519.

Government act against the background of a judicial interpretation of the Constitution already issued, it must be understood that in later cases and controversies the Court will treat its precedents with the respect due them under settled principles, including *stare decisis,* and contrary expectations must be disappointed. RFRA was designed to control cases and controversies, such as the one before us; but as the provisions of the federal statute herein invoked are beyond congressional authority, it is this Court's precedent, not RFRA, which must control.[127]

The Court found RFRA unconstitutional, concluding that Congress exceeded its authority in passing substantive legislation regarding free exercise. The Court decided that it alone had the power to define the limits of the law, and once it determined the meaning of the Constitution, no other branch of government had authority to alter the Court's decision.

To illustrate the absence of a compelling interest, consider the example of a church facing a complete ban on the sale or consumption of alcohol. Prior to 1990, the church could bring suit under the Free Exercise Clause claiming that the law burdened the free exercise of religion. Under the pre-*Smith* analysis, the church would win. For example, the church could first argue that it has a sincerely held religious belief to consume wine as part of its communion service. The government would then have the burden to show it had a compelling governmental reason to enforce the prohibition. Assuming the government's asserted interest to protect health, safety, and welfare due to the

---

[127]*Id.* at 535–36 (citation omitted).

effects of intoxication is compelling, the government must then show that it used the least restrictive means available to achieve its interest. The government could achieve this interest by controlling the sale of alcohol as it controls prescription drugs, or by limiting the amount served or intoxication levels. Consequently, a flat ban covering communion use would be unconstitutional because there would be no risk to the health, safety, or welfare of the citizens. A flat ban is not the least restrictive means, and thus, the church would win.

However, under the post-1990 *Smith* decision, the government would prevail. While the church would argue that it has a sincerely held religious belief, the government would rely upon *Smith* to state that the law is general and that it applies to both religious and nonreligious uses. If the law covers all use or consumption with no exemptions, the government would win.[128]

Currently, the only way to prevail on free exercise claims under the present constitutional interpretation is to show that the law being challenged specifically targets religion to the exclusion of other practices, allows "individualized exemptions" for secular reasons, or to combine the free exercise claim with another constitutional claim. To argue that a law specifically targets religion will be difficult since the cautious legislator will attempt to negate a true motive by drafting a general law. Proving "individualized exemptions" is much easier because any exemption from the law means that the governmental action is not neutral or generally applicable. Alternatively, it is possible in some situations to combine

---

[128]The only other possibility is to come up with some other constitutional right and then combine this right with the Free Exercise Clause.

religious free exercise challenges with a free speech, equal protection, parental rights, or other claim.

After the Supreme Court struck down the Federal RFRA, a number of federal appellate courts ruled that RFRA still applies to actions of the federal government.[129] Thus, when the federal government burdens sincerely held religious beliefs, the government must show it has a compelling reason for doing so and that it used the least restrictive means available. In the same way the federal RFRA may restrict the federal government, a majority of states have now passed state RFRAs, which serve to restrict state action burdening religious beliefs.

---

[129]*Guam v. Guerrero,* 290 F.3d 1210, 1219 (9th Cir. 2002); *Worldwide Church of God v. Philadelphia Church of God, Inc.,* 227 F.3d 1110, 1120 (9th Cir. 2000) ("We have held, along with most other courts, that the Supreme Court invalidated RFRA only as applied to state and local law."), *cert. denied,* 532 U.S. 958 (2001); *Sutton v. Providence St. Joseph Med. Ctr.,* 192 F.3d 826, 832 (9th Cir. 1999) ("Congress . . . does not enact legislation regulating the federal government pursuant to section 5 of the Fourteenth Amendment; Congress acts under that section only when regulating the conduct of the states."); *see also Kikumura v. Hurley,* 242 F.3d 950, 958 (10th Cir. 2001) (holding *Boerne* inapplicable to instances where RFRA was not being applied to states); *(In re Young) Christians v. Crystal Evangelical Free Church,* 141 F.3d 854, 858–59 (8th Cir. 1998), *cert. denied,* 525 U.S. 811 (1998) (same); *Adams v. CIR,* 170 F.3d 173, 175 n.1 (3d Cir. 1999). In general, courts that have addressed the question of constitutionality have found that RFRA is constitutional as applied to the federal government. *See In re Young,* 141 F.3d at 854; *EEOC v. Catholic Univ. of America,* 83 F.3d 455, 468–70 (D.C. Cir.1996) (finding RFRA constitutional as applied to Title VII, but relying on Fifth Circuit's decision in *Boerne*); *but see United States v. Grant,* 117 F.3d 788, 792 n.6 (5th Cir. 1997) (questioning RFRA's viability in the federal context); *In re Gates,* 212 B.R. 220 (Bankr. W.D.N.Y. 1997) (finding that *Boerne* overruled RFRA altogether). Some commentators have noted that RFRA may be unconstitutional as applied to federal law. *See* Marci Hamilton, *The Religious Freedom Restoration Act Is Unconstitutional, Period,* 1 U. PA. J. CONST. L. 1

Responding to the Supreme Court's 1997 decision on RFRA, Congress again enacted more limiting legislation. The Religious Land Use and Institutionalized Persons Act (hereinafter "RLUIPA," pronounced "rilupa"), became law in September 2000.[130] Congress exercised its power under the Commerce Clause of the United States Constitution, instead of relying on the Fourteenth Amendment. RLUIPA applies only to zoning and land marketing laws and to incarcerated persons. In this limited context, RLUIPA restored the compelling interest test.[131]

It is sad to say that the constitutional rights we enjoyed in 1990 no longer receive the same protection today. The religious liberty we all took for granted was changed with the stroke of a pen. This is not how a constitutional government was designed to operate. The Constitution is supposed to be immutable, unchangeable, and above our fluctuating human philosophies. However, because the Supreme Court assumed

---

(1998); Aurora R. Bearse, Note, *RFRA: Is It Necessary? Is It Proper?*, 50 RUTGERS L. REV. 1045 (1998); Edward J.W. Blatnik, Note, *No RFRAF Allowed: The Status of the Religious Freedom Restoration Act's Federal Application in the Wake of City of Boerne v. Flores*, 98 COLUM. L. REV. 1410 (1998); *but see* Thomas C. Berg, *The Constitutional Future of Religious Freedom Legislation*, 20 U. ARK. LITTLE ROCK L. J. 715 (1998) (arguing that RFRA is constitutional as applied to the federal government).

[130]42 U.S.C. § 2000cc.

[131]RLUIPA has been upheld as constitutional, even as applied to the states. *See Cottonwood Christian Ctr. v. Cypress Redevelop. Agency*, 218 F. Supp. 2d 1203, 1221 n.7 (C.D. Cal. 2002) (Although the constitutionality of RLUIPA was not at issue, the court stated RLUIPA does not suffer from the constitutional flaws of its RFRA predecessor.); *Freedom Baptist Church of Del. County v. Township of Middleton*, 204 F. Supp. 2d 857 (E.D. Pa. 2002) (upholding the constitutionality of RLUIPA in the context of a church zoning case); *Mayweathers v. Terhune*, No. 96–1582, 2001 WL 804140 (E.D. Cal. July 2, 2001) (upholding constitutionality of RLUIPA in a prisoner religious freedom claim).

the authority to determine the boundaries of the law and has abandoned its dedication to the original intent of the Constitution, the Constitution has lost its stability.

3. Prisoner Rights

Whether analyzed under the Free Speech or Free Exercise Clauses, the test for prisoner rights remains the same. The government must have a legitimate penological interest that is reasonably related to the government interest.[132] Courts are more deferential to prison administrators in restricting the rights of prisoners, either in their free exercise of religion or in their freedom of speech, primarily because of the penological interest at stake. The interest in punishment and security are strong governmental interests which must be balanced against the rights of the prisoner. Using this highly deferential standard, the interest of the government almost always defeats the rights of the prisoner. The test for prisoner rights can be best outlined as follows:

I. Prisoner Rights
A. Government must have a legitimate penological interest.
B. Restriction must be reasonably related to the governmental interest.

When the Religious Freedom Restoration Act[133] was given full effect, the rights of prisoners were coextensive to the rights of nonincarcerated individuals. From 1997 to 2000, the rights of prisoners reverted back to their pre-1993 status.

---

[132]*Turner v. Safley,* 482 U.S. 78 (1987); *O'Lone,* 482 U.S. at 342.
[133]42 U.S.C. § 2000bb.

However, in September 2000, the Religious Land Use and Institutionalized Persons Act became law.[134] RLUIPA has restored the compelling interest test to prisoner religious rights claims.

4. Free Speech Clause

The Supreme Court has developed more tests for the Free Speech Clause than for the Establishment Clause or the Free Exercise Clause. Any free speech analysis depends upon the nature of the forum and the type of restriction. As noted earlier, there are generally three separate kinds of forums in any free speech analysis. The three forums include a traditional, a limited or designated, or a nonpublic forum. It is critical to know the forum because the analysis depends upon the kind of forum at issue. Additionally, within each of these forums there may be four types of restrictions. The various restrictions include a content-neutral, content-based, viewpoint and prior restraint restriction. Moreover, it is also important to determine whether the restriction is being imposed by a legislatively adopted law or court-ordered injunction. The following outline overviews the Free Speech Clause analysis.

a. Legislatively Adopted Laws Restricting Speech

I. Content-neutral restriction
  A. Traditional public forum
    1. Substantial or significant governmental interest.
    2. Reasonable time, place, and manner restrictions must be narrowly tailored.
    3. Leave open ample alternative means of expression.

---

[134]42 U.S.C. § 2000cc.

   B. Limited or designated public forum
     1. Substantial or significant governmental interest.
     2. Reasonable time, place, and manner restrictions must be narrowly tailored.
     3. Leave open ample alternative means of expression.
   C. Nonpublic forum
     1. Substantial or significant governmental interest.
     2. Reasonable restrictions that are rationally related to the governmental interest.

II. Content restriction
   A. Traditional public forum
     1. Compelling governmental interest
     2. Least restrictive means available
   B. Limited or designated public forum
     1. Compelling governmental interest
     2. Least restrictive means available
   C. Nonpublic forum
     1. Substantial or significant governmental interest
     2. Reasonable restrictions that are rationally related to the governmental interest

III. Viewpoint restriction
   A. Traditional public forum
     1. Prohibited
     2. Rationale: government cannot take sides by allowing one viewpoint to the exclusion of another.
   B. Limited or designated public forum
     1. Prohibited
     2. Rationale: government cannot take sides by allowing one viewpoint to the exclusion of another.

  C. Nonpublic forum
    1. Prohibited
    2. Rationale: government cannot take sides by allowing one viewpoint to the exclusion of another.

IV. Prior restraint
  A. Presumptively unconstitutional
  B. Must have specific time for granting or refusal to grant permit
  C. Must not permit governmental discretion to grant or deny speech without specific objective standards
  D. Must provide that the government has the burden to file suit to substantiate any content-based restriction on speech[135]

Sometimes the Supreme Court has used a separate four-part test when analyzing symbolic speech. The symbolic speech test arose in the context of flag desecration. The four-part test can be summarized as follows: (1) the regulation must be within the constitutional power of the government; (2) it must further an important or substantial governmental interest; (3) the government interest must be unrelated to the suppression of speech; and (4) incidental restriction must be no greater than essential to the furtherance of that interest.[136] The Supreme Court has already indicated that this four-part test is essentially the same as the time, place, and manner test on content-neutral restrictions.[137]

---

[135]*Freedman v. Maryland,* 380 U.S. 51 (1965). If the restriction is content-neutral, the government does not have the burden of filing suit to justify its speech restriction. *Watchtower Bible and Tract Soc. of New York v. Village of Stratton,* 536 U.S. 150 (2002).

[136]*United States v. O'Brien,* 391 U.S. 367 (1968).

[137]*Ward v. Rock against Racism,* 491 U.S. 781 (1989).

b. Injunctions Restricting Speech

An injunction or court order restricting speech can either be content-neutral or content-based. A content-neutral injunction is generally one that targets specific activity rather than speech. Oftentimes a content-neutral injunction is one that attempts to restrain activity of an individual who repeatedly violated the law. A content-based injunction is one that specifically targets speech rather than activity. An injunction that targets speech is also by its very nature a prior restraint.

The standard for reviewing content-neutral injunctions requires that a heightened level of scrutiny be applied, which is a more stringent standard than the time, place, and manner test. This heightened scrutiny requires that a content-neutral injunction must not burden more speech than necessary to achieve the governmental interest at stake.[138]

A content-based injunction follows the standard content-based test. The government must have a compelling governmental interest and achieve that interest in the least restrictive means available.[139] Since a content-based injunction is also a prior restraint, it is presumptively invalid. The test for content-neutral and content-based injunctions is outlined as follows:

I. Content-Neutral Injunction
   A. Heightened level of scrutiny stricter than the content-neutral time, place, and manner test

---

[138]*Madsen v. Women's Health Ctr., Inc.,* 512 U.S. 753 (1994).
[139]*Near v. Minnesota,* 283 U.S. 697 (1931); *Better Austin v. Keefe,* 402 U.S. 415 (1971); *New York Times Co. v. United States,* 403 U.S. 713 (1971); *Carroll v. President and Comm'rs of Princess Anne,* 393 U.S. 175 (1968).

    B. Must not burden more speech than necessary to achieve its objective

II. Content-Based Injunction

    A. Presumptively invalid

    B. Must have a compelling governmental interest

    C. Must be the least restrictive means available

Rather than present a lengthy discussion of the various nuances of free speech, the application of the Free Speech Clause will be discussed throughout this book where appropriate. The free speech protection under the First Amendment is a powerful weapon in the defense of religious freedom and expression. In essence, the Free Speech Clause requires a level playing field. In other words, the government must not treat private religious expression unequally to secular expression.

Summary

The First Amendment is designed to restrain government on the one hand and protect the liberty of private parties on the other hand. The First Amendment is only applicable against the government. It is not applicable to restrain a private party. The several sections of the First Amendment include the Establishment Clause, the Free Exercise Clause, and the Free Speech Clause. To analyze any First Amendment claim, one must identify (1) the parties, (2) the forum, (3) the restriction, and (4) the test. Once the applicable test is determined, that test should be used to determine if there is a First Amendment violation.

3
STUDENTS' RIGHTS ON PUBLIC SCHOOL CAMPUSES

Freedom of Speech

STUDENTS ON PUBLIC SCHOOL CAMPUSES enjoy constitutional protection of free speech and free exercise of religion. Student speech can be prohibited only when speech activities "substantially interfere with the work of the school, or impinge upon the rights of other students."[1] In *Tinker v. Des Moines Independent School District,* the United States Supreme Court stated:

> In our system, state-operated schools may not be enclaves of totalitarianism. School officials do not

---

[1] *Tinker v. Des Moines Indep. Sch. Dist.,* 393 U.S. 503, 509 (1969) (citing *Burnside v. Byers,* 363 F.2d 744, 749 [5th Cir. 1966]).

possess absolute authority over their students. Students in school as well as out of school are "persons" under our Constitution. They are possessed of fundamental rights which the State must respect, just as they themselves must respect their obligations to the State. In our system, students may not be regarded as closed-circuit recipients of only that which the State chooses to communicate. They may not be confined to the expression of those sentiments that are officially approved. In the absence of a specific showing of constitutionally valid reasons to regulate their speech, students are entitled to freedom of expression of their views.[2]

The Supreme Court further stated, "It can hardly be argued that either students or teachers shed their constitutional rights to freedom of speech or expression at the schoolhouse gate."[3] The Court recognized that when a student is "in the cafeteria, or on the playing field, or on the campus during the authorized hours, he may express his opinions."[4] Students may exercise their constitutional right to free speech while on public school campuses before and after school, between classes, in the cafeteria, or on the playing field. Students have a constitutionally protected right to freedom of speech during noninstructional time. However, during class instruction students must conform their speech to the relevant topic being studied. While a student may talk to another student during noninstructional times about politics or religion, the student

---

[2]*Id.* at 511.
[3]*Id.* at 506.
[4]*Id.* at 512–13.

should refrain from such discussion with another student during class time unless it is relevant to the topic being studied and is done in an orderly fashion.

Students have a guaranteed right to free speech on public school campuses. When students walk on the premises of any public school, kindergarten through college, they carry with them the First Amendment protection of free speech and free exercise of religion.[5] These students do not shed their constitutional rights when they enter the schoolhouse gate.[6]

The *Tinker* case involved students in grades two through eleven who came to school wearing black armbands to symbolically protest America's involvement in the Vietnam War. The emotional reaction was certainly strong. Some of the students and faculty no doubt had family or friends who either died in the Vietnam War or who were then stationed in Vietnam. These people bristled at the sight of the black armbands. School officials demanded the students remove the armbands. When they refused, the students were threatened with suspension. The students filed suit, and in 1969 the Supreme Court ruled that students in public schools have a constitutional right to freedom of speech. Just because other students find their speech repulsive is no basis to censor the

---

[5]The students in *Tinker* included an eight-year-old second grader, an eleven-year-old fifth grader, a thirteen-year-old eighth grader, and a fifteen- and a sixteen-year-old in the eleventh grade. The students in *Board of Education of Westside Community Schools v. Mergens,* 496 U.S. 226 (1990), attended public secondary school. Public secondary schools, depending on state law, include middle schools and/or junior high schools and high schools. The students in *Widmar v. Vincent,* 454 U.S. 263 (1981), involved college students. Although the latter two cases pertained to student clubs within a public secondary school or college, these cases were based on student free speech rights.
[6]*Tinker,* 393 U.S. at 506.

speech. The only basis to restrict student free speech during noninstructional time is if it materially and substantially interferes with the ordinary operation of the school or with the rights of others.

Federal courts have the duty "to apply the First Amendment mandates in our educational system" in order "to safeguard the fundamental values of freedom of speech and inquiry."[7] Indeed, the Supreme Court has specifically stated that students may express themselves all the way "from kindergarten through high school."[8] This statement was made prior to the Supreme Court's decisions dealing with speech on college campuses, and thus, it can now rightfully be said that students have free speech rights from kindergarten through college. One federal court observed that "religious speech cannot be suppressed solely because it is religious, a principle that makes sense in the elementary school environment."[9]

Some opponents of student free speech have attempted to restrict student rights by arguing that public schools are closed, limited, or designated public forums. In using this terminology, opponents of student free speech argue that student speech activities are limited to speech condoned by the school. Some erroneously argue that schools may allow secular speech and prohibit religious speech. Others argue that student speech can be prohibited only if both secular and religious speech are equally prohibited. This is the same kind of

---

[7]*Epperson v. Arkansas,* 393 U.S. 97, 104 (1968).
[8]*Tinker,* 393. U.S. at 516.
[9]*Muller v. Jefferson Lighthouse Sch.,* 98 F.3d 1530, 1539 (7th Cir. 1996), *cert. denied,* 520 U.S. 1530 (1997).

argument that is sometimes used against student-initiated clubs. However, the analysis for student-initiated clubs is different from the analysis for student interpersonal communication. As for student-initiated clubs, schools can prohibit all student clubs so long as the prohibition on use of facilities applies to all clubs and to all use by any outside person or group.[10] In the context of student interpersonal communication, students are not requesting *use* of school facilities. To the contrary, they are commanded by law to be on the public school campus, and once there under mandate of law, schools cannot completely ban their speech.

Public schools are unique within American culture. School is the only place where citizens are commanded to be until the age of sixteen. All fifty states have compulsory education laws which require education up to the age of sixteen. Compulsory education can be satisfied by either attending a public, private, or home school. For many Americans, there is very little freedom of choice between public and private school because of monetary considerations. Consequently, most Americans have been trained in public schools. This training is not voluntary; it is mandatory. Failure to attend school until the age of sixteen may result in civil or criminal penalties. Since school is the only place in America where attendance is demanded, it would be incongruous not to recognize that students in public schools have constitutional liberties.

Freedom of speech for public school students is not only a protected right; it is also common sense. We would all

---

[10]Schools rarely close the forum to all use of facilities. Oftentimes school facilities are rented after hours as a means of generating income.

agree that when exiting the school bus on the way to class, a student has the right to converse with another student. One student can say to another student, "I like you." The same student could go even further and say, "I love you." Moreover, this student could invite a friend home after school for a birthday party. Whatever can be verbally spoken can be transferred to print. For example, this same student could pass out a Valentine card with the "I love you" message. There is no distinction between verbal or written speech. The only difference is that one creates litter, and the other does not. However, the Supreme Court has already indicated that instead of punishing all speech under the guise of prohibiting litter, the appropriate course is to punish the litterbug.[11] Everyone would admit that a student can engage in secular speech on campus. The same student can also engage in religious speech. For example, one student could tell another that "Jesus Christ loves you" and could further invite that student to an after-school religious event. This verbal message could also be transmitted in print through a gospel tract or a

---

[11]There is no difference between oral and written expression except litter. *See Organization for a Better Austin v. Keefe,* 402 U.S. 415 (1971); *Martin v. City of Struthers,* 319 U.S. 141, 145 (1943); *Jamison v. Texas,* 318 U.S. 413, 416 (1943); *Schneider v. State of N.J.,* 308 U.S. 147, 162 (1939); *Lovell v. Griffin,* 303 U.S. 444, 452 (1938). A ban on handbilling suppresses "a great quantity of speech that does not cause the evils that it seeks to eliminate." *Ward v. Rock Against Racism,* 491 U.S. 781, 800 n.7 (1989). Leafletting is a "form of religious activity [that] occupies the same high estate under the First Amendment as do worship in churches and preaching from the pulpits." *Murdock v. Pennsylvania,* 319 U.S. 105, 109 (1943). Because literature distribution is synonymous with pure speech, students have the right to distribute religious literature during noninstructional times as long as their activities do not disrupt the orderly operation of the school. *See Tinker,* 393 U.S. at 509.

church invitation. A student does not lose the constitutional right to free speech when the message is transferred to print and further does not lose the right to free speech when the message changes from secular to sacred topics. One court has stated the following:

> Public schools are dedicated, in part, to accommodate students during prescribed hours for personal intercommunication. Unless the students' speech is curriculum-related, the speech cannot be limited during those hours on the school campus without a strong showing of interference with school activities or with the rights of other students. As the Court stated, "Dedication to specific uses [including student interpersonal communication] does not imply that the constitutional rights of persons entitled to be there are to be gauged as if the premises were purely private property."[12]

According to the Supreme Court's ruling in *Tinker,* the "principal use to which the schools are dedicated is to accommodate students during prescribed hours for the purpose of certain types of activities. Among those activities is personal intercommunication among the students."[13] "The holding in *Tinker* did not depend upon a finding that the school was a public forum."[14] *Tinker* clearly acknowledged that schools, by virtue of their very existence, are dedicated to personal intercommunication among the students. Thus, in a

---

[12]*Slotterback v. Interboro Sch. Dist.,* 766 F. Supp. 280, 293 (E.D. Pa. 1991) (quoting *Tinker,* 393 U.S. at 512 n.6).
[13]*Tinker,* 393 U.S. at 512.
[14]*Rivera v. East Otero Sch. Dist.,* 721 F. Supp. 1189, 1193 (D. Colo. 1989).

sense, schools are by their very nature a designated or limited public forum for student speech and can be none other than a limited or designated public forum by virtue of the fact that they are dedicated "to accommodate students during prescribed hours."[15] One federal district court recognized this important aspect of *Tinker* by declaring:

> In the light of *Tinker*, I conclude that government intent to create public secondary schools as limited public fora, during school hours, for the first amendment personal speech of the students who attend those schools, is intrinsic in the dedication of those schools. Only when the schools cease operating is that intent negated.[16]

In other words, it is improper to analyze student-initiated speech under a forum framework, and to state, in turn, that schools can restrict the forum and thus prohibit student speech. Students are commanded by law to be on public school campuses. Once students are there, the government cannot restrict their speech unless the speech disrupts the ordinary operation of the school or interferes with the rights of other students. Schools may not prohibit student speech simply because another student objects to the content of the message. "If school officials were permitted to prohibit expression to which other students objected, absent any further justification, the officials would have a license to prohibit virtually every type of expression."[17] Additionally, the phrase,

---

[15]*Tinker*, 393 U.S. at 512.

[16]*Slotterback*, 766 F. Supp. at 293.

[17]*Clark v. Dallas Indep. Sch. Dist.*, 806 F. Supp. 116, 120 (N.D. Tex. 1992) (citing *Rivera*, 721 F. Supp. at 1189; and *Slotterback*, 766 F. Supp. at 280).

"interferes with the rights of other students," found in *Tinker,* means student speech that is sexually explicit, libelous, or defamatory toward another student.[18] Second, even if a public forum analysis were used within a public school context, schools are intrinsically dedicated to student interpersonal communication. Only when schools cease being schools is that public dedication extinguished. Just as schools cannot prohibit students from verbally speaking to one another between class, on the playing field, in the cafeteria, or during noninstructional times before or after class sessions, schools cannot prohibit other forms of student expression. "In the absence of a specific showing of constitutionally valid reasons to regulate their speech, students are entitled to freedom of expression of their views."[19] Indeed, the "vigilant protection of constitutional freedoms is nowhere more vital than in the community of American schools."[20] Finally, so long as students address the wide range of subject matters which the school allows, students may speak on the permitted subject matters from a religious viewpoint irrespective of the nature of the forum. For example, if the school allows students to pass out Valentine cards discussing the subject of love or friendship, then students may distribute religious tracts speaking of God's love. The school may not restrict the religious message by contending that others might disagree.

The Supreme Court has already rejected arguments that a school may prohibit student speech simply because others

---

[18]*Hazelwood Sch. Dist. v. Kuhlmeier,* 484 U.S. 260, 274 (1988); *Bethel Sch. Dist. v. Fraser,* 478 U.S. 675 (1986).
[19]*Clark,* 806 F. Supp. at 119 (quoting *Tinker,* 393 U.S. at 511).
[20]*Shelton v. Tucker,* 364 U.S. 479, 487 (1960).

might find it offensive. The Supreme Court could not make this point any clearer in *Tinker*:

> Any departure from absolute regimentation may cause trouble. Any variation from the majority's opinion may inspire fear. Any word spoken, in class, in the lunchroom, or on the campus, that deviates from the views of another person may start an argument or cause a disturbance. But our Constitution says we must take this risk and our history says that it is this sort of hazardous freedom—this kind of openness—that is the basis of our national strength and of the independence and vigor of Americans who grow up and live in this relatively permissive, often disputatious, society.[21]

"Undifferentiated fear or apprehension of disturbance is not enough to overcome the right to freedom of expression."[22] Regardless of the arguments presented by opponents of student speech, the Supreme Court in "*Tinker* made clear that school property may not be declared off limits for expressive activity by students."[23] Commenting on student speech in elementary schools, one court stated that "speech cannot be suppressed or discriminated against solely because it is religious. Banning religious expression, 'which the Free Exercise Clause of the First Amendment singles out for protection,' solely because it is religious is per se unreasonable."[24]

---

[21]*Tinker*, 393 U.S. at 508–09 (citations omitted).
[22]*Id.* at 508.
[23]*Grayned v. City of Rockford*, 408 U.S. 104, 118 (1972). "Tinker provides the standard for restricting student speech on campus that is not part of a school-sponsored program." *Clark*, 806 F. Supp. at 119.
[24]*Muller*, 98 F.3d at 5143–44 (citations omitted).

Harassment Policies

Some schools have adopted broad harassment policies. These policies typically prohibit "harassment" against another on account of "religion." School officials may erroneously try to use such a policy to stop one student from speaking to another student about religion. However, engaging a student in a discussion about religion when the person may be "offended" must be distinguished from repeated and hostile encounters targeted toward a particular student. While the former may not be proscribed, the latter may be restricted.

The United States Supreme Court has held that a public school may be liable for student-on-student sexual harassment *only* where school officials act with "deliberate indifference" and the harassment is so "severe" that it effectively bars the victim's access to an educational opportunity or benefit.[25] Thus, school officials may not use harassment policies to stifle the discussion of religion.

One school's harassment policy prohibited "unwelcome verbal, written or physical conduct which offends, denigrates or belittles an individual."[26] The policy stated that such harassment included, but was not limited to, unsolicited "derogatory remarks, jokes, demeaning comments or behaviors, slurs, mimicking, name calling, graffiti, innuendo, gestures, physical contact, stalking, threatening, bullying, extorting or the display

---

[25]*Davis v. Monroe County Bd. of Educ.,* 526 U.S. 629 (1999); *see also Morlock v. West Cent. Educ. Dist.,* 46 F. Supp. 2d 892 (D. Minn. 1999) (dismissing student's claim for sexual harassment because the allegations were insufficient).

[26]*Saxe v. State College Area Sch. Dist.,* 240 F.3d 200, 202 (3d Cir. 2001).

or circulation of written material or pictures."[27] The federal court, relying on the *Tinker* case, found the policy unconstitutional under the First Amendment.[28]

Literature Distribution

The Supreme Court has long recognized "that the right to distribute flyers and literature lies at the heart of the liberties guaranteed by the Speech and Press Clauses of the First Amendment."[29] "It is axiomatic that written expression is pure speech."[30] Well-settled constitutional law confirms "that the guarantee of freedom of speech that is enshrined in the First Amendment encompasses the right to distribute peacefully."[31] "From the time of the founding of our nation, the distribution of written material has been an essential weapon in the defense of liberty."[32]

The right of free speech includes the right to distribute literature.[33] In fact, the distribution of *printed* material is

---

[27]*Id.* at 203.

[28]*Id.* at 217; *see also Vega v. Miller,* 273 F.3d 460 (3d Cir. 2001) (college's sexual harassment policy was unconstitutionally vague and overbroad); *Dambrot v. Central Michigan Univ.,* 55 F.3d 1177 (6th Cir. 1995) (harassment policy used to restrict use of the word *nigger* is unconstitutional and is not a valid prohibition of fighting words); *Silva v. University of N.H.,* 888 F. Supp. 293 (D.N.H. 1994) (Sexual harassment policy infringes on First Amendment.) *But see West v. Derby Unified Sch. Dist. No. 260,* 206 F.3d 1358 (10th Cir. 2000) (upholding a student's suspension under a racial harassment policy when the student drew a rebel flag, noting that the policy adequately forecasted likely disruption by the mere presence of the flag when viewed against the history of racial unrest in the school).

[29]*ISKCON v. Lee,* 505 U.S. 672, 702–3 (1992).

[30]*Slotterback,* 766 F. Supp. at 288.

[31]*Id.*

[32]*Paulsen v. County of Nassau,* 925 F.2d 65, 66 (2d Cir. 1991).

[33]*Martin v. City of Struthers,* 319 U.S. 141 (1943).

considered pure speech.[34] Consequently, peaceful distribution of literature is protected speech.[35] Literature distribution includes anything in printed format such as brochures, pamphlets, newspapers, cards, stamps, books, and pictures that are not considered obscene.

Religious speech enjoys the same protection as political speech.[36] Indeed, the right to persuade, advocate, or proselytize a religious viewpoint is protected by the First Amendment. The Supreme Court has stated that "free trade in ideas means free trade in the opportunity to persuade to action, not merely to describe facts."[37] The burden on the government (public school) to justify an exclusion of free speech requires the government to show that the denial of speech is necessary to serve a compelling state interest and that complete denial is the least restrictive alternative to achieve that end.[38] Mere disagreement with the content of the speech is not sufficient

---

[34]*Texas v. Johnson,* 491 U.S. 397, 406 (1989) ("The Government generally has a freer hand in restricting expressive conduct than it has in restricting the written or spoken word.")

[35]*United States v. Grace,* 461 U.S. 171, 176 (1983) ("Leafletting is protected speech."); *Lovell v. City of Griffin,* 303 U.S. 444, 452 (1938) ("Liberty of circulating is as essential to [freedom of speech] as liberty of publishing; indeed, without circulation, the publication would be of little value.")

[36]*Widmar v. Vincent,* 454 U.S. 263, 269 (1981) (citing *Heffron v. ISKCON* 452 U.S. 640 (1981)); *see also Niemotko v. Maryland,* 340 U.S. 268 (1951); *Saia v. New York,* 334 U.S. 558 (1948). "No area of government may discriminate against religious speech when speech on other subjects is permitted in the same place at the same time." *Hedges v. Wauconda Comm. Unit Sch. Dist. No 118,* 9 F.3d 1295, 1297 (7th Cir. 1993) (citing *Lamb's Chapel v. Center Moriches Union Free Sch. Dist.,* 508 U.S. 384 (1993)).

[37]*Thomas v. Collins,* 323 U.S. 516, 537 (1945).

[38]*Carey v. Brown,* 447 U.S. 455, 461, 464–65 (1980); *Widmar,* 454 U.S. at 270.

reason to deny student speech.[39] Indeed, "a desire to avoid controversy might conceal a bias against a viewpoint advanced by the excluded speakers."[40]

The Supreme Court has held that a high school principal may restrict the content of a school-sponsored newspaper which was published as part of the course work for a journalism class because the newspaper was not a public forum, was part of the educational curriculum, and was a regular classroom activity.[41] However, the Court distinguished the newspaper case from literature distribution by stating:

> The question whether the First Amendment requires a school to tolerate particular student speech—the question that we addressed in *Tinker*—is different from the question whether the First Amendment re-

---

[39]*Clark,* 806 F. Supp. at 120.

[40]*Grossbaum v. Indianapolis-Marion Blvd. Auth.,* 63 F.3d 581 (7th Cir. 1995) (quoting *NAACP v. Cornelius,* 473 U.S. 788, 812 (1985)).

[41]*Hazelwood Sch. Dist. v. Kuhlmeier,* 484 U.S. 260 (1988). In *Desilets v. Clearview Regional Board of Education,* 630 A.2d 333 (N.J. Sup. Ct. 1993), a New Jersey state appeals court ruled that a school violated the First Amendment Free Speech Clause when it censored from a school-sponsored newspaper a student's movie reviews of the R-rated films *Mississippi Burning* and *Rainman.* The court reasoned that the censorship was based on the content of the movie reviews and was not associated with pedagogical concern such as grammar, writing, research, bias or prejudice, or vulgar or profane language. Since the censorship was based on the content of the movie being R-rated, the school violated the student's free speech right. The court ruled that any school newspaper censorship case must be read in light of the Supreme Court's decision in *Tinker,* 393 U.S. at 503. The court also ruled that if the school was concerned about the appearance that it endorsed R-rated movie reviews, the school could add a disclaimer to the newspaper. *But see Hosty v. Governors State Univ.,* 174 F. Supp. 2d 782 (N.D. Ill. 2001) (public university violated free speech rights of student-run newspaper which was funded by student fees when school officials attempted to shut down the paper).

quires a school affirmatively to promote particular student speech. The former question addresses educators' ability to silence a student's personal expression that happens to occur on the school premises. The latter question concerns educators' authority over school-sponsored publications, theatrical productions, and other expressive activities that students, parents, and members of the public might reasonably perceive to bear the imprimatur of the school. These activities [that is, writing an article in a school-sponsored newspaper,] may fairly be characterized as part of the school curriculum, whether or not they occur in a traditional classroom setting, so long as they are supervised by faculty members and designed to impart particular knowledge or skills to student participants and audiences.[42]

The same distinction makes literature distribution different from *Bethel School District v. Fraser,*[43] in which the Court ruled that a student was appropriately disciplined by the school authorities for the offensive tone of a nominating speech at a school assembly.[44] The difference between the Supreme Court decision in *Hazelwood* (school-sponsored newspaper), *Fraser* (an offensive nominating speech at a

---

[42]*Hazelwood,* 484 U.S. at 270–71.

[43]478 U.S. 675 (1986).

[44]Another federal court of appeals ruled that "civility" is a legitimate pedagogical concern of a school, and therefore school officials could declare a high school student ineligible to run for student office as a sanction for an offensive campaign speech delivered at a school assembly in which the student ridiculed an assistant principal. *Poling v. Murphy,* 872 F.2d 757 (6th Cir. 1989), *cert. denied,* 493 U.S. 1021 (1990).

school assembly), and *Tinker* (student-initiated speech) is important. The Court in *Hazelwood* ruled that a school could censor student speech when that speech occurred in a school-sponsored newspaper. There were two reasons the Court allowed the school to censor this speech. First, the student speech occurred in a *school-sponsored* newspaper. Faculty members participated in the production of the paper. The newspaper also contained the school logo, thus giving the appearance that the school sponsored the content of the paper. Second, the article dealt with a fellow student who had become pregnant. The article did not name the student but so specifically described the circumstances that everyone within the school knew to whom the article referred. As such, this article could have been defamatory toward the student and thus interfered with the right of a particular student under the *Tinker* analysis. Similarly, the student nominating speech in *Fraser* was also somewhat defamatory or libelous. In this particular case, the student gave a nominating speech and used sexual innuendoes, describing as it were, a sexual act between him and the student body. Moreover, the speech was given at a school-sponsored convocation during which the speaker was addressing a captive audience.

The Supreme Court, however, indicated that there is a clear difference between "whether the First Amendment requires a school to tolerate particular student speech [as was addressed in *Tinker*] and the question of whether the First Amendment requires a school affirmatively to promote particular student speech [the question addressed in *Hazelwood*]."[45] The reason the school could censor the content of the student newspaper

---

[45]*Hazelwood*, 484 U.S. at 270–71 (emphasis added).

was in part because the production of that newspaper was "supervised by faculty members and designed to impart particular knowledge or skills to student participants and audiences."[46] However, student interpersonal communication, both verbally or through printed format, has no supervision of faculty and is not designed to impart knowledge or skills to other participants or audiences. As such, the school has no reason to censor this form of student speech unless the student speech interrupts the ordinary operation of the school or interferes with the rights of other students. The Supreme Court observed that "there is a crucial difference between *government* speech endorsing religion, which the Establishment Clause forbids, and *private* speech endorsing religion, which the Free Speech and Free Exercise Clauses protect."[47]

Students may, therefore, distribute literature during noninstructional time—before, after, and between classes. As *Tinker* stated, when a student is "in the cafeteria, or on the playing field, or on the campus during the authorized hours, he may express his opinions."[48] The only compelling reason to prohibit literature distribution is when such activities substantially interfere with the work of the school or impinge upon the rights of other students.[49]

---

[46]*Id.* at 271. A federal court of appeals ruled that a school board could properly reject Planned Parenthood's advertisement for publication in high school newspapers and other school publications because in such a school-sponsored publication, the school had the right to maintain a position of neutrality on controversial issues. *Planned Parenthood of S. Nev., Inc. v. Clark County Sch. Dist.,* 941 F.2d 817 (9th Cir. 1991) (*en banc*).

[47]*Mergens,* 496 U.S. at 250.

[48]*Tinker,* 393 U.S. at 512–13.

[49]*Id.* at 509, 511. *Accord Baughman v. Freienmuth,* 478 F.2d 1345 (4th Cir. 1973); *Quarterman v. Byrd,* 453 F.2d 54 (4th Cir. 1971); *Rivera,* 721 F. Supp. at 1189.

The distribution of religious literature is a powerful evangelization tool. Students should not be intimidated from using this form of expression. Students may distribute religious literature before or after school while students are arriving on the campus. Bus stops and hallways are prime areas for the distribution of literature. Students may also distribute literature or engage in verbal speech between classes. Other times appropriate for student expression include lunchtime, in the cafeteria, or on the playing field. During noninstructional time, students have the right to express themselves. Students should not attempt to distribute literature during class time. However, outside of class time, a flat "ban on the distribution of student-initiated religious literature cannot be constitutionally justified."[50]

Sometimes the bigotry and ignorance of some school officials is astonishing. One eighth grader brought the religious newspaper *Issues and Answers* to school, planning to distribute the paper to her fellow students during noninstructional time. She asked the assistant principal for permission to distribute the

---

[50]*Widmar,* 454 U.S. at 269–70. It should be noted that distribution of literature by outside groups is treated differently from distribution of literature by students. Though some courts have ruled in favor of Gideons, others have ruled that Gideons may not come on public school campuses for the purpose of distributing Bibles. Cf. *Peck v. Upshur County Bd. of Educ.,* 941 F. Supp. 1465 (N.D.W. Va. 1996), *aff'd in part, rev'd in part,* 155 F.3d 274 (4th Cir. 1998) (Gideons may distribute Bibles on public school campuses.); *Schanou v. Lancaster County School Dist.,* 863 F. Supp. 1048 (D. Neb. 1994), *vacated and remanded,* 62 F.3d 1040 (8th Cir. 1995) (same) *with Berger v. Rensselaer Cent. Sch. Corp.,* 982 F.2d 1160 (7th Cir.), *cert. denied,* 508 U.S. 911 (1993) (Gideons may not distribute Bibles on public school campuses.); *Meltzer v. Board of Pub. Instruction of Orange County,* 548 F.2d 559 (5th Cir. 1977), *aff'd in part, rev'd in part on reh'g,* 577 F.2d 311 (5th Cir. 1978) (*en banc*), *cert. denied,* 439 U.S. 1089 (1979) (same).

literature. After reviewing the contents of the paper and noting that it was religious and contained Bible verses, the assistant principal responded that students were not permitted to bring Bibles, religious literature, or literature that quoted the Bible on public school campuses. Therefore, the request for distribution was flatly denied. Liberty Counsel represented this student and filed suit against the school board for denial of the student's free speech rights. The day after filing suit, one school board member was quoted by the media as saying that religion had no place on public school campuses and that students had no right to bring religious literature to school. This statement by the board member was later retracted when the school board agreed with Liberty Counsel's position that the student had a First Amendment right to distribute her literature before and after class, in between classes, in the cafeteria, or on the playing field.[51]

Following school board policy, the principal for the Milwaukee High School for the Arts told students that they could no longer refer to their Bible club as Christian Fellowship because the word *Christian* violated the "separation of church and state."[52] Instead, the school advised the students they must refer to themselves as "CF."[53] As if that were not enough, when Heather, Jolie, and Sarah sought

---

[51]*Beach v. School Bd. of Leon County,* No 93–40048 (N.D. Fla. filed Feb. 9, 1993).

[52]For a discussion of the phrase "separation of church and state" and how it has been misused, see Mathew D. Staver, TAKE BACK AMERICA 33–44 (2000). *See generally* Daniel L. Dreisbach, THOMAS JEFFERSON AND THE WALL OF SEPARATION BETWEEN CHURCH AND STATE (2002).

[53]*Knutson v. Milwaukee Pub. Sch.,* No. 97-CV-143 (E.D. Wis. filed Feb. 13, 1997).

permission to hang a poster on the club bulletin board and to distribute a pledge card to other students on Valentine's Day in support of a True Love Waits campaign, school officials denied permission because the pledge contained the word *God*. Throughout the country, many high school students promote the True Love Waits campaign, which is designed to encourage other students to remain sexually abstinent until entry into a biblical marriage. The card pledges support to family, friends, future spouse, future children, and to God. Although the other clubs were allowed to put up secular posters on the bulletin board and distribute secular literature, school board policy stated that no religious literature could be posted on bulletin boards or distributed by students. Fortunately Liberty Counsel was able to intervene on behalf of these students. On February 12, it became apparent that the school would not budge in its position. Several attorneys began working on this case in the late afternoon and worked throughout the night and until midday on February 13. A federal lawsuit containing approximately one and one-half inches of typed legal research was sent via the Internet to Milwaukee. The documents were printed, signed by the parties, and delivered to the federal court at 4:15 p.m., just fifteen minutes before the court closed. On the morning of February 14 at 11:15 a.m., a federal judge entered an emergency restraining order which allowed the students to hang their posters and distribute the pledge cards. At the end of the day, one girl approached Sarah expressing interest in the pledge, but during the course of the conversation, the student hung her head down and said, "I can't sign the pledge because I'm not a virgin." Sarah responded that God forgave her past, and she could pledge from that time forward to remain sexually abstinent until she entered a biblical marriage. At that moment the girl's face lit up, and she signed the pledge. Certainly literature distribution is a powerful tool, and in this case, at least one student may have begun a new chapter in her life.[54]

In another case second-grader Morgan Nyman was told by the principal at the direction of the school board that she could not pass out her Valentine cards because her cards contained religious messages, such as "Jesus loves you. Pass it on."[55] The other students were permitted to pass out their cards containing secular messages. After Liberty Counsel filed suit, the story became the top news item, with the local television networks displaying enlarged pictures of the cards. Thus, instead of a few students receiving Morgan's cards, hundreds of thousands of people heard her message. The school later agreed with Liberty Counsel's position and redrafted the school board policy.

Some schools have attempted to regulate student literature distribution by requiring that all literature be reviewed by school officials prior to distribution. However, the requirement of giving advance notice of a student's intent to speak inherently inhibits free speech.[56] The Supreme Court has stated that prior notification is "quite incompatible with the requirements of the First Amendment."[57] Indeed, the "simple knowledge that one must inform the government of his desire to speak and must fill out appropriate forms and comply with

---

[54]In 2004, Liberty Counsel launched the Day of Purity to promote abstinence outside of marriage. For more information, visit www.DayofPurity.org.

[55]*Nyman v. School Bd. of Kettle Moraine,* No.01–285 (E.D. Wis. filed Mar. 22, 2001).

[56]*NAACP v. City of Richmond,* 743 F.2d 1346 (9th Cir. 1984).

[57]*Thomas v. Collins,* 323 U.S. 516, 540 (1945).

applicable regulations discourages citizens from speaking freely."[58] Certainly the "delay inherent in advance notice requirements inhibits [free speech by] outlawing spontaneous expression."[59] The Supreme Court has further noted that when "an event occurs, it is often necessary to have one's voice heard promptly, if it is to be considered at all."[60]

Most of these school policies requiring advance notice prior to distribution are insufficient because they lack specific guidelines. These policies often leave much discretion to the school officials so as to allow them to censor the speech without using objective criteria. These pre-distribution review requirements are presumptively invalid because, essentially, they require a license from the government prior to speaking.[61] One case concluded that a one-day advanced notification requirement was unconstitutional.[62] In striking down an advanced notification requirement, a federal court noted that "a policy which subjects all nonschool-sponsored communications to predistribution review for content censorship violates the First Amendment. . . . [N]o . . . content control is justified for communication among

---

[58]*City of Richmond,* 743 F.2d at 1355 (citing *Rosen v. Port of Portland,* 641 F.2d 1243 [9th Cir. 1981]).

[59]*City of Richmond,* 743 F.2d at 1355.

[60]*Shuttlesworth v. City of Birmingham,* 394 U.S. 147, 163 (1969).

[61]"It is well established that in the area of freedom of expression an overbroad regulation may be subject to facial review and invalidation, even though its application in the case under construction may be constitutionally unobjectionable." *Forsyth County v. Nationalist Movement,* 505 U.S. 123, 129 (1992); *see also Secretary of State of Md. v. Joseph Munson Co.,* 467 U.S. 947 (1984); *Shuttlesworth v. Birmingham,* 394 U.S. 147 (1969); *Freedman v. Maryland,* 380 U.S. 51 (1965); *Talley v. California,* 362 U.S. 60 (1960); *Abramson v. Gonzalez,* 949 F.2d 1567 (11th Cir. 1992); *Sentinel Communications Co. v. Watts,* 936 F.2d 1189 (11th Cir. 1991).

[62]*Rosen,* 641 F.2d at 1243 (dealing with an international airport).

students which is not part of the educational program."[63] The "majority of courts of appeals considering policies similar to the one at issue here [a predistribution review policy] found them violative of the First Amendment because they were overly broad and inadequately focused on avoidance of disruption and interference with school discipline."[64]

Reviewing a predistribution review literature distribution policy within the context of the public school, a federal court found such a policy unconstitutional because it gave school officials "unfettered discretion."[65] The court further stated that such a policy gave

the government the power to suppress speech in advance, while imposing no time limits or other procedural obligations on school officials that would

[63]*Burch v. Barker,* 861 F.2d 1149, 1157 (9th Cir. 1988).
[64]*Id.* at 1155. The Seventh Circuit stated in *Fujishima v. Board of Education,* 460 F.2d 1355, 1358 (7th Cir. 1972), that "*Tinker* in no way suggests that students may be required to announce their intentions of engaging in certain conduct beforehand so school authorities may decide whether to prohibit the conduct." The following courts have struck down prior review policies in secondary schools: *Riseman v. School Comm. of the City of Quincy,* 439 F.2d 148 (1st Cir. 1971); *Eisner v. Stamford Board of Education,* 440 F.2d 803 (2d Cir. 1971); *Quarterman,* 453 F.2d at 453; *Baugman v. Board of Education,* 478 F.2d 1345 (4th Cir. 1973); *Nitzberg v. Parks,* 525 F.2d 378 (4th Cir. 1975); *Shanley v. Northeast Independent School District,* 462 F.2d 960 (5th Cir. 1972); *Fujishima v. Board of Education,* 460 F.2d 1355 (7th Cir. 1972); *Hedges,* 9 F.3d at 1295; *Burch,* 861 F.2d at 1149. *See also Johnston-Leohner v. O'Brien,* 859 F. Supp. 575 (M.D. Fla. 1994); *Slotterback,* 766 F. Supp. at 280; *Rivera,* 721 F. Supp. at 1189; *Nelson v. Moline Sch. Dist.,* 725 F. Supp. 965 (N.D. Ill. 1989); *Sullivan v. Houston Indep. Sch. Dist.,* 333 F. Supp. 1149 (S.D. Tex. 1971); *Zucker v. Panitz,* 299 F. Supp. 102 (S.D.N.Y. 1969). *But see Muller,* 98 F.3d at 1530 *and Bystrom v. Fridley High Sch.,* 822 F.2d 747(8th Cir. 1987) (upholding a very detailed prior review policy, but noting that such a policy could not apply to colleges or universities).
[65]*Rivera,* 721 F. Supp. at 1198.

insure that speech is suppressed to the minimum extent possible, or that the speech is supported for good and expressed reasons, rather than at the whim of school officials. This policy gives the school authorities the power to extinguish the right of students to speak through inaction and delay.[66]

In a case brought on behalf of a fifth-grade student whose literature was confiscated by a school principal, Liberty Counsel argued that the policy placed an impermissible restraint on free speech. The school argued that it must prereview the literature for religious content. The court stated: "It is beyond dispute that the school policy imposes a prior restraint on speech. It is also beyond dispute that the restraint is based on content, for only after reviewing content does the school decide whether particular materials may be distributed."[67]

Recognizing that public school students, including fifth graders, have the right to free speech, the court declared:

In order for the State in the person of school officials to justify prohibition of a particular expression of opinion, it must be able to show that its action was caused by something more than a mere desire to avoid the discomfort and unpleasantness that always accompany an unpopular viewpoint.[68]

Following *Tinker,* a school seeking to impose a content-based prior restraint on student speech must show that the

---

[66]*Id.*
[67]*Johnston-Loehner,* 859 F. Supp. at 579.
[68]*Id.* at 580.

restricted speech would materially and substantially interfere with school operations or with the rights of other students. Speculative fear is insufficient to sustain a content-based prior restraint on student speech.[69]

The courts have disdained predistribution review policies because they essentially allow the government to suppress speech in advance. Policies that do not contain time limits in which the government official has to grant or deny the request essentially allow for the suppression of speech either by inaction or delay. One federal court of appeals stated that "*Tinker* in no way suggests that students may be required to announce their intentions of engaging in certain conduct beforehand so school authorities may decide whether to prohibit the conduct."[70] These predistribution review policies are essentially a licensing law, and the Supreme Court has made "clear that a person faced with such an unconstitutional licensing law may ignore it and engage with impunity in the exercise of the right of free expression for which the law purports to require a license."[71] A policy which requires students to present their literature for predistribution review is unconstitutional.[72]

Going back to the common-sense approach mentioned earlier regarding student speech, it would be laughable for

---

[69]*Id.* at 580.

[70]*Fujishima,* 460 F.2d at 1358.

[71]*Shuttlesworth,* 394 U.S. at 151.

[72]*But see Muller,* 98 F.3d at 1530; *Hedges,* 9 F.3d at 1295. In *Hedges* the Seventh Circuit upheld a policy requiring prior review of literature distributed in quantities greater than ten. However, this decision is flawed and is inconsistent with Supreme Court cases regarding prior literature distribution. Moreover, the majority of the federal appellate courts are not in agreement with the Seventh Circuit.

any school to require students to reveal the content of their *verbal* communication to public officials prior to engaging in conversation during noninstructional time. When entering the school, a student is not required to announce to the principal the content of all verbal speech that will occur during the day. A student does not need permission to tell another student, "I like you." It is both unconstitutional and ludicrous for a school to impose such a requirement. Additionally, it is likewise unconstitutional and ludicrous to require prior review of speech simply because it is transformed to the printed page.

Some schools may argue that their restrictive policies do not violate student free speech so long as the students can exercise their free speech off campus or so long as they can place literature in a designated rack within the school. However, the Supreme Court has stated that "one is not to have the exercise of his liberty of expression in appropriate places abridged on the plea that it may be exercised in some other place."[73] One school argued that it must prohibit student distribution of literature because to allow it would violate the Establishment Clause or the so-called separation of church and state. The school allowed the distribution of literature but only if it were placed at a specific designated location. A court reviewing this situation ruled that the designated location restriction created an Establishment Clause problem which the school attempted to avoid.[74] It is unreasonable to

---

[73]*Schneider,* 308 U.S. at 163.
[74]*Johnston-Loehner,* 859 F. Supp. at 575. The Establishment Clause is not implicated by student-initiated literature distribution during noninstructional time. When the school sought to restrict student literature distribution by requiring that the literature be "distributed" only in a placement

require students to speak only at a designated location. Just as it would be ridiculous to require students to go to a designated location in order to pass out a love note or directions, it is unreasonable to require students to place their religious literature at a designated location. Verbal speech is equivalent to written speech. The two should be treated equally. The only difference between them is litter. However, schools should prohibit the one who litters and not use littering or some other invalid reason to restrict speech in general.[75] A ban on handbilling would suppress "a great quantity of speech that does not cause the evils that it seeks to eliminate."[76] Leafletting is a "form of religious activity [that] occupies the same high estate under the First Amendment as do worship in churches and preaching from the pulpits."[77]

Some schools have attempted to restrict student-initiated speech on the basis that it violates the Establishment Clause of the First Amendment, or the so-called "separation of church and state." In one case Liberty Counsel represented a fifth-grade student whose principal confiscated and destroyed her religious tracts. The school argued that if it allowed the young girl to distribute material to her fellow classmates, the other students would perceive that the school was endorsing the message within these tracts, and since the school was prohibited from endorsing or promoting religion,

---

rack provided by the school, the school created, rather than avoided, an Establishment Clause violation.

[75]See *Organization for a Better Austin v. Keefe,* 410 U.S. at 415; *Martin,* 319 U.S. at 145; *Jamison,* 318 U.S. at 416; *Schneider,* 308 U.S. at 162; *Lovell,* 303 U.S. at 452.

[76]*Ward,* 491 U.S. at 789–99.

[77]*Murdock,* 319 U.S. at 109 (1943).

the distribution of these tracts would violate the Establishment Clause. The federal court ruled that the school board's "asserted interest in avoiding violation of the Establishment Clause is invalid because permitting student distribution of religious materials does not violate the Establishment Clause."[78]

The school district's reasoning was, of course, flawed. Students as well as school officials have the affirmative protection of the First Amendment Free Speech and Free Exercise Clauses. However, only teachers and school officials are restricted by the Establishment Clause from promoting their religion. The Establishment Clause applies only to governmental entities. It does not apply to individuals who are not associated with the government. Therefore, students do not have the restriction imposed by the Establishment Clause. Students cannot establish a religion. Only governmental entities and their agents can establish a religion. Consequently, students have all the affirmative protection of the Free Speech and Free Exercise Clauses of the First Amendment and do not have any restriction or prohibition of the Establishment Clause. While schools and their agents are prohibited from actively promoting and proselytizing a particular religious tenet, students have absolutely no prohibition in this regard. The Supreme Court has already recognized that "there is a crucial difference between *government* speech endorsing religion, which the Establishment Clause forbids, and *private* speech endorsing religion, which the Free Speech and Free Exercise Clauses protect."[79] One court, rejecting a school's

---

[78]*Johnston-Loehner*, 859 F. Supp. at 579.
[79]*Mergens*, 496 U.S. at 250.

argument that it must censor religious literature, stated the following:

> Just as bellicose bystanders cannot authorize the government to silence a speaker, so ignorant bystanders cannot make censorship legitimate. . . . Schools may explain that they do not endorse speech by permitting it. If pupils do not comprehend so simple a lesson, then one wonders whether . . . schools can teach anything at all. Free speech, free exercise, and the ban on establishment are quite compatible when the government remains neutral and educates the public about the reason. . . .
>
> Misperceptions of endorsement may be dealt with by steps to increase the students' understanding of our constitutional structure, and students' speech will *itself* dissipate any perception of endorsement—for students will disagree among themselves, and the audience will understand that the school does not endorse incompatible positions.[80]

"It is only when individuals seek to observe their religion in ways that unduly involve the government that their expressive rights may be circumscribed."[81] There has never been any case in which student-initiated speech has constituted a violation of the Establishment Clause.

A Texas court flatly rejected the Establishment Clause argument on the basis that the Establishment Clause "is not a restriction on the rights of individuals acting in their private lives."[82]

---

[80]*Hedges,* 9 F.3d at 1299.
[81]*Berger,* 982 F.2d at 1168.
[82]*Clark,* 806 F. Supp. at 121. *Accord Mergens,* 496 U.S. at 226; *Rivera,* 721 F. Supp. at 1195.

Another court has also rejected this argument by stating:

> The Establishment Clause is a limitation on the power of governments; it is not a restriction on the rights of individuals acting in their private lives. The threshold question in any Establishment Clause case is whether there is sufficient governmental action to invoke the prohibition. In *Bethel* and *Hazelwood,* the Supreme Court recognized a distinction between school-affiliated speech and the private speech of students. It is clear that the mere fact that student speech occurs on school property does not make it government supported. It is undisputed in this case that the students are not government actors, are not acting in concert with the government, and do not seek school cooperation or assistance with their speech. Accordingly, the Establishment Clause simply is not implicated.[83]

The Supreme Court has already recognized a distinction between student-initiated speech and school-sponsored speech.[84] One federal district court clearly distinguished school-sponsored speech from student-initiated speech by pointing out that the "standard for reviewing the suppression of . . . school-sponsored speech [is governed] by *Hazelwood,* and all other speech by *Tinker.*"[85]

---

[83]*Rivera,* 721 F. Supp. at 1195; *see also Clark,* 806 F. Supp. at 121; *Thompson v. Waynesboro Area Sch. Dist.,* 673 F. Supp. 1379 (M.D. Pa. 1987).
[84]*Hazelwood,* 484 U.S. at 270–71.
[85]*Chandler v. McMinnville Sch. Dist.,* 978 F.2d 524, 529 (9th Cir. 1992).

Clothing

Expressive activity through the wearing of clothing that has writing, or items such as crosses or religious jewelry which do not substantially interfere with the work of the school or impinge upon the rights of other students also retains First Amendment protection. The *Tinker* case involved students wearing black armbands to school as a symbolic protest to the Vietnam War. The Supreme Court held that such expression was protected by the First Amendment.[86]

The analysis used for clothing is essentially the same analysis used for literature distribution. The main difference between the two is that the former speech is carried into the classroom while the latter can be limited to noninstructional time. As a result of this difference, schools can enact neutral uniform policies which require all students to wear the same clothing and which ban all words or symbols.[87] However, even a uniform dress policy that is selectively applied to unwanted messages violates the First Amendment.[88] If the dress policy allows secular words, symbols, or jewelry, then students have the right to wear articles of clothing bearing religious messages.[89]

---

[86]*Tinker,* 393 U.S. at 506, 511.

[87]*Littlefield v. Forney Indep. Sch. Dist.,* 268 F.3d 275 (5th Cir. 2001) (upholding uniform dress code which allowed an opt out for religious reasons); *Canady v. Bossier Parish Sch. Bd.,* 240 F.3d 437 (5th Cir. 2001); *Long v. Board of Educ. of Jefferson County,* 121 F. Supp. 2d 621 (W.D. Ky. 2000); *Boroff v. Van Wert City Bd. of Educ.,* 220 F.3d 465 (6th Cir. 2000); *Phoenix Elementary Sch. Dist. No. 1 v. Green,* 943 P.2d 836 (Ariz. Ct. App. 1997).

[88]*Castornia v. Madison County Sch. Bd.,* 246 F.3d 536 (6th Cir. 2000) (involving a rebel flag).

[89]Guidance on Constitutionally Protected Prayer in Public Elementary and Secondary Schools, 68 Fed. Reg. 9645–01 (2003) (available at www.lc.org/misc/Education.html) (hereinafter 68 Fed. Reg. 9645–01 (2003)).

Printed words on clothing such as T-shirts are a form of free speech. Just like the students in *Tinker* who wore black armbands protesting involvement in the Vietnam War, students have the right to wear words or symbols on their clothing. Student expression may be limited only if it interferes with the ordinary operation of the school or with the rights of other students. In the case of interfering with the rights of other students, the issue is whether the wording is defamatory or libelous to another student, not whether it is offensive.[90] Simply because another student disagrees with the content of the message does not permit the school to restrict the wearing of the shirt.

One student contacted Liberty Counsel after listening to a national radio broadcast on this topic. The student apparently had worn a T-shirt to school with a pro-life message. The principal ordered her to change clothes and not wear the shirt again. The shirt had the message "God created woman with a womb, not a tomb." Liberty Counsel instructed the student that she should respect those in authority over her, but this situation involved her religious conviction and her right to speak under the First Amendment. Therefore, the student was advised that she had a right to wear the shirt to school. When she later showed up at school wearing the shirt, the principal questioned her, stating, "Why are you wearing that T-shirt again?" The student responded, "Because my attorney said I have a constitutional right to do so." That was the end of the discussion. After contacting the superintendent, the principal agreed that the student had the right to wear the shirt. In one

---

[90]*Clark,* 806 F. Supp. at 120.

case, junior high school students designed T-shirts, on the back of which was printed: "The best of the night's adventures are reserved for people with nothing planned."[91] School officials told the students to remove the T-shirts because the officials believed the message promoted an alcohol advertisement. However, the students contended that the T-shirt was meant to convey a message of being spontaneous and having fun. The federal court found that the students' speech was "presumptively protected by the First Amendment."[92] The court further noted that the T-shirts worn during regular school hours did not bear the imprimatur or sponsorship of the school, and therefore neither the *Hazelwood* case (the school newspaper case) nor the *Fraser* case (the nominating speech case) applied. Finally, the court ruled that a forum analysis was not appropriate and that the proper test was to apply *Tinker*.[93] The court, therefore, concluded that the students had a First Amendment right to wear the T-shirts, and they could not be prohibited unless there was evidence of "substantial disruption or material interference with school activities."[94]

During a school-sponsored diversity week at Woodbury High School in Minnesota, Elliot Chambers wore a sweatshirt emblazoned with the message "Straight Pride." On the back

---

[91]*McIntire v. Bethel Indep. Sch. Dist.*, 804 F. Supp. 1415, 1422 (W.D. Ok. 1992).

[92]*Id.* at 1424; *see also Roth v. United States*, 354 U.S. 476, 484 (1957) ("All ideas having even the slightest redeeming social importance—unorthodox ideas, controversial ideas, even ideas hateful to the prevailing climate of opinion—have the full protection of the guarantees [of the First Amendment].")

[93]*McIntire*, 804 F. Supp. at 1427.

[94]*Id.* at 1420.

of the shirt was a symbol of a man and a woman holding hands. School officials demanded the sweatshirt be removed because, they contended, the message might "offend" other students. The court ruled that the student had a right to wear the shirt with his own message even though it conflicted with the school's diversity week message.[95]

One court found that a middle school violated the rights of students by punishing them for wearing "SCAB" buttons to protest replacement teachers during a strike.[96] The court found the school did not prove that the buttons were "inherently disruptive" to school activities under the *Tinker* standard. Another court found that a Texas school violated the First Amendment when it applied a dress policy prohibiting gang-related apparel to a devout Roman Catholic and prohibited the student from wearing a rosary.[97]

Wearing T-shirts with messages or symbols on the back allow the message to be viewed by others throughout the school day, especially by those sitting behind the student in class. During class, discussion about the message is probably inappropriate, but after class or in between class, discussion of the message is appropriate. Articles of clothing or jewelry provide many expressive opportunities.

Hair and Headwear

Hair dress is important to certain religious beliefs. School dress codes requiring males to have short hair may conflict

---

[95]*Chambers v. Babbitt,* 145 F. Supp.2d 1068 (D. Minn. 2001).
[96]*Chandler,* 978 F.2d at 524.
[97]*Chailfoux v. New Caney Indep. Sch. Dist.,* 976 F. Supp. 659 (S.D. Tex. 1997).

with the beliefs of some Native American students. One federal court ruled that it is unconstitutional for a school to require Native American male students to have short hair contrary to their religious beliefs. Some Native Americans believe that short hair may only be worn to show mourning when a close family member dies. Since wearing long hair for males of certain religious beliefs may actually be a First Amendment expressive activity, some dress codes may be ruled unconstitutional.[98] In order to object to a dress code, the student must have a sincerely held religious belief that is negatively impacted by the code. The school should then take efforts to accommodate the student's religious belief.

Class Discussions and Reports

Students may ask questions or even respectfully challenge teachers during class when the subject matter being taught is disagreeable. Students may give religious verbal or written reports or projects. While student speech is protected by the First Amendment, a student cannot stand up in a math class and begin speaking about religion if the speech has no relation to the topic being studied.[99] However, if the subject

---

[98]*Alabama and Coushatta Tribes of Texas v. Trustees of the Big Sandy Indep. Sch. Dist.,* 817 F. Supp. 1319 (E.D. Tex. 1993). *But see Isaacs v. Board of Educ. of Howard County,* 40 F. Supp. 2d 335 (D. Md. 1999) (upholding a school's "no hats" policy against a challenge by a student wanting to wear a head wrap celebrating African cultural heritage, where policy made exceptions for religious headgear such as yarmulkes and Muslim hijab, including head scarves).

[99]*Walz v. Egg Harbor Township Bd. of Educ.,* 187 F. Supp. 2d 232 (D.N.J. 2002) (school allowed distribution outside classroom and after school hours but prohibited in-class distribution).

matter is evolution, the student can certainly ask questions regarding creation science or abrupt appearance and can even respectfully disagree with the teacher. The student may express views on any subject being taught so long as the expression is consistent with the subject matter being discussed at that time.

If students are asked to give verbal or written reports, they may give these reports on religious matters, so long as the work product is within the parameters of the assignment. Students may express their religion in school assignments. For example, in a literature class, if students are required to read a book and give a written or oral report, a student may read a religious book and give a report on this book. If a teacher prohibited the student from giving the report solely because the content of the report was religious, this would be a violation of the student's free speech and free exercise rights.[100]

The United States Department of Education issued guidelines entitled *Guidance on Constitutionally Protected Prayer*

---

[100]*But see C. H. v. Oliva*, 226 F.3d 198 (3d Cir. 2000) (*en banc*), *cert denied*, 533 U.S. 915 (2001); *Hood v. Medford Township Bd. of Educ.*, 533 U.S. 915 (2001) (the appellate court decision regarding a kindergartner wanting to read a religious book was divided by a six to six vote, but the court allowed the young girl to amend her complaint); *DeNooyer v. Livonia Pub. Schs.*, 799 F. Supp. 744 (E.D. Mich. 1992), *aff'd sub nom, DeNooyer v. Merinelli*, 12 F.3d 211 (6th Cir. 1993), *cert. denied*, 511 U.S. 1031 (1994) (A school may prohibit a second-grade student from showing videotape when the assignment required oral presentations.); *Duran v. Nitsche*, 780 F. Supp. 1048 (E.D. Pa. 1991), *appeal dismissed, vacated*, 972 F.2d 1331 (3d Cir. 1992) (A fifth-grade teacher may prohibit a student from giving an oral presentation to her class about her belief in God because, even though the teacher allowed oral presentations, the classroom was not open for all forms of discussion.).

in Public Elementary and Secondary Schools.[101] Addressing the topic of student assignments, these guidelines state the following:

> Students may express their beliefs about religion in the form of homework, artwork, and other written and oral assignments free of discrimination based on the religious content of their submissions. Such home and classroom work should be judged by ordinary academic standards of substance and relevance, and against other legitimate pedagogical concerns identified by the school.[102]

School officials who choose to ignore the Department of Education guidelines risk losing their federal funding. Public schools must certify compliance with the guidelines annually with their state department of education. Each state must report noncomplying schools. Complaints regarding schools not complying with the federal guidelines may be filed with both the state education office and the United States Department of Education.

One parent contacted Liberty Counsel stating that his seventh-grade son could not use the word *God* in his oral class presentation because to do so would violate the "separation of church and state." Incredibly, the teacher required the seventh-grade boy to reverse the "d" with the "G" every time the word appeared. Although the other students were allowed to give their oral presentations without censorship, this

---

[101]68 Fed. Reg. 9645-01 (2003) (available at www.lc.org/nisc/Education.html).
[102]*Id.*

student was required to say "dog" every time his written speech mentioned "God." Unbelievable as it seems, this is the battlefield public school students enter every day. The teacher was unquestionably wrong and unfortunately sent a horrible message to the entire class.

In addition to the right to express a message, students may object to participating in certain kinds of class assignments if the activity violates a sincerely held religious belief. If a class project, assignment, or activity violates a student's sincerely held religious belief, the student may opt out and request alternative accommodations.[103]

Students and parents may object to various curricula on several grounds. One challenge to religiously objectionable curriculum is to assert free exercise and parental rights. The student or parent must first have a sincerely held religious belief that is substantially burdened by the curriculum. Once this threshold is reached, the school must show it has a compelling reason for disallowing an opt-out and that its refusal to allow an opt-out is the least restrictive means available. Generally, a school should allow the student to opt out of religiously objectionable instruction.

Challenges to the entire curriculum are generally not successful, but challenges to portions of classroom instruction may be appropriate. One federal court rejected a challenge to the entire school curriculum in which parents argued that the curriculum promoted secular humanism.[104] Challenges

---

[103]State law often requires parental notice and/or opt-out provisions for sex education or HIV/AIDS instruction.
[104]*Mozert v. Hawkins County Bd. of Educ.*, 827 F.2d 1058 (6th Cir. 1987), *cert. denied*, 484 U.S. 1066 (1988).

to the entire curriculum based upon allegations that it promotes the religion of secular humanism have failed for two reasons. First, courts have found the task of defining secular humanism difficult. Second, courts are reluctant to strike down an entire curriculum since that would substantially interfere with the educational process and create a huge void with nothing to fill the instructional time. Moreover, courts are reluctant to strike down an entire curriculum based on one person's religious belief for fear that another person will have a different religious viewpoint, and the schools will be caught in a quagmire.

Not only are courts reluctant to throw out an entire curriculum, courts are also reluctant to strike down specific courses. A federal court of appeals ruled against parents challenging curriculum on the basis that the students were required to learn witchcraft and create poetic chants.[105]

In an outrageous case, a federal appeals court rejected a challenge brought by parents who claimed that their rights were violated when their children were subjected to a sexually explicit presentation put on by a private organization called Hot, Sexy and Safer Productions, Inc.[106] The parents complained that their children had been mentally raped when they were required to go to a mandatory convocation reportedly on sex education. However, instead of objectively overviewing sex education issues, the outside organization called students from the audience, placed huge condoms over their entire body and then licked the condoms.

---

[105]*Brown v. Woodland Joint Unified Sch. Dist.*, 27 F.3d 1373 (9th Cir. 1994).
[106]*Brown v. Hot, Sexy and Safer Prod., Inc.*, 68 F.3d 525 (1st Cir. 1995), *cert. denied*, 516 U.S. 1159 (1996).

Comments were also made regarding the kinds of pants boys should wear, their physical features, genitalia, masturbation, and homosexuality. The students were shocked and horrified, and yet the court rejected the constitutional challenge that parental rights had been violated by subjecting these students to this unwarranted mental rape.[107]

Although not raising religious objections, two federal courts ruled that compulsory community service requirements do not violate due process or parental rights.[108] In both of these cases, the school boards enacted regulations requiring students to perform community service prior to graduation. The students and parents raised objections based on due process, interference with parental rights, and violation of the Thirteenth Amendment, which prohibits involuntary servitude. The courts found that none of these claims had merit. However, these cases did not raise religious objections, and it may be arguable in some cases that mandatory community service would violate sincerely held religious beliefs. This would certainly be true if the choices presented for community service required the student to participate in religiously objectionable activities.

---

[107]A majority of states now require parental notice and/or consent for sex education. A New York State court ruled that a condom distribution program violated state law when the schools failed to get the parents' prior consent to distribute the condoms. *Alfonso v. Fernandez,* 606 N.Y.S.2d 259 (1993) (ruling that the condom distribution fell under the state statute dealing with health services which required parental consent).

[108]*Immediato v. Rye Neck Sch. Dist.,* 73 F.3d 454 (2d Cir.), *cert. denied,* 519 U.S. 813 (1996); *Herndon v. Chapel Hill-Carrboro City Bd. of Educ.,* 89 F.3d 174 (4th Cir. 1996), *cert. denied,* 519 U.S. 1111 (1997).

Access to Books and Films

The Supreme Court has declared that a student's "right to receive ideas is a necessary predicate to the recipient's meaningful exercise of his or her own right of speech."[109] While a school may not be forced to place a book in the library, once a book is placed there, the discretion to remove the book is circumscribed by the First Amendment. The book may not be removed solely because the school disagrees with the content. However, the book could be removed if it lacked "educational suitability" or if it contained pervasive vulgarity.[110] Similarly, the Bible cannot be removed from a library on the basis of its religious content.[111] Finally, although a school has wide latitude in the selection and retention of curriculum, content-neutral criteria may be necessary to remove a book or film from the curriculum.[112]

One student called Liberty Counsel because her library did not have any pro-life literature. She obtained certain books and donated them to her school library, and the library accepted the books, placing them on the library shelves. Once accepted, the library has certain restrictions on removing the books. Books cannot be removed simply because the content of the speech is disagreeable or offensive. The so-called political correctness movement often seeks to remove certain speech that offends various classes of society. Such action may violate the First Amendment and should be resisted.

---

[109]*Board of Educ., Island Trees Union Free Sch. Dist. No. 26 v. Pico,* 457 U.S. 853, 867 (1982).

[110]*Id.* at 871.

[111]*But see Roberts v. Madigan,* 702 F. Supp. 1505 (D. Colo. 1989), *aff'd,* 921 F.2d 1047 (10th Cir. 1990), *cert. denied,* 505 U.S. 1218 (1992).

[112]*Pratt v. Independent Sch. Dist.,* 670 F.2d 771 (8th Cir. 1982).

Another individual contacted Liberty Counsel concerned that the school principal had told her that a Bible could not be in the school library because it violated the so-called "separation of church and state." This is absolutely untrue. Schools may and should have religious literature in their libraries. Schools that remove religious material simply because the content is religious violate the First Amendment, because such decisions target the content of the literature.

Student Fees

Any student who has attended college is familiar with mandatory student fees. These fees are paid by students and are used by the school for a multitude of reasons. Schools may not discriminate in the disbursement of the fees. Students may challenge mandatory fee schemes if the distribution mechanism established by the school discriminates based on viewpoint.

The University of Virginia is one of the nation's oldest schools. Like other schools, the University of Virginia imposed mandatory student fees. Recognized student groups were entitled to apply for funds from the Student Activities Fund to assist their student club. Although the University funded fifteen student newspapers, along with a Jewish and a Muslim student group, it refused to fund a newspaper published by Wide Awake Productions because it was Christian.[113] The University took the position that the Jewish and Muslim clubs were not religious, but cultural. The school believed that it

---

[113]*Rosenberger v. Rector and Visitors of the Univ. of Va.,* 515 U.S. 819 (1995).

was prohibited by the Constitution from funding any religious organization. The United States Supreme Court rejected the University of Virginia's argument and ruled that the University must fund the Christian publication because failure to do so would violate the First Amendment. The Court noted:

It is axiomatic that the government may not regulate speech based on its substantive content or the message it conveys. Other principles follow from this precept. In the realm of private speech or expression, government regulation may not favor one speaker over another. Discrimination against speech because of its message is presumed to be unconstitutional. These rules informed our determination that the government offends the First Amendment when it imposes financial burdens on certain speakers based on the content of their expression. When government targets not subject matter but particular views taken by speakers on a subject, the violation of the First Amendment is all the more blatant. Viewpoint discrimination is thus an egregious form of content discrimination. The government must abstain from regulating speech when the specific motivating ideology or the opinion or perspective of the speaker is the rationale for the restriction.[114]

The University of Virginia also argued that this case involved the disbursement of funds, and since funds were scarce, the University was justified in restricting funds from

---

[114]*Id.* at 828–29 (citations omitted).

certain groups. However, the Supreme Court rejected this argument stating that "government cannot justify viewpoint discrimination among private speakers on the economic fact of scarcity."[115] The Court responded with the following:

> Vital First Amendment speech principles are at stake here. The first danger to liberty lies in granting the State the power to examine publications to determine whether or not they are based on some ultimate idea and, if so, for the State to classify them. The second, and corollary, danger is to speech from the chilling of individual thought and expression. That danger is especially real in the University setting, where the State acts against a background and tradition of thought and experiment that is at the center of our intellectual and philosophic tradition. In ancient Athens, and, as Europe entered into a new period of intellectual awakening, in places like Bologna, Oxford, and Paris, universities began as voluntary and spontaneous assemblages or concourses for students to speak and to write and to learn. The quality and creative power of student intellectual life to this day remains a vital measure of a school's influence and attainment. For the University, by regulation, to cast disapproval on particular viewpoints of its students risks the suppression of free speech and creative inquiry in one of the vital centers for the nation's intellectual life, its college and university campuses.[116]

---

[115]*Id.* at 835.
[116]*Id.* at 835–36 (citations omitted).

The Supreme Court found that allowing the Christian student group access to student fees does not violate the Establishment Clause of the First Amendment. Disbursement of the student fees is neutral toward religion in that the fees are available to all student clubs. The University would not be singly funding religion. Moreover, these fees come from students, not the University.[117] The Court pointed out the following:

> It does not violate the Establishment Clause for a public university to grant access to its facilities on a religion-neutral basis to a wide spectrum of student groups, including groups which use meeting rooms for sectarian activities, accompanied by some devotional exercises. This is so even where the upkeep, maintenance, and repair of the facilities attributed to those uses is paid from a student activities fund to which students are required to contribute. The government usually acts by spending money.[118]

The Court noted that there is no constitutional violation for a university to allow access to its facilities on a neutral basis. If a school created a printing room and allowed access to the printers by secular groups, it must allow access to the same printers by Christian groups. Additionally, if the school takes student funds and pays a third party off campus to print student newspapers for secular groups, it must also provide the same funds to pay other third party printers off campus to print a newspaper for a Christian group.[119]

---

[117]*Id.* at 840–41.

[118]*Id.* at 842–43 (citations omitted).

[119]*Id.* at 843–44.

The Supreme Court's decision is clear. Public schools, whether at the college level or lower, may not discriminate in the disbursement of student funds. Christian groups have just as much right to apply for and receive student funds as secular student groups.

Some students may object to the *payment* of a portion of their student fees because of how these funds are used. For example, some student funds are used to provide health insurance for students which may include coverage for abortion. Other portions of the funds may go to political causes advocated by the school which are contrary to sincerely held religious beliefs. Students may raise objections to mandatory fee schemes if the distribution mechanism set up by the school discriminates based on the viewpoint of the applicant. Although the Supreme Court ruled that schools may impose a mandatory fee scheme, the Court also ruled the distribution of fees must be viewpoint-neutral.[120] The Court first noted that if a university conditions the opportunity to receive a college education on an agreement to support objectionable, extracurricular expression by other students, such action would infringe on free speech.[121] The Court then observed that a college or university must provide protection to the First Amendment rights of students and that "the standard of protection for objecting students . . . is the requirement of viewpoint neutrality in the allocation of funding support."[122] In other words, while a college or university may impose mandatory fees, the

---

[120]*Board of Regents of the Univ. of Wisconsin Sys. v. Southworth,* 529 U.S. 217 (2000); *see also Goehring v. Brophy,* 94 F.3d 1294 (9th Cir. 1996) (students failed to establish that the University's health insurance system imposed a substantial burden on their free exercise of religion).
[121]*Id.* at 231.
[122]*Id.* at 233.

disbursement of fees to student activities must be made equally available to all viewpoints. If the disbursement discriminates against viewpoint, then the fee scheme is unconstitutional.[123]

Advertisements in School Newspapers and Yearbooks

Frequently, a public school newspaper or yearbook will print paid advertisements. One federal court found that while state action existed in the publication of a school-sponsored newspaper, the school could reject a Planned Parenthood ad that was contrary to school policy.[124] However, another court found no state action existed when the newspaper was run by a student editorial board, and thus no constitutional challenge could be waged over the decision by the students to reject an ad.[125]

In contrast, another federal court held that where a state university's campus newspaper was open to commercial and some political and service advertisements, the school could not constitutionally reject an ad describing the university employees' union.[126] Yet another court ruled that a university created a limited public forum in the yearbook and that efforts to restrict its publication violated the First Amendment.[127]

---

[123]Many mandatory fee schemes violate the First Amendment because the disbursements typically go toward ultraliberal causes. Conservative and Christian causes oftentimes receive little funding. See *Southworth v. Board of Regents of the Univ. of Wis. Sys.*, 307 F.3d 566 (7th Cir. 2002).

[124]*Planned Parenthood of S. Nev. v. Clark County Sch. Dist.*, 941 F.2d at 817.

[125]*Yeo v. Town of Lexington*, 131 F.3d 241 (1st Cir. 1997).

[126]*Lee v. Board of Regents of State College*, 441 F.2d 1257 (7th Cir. 1971).

[127]*Kincaid v. Gibson*, 236 F.3d 342 (6th Cir. 2001).

In summary, first determine whether the newspaper or year-book is student run or school sponsored. If school sponsored and edited, then there may be a constitutional claim. However, secondary schools have more leeway to reject ads inconsistent with school policy than institutions of higher learning.

Release Time

Release time programs allow public school students a certain time each week to leave school to attend religious instruction.[128] The instruction must be given by nonschool personnel off campus.[129] Portable instruction sites must not be on school premises, and no academic credit should be given for such instruction.[130] Finally, the printing cost of attendance cards should be borne by the religious institution providing the instruction,[131] and elective credit should not be given.[132]

The Pledge of Allegiance

The Pledge of Allegiance has been attacked in court in two different ways. The first attack has been from a free

---

[128]*Zorach v. Clauson,* 343 U.S. 306 (1952).

[129]*Lanner v. Wimmer,* 662 F.2d 1349 (10th Cir. 1981).

[130]*Doe v. Shenandoah County Sch. Bd.,* 737 F. Supp. 913 (W.D. Va. 1990). One court enjoined a release time program where the school the students who remained on campus were required to read and study and were banned from playing because the school did not want to discourage participation in the release time event. *See Moore v. Metropolitan Sch. Dist. of Perry Township,* No. IP00-C-1859, 2001 WL 243292 (S.D. Ind. Feb. 7, 2001).

[131]*Lanner,* 662 F.2d at 1349.

[132]*Id. See also Minnesota Fed. of Teachers v. Nelson,* 740 F. Supp. 694 (D. Minn. 1990).

exercise standpoint, and the second has been from an Establishment Clause position. The first challenge was upheld while the second was rejected.

Jehovah's Witnesses have a sincerely held religious belief against saluting flags, which they consider to be idols. The United States Supreme Court ruled that a Jehovah's Witness should be excused from the requirement of saluting the flag.[133] Indeed, anyone who opposes saluting the flag should be excused from the requirement without regard to whether the refusal is religious or nonreligious. To compel a student to salute the flag may violate free exercise and free speech rights by virtue of the state compelling a specific type of speech.

The United States Supreme Court case deciding the flag salute issue with regard to Jehovah's Witnesses occurred in 1943. However, in 1954, the Pledge of Allegiance was amended to add the phrase "under God." In 1992 an atheist brought suit against an Illinois school board claiming that the flag salute was an unconstitutional establishment of religion by the state because it required individuals, at the direction of the state, to confess belief in God. The federal appeals court found that the Pledge was "a secular rather than sectarian vow" and, therefore, did not violate the First Amendment Establishment Clause.[134] The court ruled that the Pledge was constitutional, merely recognizing "the historical fact that our Nation was believed to have been founded 'under God.'"[135] The court additionally stated that "reciting the pledge may be no more of a religious exercise than reading aloud Lincoln's

---

[133]*West Virginia State Bd. of Educ. v. Barnette,* 319 U.S. 624 (1943).
[134]*Sherman v. Community Consol. Sch. Dist.,* 980 F.2d 437 (7th Cir. 1992), *cert. denied,* 508 U.S. 950 (1993).
[135]*Id.* at 447.

Gettysburg Address, which contains an allusion to the same historical fact."[136] Students in public schools should have the option to refuse to say the Pledge of Allegiance. Without this option, there may be a constitutional violation.

Equal Access on Public School Campuses

EQUAL ACCESS ACT

Students have the right to meet on campus under both the First Amendment and the federal law known as the Equal Access Act of 1984 (hereinafter the "Act").[137] The Act was affirmatively upheld by the Supreme Court in 1990.[138] If a public secondary school receives federal funds and allows one or more noncurriculum-related student groups to meet on campus, then the school cannot prohibit other noncurriculum-related student groups from meeting on campus unless such

---

[136]*Id.* In *Elk Grove Unified School District v. Newdow,* 124 S. Ct. 2301 (2004), the United States Supreme Court threw out a challenge to the words "under God" in the Pledge. The Ninth Circuit Court of Appeals had ruled that the words "under God" in the Pledge violated the Establishment Clause. *See Newdow v. U.S. Congress,* 292 F.3d 597 (9th Cir. 2002). The Supreme Court threw out the case without deciding the constitutional issue.

[137]20 U.S.C. §§ 4071-74. The U.S. Department of Education's *Guidance on Constitutionally Protected Prayer in Public Elementary and Secondary Schools* reminds school officials that religious student groups "must be given the same access to school facilities for assembling as is given to other non-curricular groups, without discrimination because of the religious content of their expression." Complaints regarding noncompliance with the Department's guidelines may be filed with the state department of education and may result in the denial of federal funding to the offending school district. *See* http://www.lc.org/misc/Education.html.

[138]*Mergens,* 496 U.S. at 226.

clubs "materially and substantially interfere with the orderly conduct of educational activities within the school."[139] A non-curriculum-related student group is interpreted broadly to mean "any student group that does not *directly* relate to the body of courses offered by the school."[140] The Court indicated that

> a student group directly relates to a school's curriculum if the subject matter of the group is actually taught, or will soon be taught, in a regularly offered course; if the subject matter of the group concerns the body of courses as a whole; if the participation in the group is required for a particular course; or if participation in the group results in academic credit.[141]

Examples of noncurriculum-related groups are chess clubs, stamp collecting clubs, or community service clubs.

Equal access means exactly what it says—equal access to every facility of the school which is used by at least one or more noncurriculum-related student groups. Equal access includes use of classroom facilities, copy machines, intercom systems, bulletin boards, a school newspaper, yearbook pictures, annual club fairs, an internal bank account, or any other benefit provided to a secular club.[142]

The application of the Act is simple: all groups must be treated equally without discrimination. Religious and political

---

[139]*Id.* at 236, 241.

[140]*Id.* at 239.

[141]*Id.* at 239–40.

[142]As for use of bulletin boards and yearbooks, the school can designate space to "noncurriculum-related student clubs," thus avoiding the appearance of school endorsement.

groups must be treated equally with other social or activity groups. According to the United States Supreme Court in *Mergens,* Congress passed the Act in order "to prevent discrimination against religious and other types of speech."[143]

In the *Mergens* case, the Westside High School already allowed a Christian club to meet informally in the school facilities after school hours. However, the Christian club was denied official recognition, which recognition allowed other student clubs to be a part of the Student Activities Program and permitted access to the school newspaper, bulletin boards, the public address system, and the annual club fair. According to *Mergens,* since the Westside High School officially recognized other noncurriculum-related student groups and allowed those groups access to the school newspaper, bulletin boards, public-address system, and the annual club fair, but did not allow the same privileges to the Christian club, the school violated the Act. Thus, if any club is given access to use school facilities, then a school must allow the same access to other groups. As one group is treated, all groups must be treated. In *Mergens,* the Court noted the following:

> *[The students] seek equal access in the form of official recognition by the school.* Official recognition allows student clubs to be part of the Student Activities Program and carries with it access to the school newspaper, bulletin boards, the public address system, and the annual Club Fair. *We hold that Westside's denial of [the students'] request to form a*

---

[143]*Mergens,* 496 U.S. at 249.

Christian club denied them "equal access under the Act."[144]

Following the *Mergens* case, one school reluctantly allowed the Christian club to meet on campus but informed the club that it could only meet after school hours, while allowing the secular student clubs to meet throughout the school day. The school argued that it allowed equal access to school facilities, just at different times. However, the federal court of appeals easily saw through this thinly guised form of discrimination and ruled that equal access means student clubs must be treated equally. In other words, if the school allows the secular clubs to meet during the day, it must also allow the Christian clubs to meet throughout the day.[145]

Additionally, another federal court found that a high school discriminated against Christian clubs when it allowed the secular clubs to meet during the lunch hour but denied the Christian clubs the same right. The Court ruled that lunch time was considered noninstructional time, and because the school allowed the secular clubs to meet during the lunch hour, it must also allow the Christian clubs to meet during the same time period.[146]

In another case, the school board developed a nondiscrimination policy, requiring that no student-initiated club could discriminate against any person wishing to hold office on the basis of race, sex, national origin, and *religion*. The

---

[144] *Id.* at 247 (emphasis added).

[145]*Good News/Good Sports Club v. School Dist. of City of Ladue,* 28 F.3d 1501 (8th Cir. 1994), *cert. denied,* 515 U.S. 1173 (1995).

[146]*Ceniceros v. Board of Trustees of the San Diego Unified Sch. Dist.,* 106 F.3d 878 (9th Cir. 1997).

policy prohibited discrimination on the basis of race, color, national origin, creed or religion, marital status, sex, age, or handicap condition.

When the Christian group refused to put this nondiscrimination clause in their constitution, the school refused to allow the club access. The school argued that it treated all clubs equally and that all clubs were prohibited from discriminating against potential officers. However, the Christian club argued that if it were not allowed to discriminate on the basis of religion, then the Christian club could essentially face a situation where someone running for office in their Christian club could be an atheist or a Satanist. Fortunately, the federal court agreed and found this nondiscrimination policy unconstitutional because it would essentially obliterate the unique essence of a Christian club.[147]

1. Application of Equal Access Act

The Act provides a safe harbor in which a school may operate. The Act should be viewed as a floor and not a ceiling. In other words, it presents the bare minimum that a school may provide to student groups, but a school may grant even more rights to student groups than the Act requires.

The Act applies to (1) any public secondary school (2) which receives federal funds and (3) has a limited open forum. Identifying a public school providing secondary education receiving federal funds is easy. A limited open forum occurs "whenever such school grants an offering to or opportunity for

---

[147]*Hsu v. Roslyn Union Free Sch. Dist. No. 3,* 85 F.3d 839 (2d Cir.), *cert. denied,* 519 U.S. 1040 (1996).

one or more noncurriculum-related student groups to meet on school premises during noninstructional time."[148]

The Supreme Court in *Mergens* defined a noncurriculum-related student group "broadly to mean any student group that does not *directly* relate to the body of courses offered by the school."[149] The Court further stated:

> A student group directly relates to a school's curriculum if the subject matter of the group is actually taught, or will soon be taught, in a regularly offered course; if the subject matter of the group concerns the body of courses as a whole; if participation in the group is required for a particular course; or if participation in the group results in academic credit.[150]

A student government group would generally relate directly to the curriculum to the extent that it addresses concerns or solicits opinions and formulates proposals pertaining to the body of courses offered by the school. If participation in the school band or orchestra were required for the band or orchestra classes or resulted in academic credit, then such groups would directly relate to the curriculum. One court ruled that a school may not get around the Act by attempting to label the secular clubs as "curriculum-related."[151] On the other hand, some examples of noncurriculum-related student groups include, but are by no means limited to, the chess club, a stamp collecting club, a community service club, camera club,

---

[148]20 U.S.C. § 4071(b).
[149]*Mergens*, 496 U.S. at 239.
[150]*Id.* at 239–40.
[151]*Van Schoick v. Saddleback Valley Unified Sch. Dist.*, 104 Cal. Rptr. 2d 562 (2001).

diving club, music groups, Key Club, debate groups, business groups, political groups, and religious groups.[152]

2. Organizing a Student Club

Under the Act a student club must be initiated by the students. Once initiated, the student group, regardless of size or purpose, must be given treatment equal to all existing clubs. If the school requires a constitution or a statement of purpose from the other clubs, then a constitution or a statement of purpose may also be required of the new club. The school may require a faculty member or any other school employee to be a sponsor of the group if a sponsor is required of the already existing groups. The school faculty member or employee may attend the student meetings. The basic principle is that the student group must be initiated and predominantly led by students, although the students bring in outside speakers.

3. Equal Access Act and Disruptive Clubs

A concern was raised during the legislative hearings on the Act that equal access would allow groups in public schools who promote racism, hate, or disruptive activity.[153] The Act has been in effect since 1984, yet an influx of disruptive hate groups disturbing schools has not occurred.

The Act specifically indicates that it shall not "be construed to limit the authority of the school, its agents or

---

[152]See Mergens, 496 U.S. at 240; Bender v. Williamsport Area Sch. Dist., 741 F.2d 538, 549 n.18 (3d Cir. 1984), vacated on other grounds, 475 U.S. 534 (1986); Student Coalition for Peace v. Lower Merion Sch. Dist., 633 F. Supp. 1040, 1042 (E.D. Pa. 1986); 130 CONG. REC. H7732 (daily ed. July 25, 1984) and 130 CONG. REC. S8365 (daily ed. July 27, 1984).

[153]See Act of Nov. 1, 1978, Pub. L. No. 95-561, 1978 U.S.C.C.A.N. (92 Stat.) 2143.

employees, to maintain order and discipline on school premises, to protect the well-being of students and faculty, and to assure that attendance of students at meetings is voluntary."[154] If a group substantially interferes with the normal operation of the school or is disruptive, the school, under the Act, is free to prohibit such a group from meeting on campus. The school must be able to show that the group is, in fact, disruptive. A simple fear that a group may be disruptive in the future is not enough to support denial of equal access, but actual or threatened disruption by a group may be enough to restrict equal access.[155] Satanic, occultic, racist, and hate groups may at some time cause disruption, but time has shown that schools have not seen an influx of these groups. Simply because some students or faculty disagree with the content of a group's speech is not enough to prohibit that group from equal access. However, if such a group is disruptive to the ordinary operation of the school, then the administrators retain the authority under the Act to maintain an orderly operating school. A school cannot deny access to a group simply because the content of the group's speech is distasteful or offensive. Moreover, a school cannot deny access to a group merely because an affiliate or parent organization at some other location has been shown to be disruptive.[156] The United States Supreme Court has stated:

---

[154]20 U.S.C. § 4071(f).

[155]One court ruled that a high school may not ban a homosexual club if other clubs are permitted on campus. *East High Gay/Straight Alliance v. Board of Educ. of Salt Lake City Sch. Dist.,* 81 F. Supp. 2d 1166 (D. Utah 1999).

[156]*Healy v. James,* 408 U.S. 169 (1972).

Among the rights protected by the First Amendment is the right of individuals to associate to further their personal beliefs. While the freedom of association is not explicitly set out in the Amendment, it has long been held to be implicit in the freedoms of speech, assembly, and petition.[157]

The Supreme Court also observed the following:

It should be obvious that the exclusion of any person or group—all-Negro, all-Oriental, or all-white—from public facilities infringes upon the freedom of the individual to associate as he chooses. . . . The associational rights which our system honors permit all white, all black, all brown, and all yellow groups to be formed. They also permit all Catholic, all Jewish, or all agnostic clubs to be established. Government may not tell a man or woman who his or her associates must be. . . . The freedom to associate applies to the beliefs we share, and to those we consider reprehensible. It tends to produce the diversity of opinion that oils the machinery of democratic government and insures peaceful, orderly change.[158]

On one university campus, a school tried to prohibit the formation of a student group because its national affiliate or parent organization was known to have violent or disruptive behavior. Yet there was no evidence that the local student group had

---

[157]*Id.* at 181.
[158]*Gilmore v. City of Montgomery,* 417 U.S. 556, 575 (1974) (quoting *Moose Lodge No. 107 v. Irvis,* 407 U.S. 163, 179–80 (1972) (Douglas, J., dissenting)).

caused violent or disruptive behavior. The school denied access to the student group simply because of the affiliation with its national parent. The United States Supreme Court ruled that denying access to this student group based on the activities of other individuals was a violation of the First Amendment.[159] Consequently, though school administrators have the right to maintain an orderly process on campus, mere distaste for the content of the student group's speech or an undifferentiated fear of disruption is not enough to prohibit access. Moreover, it is not enough to prohibit access simply because some other parent or affiliate organization similar to the one seeking access is known to be violent or disruptive. Certainly schools can prohibit violent or disruptive groups, but the school must have specific information to support the violent or disruptive behavior of the particular group requesting access.

4. Equal Access Act and the Constitution

On June 4, 1990, the Supreme Court of the United States upheld the constitutionality of the Act.[160] Specifically, the *Mergens* case ruled that the Act was not prohibited by the First Amendment Establishment Clause. Although the Supreme Court in 1986 hinted that the Act was constitutional in the case of *Bender v. Williamsport Area School District*,[161] the *Mergens* case in 1990 left no doubt as to the constitutionality of the Act.[162]

---

[159]*Healy,* 408 U.S. at 169.
[160]*Mergens,* 496 U.S. at 226.
[161]*Bender,* 475 U.S. at 534.
[162]*Mergens,* 496 U.S. at 226.

5. Guidelines for Starting an Equal Access Act Club

The following are suggested steps for starting an Equal Access Act club. These steps are not required by the Act. They are presented here only to illustrate practical guidelines.

1. A club must be initiated by a student. One student should talk to friends to see if there is an interest in starting a club. The students should share ideas about the club. What will the club do? What will the name of the club be? What is the club's purpose? How often will the club meet?

2. After the idea of the club has been formulated, one or two students should ask a school employee to be its sponsor. Meet with the sponsor to share your ideas. Not all schools require a sponsor, so talk to members of other clubs to see if they have a sponsor.

3. Prepare a constitution which states the club's name and purpose. A constitution can be anything from one paragraph to several pages.[163]

4. One or two student leaders of the club should meet with the principal or one of the vice principals in charge of clubs. Present your request to form a club and your constitution at this meeting.

5. The school should then consider your request and give you guidance for beginning your meetings.

EQUAL ACCESS UNDER THE FIRST AMENDMENT

While the Equal Access Act has been a powerful weapon for student clubs, the First Amendment provides additional

---

[163] Liberty Counsel will provide a model constitution upon request.

rights not covered by the Act. The Act should be thought of as a law that provides basic rights. Issues not covered by the Act, or not commanded by the federal law, are often commanded by the First Amendment. For example, while the Act requires the club to be student-initiated and student-led, the First Amendment may allow the club to be adult-initiated and adult-led. The Act applies to clubs desiring to meet during "noninstructional" time.[164] The First Amendment applies any time the school allows other clubs or groups to meet, which could include instructional time. Furthermore, while the Act applies to "secondary schools," which each state typically defines as high school, middle and junior high, the First Amendment applies to all grade levels, including elementary.

In *Good News Club v. Milford Central School District,*[165] the United States Supreme Court ruled that a public school which allows use of its facilities to secular groups may not discriminate against religious groups. The *Good News Club* case involved an adult-initiated and adult-led, after-school religious club sponsored by Child Evangelism Fellowship. Public school teachers may also participate in religious clubs and organizations after class when community groups are allowed to use school facilities. A federal appeals court ruled that a teacher's participation in a Good News Club held on school property constituted private speech. As a result, the district could not forbid the teacher from teaching a Good News Club immediately after school in the same school

---

[164]20 U.S.C. §§ 4071(b), 4072(4). Noninstructional time includes time set aside by the school before actual classroom instruction begin or ends.
[165]533 U.S. 98 (2001).

where she taught during the day.[166] *Wigg v. Sioux Falls School District 49-5*, 382 F.3d 807 (8th Cir. 2004), *reh'g and reh'g en banc denied*. Good News Clubs are designed for children ages five to twelve. These clubs teach morals and character development from a Christian viewpoint. A typical Good News Club meeting includes Bible reading, Scripture memorization, prayer, singing, stories about biblical or modern people, and games. The Milford school district argued that the school must ban the club from meeting on campus because (1) the club engaged in religious instruction, and (2) the young elementary students would mistakenly believe the school endorsed religion, especially since the club met immediately after the last bell.

The Court rejected all these arguments and found that the school's "exclusion of the Club on the basis of its religious viewpoint constitutes unconstitutional viewpoint discrimination."[167] The Court also rejected the argument that the school was required to discriminate against the Christian Club because state law mandated such discrimination.[168] Thus, a school may not argue that the state law, or even the state constitution, provides for strict separation of church and state because the Free Speech Clause of the United States Constitution would preempt any state law to the contrary.[169] Noting that the Good News Club sought "nothing more than to be treated neutrally and given access to speak about the same topics as . . . other clubs," the Court ruled that "the

---

[166]*Wigg v. Sioux Falls School District 49–5*, 382 F.3d 807 (8th Cir. 2004), *reh'g and reh'g en banc denied*.

[167]*Id.* at 107 n.2.

[168]*Id.*

[169]*Id. See also Prince v. Jacoby*, 303 F.3d 1074 (9th Cir. 2002).

school could not deny equal access to the Club for any time that is generally available for public use."[170] The Court also found that allowing adults on campus immediately after school to teach Christian principles to elementary students did not violate the Establishment Clause. The mere fact that some might perceive that the school endorsed religion by allowing the Christian club on campus or the possibility that only religious groups may choose to use the facilities at a particular time, was irrelevant.[171]

Following the lead of the Supreme Court's opinion in the *Good News Club* case, other federal courts similarly recognized that the First Amendment grants broader rights than the Equal Access Act.[172] In the *Prince* case, the school allowed a Christian Bible club called World Changers to meet on campus after school hours.[173] However, the school treated the religious club differently from other clubs. The school withheld money to fund club activities, denied the club participation in fund-raising events such as the annual Club Fair and the school auction, denied the club free access to the yearbook, prohibited the club from meeting during school hours, did not allow the publicizing of club events (including posting flyers throughout the school instead of on a single bulletin board and access to the public-address system) and denied the club access to school supplies, copiers, audiovisual equipment, and the use of vehicles for field trips. The court

---

[170]*Good News/Good Sports Club,* 533 U.S. at 114 n.5.
[171]*Id.* at 119.
[172]*Culbertson v. Oakridge Sch. Dist.* No. 76, 258 F.3d 1061 (9th Cir. 2001) (public school may not ban the Christian Good News Club from meeting immediately after school on an elementary school campus).
[173]*Prince,* 303 F.3d at 1077.

found that either under the Equal Access Act, or the broader rights protected by the First Amendment, a denial of these benefits to the religious club is unconstitutional.

The court in *Prince* stated that "equal access" under the Equal Access Act means that "religiously-oriented student activities must be allowed under the same terms and conditions as other extracurricular activities."[174] The court addressed each one of the issues separately and noted that "discriminatory actions in the form of harassment or unequal penalties, as well as clear cut denial, constitute a violation of the law."[175]

Two different kinds of funds were analyzed by the court. The court first addressed the funds that were generated by the sale of student cards, which cost $20 and entitled the holder to participate in school sports and to receive various discounts. This particular fund also was generated by the selling of crafts at annual club fairs, participating in the school auction, and through other fund-raising activities, such as candy sales and car washes. The other student clubs were allowed access to these funds, but the religious club was denied the same access. The court concluded that "by denying them equal access to those funds,"[176] the school violated the Equal Access Act. The school also violated the Act "when it prohibits [the religious club] from engaging in or charges them to participate in other fund-raising activities, including the auction and the craft fair, on an equal basis with other [student] groups."[177]

---

[174]*Id.* at 1081.
[175]*Id.*
[176]*Id.* at 1086.
[177]*Id.*

In *Prince,* the school also denied the religious club free access to the yearbook and instead charged them advertising fees to appear in the publication. The court noted that it is "unlawful viewpoint discrimination" under the Act to allow other noncurriculum student clubs to appear in the yearbook free of charge while requiring the religious club to pay a fee.

The school also prohibited the religious club equal access to the public-address system and limited the club to a single bulletin board. The court found this discriminatory treatment violated the Act and stated, "We hold that the Act requires the School District to afford the World Changers the same access to the public address system and bulletin boards enjoyed by ASB groups to publicize their activities."[178]

Noncurriculum clubs were allowed to meet during what the school termed "student/staff" time, which is "a scheduled class where attendance is taken, and where no formal classroom instruction takes place, except on a voluntary, individual basis."[179] The court stated that although the Equal Access Act did not require the school to permit the religious club to meet during the school day when attendance was mandatory, the First Amendment is broader than the Equal Access Act and *does* require the school to allow the Christian club to meet at the same time other noncurriculum, secular clubs meet.[180]

The court noted that the use of school supplies, audio-visual equipment and the use of school vehicles involved

---

[178]*Id.* (ASB stands for an Associated Student Body club, which were noncurriculum-related).
[179]*Id.* at 1087.
[180]*See id.* at 1089, 1092.

direct funding by the school and was not generated by club fund-raising activities. While the court held that the Equal Access Act did not require the school to provide religious clubs with use of school supplies, audiovisual equipment, and the use of school vehicles, the broader provisions of the First Amendment did require the school to provide equal access to these benefits.[181]

An issue that sometimes arises involves the distribution of information to announce the meetings of Good News Clubs or other after-school, religious meetings. The same principles already set forth equally apply to distributing such announcements.

In *Child Evangelism Fellowship of Maryland, Inc. v. Montgomery County Public Schools*,[182] the federal appeals court ruled that a school district must allow the Good News Club informational flyers to be distributed by teachers to students. The school district permitted many after-school organizations to give informational flyers to teachers for distribution to the students. However, the district refused to permit distribution of the Good News Club flyers, stating that the flyers were religious and contained a proselytizing message. The court rejected this argument, finding that it is impermissible to discriminate against the religious viewpoint of the Good News Club. Thus, if the school permits informational flyers of secular organizations to be distributed to parents through the students, then the school must also allow the distribution of flyers by religious organizations.

---

[181]*See id.* at 1092.
[182]373 F.3d 589 (4th Cir. 2004).

Similarly, in *Child Evangelism Fellowship of New Jersey Inc. v. Stafford Township School District,*[183] a federal court of appeals held that the district engaged in "viewpoint-based religious discrimination" by refusing to allow faculty to distribute flyers for Good News Clubs. The court ruled that the district must treat Child Evangelism Fellowship like other community organizations with respect to the distribution and posting of materials and participation in school events.

In *Hills v. Scottsdale Unified School District No. 48,*[184] the school district refused to distribute to students a brochure announcing a Christian summer camp that offered classes on "Bible Heros" and "Bible Tales." Although the school distributed information to the students regarding other after-school, secular programs, the school would not distribute the brochures regarding the summer camp because of its religious character. The court of appeals in *Hills* ruled that the school violated the First Amendment by refusing to give equal treatment to the religious event. The court stated: "If an organization proposes to advertise an otherwise permissible type of extra-curricular event, it must be allowed to do so, even if the event is obviously cast from a particular religious viewpoint."[185] Thus, if the school distributes information about after-school, secular programs or events to students, it must also distribute information to students regarding after-school, religious events.

In *Rusk v. Crestveiw Local School District,*[186] a federal court of appeals found that a school district's practice of

---

[183]386 F.3d 514 (3d Cir. 2004).
[184]329 F.3d 1044 (9th Cir. 2003).
[185]*Id.* at 1052.
[186]379 F.3d 418 (6th Cir. 2004).

distributing flyers advertising activities sponsored by religious groups did not violate the Establishment Clause. The Crestview Elementary School occasionally distributed flyers regarding after-school programs sponsored by various groups, including the American Red Cross, the 4-H Club, sports leagues and local churches. Some of the flyers described religious activities such as Bible stories, "crafts and songs that celebrate God's love," and one program that was "Rated Religious." Although the recipients were elementary students and their parents, the court found that the practice of distributing flyers regarding after-school, religious activities is permissible under the First Amendment.[187]

One final important difference between the Act and the First Amendment involves the question of what triggers the legal protection. The Act is triggered whenever (1) a public secondary school (2) which receives federal funds (3) allows at least one noncurriculum-related student club on campus. The First Amendment is triggered whenever (1) any public facility (2) allows use of its facilities for certain persons or groups to conduct meetings. The First Amendment, therefore, applies to all schools, regardless of grade level and irrespective of whether the public school receives federal funds. The First Amendment is triggered even if the school has no noncurriculum-related student clubs, so long as the school allows any public use of its facilities. Thus, any club organized primarily for students should rely on both the Act and

---

[187]For more information on equal access to public facilities in general, and discriminatory fee schemes in particular, see chapter 8 entitled "use of Public Facilities." *See also* Mathew D. Staver, *Equal Access*, available by contacting Liberty Counsel at www.lc.org or at 1-800-671-1776.

the First Amendment for protection. Rights not covered by the Act may be covered by the First Amendment.

Summary

Students on public school campuses do not shed their constitutional rights at the schoolhouse gate. Before, after, in between classes, during the lunch period, and on the playing field, students have the First Amendment right to free speech and freedom of religion. Student speech can be exercised during noninstructional time so long as it is not disruptive to the ordinary operation of the school. Students can communicate with each other verbally, through literature, through jewelry, or through clothing with inscribed messages.

During class discussions, students have a constitutional right to ask questions and discuss religious issues so long as the questions or discussion are related to the curriculum being studied. Students have the First Amendment right to express themselves through projects or reports. To allow other students to present secular reports while prohibiting religious reports is to show hostility toward religion, which the Constitution forbids.

The First Amendment rights of students also permit them to have access to various books and films. Schools may not remove books or films from libraries if the decision to remove them is based upon the content of the message. Students also have free exercise rights, which allow them to participate in a school release time program, where students leave campus for off-site religious instruction.

Schools cannot compel a student to say a pledge of allegiance to a flag if the student has a sincerely held religious belief prohibiting the student from saying a pledge or simply objects to the pledge for nonreligious reasons. The Pledge of Allegiance is clearly constitutional, and schools may require its recitation in the classroom so long as the opt-out opportunity is recognized.

Finally, the First Amendment permits students to gather together in student clubs. The Equal Access Act requires schools to treat all clubs equally. Even if the Equal Access Act did not exist, the First Amendment still grants First Amendment free speech rights for students to form student clubs. Under the Act, if a school allows any noncurriculum-related club, it must allow all noncurriculum-related student clubs, even if the content of their speech is religious. All clubs must be treated equally. However, the First Amendment provides broader rights than are afforded under the Act. Thus, if a school allows any public use of its facilities, then the school cannot discriminate against the religious viewpoint of any person or club. Moreover, while the Act applies to secondary schools and requires the clubs to be student-initiated and student-led, the First Amendment applies to *all* schools and provides that the clubs can be adult-initiated and adult-led.

Students are clearly protected by the Constitution while on public school campuses, and they may exercise their religious and free speech rights by sharing their faith with other students. These liberties are important rights which must be exercised and protected.

4
TEACHERS' RIGHTS ON PUBLIC SCHOOL CAMPUSES

Classroom as the Battleground

PUBLIC SCHOOL TEACHERS often find themselves in difficult positions. Most teachers sincerely want the best for their students. Unfortunately, they work in often combative, even litigious, environments. For the most part, discipline has all but disappeared under the threat of lawsuits. Child abuse allegations against public school teachers have increased. Trying to protect their school, administrators often side with parents rather than teachers in student-teacher disputes. The classroom is becoming more violent and disruptive. Many school administrators are so cautious that they have erroneously erased all traces of religion. Some have run roughshod over teachers while others have attempted to squelch all discussion of religion. Many are simply uninformed about the basics of constitutional rights.[1]

The public school has become a battleground for religion. John Dunphy, a secular humanist, wrote in *The Humanist* magazine:

> I am convinced that the battleground for humankind's future must be waged and won in the public school classroom by teachers who correctly perceive their role as the proselytizers of a new faith: a religion of humanity that recognizes and respects the spark of what theologians call divinity in every human being. These teachers must embody the same selfless dedication as the most rabid fundamentalist preacher, for they will be ministers of another sort, utilizing a classroom instead of a pulpit to convey humanist values in whatever subjects they teach regardless of the educational level—preschool daycare or large state university. The classroom must and will become an arena of conflict between the old and the new—the rotting corpse of Christianity together with all its adjacent evils and misery and the new faith of humanism, resplendent in its promise of a world in which the never realized Christian idea of "love thy neighbor" will be finally achieved.[2]

---

[1] A survey of 900 school administrators and 902 teachers found that "roughly one in five cannot recall any of the five freedoms" guaranteed under the First Amendment. The survey was conducted in 2001 by the Center for Survey Research and Analysis at the University of Connecticut and was reported at http://www.freedomforum.org/.

[2] John Dunphy, *A Religion for a New Age*, THE HUMANIST, Jan.–Feb. 1982, at 26.

John Dewey, the so-called father of modern education, hoped to replace sectarian religion with "a religious faith that shall not be confined to sect, class, or race."[3] Some have referred to the religion envisioned by John Dewey as a religion of secular humanism. Indeed, the Supreme Court has recognized secular humanism as a religion.[4] As a result of the secularization of public education, many teachers have the mistaken view that religion is forbidden on public school campuses.

Notwithstanding the confusion over religion, teachers still have constitutionally protected liberties and should exercise them. Teachers play a critical role in educating future generations. Indeed, schools were originally founded to instill religious principles.[5] With the exception of the University

---

[3]John Dewey, A COMMON FAITH 86–87 (Yale U. Press 1934).

[4]*Torcaso v. Watkins,* 367 U.S. 488 (1961).

[5]The first compulsory education law was enacted by the Colony of Massachusetts in 1647. *See* COLONIAL ORIGINS OF THE AMERICAN CONSTITUTION 129 (Donald Lutz, ed., Liberty Fund 1998). Known as "The Olde Deluder Satan Act," the law required universal education in order to teach children how to read the Scriptures. Next to the Bible, *The New England Primer* was the beginning textbook for students, instructing them on the alphabet, grammar, and religion. This book contained what is known as "The Shorter Catechism" which instructed public school children in religious doctrine by means of questions and answers. Forty questions dealt specifically with the Ten Commandments. For two hundred years of American education from the 1700s to the early 1900s, almost every child entering school studied from the pages of this fascinating book. On July 13, 1787, the Continental Congress reenacted the Northwest Ordinance which proclaimed: "Religion, morality, and knowledge, being necessary to good government and the happiness of mankind, schools and the means of education shall be forever encouraged." ORD. OF 1789, art. A3 (July 13, 1789), *reprinted in* DOCUMENTS ILLUSTRATIVE OF THE FORMATION OF THE UNION OF AMERICAN STATES 52 (Charles C. Tansell ed., 1927); *see also An Act to Provide for the Government of the Territory Northwest of the River Ohio (Northwest Ordinance),* Ch. 8, 1 Stat. 50–51 (Peter's ed. 1845).

of Pennsylvania, every collegiate institution prior to the Revolutionary War was established by some branch of the Christian church.

The Greek philosopher Aristotle understood the importance of teaching when he stated, "All who have meditated on the art of governing mankind are convinced that the fate of empires depends on the education of youth."[6] Martin Luther once stated that he was

> afraid that schools will prove to be great gates of hell, unless they diligently labor in explaining the Holy Scriptures, engraving them in the hearts of youth. I advise no one to place his child where the Scriptures do not reign paramount. Every institution in which men are not increasingly occupied with the word of God must become corrupt.[7]

Teachers are in a unique position to inculcate values for the next generation. Under the present constitutional makeup, teachers still have great latitude in reviewing religious topics. As the former United States Secretary of Education recognized, "Public schools must treat religion with fairness and respect."[8] The United States Supreme Court has observed: "It can hardly be argued that either students or teachers shed their constitutional rights to freedom of speech or expression at the schoolhouse gate."[9]

---

[6]Aristotle, 384–322 B.C.

[7]Martin Luther, "To the Christian Nobility of the German Nation Concerning the Reform of the Christian Estate," in *What Luther Says*, § 1327 (Ewarl Plass, ed., Concordia Publishing 1972).

[8]Richard W. Riley, U.S. Secretary of Education, *Statement on Religious Expression* (http://www.ed.gov/Speeches/08–1995/religion.html).

[9]*Tinker v. Des Moines Indep. Sch. Dist.*, 393 U.S. 503, 506 (1969).

Teacher as Individual and State Agent

Although the First Amendment of the Constitution initially restricted the authority of the federal government and not the states, the United States Supreme Court, in 1940, nevertheless applied the First Amendment to the states through the Fourteenth Amendment.[10] The First Amendment is now interpreted to protect the free exercise of religion of individuals and to prohibit the establishment of religion by state and federal entities.

Teachers are in a unique position because they are both individuals *and* agents of the state. Consequently, the First Amendment serves to protect their freedom of speech and free exercise of religion and to prohibit them from establishing a religion.[11] In other words, since teachers are employees of the state, they are, in a sense, an extension of the state. As such, the First Amendment Establishment Clause, which prohibits the government from establishing a religion, places certain restrictions on teachers' activities in matters of religion.

---

[10]*Cantwell v. Connecticut,* 310 U.S. 296 (1940) (Free Exercise Clause); *Everson v. Board of Educ.,* 330 U.S. 1 (1947) (Establishment Clause); *Illinois ex rel. McCollum v. Board of Educ. of Sch. Dist. No. 71,* 333 U.S. 203 (1948) (same).

[11]Originally the term "establishment of religion" referred to the federal government establishing a national religion or national church. The First Amendment prohibited the federal government from establishing such a national church. While the individual states could establish their own religion, the federal government had no jurisdiction in this matter. However, this term has been interpreted over time by the United States Supreme Court to mean endorsement or promotion of religion. Essentially, the Supreme Court has required that the government remain neutral in matters of religion, neither inhibiting, nor promoting religion. Applying this concept of neutrality to the public school teacher means that the teacher must not only be neutral but objective when overviewing religious topics. Consequently,

On the other hand, teachers do not lose their rights to free speech and freedom of religion simply because they are employees of the state. Teachers' freedom of religion rights are also protected by other federal laws.[12]

The First Amendment has been interpreted to mean that a state may not affirmatively promote or proselytize a particular religious viewpoint, but neither may the state be hostile toward religion. Thus, while teachers may not encourage students to accept Jesus Christ as Lord and Savior, teachers may not try to convince students that Jesus is a fictional character. Teachers may objectively overview the teachings of Jesus as long as the overview is consistent with the subject matter being taught.[13]

Asserting Your Rights

The teacher is protected by the Constitution and should assert constitutional protection when deemed appropriate. A teacher can assert not only constitutional rights but also the status of tenure, which should at least guarantee notice and opportunity for a hearing in the event of a complaint.[14]

---

a teacher should not ignore, nor should a teacher actively proselytize, a particular religion or faith. To ignore, censor, or denigrate religion is just as prohibited by the Supreme Court's interpretation as is active promotion or proselytizing of religion by government. For a discussion on the origin and meaning of the phrase "separation of church and state," see Mathew D. Staver, TAKE BACK AMERICA 33–44 (2000).

[12]In addition to having constitutional rights and obligations, teachers are public employees and therefore have rights under state and federal employment laws. See chapter 14 in this book entitled "Religious Rights in the Workplace."

[13]See Brown v. Woodland Joint Unif. Sch. Dist., 27 F.3d 1373, 1380, (9th Cir. 1994) ("A reenactment of the Last Supper or a Passover dinner might be permissible if presented for historical or cultural purposes.").

[14]On occasion the apostle Paul used his status as a Roman citizen to his

FREEDOM OF SPEECH

Teachers have the constitutional right to free speech while on a public school campus.[15] Neither students nor teachers "shed their constitutional rights to freedom of speech or expression at the schoolhouse gate."[16] A teacher can discuss religious topics with other teachers in the school lounge or between classes. If a school allows its facilities to be used by teachers for meetings unrelated to the curriculum, it probably cannot prohibit teachers from meeting with other teachers during noninstructional time solely on the basis of religion.[17]

Clearly, during nonschool hours and while off school property, teachers are individual citizens and not actors of the state. As such, they enjoy the affirmative protection of the Free Speech and Free Exercise Clauses. In this context they are not actors of the state and, therefore, do not have the restrictions imposed by the First Amendment Establishment Clause.[18]

While on school campus but before or after school hours, teachers may have certain restrictions imposed by the First

---

benefit. *See* Acts 22:25. Indeed, Paul used his status as a Roman citizen to have his case heard in Rome before Caesar where he stated "I am standing before Caesar's tribunal, where I ought to be tried." Acts 25:10.

[15]*Tinker,* 393 U.S. at 506.

[16]*Id.*

[17]*Cf. Widmar v. Vincent,* 454 U.S. 263 (1981); *May v. Evansville-Vanderbaugh Sch. Corp.,* 787 F.2d 1105 (7th Cir. 1986); *Police Dep't of Chicago v. Mosley,* 408 U.S. 92 (1972).

[18]*See Wigg v. Sioux Falls Sch. Dist. 4–5,* 382 F.2d 807 (8th Cir. 2004) (teacher may lead elementary students in prayer after school on school property). *See also Daugherty v. Vanguard Charter Sch. Academy,* 116 F. Supp. 2d 897 (W.D. Mich. 2000) (teachers may meet together for prayer).

Amendment Establishment Clause.[19] In this context courts often balance the interest of the teachers against the interest of the school.[20]

Some courts have considered the age and impressionability of students.[21] The younger the student, the more careful the teacher must be in matters of religion. The courts have reasoned that younger students are not easily able to separate the acts of the teacher from the acts of the school. The courts have considered that older students have the capability of making a distinction between the teacher as an individual and the actions of the school. Unfortunately, no clear line has been drawn as to when this age differential changes. No matter the age, however, teachers may not proselytize students in a captive setting. For example, if several teachers were to congregate before school in a classroom to pray, the teachers could not invite students and could not publicize the meeting to the students. To do so may give the impression that the school is affirmatively promoting religion. However, a

---

[19]See, e.g. Marchi v. Board of Coop. Educ. Svc. of Albany, 173 F.3d 469 (2d Cir. 1999) (special education teacher prohibited from expressing religious viewpoint as part of instructional program); Peloza v. Capistrano Unif. Sch. Dist., 37 F.3d 517 (9th Cir. 1994) (teacher prohibited from discussing his religious views with students at school); Bishop v. Aronov, 926 F.2d 1066, 1077 (11th Cir. 1991) (university professor required to stop interjecting his personal religious beliefs into class discussions); Downs v. Los Angeles Unified Sch. Dist., 228 F.3d 1003 (2000) (teacher did not have First Amendment right to post personal viewpoint on school bulletin board that was used for official purposes).

[20]See, e.g. Bishop v. Aronov, 926 F.2d at 1072, 1074) (stating there is "no substitute for a case-by-case inquiry into whether the legitimate interests of the authorities are demonstrably sufficient to circumscribe a teacher's speech").

[21]See, e.g. Roberts v. Madigan, 921 F.2d 1047 (10th Cir. 1990) (teacher prohibited from silently reading personal Bible while fifth graders were in class).

teacher does not have to be so paranoid as to avoid a student's religious inquiry.

TEACHING ABOUT RELIGION

Academic freedom is "the principle that individual instructors are at liberty to teach that which they deem to be appropriate in the exercise of their professional judgment."[22] According to the Supreme Court, academic freedom "is a special concern of the First Amendment."[23] However, academic freedom is not absolute. A teacher cannot use the classroom to indoctrinate students in religious faith, but a teacher is free to disseminate information in an objective manner so long as the information is reasonably related to the subject matter being taught in the curriculum.[24] Therefore, academic freedom, or the right to free speech, permits an objective discussion of religion as it relates to the curriculum. In fact, no subject can be thoroughly taught without some discussion of religion.[25]

The teacher would probably be prohibited from talking about a biblical reason for sexual abstinence before marriage in a math class, but a teacher in a health class may discuss

---

[22]*Edwards v. Aguillard,* 482 U.S. 578, 586 n.6 (1987).

[23]*Keyishian v. Board of Regents,* 385 U.S. 589, 603 (1967).

[24]Free speech or academic freedom is not unlimited. *Cf. Krizek v. Cicero-Stickney Township High Sch. Dist.,* 713 F. Supp. 1131 (N.D. Ill. 1989). (School did not renew the contract of a nontenured teacher who showed an R-rated film during class.)

[25]"The fact is that, for good or for ill, nearly everything in our culture worth transmitting, everything which gives meaning to life, is saturated with religious influences, derived from paganism, Judaism, Christianity—both Catholic and Protestant—and other faiths accepted by a large part of the world's peoples. One can hardly respect a system of education that would leave the student wholly ignorant of the currents of religious thought that move the world society for a part in which he is being prepared." *McCollum,* 333 U.S. at 236 (Jackson, J., concurring).

sexual abstinence, including various religious views on sexual abstinence. Biblical literature can be discussed in literature class but probably not in a math class. However, it is permissible to discuss numerology in math class. The Egyptians used mathematics as part of their religion. Both Old and New Testaments use numbers and mathematical formulas to represent symbolic meanings.[26] If the content of speech is consistent with the course being studied, the teacher may objectively overview religious contributions and viewpoints dealing with the issue.

Certainly schools have "important, delicate and highly discretionary functions" to perform.[27] These functions, however, must be performed "within the limits of the Bill of

---

[26]For example, the numbers 3 and 7 occur throughout the Bible. The number 12 is also frequently used. This number plays an integral role when describing the new heaven, which when measured, forms a perfect cube. *See* Revelation 21:9–21. Some ancient Hebrews often assigned mathematical significance to the Hebrew alphabet. This is done in different ways. One way is to assign a number to each successive letter of the alphabet. One example is the name David. In Hebrew it is spelled Dwd. The daleth or d is the fourth letter in the Hebrew alphabet. The waw or w is the eighth letter in the Hebrew alphabet. When added together, David's name equates to the number 14. This is probably the reason that the first chapter of Matthew describes three series of fourteen generations, fourteen from Abraham to David, fourteen from David to the Babylonian deportation, and fourteen from the Babylonian deportation to Christ. *See* Matthew 1:1–17. Actually, there are more than fourteen generations if every individual is counted, but when one understands how genealogies were counted in the Old Testament, the number 14 makes perfect sense. Counting genealogies did not mean counting every single individual in the lineage. Rather, genealogies highlight certain individuals throughout time which show a link from the past to the present. One final example of numerology used in the Bible is the infamous "666," which is the mark of the beast. *See* Revelation 13:18.

[27]*West Virginia State Bd. of Educ. v. Barnette*, 319 U.S. 624, 637 (1943).

Rights."[28] "The vigilant protection of constitutional freedoms is nowhere more vital than in the community of American schools."[29] Since the "classroom is peculiarly the marketplace of ideas,"[30] teachers may lead robust discussions and present information, including religious information, in an objective manner.

One of my teacher friends taught space technology in a public high school. His innovation earned him "teacher of the year." He used unique teaching techniques in the classroom, including having his class directly linked to the space shuttle and communicating with the astronauts on board. This class addressed topics related to space technology, including the technology used in laser-guided bombs during the Persian Gulf War, astronomy, satellite hookups, and other forms of technology.

During the Persian Gulf War, this teacher focused on the technology used by the military. During one discussion, he brought up the issue of war in the Middle East, which naturally led to a discussion regarding the various confrontations among the warring religious sects. It is virtually impossible to address the Persian Gulf War without looking at the religious and cultural issues involved.

This teacher also focused on astronomy and, as such, must address the Big Bang theory and the origin of the universe. This theory is replete throughout many science books, and even after its repudiation by some well-known scientists, many science books continue to rely on this theory. A good

---

[28]Id. at 637.
[29]Shelton v. Tucker, 364 U.S. 479, 487 (1960).
[30]Keyishian, 385 U.S. at 603 (1967).

teacher brings up this information, critiques it, and then the natural question arises as to what other theories have been put forth regarding the origin of the universe. Within this context, the teacher may overview theories of abrupt appearance or punctuated equilibrium. As Wendell Bird has shown in his two-volume work entitled *The Origin of the Species Revisited,*[31] abrupt appearance can be taught as science. The theory of abrupt appearance is a classic example of a topic that can be objectively overviewed in class.[32] Abrupt appearance does not need to use the Bible as the textbook.

---

[31]Wendell R. Bird, 1–2 THE ORIGIN OF THE SPECIES REVISITED (NY: Philosophical Library, 1989).

[32]The United States Supreme Court struck down the State of Arkansas' antievolution statute which prohibited the teaching of evolution within public schools because the court found that the primary purpose of this statute was religious and had no objective secular basis. *Epperson v. Arkansas,* 393 U.S. 97 (1968). The Supreme Court ruled in *Edwards v. Aguillard,* 482 U.S. 578 (1987), that a state could not mandate the teaching of creationism by requiring that creation theories be taught whenever evolutionary theories are taught. The principle in this case was that the state statute had primarily a religious and not a secular aspect, which indeed required the teaching of creationism. It is an entirely different matter when a teacher objectively overviews origin of the universe theories without religious advocacy. A federal appeals court has ruled that a principal may prohibit a teacher from teaching nonevolutionary theories of creation in the classroom without violating the teacher's First Amendment rights. *Webster v. New Lenox Sch. Dist.,* 917 F.2d 1004 (7th Cir. 1990). In the *Webster* case the issue was not so much whether teaching evolutionary creation violates the First Amendment Establishment Clause, but whether a principal had the right to control the curriculum within the school contrary to the individual desires of teachers within that school. The court noted the essence of the case was that "an individual teacher has no right to ignore the directives of duly appointed education authorities." *Id.* at 1008. The court further noted that the teacher had "not been prohibited from teaching any nonevolutionary theories or from teaching anything regarding the historical relationship between church and state" but that the teacher was merely prohibited from "religious advocacy." *Id.* at 1006.

However, when overviewing theories of the origin of the universe, the astute teacher may present evidence proffered for evolution and for abrupt appearance.[33] In the final analysis, neither can be scientifically proven. Both theories must be accepted by faith. However, when discussing the scientific data, in order to overview the entire subject adequately, cultural and religious views may be discussed in an objective manner. Many religions have theologies regarding creation in addition to the Judeo-Christian religion. Egyptian theology on this matter can be found in *The Memphite Theology of Creation*.[34] Likewise, the Akkadians, as well as those in the Far East, had creation epics.

Similarly, when studying geographical topography such as the Grand Canyon, the theory of deluge must be overviewed. The Sumerians, the Akkadians, and the Babylonians all had similar flood stories.[35] To ignore this rich religious and cultural history is to neglect the topic and to cheat the students of a broad education.[36]

No topic can be adequately studied without objectively overviewing religious contributions. When studying sociology,

---

[33]*See Daugherty,* 116 F. Supp. 2d at 897 (permitting teachers to question evolution).

[34]1 THE ANCIENT NEAR EAST 1 (James B. Pritchard, ed., Princeton U. Press, 1958).

[35]*Id.* at 28, 31; READINGS IN ANCIENT HISTORY FROM GILGAMESH TO DIOCLETIAN 12 (N. Bailkey, ed., Lexington, MA: D.C. Heath & Co., 1976).

[36]One of the best videos addressing a modern-day catastrophe which may give insight to the theory of deluge has been produced by the Institute for Creation Research regarding the eruption of Mt. St. Helens. The video, entitled "Mt. St. Helens: Explosive Evidence for Catastrophe" is worth viewing and is highly recommended. Information may be obtained by writing ICR, 10946 Woodside Ave. N., Santee, CA 92071, calling (619) 448-0900, or on the Internet at www.icr.org.

demographic studies may be brought in showing the geographical distribution of the various religious faiths. Demographic maps of the United States showing the distribution of religious faiths within the states are very informative. Such maps are certainly relevant to sociology, history, and political science. Religious contributions and musical compositions may be studied in music class. Religious art may be studied in art class. History and political science cannot be studied properly without considering the Roman Catholic, Protestant, evangelical, or charismatic impacts. Literature cannot be adequately studied without considering religious influences. For example, today's book format arose out of Christian evangelization. Prior to the formation of books, Old Testament Scriptures were contained on bulky scrolls. The New Testament Christians cut these scrolls in pieces and sewed the edges together to form a codex, now known as a book. Printing presses were developed primarily to reproduce the Bible. In short, no subject matter can be taught adequately without considering and overviewing the impact of religion. Teachers have a constitutional right to teach about religion and should not shirk their responsibility to do so.

In *School District of Abington Township v. Schempp,*[37] the Supreme Court stated that study of the Bible or religion, when presented objectively as part of a secular program of education, is consistent with the First Amendment. The United States Department of Education has issued Guidelines on Religious Expression in Public Schools, noting that the Bible may be taught in school and that a teacher may instruct

---

[37]374 U.S. 203 (1963).

the class about religious influences relevant to the subject matter being discussed.[38]

The Bible can be studied as literature in a literature course.[39] Religious literature can be used in any course in which the message is relevant to the subject matter.

The Bible is an excellent literary source. For example, the entire book of Lamentations is written in acrostic form. An acrostic is a mnemonic device using the twenty-two letters of the Hebrew alphabet. Chapter 1 of Lamentations contains twenty-two verses, and each verse successively begins with the corresponding letter of the alphabet. Verse 1 begins with the aleph (A), the first letter of the alphabet. Verse 2 begins with the beth (B), the second letter of the alphabet. Verse 22 ends with a tau (T), the last letter of the Hebrew alphabet. Chapter 2 continues this sequence and also contains 22 verses. Chapter 3, the middle chapter, triplicates the Hebrew alphabet. This chapter contains sixty-six verses, the alphabet multiplied by three. These verses follow the alphabet in sequence but are grouped in threes. Verses 1, 2, and 3 begin with the first letter

---

[38]Regarding teaching about religion in schools, the guidelines, first released in 1995 and then again in 1999, state:

> Public schools may not provide religious instruction, but they may teach *about* religion, including the Bible or other scripture: the history of religion, comparative religion, the Bible (or other scripture)-as-literature, and the role of religion in the history of the United States and other countries all are permissible public school subjects. Similarly, it is permissible to consider religious influences on art, music, literature, and social studies.

See http://www.ed.gov/Speeches/08-1995/religion.html and http://www.ed.gov/inits/ religionandschools/.

[39]An excellent resource is Leland Ryken, THE BIBLE AS LITERATURE (1974). This book was published by Zondervan. Although this book may be out of print, there are many similar available resources.

of the alphabet while verses 4, 5, and 6 begin with the second letter of the Hebrew alphabet and so on. Chapter 4 again contains twenty-two verses, each starting with the successive letter of the alphabet. Chapter 5, though containing twenty-two verses, departs from the acrostic pattern.

The most famous acrostic of all is Psalm 119. This psalm contains twenty-two sections, each section containing eight verses. The first eight verses begin with the first letter of the Hebrew alphabet while the second series of eight verses begin with the second letter of the Hebrew alphabet and so on.

Hebrew literature also contains parallelisms. Approximately one-third of the Old Testament and parts of the New Testament are written in poetry. By and large there is no rhyme in terms of sound as we know it in English. Hebrew rhyme is based on thought parallelisms. For example, synonymous parallelism is found in Isaiah 1:3 where the same thought is expressed in successive stichs: "The ox knows its owner, and the ass its master's crib." The "ox" is equivalent to the "ass," and the "owner" is equivalent to the "master." Another example is found in Amos 5:24. Antithetic parallelism means that the second stich is in contrast to the first, as found in Psalm 1:6, "For the LORD knows the way of the righteous, but the way of the wicked will perish." In Matthew 7:18, Jesus stated: "A sound tree cannot bear evil fruit, nor can a bad tree bear good fruit." The most famous one of all is in Matthew 10:39 where Jesus declared: "He who finds his life will lose it, and he who loses his life for my sake will find it." Formal or synthetic parallelism contains neither repetition nor contrasted assertions but is where the first stich is carried further in thought through the second stich. Psalm 14:2 is an example: "The LORD looks down from heaven upon the children of men." Climactic parallelism is found in Psalm 28:1 where the second stich echoes or repeats the first part of the stich and adds to it an element of thought such as the following: "Ascribe to the Lord, oh heavenly beings, ascribe to the Lord glory and strength." These examples are what is known as Internal Parallelism. Examples of External Parallelism are found between dystichs, such as that found in Isaiah 1:27–28:

> Zion shall be redeemed by Justice,
> And those in her who repent, by righteousness.
> But rebels and sinners shall be destroyed together,
> And those who forsake the Lord shall be consumed.

The first stich (first two lines) speaks of redemption using synonymous terms of "justice" and "righteousness." The second stich (second two lines) contrasts the thought of the first stich and speaks of destruction using synonymous terms such as "destroyed" and "consumed."

Hebrew poetry also has meter, with the most frequent pattern being 3:3, which is a dystich with three stressed syllables in each stich. An example is found in Job 14:1–2. The shorter 2:2 meter is used to convey intense emotion and urgency as found in Isaiah 1:16–17. The 3:2 pattern is known as the Qinah or the Lament or dirge meter. This is the prevailing meter used in the book of Lamentations. An example is also found in Amos 5:2. Other, but less frequently used, patterns are 4:4, 2:2:2, and 3:3:3. In the original Hebrew, alliteration is found in Psalm 122:6–7, where the effect of the passage is gained by juxtaposition of words or syllables which begin with the same consonant.

Assonance is found in Psalm 90:17, where the same vowel sound is often deliberately repeated. An interesting concept is found in Judges 5:2 known as onomatopoeia, where the writer uses words which actually sound like the described activity. This is the Song of Deborah describing the galloping of horses. The Hebrew words, when spoken together, sound like the galloping of horses' hooves. Paranomasia, or a play on words, is aptly found in Isaiah 5:7. There Isaiah says that God looked for "justice" (mishpat), but instead he found only "bloodshed" (mispah); he looked for "righteousness" (sedhaqah) but instead found only a "cry" (seaqah).

Clearly the Bible is a fascinating literary book. The Chronicles of Narnia is also a work that can be studied from a literary point of view. When studying religious works from a literary standpoint, the teacher should be objective. Indeed, to ignore religious literature, including the Bible, ignores a vast amount of educational material and ultimately is to the detriment of the student.

Symbols, Music, Art, Drama, and Literature

The constitutional principle regarding symbols, music, art, drama, or literature, whether in public school or in association with other public entities, is simple—mix the secular and the sacred. In other words, if a public entity, or a teacher as an agent of that entity, displays or presents a secular aspect or purpose along with the religious symbol, music, art, drama, or literature, then the display or the presentation is considered constitutional. For example, a publicly sponsored nativity scene without any other accompanying symbols on public property would be unconstitutional. However, the same nativity scene becomes constitutional when secular symbols of the holiday are presented in the same context. A nativity scene in the classroom follows the same guidelines. A school-sponsored Christmas concert on a public school campus containing only Christian music would be unconstitutional, but Christian Christmas songs mixed with secular songs of the holiday make the presentation constitutional.[40] In art class the teacher can overview religious art so long as secular art is also discussed. Religious literature can be read and studied so long as it is objective and combined with other secular aspects of literature.

Probably the best illustration of the permissibility for the use of symbols, music, art, drama, and literature within the public school system is the school board policy of Sioux Falls School District in Sioux Falls, South Dakota. This policy has been court tested and serves as an example to other schools. The school policy begins by stating that tolerance and understanding should be promoted and that "students and staff members should be excused from participating in practices which are contrary to their religious beliefs" unless there are clear, overriding concerns that would prevent excusal.[41]

The policy also states the following:

1. The several holidays throughout the year which have a religious and a secular basis may be observed in the public schools.

---

[40]*See Bauchman v. West High Sch.,* 132 F.3d 542 (10th Cir. 1997), *cert. denied,* 524 U.S. 953.
[41]*Florey v. Sioux Falls Sch. Dist. 49-5,* 619 F.2d 1311, 1319 (8th Cir. 1980), *cert. denied,* 449 U.S. 987 (1980).

2. The historical and contemporary values and the origin of religious holidays may be explained in an unbiased and objective manner without sectarian indoctrination.

3. Music, art, literature, and drama having religious themes or bases are permitted as part of the curriculum for school-sponsored activities and programs if presented in a prudent and objective manner and as a traditional part of the cultural and religious heritage of the particular holiday.

4. The use of religious symbols such as a cross, menorah, crescent, Star of David, creche, symbols of Native American religions or other symbols that are part of a religious holiday [are] permitted as a teaching aid or resource provided such symbols are displayed as an example of the cultural and religious heritage of the holiday and are temporary in nature. Among these holidays are included Christmas, Easter, Passover, Hanukkah, St. Valentine's Day, St. Patrick's Day, Thanksgiving and Halloween.

5. The school district's calendar should be prepared so as to minimize conflicts with religious holidays of all faiths.[42]

The same school board policy also correctly addresses religious literature in the curriculum as follows:

Religious institutions and orientations are central to human experience, past and present. An education excluding such a significant aspect would be incomplete. It is essential that the teaching about and not of

---

[42]*Id.* at 1319–20.

religion be conducted in a factual, objective and respectful manner.[43]

The policy then outlines the following:

1. The District supports the inclusion of religious literature, music, drama, and the arts in the curriculum and in school activities provided it is intrinsic to the learning experience in the various fields of study and is presented objectively.

2. The emphasis on religious themes in the arts, literature and history should be only as extensive as necessary for a balanced and comprehensive study of these areas. Such studies should never foster any particular religious tenets or demean any religious beliefs.

3. Student-initiated expressions to questions or assignments which reflect their beliefs or nonbeliefs about a religious theme shall be accommodated. For example, students are free to express religious belief or nonbelief in compositions, art forms, music, speech and debate.[44]

The above-cited school board policy of the Sioux Falls School District is presented here because it concisely and correctly outlines the parameters for the celebration of religious holidays; the display of symbols; the performance of music, art, or drama; and the study of religious literature within the public school system. The constitutionality of this school board policy has been upheld by Federal court of appeals. As it pertains to religious literature within the public

[43]*Id.* at 1320.
[44]*Id.*

school system, the United States Supreme Court declared that the "study of the Bible or of religion, when presented objectively as a part of a secular program of education," is consistent with the First Amendment.[45] Indeed, the Supreme Court has reiterated that the Bible may constitutionally be used as an appropriate study of history, civilization, ethics, comparative religion, or the like.[46] In other words, a public school teacher may teach about religion in an objective manner but should avoid promoting belief in a particular religion and should likewise avoid degrading or showing hostility toward any religion.

Commenting on religious themes in public schools, the federal court noted in the *Florey* case, "The close relationship between religion and American history and culture has frequently been recognized by the Supreme Court of the United States. . . . Total separation (between church and state) is not possible in an absolute sense."[47] The court declared that "the Constitution does not necessarily forbid the use of materials that have a 'religious basis.' Government involvement in an activity of unquestionably religious origin does not contravene

---

[45]*Abington Township,* 374 U.S. at 225.

[46]*Stone v. Graham,* 449 U.S. 39, 42 (1980). The Supreme Court in *Stone* struck down the display of the Ten Commandments on a classroom bulletin board because, standing alone in the absence of a secular context, it was not integrated into the school curriculum, where the Bible may constitutionally be used as an appropriate study of history, civilization, ethics, comparative religion, or the like. Presumably, if the Ten Commandments were displayed on the bulletin board in association with other secular symbols of law-based society, the Supreme Court may well have ruled the display to be constitutional.

[47]*Florey,* 619 F.2d at 1313–14 (quoting *Lemon v. Kurtzman,* 403 U.S. 602, 614 (1971)).

the Establishment Clause if its 'present purpose and effect' is secular."[48]

Public performance of religious songs is a legitimate part of secular study. "We view the term 'study' to include more than mere classroom instruction: public performance may be a legitimate part of secular study."[49] "To allow students only to study and not to perform (religious art, literature and music, when) such works . . . have developed an independent secular and artistic significance, would give students a truncated view of our culture."[50]

In response to the argument that certain Christmas songs will have a religious effect on the listener, the *Florey* court stated, "It would be literally impossible to develop a public school curriculum that did not in some way affect the religious or nonreligious sensibilities of some of the students or their parents."[51] The court also rejected the argument that singing Christian carols would entangle the school with religion.[52] Certainly, "music without sacred music, architecture minus the Cathedral, or painting without the Scriptural themes would be eccentric and incomplete, even from a secular view."[53]

In *Doe v. Duncanville Independent School District*,[54] a federal court held that a public high school choir's adoption of the song, "The Lord Bless You and Keep You," as its theme

---

[48]*Id.* at 1315 (quoting *McGowan v. Maryland*, 366 U.S. 420 (1961)).
[49]*Id.* at 1316.
[50]*Id.* (quoting *Florey v. Sioux Falls School District* 49–5, 464 F.Supp. 911 (D.S.D. 1979)).
[51]*Id.* at 1317.
[52]*Id.*
[53]*McCollum*, 333 U.S. at 236 (Jackson, J., concurring).
[54]70 F.3d 402 (5th Cir. 1995).

song, did not violate the Establishment Clause and was constitutional. The religious song had been the school's theme song for twenty years. Even more importantly, in *Doe* the song was sung every Friday during practice, at the end of some performances and choral competitions, and on the bus to and from performances, which the students were "required to sing."[55]

The court found that 60 to 75 percent of serious choral music is based on sacred themes or text. "Given the dominance of religious music in this field, [the school district] can hardly be presumed to be advancing or endorsing religion by allowing its choirs to sing a religious theme song."[56] The court noted the obvious, stating:

As a matter of statistical probability, the song best suited to be the theme is more likely to be religious than not. Indeed, to forbid DISD from having a theme song that is religious would force DISD to disqualify the majority of appropriate choral music simply because it is religious. Within the world of choral music, such a restriction would require hostility, not neutrality, toward religion.[57]

In *Bauchman v. West High School*,[58] another federal court held that singing songs with Christian lyrics, including "The Lord Bless You and Keep You" and "Friends," was constitutional even in settings such as graduation ceremonies and

---

[55]*Id.* at 404, 407.
[56]*Id.* at 407.
[57]*Id.* (emphasis added).
[58]132 F.3d 542 (10th Cir. 1997).

concerts at churches.[59] "The Constitution does not require that the purpose of every government-sanctioned activity be unrelated to religion."[60] "Courts have long recognized the historical, social and cultural significance of religion in our lives and in the world, generally."[61] Consequently, the court concluded that in order to show an improper purpose, the plaintiff "must allege facts indicating the defendants have no 'clearly secular purpose' for selecting songs with religious content and requiring the choir to perform in religious venues."[62] The court found that there was a secular purpose for singing religious songs, even if they were performed at religious venues.[63]

> Here, we discern a number of plausible secular purposes for the defendants' conduct. For example, it is recognized that a significant percentage of serious choral music is based on religious themes or text. Any choral curriculum designed to expose students to the full array of vocal music culture therefore can be expected to reflect a significant number of religious songs. Moreover, a vocal music instructor would be expected to select any particular piece of sacred choral music, like any piece of secular choral music, in part for its unique qualities useful to teach a variety of vocal music skills (i.e., sight reading, intonation, harmonization, expression.). *Plausible secular reasons*

---

[59]*Id.* at 547.
[60]*Id.* at 553.
[61]*Id.* at 554.
[62]*Id.*
[63]*Id.*

also exist for performing school choir concerts in churches and other venues associated with religious institutions. Such venues often are acoustically superior to high school auditoriums or gymnasiums, yet still provide adequate seating. Moreover, by performing in such venues, an instructor can showcase his choir to the general public in an atmosphere conducive to the performance of serious choral music.[64]

The court also stated that the possibility some member of the public might be offended is no reason to censor the religious theme.

> The Establishment Clause prohibits only those activities which, in the eyes of a reasonable observer, advance or promote religion or a particular religious belief. This is an objective inquiry, not an inquiry into whether a particular individual might be offended by the content or location of the Choir's performance, or consider such performances to endorse religion.[65]

The reasonable observer must be a person with knowledge of the facts surrounding the community in which the activities happened. "We believe a reasonable observer aware of the purpose, context and history of public education . . . and the traditional and ubiquitous presence of religious themes in vocal music . . . would not perceive the religious music to be the advancement or endorsement of religion."[66]

---

[64]*Id.* (emphasis added).
[65]*Id.*
[66]*Id.*

In summary, religious symbols, music, art, drama, and literature may clearly be taught and presented in public school, so long as the presentation is done in an objective manner consistent with the topic or the holiday occasion. Contrary to some popular opinion, religious Christmas carols are still permitted in the public school; religious art, drama, and literature are still permitted as part of the curriculum; and religious symbols are still permissible. The key is to present the information, display, or performance objectively and in combination with other secular aspects surrounding the holiday or subject matter. To exclude religion from public school creates an atmosphere of hostility, rather than neutrality, toward religion. Clearly the First Amendment demands accommodation and absolutely forbids hostility.

Answering Questions Posed by Students

Teachers are frequently asked questions related to the subject matter being studied and about their personal opinions. What if, following the 9/11 terrorist attack a teacher is asked how he or she copes with the tragedy? Must a teacher remain silent because the question evokes some discussion about the teacher's personal faith? Absolutely not! Teachers may respond to questions raised by students. To answer every question except those which require some response touching on religion would evince discrimination or hostility toward religion rather than the constitutionally mandated neutrality. A teacher may preface the remarks by noting that the answer reflects a personal opinion.

Religious Holidays

The Supreme Court has upheld the display of religious symbols on public property if the context of the religious symbols has other nonreligious symbols that acknowledge the secular aspects of the holiday.[67] The classic example is a nativity scene in the context of a Christmas tree, a menorah, or a Santa Claus. The nativity scene should be in close proximity to a secular symbol.

The Eighth Circuit Court of Appeals ruled in 1980 that a school Christmas program may include religious carols so long as they are presented "in a prudent and objective manner and as a traditional part of the cultural and religious heritage of the particular holiday."[68] The Supreme Court has long ago acknowledged that "music without sacred music, architecture minus the cathedral, or painting without the Scriptural themes would be eccentric and incomplete, even from a secular view."[69] Teachers should not shun celebrations of religious holidays. This includes permitting students to give reports, whether oral or written, on religious holidays or topics. This also includes the display of a nativity scene within the classroom setting. A nativity scene is certainly permissible in a classroom setting if, within the same nativity scene setting, secular symbols of Christmas are also displayed. For example, a teacher can display a nativity scene so long as

---

[67]*Lynch v. Donnelly,* 465 U.S. 668 (1984); *County of Allegheny v. ACLU,* 492 U.S. 573 (1989); *see also ACLU of N.J. v. Schundler,* 168 F.3d 92 (3d Cir. 1999) (appeals court upheld display of nativity scene along with Kwanzaa symbols, sled, figures of Frosty the Snowman and Santa Claus, and two signs referring to cultural and ethnic diversity).

[68]*Florey,* 619 F.2d at 1311.

[69]*McCollum,* 333 U.S. at 236 (Jackson, J., concurring).

secular symbols are displayed within the same context, such as a Christmas tree, Santa Claus, or a reindeer. Jewish celebrations of Hanukkah may also be displayed.[70]

Clothing and Jewelry

Teachers should be permitted to wear religious symbols. Like the students in *Tinker v. Des Moines Independent School District,* a federal appeals court permitted teachers to wear black arm-bands in symbolic protest to the Vietnam War.[71]

In contrast to a student's ability of free expression through articles of clothing, a teacher has a few limitations.[72] If the content of the message is not religious, a teacher probably has greater latitude to wear clothing with inscribed words. However, the First Amendment Establishment Clause places certain restrictions on a teacher with respect to promoting religion. Nevertheless, a teacher should be able to wear religious articles of clothing or jewelry. Clothing with religious writing moves into a gray area. The more objective the writing without promoting a religious view, the more likely the teacher is able to wear the article of clothing.

---

[70]The background of Hanukkah can be found by reading the Apocryphal book of Maccabees, which describes the Jews taking back and cleansing the temple from the Syrians on Kislev 25, or the ninth month of the Jewish calendar. 1 *Maccabees* 4.

[71]*James v. Board of Educ.,* 461 F.2d 566 (2d Cir. 1972), *cert. denied,* 409 U.S. 1042 (1972), *reh'g denied,* 410 U.S. 947 (1973), *withdrawn,* 515 F.2d 504 (1975).

[72]*See Downing v. West Haven Bd. of Educ.,* 162 F. Supp. 2d 19 (D. Conn. 2001) (an uncommon case where a teacher was prohibited from wearing a "Jesus 2000" T-shirt).

In one case, a school allowed teachers to wear T-shirts to class on Spirit Day, a day when students and teachers acknowledged the various student-initiated clubs on campus. Teacher-sponsors and others were permitted to wear T-shirts of the various clubs, but the school prohibited some teachers from wearing the Fellowship of Christian Athletes' T-shirt, claiming that to allow teachers to wear these shirts would violate the "separation of church and state." Liberty Counsel intervened and the teachers were allowed to wear the Fellowship of Christian Athletes shirts along with other teachers who wore the secular club T-shirts. In this case, to discriminate against a teacher solely because of the content of the message while allowing other teachers to wear secular messages violated the First Amendment. Whether clothes or jewelry, Christian teachers should receive equal treatment as that afforded other teachers who wear articles of clothing or jewelry with secular messages.

Outside Speakers

Teachers may bring in outside speakers to present views on a particular topic. The teacher can even use a debate format to present both sides of an issue. This avoids the problem of the school endorsing the speaker and allows for experts in various areas to present information to students. However, a debate format is not necessary for a teacher to bring an outside speaker on campus to present a particular view. A teacher may bring an outside speaker to present a view opposing the teacher or one in support of the teacher. There is no requirement that both sides of a topic be presented. Since the outside speaker is not an agent of the state, the speaker may address controversial topics and state an opinion on these topics. The teacher should avoid a regular pattern of inviting outside speakers to present only one viewpoint, and the school should not pay for or sponsor the outside speaker.[73] However, the school may pay a speaker to come on campus to present a message dealing with sexual abstinence or drug abuse. Such a message, while having moral and social concerns, also has religious concerns. The speaker may talk about all the concerns touching this topic. The only time a school should avoid paying for a speaker is if the speaker is brought to campus for the sole purpose of presenting a specific sectarian view that could be construed as proselytizing or evangelism.

Student Bible Clubs

Student clubs are governed by the First Amendment and the federal law known as the Equal Access Act (hereinafter Act).[74] The protections afforded by the First Amendment are in most cases broader than those provided under the Act.[75] The Act only applies to public secondary schools and typically does not apply to elementary schools. In contrast, the First Amendment applies to all schools. From the teacher's perspective, the First Amendment should be primarily relied upon if the club meets outside of school hours, while the Act should be relied upon if the club meets during the school

---

[73]*Wilson v. Chancellor,* 418 F. Supp. 1358 (D. Or. 1976).
[74]20 U.S.C. §§ 4071 *et seq.*
[75]*See Prince v. Jacoby,* 303 F.3d 1074 (9th Cir. 2002). This case undertook an excellent analysis of the different protections afforded by the First Amendment and the Act.

day. During the school day, the teacher continues to wear the hat of a public school employee. After school hours, the teacher wears the hat of a private citizen.

Under the Act, a school may require that student-initiated, religious clubs have a teacher sponsor. Schools may require a sponsor for religious clubs only if the same requirements are made of secular clubs. The provision of a school sponsor does not mean that the school endorses the club.[76] The employee or agent of the school should be present at such religious meetings "only in a nonparticipatory capacity."[77] This "nonparticipatory" attendance means that the school employee should not actively lead or direct the group. The club must be student-initiated and student-led, which means that the activity must primarily be the activity of the students and not of the school. School sponsors can give advice and counsel, but the clubs should remain student-initiated and student led. However, school employees may invite the students to their homes, and in the off-campus setting they may take an active role.

If the club meets outside school hours, whether on or off campus, the restrictions that the club be student-initiated or student-led, including the requirement that the teacher be present in a "nonparticipatory capacity," do not apply. The Supreme Court in the *Good News Club*[78] case found that a school violated the First Amendment when it denied an after-school Christian club the right to meet on campus to conduct

---

[76]20 U.S.C. § 4072(2).

[77]20 U.S.C. § 4071(c)(3).

[78]*Good News Club v. Milford Central Sch. Dist.*, 533 U.S. 98 (2001); see also *Culbertson v. Oakridge Sch. Dist. No. 76*, 258 F.3d 1061 (9th Cir. 2001).

an adult-led club for elementary students. This case is significant for several reasons. First, the club was a religious club at the elementary level. Second, the club was adult initiated and adult led. Third, the meeting began immediately after school ended. Fourth, the Court rejected the argument that the young elementary students might be confused and assume that the club was a school function. The Court noted that the Good News Club required the students to obtain a signed parental permission slip in order to attend the meetings. Thus, the Supreme Court reasoned that the religious meeting should not be viewed from the child's perspective but from the perspective of the adult parent or guardian. Thus, a federal court of appeals ruled that a public elementary school teacher may participate after school in leading a Good News Club on the same campus where the teacher works during the school day.[79]

Summary

Teachers on public school campuses are protected by the First Amendment Free Speech and Free Exercise Clauses. Teachers are also limited by the First Amendment Establishment Clause. Teachers retain the constitutional right to bring information to the classroom that is related to the curriculum being taught. The more relevant the information to the curriculum, the stronger the constitutional protection. Teachers may objectively instruct about religion but should be careful not to proselytize. Every subject taught in public school has in some way been impacted by religion. To ignore

---

[79]*Wigg,* 382 F.2d at 807.

religion is to render a disservice to the curriculum being taught and to the students.

Teachers may be sponsors of religious clubs. If the club meets during the school day, the Equal Access Act may require the club to be student initiated and student led and may further require that the teacher be present in a nonparticipatory capacity. However, if the club meets outside school hours, whether on or off campus, the First Amendment provides greater protection. Such clubs may be adult initiated and adult-led, and teachers may take an active role in the club. To ensure that students will not misperceive the teacher's role, the students should obtain a parental permission slip which acknowledges that the teacher is acting as a private citizen and not on behalf of the students.

5
PRAYERS AT PUBLIC ASSEMBLIES

PRAYER AT PUBLIC MEETINGS predates our Constitution and is replete throughout America's history. Prior to the early 1960s, there was little controversy regarding prayer at public events. Until that time there had been no successful legal challenge to public prayers. Ever since the United States Supreme Court first addressed public prayers, courts have rendered conflicting decisions. Oftentimes these decisions depend largely on factual circumstances. These circumstances include the particular event in question, the extent of the state's control over the content of the message, the audience, and the participants. This chapter overviews prayers in public school classrooms, athletic events, graduation prayers, prayers in the courtroom, legislative prayers, and prayers offered before county, municipal, or school board meetings.

Public School Classrooms

There are three types of public school classroom prayers. The first includes prayers composed by public school officials. The second deals with statutes authorizing a moment of voluntary prayer. The final type involves statutes, rules, or policies authorizing a moment of silence.

STATE-COMPOSED OR STATE-LED PRAYERS

The first case dealing with school prayer reached the United States Supreme Court in 1962. The case, known as *Engel v. Vitale*,[1] involved a prayer composed by the Board of Regents for the New York public schools. The prayer stated as follows: "Almighty God, we acknowledge our dependence upon Thee, and we beg Thy blessings upon us, our parents, our teachers and our Country."[2] The parents of ten students brought suit against the public school and the Board of Regents arguing that the state-composed prayer was a violation of the Constitution. The Supreme Court agreed and stated:

> We think the constitutional prohibition against laws respecting an establishment of religion must at

---

[1] 370 U.S. 421 (1962). Prayer was commonplace in public schools from the founding of America. The first printed textbook in America was *The New England Primer*. This book profoundly influenced American education. For nearly two hundred years, from the 1700s to the early 1900s, almost every student entering public or private school learned about the alphabet, grammar, and religion from the pages of this book. Those who drafted, debated, and voted on the First Amendment along with all the Founding Fathers probably read this book. Public school students were taught the Lord's Prayer along with the Infant's Morning and Evening Prayers. Those who know most about the First Amendment did not believe that prayer in school established a religion.

[2] *Id.* at 422.

least mean that in this country it is no part of the business of government to compose official prayers for [students] to recite as part of a religious program carried on by government.³

From 1962 to the present, the United States Supreme Court has consistently ruled that state-composed and state-led prayers in the public school classroom violate the First Amendment Establishment Clause.

In 1963 the Supreme Court considered a case involving state-mandated Bible readings and the recitation of the Lord's Prayer by a state official at the beginning of the school day. In *School District of Abington Township v. Schempp,*⁴ the Court ruled that it was unconstitutional for state officials to read the Bible to public school students followed by the recitation of the Lord's Prayer at the beginning of each day.⁵ School officials were charged with selecting various Bible verses and reading these verses at the beginning of each school day. The students were then asked to recite the Lord's Prayer in unison. The Court ruled that both of these practices violated the First Amendment Establishment Clause.⁶ However, the Court noted that the Bible could be studied as literature, and religion could be studied in a religious history class.

MOMENT OF VOLUNTARY PRAYER

The primary case involving voluntary prayer decided by the Supreme Court is *Wallace v. Jaffree.*⁷ The state of Alabama

---

³*Id.* at 425.
⁴374 U.S. 203 (1963).
⁵*Id.* at 211.
⁶*Id.* at 223.
⁷472 U.S. 38 (1985).

passed a law in 1978 authorizing a one-minute period of silence in all public schools "for meditation." In 1981 the state passed another law authorizing a period of silence "for meditation or voluntary prayer," and in 1982 the state amended the law to authorize teachers to lead "willing students" in a prescribed prayer to "almighty God . . . the Creator and Supreme Judge of the world."[8] A lower federal court ruled that the statute allowing a time for meditation was constitutional.[9] This part of the decision was never appealed and accordingly was not before the Supreme Court for determination. The Supreme Court considered two parts of the statute: (1) the 1981 statute authorizing meditation or voluntary prayer and (2) the 1982 statute authorizing teachers to lead willing students in a prescribed prayer.

In reviewing the statute, the Supreme Court considered the state legislative debates prior to its adoption. Apparently Senator Donald Holmes was one of the main sponsors of the bill. He stated during the legislative debate that the intent behind the statute was "to return voluntary prayer" to the public schools.[10] The Court, therefore, ruled that the Alabama law was a veiled attempt to circumvent the 1962 and 1963 *Engel* and *Schempp* decisions and struck down the law as a violation of the Establishment Clause.

It is extremely important to note the exact parameters of the Supreme Court's opinion. The Supreme Court did not rule on the constitutionality of a moment of silence. The issues before the Court were a moment of "voluntary prayer" and

---

[8]*Id.* at 40.
[9]*Jaffree v. James,* 554 F. Supp. 1130, 1132 (S.D. Ala. 1982).
[10]*Wallace v. Jaffree,* 472 U.S. 38, 57 (1985).

another statute dealing with authorization of teachers to lead students in a specific state-composed prayer. Both of these statutes were struck down as unconstitutional.

In another case, the Louisiana legislature amended a statute that provided for a moment of "silent prayer or meditation" by deleting the word *silent*. The sponsor of the amendment stated its purpose was to "allow verbal prayer in schools."[11] The court struck down the law, stating that the amendment and the statements by the sponsor "demonstrate[d] that the sole purpose of the amendment was to return verbal prayer to the public schools."[12]

In 2000 the Commonwealth of Virginia enacted a law that established a "minute of silence" in all public schools so that "each pupil may, in the exercise of his or her individual choice, meditate, pray, or engage in any other silent activity which does not interfere with, distract, or impede other pupils in the like exercise of individual choice."[13] In upholding the law, the federal court observed that the First Amendment

> Religion Clauses must not be interpreted with a view that religion be suppressed in the public arenas in favor of secularism. . . . The Constitution "does not require total separation of Church and State." . . . Not only is the government permitted to accommodate religion without violating the Establishment Clause, at times it is *required* to do so.[14]

---

[11]*Doe v. Ouachita,* 274 F.3d 289, 294 (5th Cir. 2001).
[12]*Id.* at 294–95.
[13]*Brown v. Gilmore,* 258 F.3d 265, 270 (4th Cir.), *cert denied,* 534 U.S. 996 (2001) (quoting VA. CODE § 22.1–203).
[14]*Id.* at 274.

The court distinguished this case from the *Wallace* decision discussed above on the basis that there was no evidence the Virginia legislature acted in open defiance of the federal Constitution. During the debates, the legislators discussed the current case law, but no one made statements about returning verbal state-led prayer to school. Additionally, the law allowed for both a moment of silence and a moment of voluntary silent prayer. The statute was thus clear that the minute could be used for either secular or religious silent reflection.

MOMENT OF SILENCE

Although the United States Supreme Court has never directly ruled on a moment of silence statute, its 1985 opinion in *Wallace v. Jaffree*[15] suggests that moment of silence statutes, rules, or policies are constitutional. Justice Stevens wrote the opinion in *Wallace v. Jaffree* striking down the state laws requiring a moment of voluntary prayer and a law authorizing teachers to lead students in a state-composed prayer. In *Wallace v. Jaffree,* Justice O'Connor stated that the prior Supreme Court opinions of *Engel* and *Schempp* were not dispositive of the constitutionality of moment of silence laws.[16] In this regard she stated:

> A state-sponsored moment of silence in the public schools is different from state-sponsored vocal prayer or Bible reading. First, a moment of silence is not inherently religious. Silence, unlike prayer or Bible reading, need not be associated with a religious

---

[15]*Wallace,* 472 U.S. at 38.
[16]*Id.* at 71.

exercise. Second, a pupil who participates in a moment of silence need not compromise his or her beliefs. During a moment of silence, a student who objects to prayer is left to his or her own thoughts, and is not compelled to listen to the prayers or thoughts of others. For these simple reasons, a moment of silence statute does not stand or fall under the Establishment Clause according to how the court regards vocal prayer or Bible reading.[17]

Justice O'Connor cited Justice Brennan's concurring opinion in *Schempp* as follows:

> The observance of a moment of reverent silence at the opening of class "may serve" the solely secular purpose of the devotional activities without jeopardizing either the religious liberties of any members of the community or the proper degree of separation between the spheres of religion and government.[18]

The United States Supreme Court has never directly addressed a statute dealing with a moment of silence, but Justice O'Connor's opinion regarding the constitutionality of a moment of silence found support from a majority of the Court. In fact, Chief Justice William Rehnquist went further and suggested that the Supreme Court should recede from its 1962 and 1963 opinions striking down state-led and state-composed prayers.[19]

---

[17]*Id.* at 72 (O'Connor, J., concurring).
[18]*Id.* at 72–73 (quoting *Abington Township,* 374 U.S. at 281). Justice Powell also agreed that "some moment of silence statutes may be constitutional."
[19]*Wallace,* 472 U.S. at 91 (Rehnquist, J., dissenting).

In 1994 the Georgia legislature enacted the Moment of Quiet Reflection in Schools Act.[20] Under the Act, the teacher in charge of the public school classroom at the opening of each school day was required to conduct "a brief period of quiet reflection for not more than 60 seconds with the participation of all pupils therein assembled."[21] Prior to the start of the 1994–95 school year, a school teacher in the Gwinnett County School District expressed concerns about implementing the Act. The teacher wrote a letter to the superintendent who responded with a letter that had been sent to all the school principals. In the letter, the superintendent advised the principals to remind teachers and administrators not to suggest or imply that students should or should not use this time for prayer. Students were free to use this time for prayer if they chose, but the school did not tolerate any coercion by school officials in this manner. At the beginning of the school day on August 22, 1994, the principal for South Gwinnett High School made various announcements over the intercom. Following the announcements, the principal stated: "Let us take a few moments to reflect quietly on our day, our activities, and what we hope to accomplish."[22] In contravention of the Act, the school teacher told his class that each student may do as he/she wished, but he was going to continue with his lesson. The teacher was later fired for failure to comply with the Act. The teacher then brought suit against the school board, alleging that the Quiet Reflection Act violated the First

---

[20]GA. CODE ANN. § 20–2–1050 (1996).
[21]GA. CODE ANN. § 20–2–1050(a).
[22]*Bown v. Gwinnett County Sch. Dist.,* 112 F.3d 1464, 1468 (11th Cir. 1997).

Amendment Establishment Clause. Yet the federal court of appeals found the Act constitutional.[23]

In summary, state-composed and state-mandated prayers in public schools have been ruled unconstitutional. Moments of voluntary "prayer" have been ruled unconstitutional. However, courts consider moment of silence statutes or policies constitutional.

STUDENT-LED CLASSROOM PRAYER

Even after the Supreme Court decision in 1962, many public schools in the State of Mississippi continued to allow prayer in the classroom. For example, students in Pontotoc County regularly offered prayer over the intercom. At North Pontotoc Attendance Center, the Aletheia Club announced the times and places of its meeting over the intercom and also offered prayers and read devotionals. In 1996 a Mississippi federal court ruled that these prayers, delivered by students via intercom to the classrooms, were unconstitutional.[24] The court found that the students in the classroom were a captive audience and that the school intercom had not been generally opened to student speech. Although the court acknowledged

---

[23]The court found that the Act had a secular purpose, that it did not have the primary effect of advancing religion, and that it did not foster excessive governmental entanglement with religion. The court stated that "even if some legislators were motivated by a conviction that religious speech in particular was valuable and worthy of protection, that alone would not invalidate the Act, because what is relevant is the legislative purpose of the statute, not the possibly religious motives of the legislators who enacted the law." *Bown,* 112 F.3d at 1471–72 (quoting *Board of Educ. of Westside Community Schs. v. Mergens,* 496 U.S. 226, 249 [1990]).

[24]*Herdahl v. Pontotoc County Sch. Dist.,* 933 F. Supp. 582 (N.D. Miss. 1996).

that in some cases a school "may have a valid argument that it has created a forum to permit announcements at the school and student activities,"[25] the facts in the Pontotoc case indicated that the school had not allowed the intercom system to be used as a "soap box for the religious, social or political expressions of members of the student body who want to preach, teach or politicize over the intercom system."[26]

The legislature and the student body quickly reacted to the judge's ruling by passing a statute that purported to permit prayer on any public school property so long as it was nonsectarian, nonproselytizing, student-initiated, voluntary prayer. The legislation attempted to do what the students did through the intercom system. However, a federal court of appeals found that statute unconstitutional as well.[27]

The student body was not content with the result of the court or legislative remedies. Representatives of the student body approached school officials requesting permission to use the auditorium or gymnasium to hold voluntary student prayer meetings in the morning before the start of the school day.[28] The students therefore began using the gymnasium and auditorium for these large prayer meetings. The school board voted to move the school day back several minutes to allow the students to meet prior to the start of the official

---

[25]*Id.* at 589.

[26]*Id.*

[27]*Ingebretsen v. Jackson Pub. Sch. Dist.*, 88 F.3d 274 (5th Cir.), *cert. denied,* 519 U.S. 965 (1996).

[28]Actually, the *Herdahl* case, which struck down the intercom prayer and ruled that no forum had been created through the intercom system, added language that suggested the students could voluntarily meet together to pray. This could include the younger students so long as they had parental consent.

day. Approximately 95 percent of the entire student body attended the student-led morning prayer meetings. As a result of the litigation, more students gathered for prayer than at any time in the school's history. Since the event is student-led, voluntary, and held outside mandatory class hours, it is clearly constitutional.

Athletic Events and Assemblies

In 2000 the Supreme Court struck down an athletic event prayer policy in which public school officials controlled the content of the message and thus assured that the message would always include prayer.[29] However, the Court was quick to acknowledge that "nothing in the Constitution . . . prohibits any public school student from voluntarily praying at any time before, during, or after the school day."[30] The Court also noted that the First Amendment does not "impose a prohibition on all religious activity in our public schools."[31] Once the specific facts of this case are considered, the principle is clear: a policy or practice whereby the government remains neutral by allowing a message of the speaker's choice, including a religious message, is constitutional.

The *Santa Fe* case involved four separate school board policies. The first policy dealt with graduation prayer. The senior class could vote on whether to include a "nonsectarian" and "nonproselytizing" invocation and benediction as part of graduation. If the class voted to do so, two seniors were

---

[29]*Santa Fe Indep. Sch. Dist. v. Doe,* 530 U.S. 290 (2000).
[30]*Id.* at 313.
[31]*Id.*

elected by the class to deliver the prayers. A second policy eliminated the requirement that the prayers be "nonsectarian" and "nonproselytizing." A third policy dealt specifically with invocations at football games and was patterned after the graduation policies, except that the student chosen to deliver the invocation would be the same student for each and every home game. The final football game prayer policy omitted the word *prayer* and replaced it with the words *messages, statements,* and *invocations.* However, the person chosen to deliver the invocation "message" was the same person selected under the prior "prayer only" policy.

Under the *Santa Fe* policies, the only "message" which a chosen student could deliver was prayer. If the students voted against an invocation, then no message was permitted. If the students voted in favor of an invocation, then the policy required that the content of the message include only prayer. Thus, the school policy predetermined the content of the message. The Court was not concerned with the fact that the policy granted only one student access to the stage at a time.[32] The Court suggested that students may speak on religious topics during school-sponsored events so long as their message is not controlled and directed by school officials.[33] Thus, an athletic event policy is constitutional if it both allows (1) students to vote on whether to include a "message" at an athletic event and leaves the choice of the message entirely up to the student, or (2) students or other speakers to deliver a message, the content of which is the free choice of

---

[32]*Id.* at 304.

[33]*Id.* at 302–04, 313. *See also Adler v. Duval County Sch. Bd.,* 250 F.3d 1330 (11th Cir. 2001) (*en banc*), *cert denied,* 531 U.S. 801 (2002).

the speaker. The difference between the first and second option is a popular vote. Under the first option, students vote on whether to include a message and, if so, then vote on the messenger. The second option does not include a vote and is designed to cover any student or outside speaker who is selected by school officials using religion-neutral or secular criteria. In other words, the person is not selected for the purpose of delivering a religious message. Rather, the person is selected because the student is, for example, senior class president, homecoming queen candidate, student government president, captain of the team, or a community or business leader. This option merely covers a person's spontaneous religious message which was not preordained or coerced by school officials.

Prior to the Supreme Court's *Santa Fe* ruling in 2000, several other lower federal courts had already grappled with prayers at athletic events. Based on the *Santa Fe* case, some of these decisions may no longer be valid. In 1989 a federal court of appeals ruled that prayer at a public high school football game was unconstitutional.[34] From 1947 to 1986 an announcer introduced the invocation speaker and usually identified the church affiliation. The student government originally invited the invocation speakers, but in 1950, local ministers began to give the invocations. In the early 1970s, an assistant football coach delegated the task of furnishing invocation speakers to a Presbyterian clergyman. From the early 1970s to 1986, the same clergyman recruited invocation

---

[34]*Jager v. Douglas County Sch. Dist.,* 862 F.2d 824 (11th Cir. 1989), *cert. denied,* 490 U.S. 1090 (1989).

speakers from the Douglas County Ministerial Association, whose membership consisted exclusively of Protestant Christian ministers. In 1986, in response to a complaint by a student, a so-called equal access plan was developed permitting the various school clubs and organizations to designate club members to give the invocation, including any student, parent, or school staff member. This "prayer only" policy was struck down.[35] However, the same federal appeals court later upheld the rights of students to deliver voluntary prayer at school-sponsored events and noted that this football game policy was unconstitutional because it provided for "*invocations* and *only* invocations at school sporting events."[36] Therefore, a policy in which the school does not direct the content of the message would be upheld.

Another federal court ruled that the First Amendment did not permit the student council to begin assemblies with prayer.[37] In this case, the student council officers conducted various assemblies throughout the school year under the guidance and direction of the school principal. Students who did not wish to attend could report to a supervised study hall. With the permission of the principal, the student council was permitted to open their assemblies with prayer and Bible readings of their choosing. A time was set aside on the agenda, and the student council selected one member of the student body to say a prayer. Nevertheless, the court ruled

[35]*Id.* at 832–33.
[36]*Chandler v. James,* 180 F.3d 1254, 1259 (11th Cir. 1999), *cert. granted, vacated and remanded sub nom, Chandler v. Siegelman,* 530 U.S. 1256 (2000), *judgment reinstated,* 230 F.3d 1313 (11th Cir. 2000).
[37]*Collins v. Chandler Unified Sch. Dist.,* 644 F.2d 759 (9th Cir.), *cert. denied,* 454 U.S. 863 (1981).

that prayer in this context was unconstitutional because the school authorized the content of the message to specifically include prayer. Had the student message been spontaneous, or had the school opened the format for the students to select any topic of choice, the outcome would have been different.

Another federal court addressed the issue of prayer led by coaches of athletic teams and came to a similar conclusion as did the court regarding prayers before public high school football games. In *Doe v. Duncanville Independent School District*,[38] a girls' basketball coach regularly began and ended practice with a team recitation of the Lord's Prayer. At one of the first basketball games, the Lord's Prayer was recited in the center of the court at the end of the game, the girls on their hands and knees with the coach standing over them, all with bowed heads. Before away games, the coach would lead the team in prayer prior to leaving the school and before exiting the bus upon the team's return. A seventh-grade basketball player objected to these prayers and filed suit. The court ruled that the recitation of the Lord's Prayer in this manner violated the First Amendment Establishment Clause because the coach, as an agent of the school, had actually "composed" a prayer.[39] This case is slightly different from cases regarding students or outside speakers, because the teacher or coach is considered a mouthpiece for the school, and thus the prayer is deemed to be government prayer rather than private speech.

When considering the impact of the above rulings, a number of factors should be noted. First, these cases deal with

---

[38]994 F.2d 160 (5th Cir. 1993).
[39]*Id.* at 165.

public secondary schools. The rulings may not apply to post-secondary schools in light of the age differences. In the context of the First Amendment Establishment Clause, courts have often considered the age of the students. The older the student, the less risk the religious practice will be perceived as establishing a religion. Second, the cases involving prayer before a public high school football game and the prayers composed and led by the basketball coach are similar to the 1962 and 1963 Supreme Court rulings in *Engel* and *Schempp*. The case of the high school basketball coach is similar to the state of New York's ruling in the 1962 *Engel* case, when the school composed the prayer. Third, none of these cases address a moment of silence. Moments of silence do not inject the government into religion. Finally, these cases deal with "prayer only" policies or practices. If students were leading the prayer at these athletic events in conjunction with other student-initiated, nonreligious speech, then to prohibit the students from the religious speech will likely violate their First Amendment free speech rights. In other words, if students were allowed to speak at the athletic events or other assemblies on a variety of topics, then students would be able to engage in religious speech to the same extent they engage in secular speech. To prevent student speech because it is religious, while allowing secular speech, violates the First Amendment.

Graduation Prayers

The United States Supreme Court decision in *Lee v. Weisman*[40] has caused some confusion as to whether prayers are permissible at public school graduation ceremonies.

---

[40]505 U.S. 577 (1992).

While prayers have been restricted at public school graduations, they have not been completely prohibited. It is important to know what the Court did and did not say.

WHAT IS PROHIBITED?

To understand what is presently prohibited by the United States Supreme Court decision in *Lee v. Weisman,* it is important to know some of the history regarding the case. The Supreme Court's decision focused on the following three factors: (1) the school principal decided that an invocation and benediction would be given at the ceremony and placed prayer on the agenda; (2) the principal chose the religious participant; and (3) the principal provided the clergyman with a copy of *Guidelines for Civic Occasions,* produced by the National Council of Christians and Jews, outlining suggestions for delivering nonsectarian prayers. The Court found that these three factors placed the school in the position of guiding and directing the content of the prayer during a public ceremony.

What the Supreme Court prohibited can be summarized as follows: School officials cannot direct that prayer be part of a public school graduation ceremony, select a religious participant for the express purpose of delivering a prayer, and give guidelines on how to say a nonsectarian, nonproselytizing prayer. In practical terms, a public school cannot invite a clergyman to say a prayer at a graduation ceremony and direct the content or manner of the prayer. As an additional note, the *Lee* decision does not affect graduation prayers at postsecondary schools, that is, the college or university level.[41]

---

[41] *Tanford v. Brand,* 104 F.3d 982 (7th Cir. 1997), *cert. denied,* 522 U.S. 814 (1997). (Students at university level are mature enough to understand that

The Supreme Court did not ban all prayers at graduation. In fact, the Court stated that its ruling was limited to the facts of that particular case.[42] Therefore, any change in the factual situation presented in *Lee* might change the outcome. Justice Scalia wrote in his dissenting opinion that merely adding a disclaimer to the graduation program would make the same set of facts constitutional.[43] Justice Scalia stated the following:

> All that is seemingly needed is an announcement, or perhaps a written insertion at the beginning of the graduation program, to the effect that, while all are asked to rise for the invocation and benediction, none is compelled to join in them, nor will be assumed, by rising, to have done so. That obvious fact recited, the graduates and their parents may proceed to thank God, as Americans have always done, for the blessings He has generously bestowed on them and on their country.[44]

Obviously the United States Supreme Court has not taken the position that all graduation prayer is unconstitutional. Indeed, the Court noted the following:

> We recognize that, at graduation time and throughout the course of the educational process, there will be instances when religious values, religious

---

a prayer delivered by a clergy at a state university graduation ceremony is not an establishment of religion, and therefore such prayer is constitutional.) *See also Chaudhuri v. Tennessee,* 130 F.3d 232 (6th Cir. 1997), *cert. denied,* 523 U.S. 1024 (1998).

[42]*Lee,* 505 U.S. at 587.

[43]*Id.* at 645 (Scalia, J., dissenting).

[44]*Id.*

practices, and religious persons will have some interaction with the public schools and their students.[45]

The United States Supreme Court recognized that "a relentless and all-pervasive attempt to exclude religion from every aspect of public life could itself become inconsistent with the Constitution."[46] The Court in *Lee v. Weisman* was concerned that school officials were actively involved in placing prayer on the agenda, inviting a religious clergyman to speak for the purpose of prayer, and giving the clergyman specific guidelines for saying nonsectarian prayers. Prayer can still be conducted at public school graduations if school officials use secular criteria to invite the speaker, and once there, the speaker voluntarily prays. A valedictorian, salutatorian, or class officer can also voluntarily pray as part of the ceremony. The student body can elect a class chaplain or elect a class representative for the specific purpose of prayer. Part of the school program can be given over to the students and therefore be student-led and student initiated. A parent and/or student committee can create and conduct part of the ceremony and, therefore, avoid state involvement. The ceremony can be conducted off the school premises by private individuals, and therefore no state involvement would occur. The school may also adopt a free speech policy which allows the senior class an opportunity to devote a few minutes of the ceremony to uncensored student speech that can be secular or sacred. Finally, private individuals can sponsor public school graduations on or off the public campus.

---

[45]*Id.* at 598–99.
[46]*Id.*

What Is Permitted?

Prayer is still permissible during public school graduation. Postsecondary schools (colleges and universities) may continue to invite clergy to deliver a prayer at graduation. The restrictions on prayer during graduation at a public secondary school do not apply at the postsecondary level.[47] Courts have reasoned that students in postsecondary schools are less impressionable, more mature, and can better understand that the prayer offered by a student or an outside clergyperson does not necessarily represent the school, thus removing some of the restrictions secondary schools maintain. While secondary schools (middle, junior high and high school) face more restrictions than postsecondary schools, they still retain several options for the continuation of prayer.

1. Option One—Student Messages

Following the Supreme Court's 1992 decision in *Lee v. Weisman,* some school districts reacted by adopting "prayer only" policies for student speakers.[48] Some federal courts

---

[47]*Tanford,* 104 F.3d at 982; *Chaudhuri v. Tennessee,* 886 F. Supp. 1374 (M.D. Tenn. 1995) *cert. denied,* 522 U.S. 814 (1997).

[48]The first case involving a "prayer only" policy for students is *Jones v. Clear Creek Independent School District,* 977 F.2d 963 (5th Cir. 1992), *cert. denied,* 508 U.S. 967 (1993). The Supreme Court handed down the decision in *Lee v. Weisman* on June 24, 1992, and the *Jones* decision was rendered on November 24, 1992. The High Court refused to hear the *Jones* appeal on June 7, 1993. Thus, it appeared that the Supreme Court would uphold a "prayer only" policy so long as the messenger was a student. However, the Court's 2000 decision in *Santa Fe* now indicates that "prayer only" policies may also be called into question. Note that the Fifth Circuit Court of Appeals has since reaffirmed the *Jones* decision. *See Ingebretsen,* 88 F.3d at 274. The next case dealing with student prayers is *Harris v. Joint School District No. 241,* 821 F. Supp. 638 (D. Idaho 1993), *modified,* 41 F.3d 447

have upheld such policies while others have not.[49] However, based on the Supreme Court decision in *Santa Fe* regarding prayers during athletic events, it appears that the Court would strike down a "prayer only" policy. Instead, a policy which allows students to select a message of choice without input, direction or censorship from school officials meets every concern expressed by the High Court. Such a policy was at issue

(9th Cir. 1994), *vacated as moot,* 515 U.S. 1154 (1995). However, the Supreme Court set aside the ruling because the students had graduated, and the case became moot. Later, the same Ninth Circuit Court of Appeals upheld a policy which allowed the top four academic students to deliver an uncensored "message" of the student's choice. *See Doe v. Madison Sch. Dist. No. 321,* 147 F.3d 832 (9th Cir. 1998), *vacated on other grounds,* 177 F.3d 789 (9th Cir. 1999) (*en banc*). The same court then set aside this ruling on the basis that the case had become moot due to graduation. The next time the Ninth Circuit considered a graduation prayer case was in *Cole v. Oroville Union High School District,* 228 F.3d 1092 (9th Cir. 2000). In *Cole,* the court ruled against a student who sought to force the school to allow him to pray at graduation. The next case was *Adler v. Duval County School Board,* 851 F. Supp. 446 (M.D. Fla 1994), *aff'd in part and vacated in part,* 112 F.3d 1475 (11th Cir. 1997), *reh'g denied,* 120 F.3d 276 (11th Cir. 1997). The court in *Adler* upheld a student "message" policy, but when the ACLU appealed the matter, the appeals court vacated the case because of mootness due to the fact the students had already graduated. Note that Karen Adler was the student in the 1994 *Adler* case. Her younger sister, Emily, later refiled the same case in 1998. This later series of rulings upheld the "message" policy and will be further addressed below. In *ACLU v. Black Horse Pike Regional Board of Education,* 84 F.3d 1471 (3d Cir. 1996) (*en banc*), the court struck down a "prayer only" policy. The most well-reasoned cases which upheld student prayers at graduation include *Adler,* 250 F.3rd at 1330, *Chandler v. James,* 180 F.3d at 1254, and *Chandler v. Siegelman,* 230 F.3d at 1313. These cases will be further discussed below.
[49]As noted above, the Fifth Circuit Court of Appeals has upheld a student "prayer only" policy provided the prayer is nonsectarian and nonproselytizing. The Fifth Circuit covers the states of Texas, Louisiana, and Mississippi. The Third and Ninth Circuits have ruled against such policies. The Third Circuit governs Pennsylvania, Delaware, New Jersey, and the Virgin Islands. The Ninth Circuit governs California, Washington, Oregon, Nevada, Arizona, Idaho, Montana, Hawaii, Alaska, and Guam.

in the case of *Adler v. Duval County School Board.*[50] The full policy states as follows:

    1. The use of a brief opening and/or closing message, not to exceed two minutes, at high school graduation exercises shall rest within the discretion of the graduating senior class.

    2. The opening and/or closing message shall be given by a student volunteer, in the graduating senior class, chosen by the graduating senior class as a whole.

---

[50]250 F.3d 1330 (11th Cir. 2001), cert. denied, 534 U.S. 1065 (2001). This case began in 1994 when Karen Adler challenged a school policy allowing students to deliver uncensored messages at graduation. Liberty Counsel intervened and defended the school policy. The court upheld the policy. *See Adler,* 851 F. Supp. at 446. She appealed the case, and it was argued twice (1995 and 1996) before the Eleventh Circuit Court of Appeals. In 1997, the court dismissed the case as moot because Karen Adler had already graduated. *See Adler,* 112 F.3d at 1475. In 1998, her younger sister, Emily, filed the identical suit against the policy. Again, the court upheld the policy, and the case was appealed. *See Adler v. Duval County Sch. Bd.,* 174 F.3d 1236 (11th Cir. 1999). This time the court ruled in a 2-to-1 decision against the policy. Liberty Counsel immediately asked the full panel of judges to rehear the case and set aside the ruling. Three weeks after the ruling, the full panel of twelve judges set aside the ruling and agreed to rehear the case. After arguing the case before the twelve judges, the court on March 15, 2002 ruled 10–2 in favor of the policy. *See Adler v. Duval County Sch. Bd.,* 206 F.3d 1070 (11th Cir. 2000) (*en banc*). Then on June 19, 2000, the Supreme Court handed down the *Santa Fe* case involving prayers at football games. *See Santa Fe,* 530 U.S. at 290. The ACLU appealed the *Adler* case, and the High Court, while not ruling on the case, vacated the opinion and sent the case back down to the Eleventh Circuit to consider whether *Santa Fe* affected its decision. *See Adler,* 531 U.S. at 801. On May 11, 2001, the Eleventh Circuit issued its opinion in an 8–4 ruling again upholding the policy, stating that the Santa Fe decision did not change the outcome. *See Adler,* 250 F.3d at 1330. The ACLU appealed the case one more time, arguing the *Santa Fe* decision meant that all prayers by students at school-sponsored event were unconstitutional. On December 10, 2001, the Supreme Court refused to hear the case and thus allowed the decision upholding the message policy to stand. *See Adler,* 534 U.S. at 1065.

3. If the graduating senior class chooses to use an opening and/or closing message, the content of that message shall be prepared by the student volunteer and shall not be monitored or otherwise reviewed by school officials, its officers, or employees.[51]

During the first year in which the above policy was operative within the school district, ten of the seventeen high schools opted for messages that constituted various forms of religious prayer. The remaining seven schools had either no message at all, or their message was entirely secular in nature.[52] The policy allowed the senior class to vote on whether to include an opening and/or closing student "message" at graduation. If the students voted to include a message, then the senior class elected a student to deliver the message, the content of which was entirely the student's decision. Under this policy, students could deliver a secular or religious message or no message at all. School officials were prohibited from directing, reviewing or censoring the message. The *Adler* Court observed the following about the school policy:

> The Duval County policy, unlike the Santa Fe policy, does not subject the issue of prayer to an up-or-down vote; students do *not* vote on whether prayer, or its equivalent, should be included in graduation ceremonies. Rather, students vote on two questions that do not expressly or inherently concern prayer: (1) whether to permit a student "message" during the ceremony, and (2) if so, which student is to deliver the message. . . .

---

[51]*Adler,* 250 F.3d at 1332.
[52]*Id.* at 1339.

Although it is possible that under Duval County's policy the student body may select a speaker who then chooses *on his or her own* to deliver a religious message, that result is not preordained, and more to the point would not reflect a "majority" vote to impose religion on unwilling listeners. Rather, it would reflect the uncensored and wholly unreviewable decision of a single student speaker.[53]

Commenting on school policies that provide prayer as the only option, one federal court observed the following:

When the State *commands* religious speech, it steps over the Constitution to establish religion. In each of these cases, it is the *State's decision to create an exclusively religious medium* which violates the Establishment Clause; not the private parties' religious speech. It is not the "permitting" of religious speech which dooms these policies, but rather the *requirement* that the speech be religious, i.e., invocations, benedictions, or prayers.[54]

Since "genuinely student-initiated religious speech is private speech endorsing religion, it is fully protected by both

---

[53]*Id.* at 1338–39.

[54]*Chandler,* 180 F.3d at 1259. This case was decided on July 13, 1999. During the appeal, the U.S. Supreme Court handed down the *Santa Fe* football game prayer case. In light of this case, the High Court vacated the *Chandler* decision and sent it back to the Eleventh Circuit Court of Appeals to consider whether the *Santa Fe* ruling affected the outcome of *Chandler.* The appeals court considered *Santa Fe* and issued another ruling reinstating the Chandler decision, stating that nothing in *Santa Fe* changed the outcome. *See Chandler,* 230 F.3d at 1313. The case was again appealed, but this time the Supreme Court refused to hear the case and allowed the decision to stand.

the Free Exercise and the Free Speech Clauses of the Constitution."[55] The same court also observed that the "Constitution does not require a complete separation of church and state such that religious expression may not be tolerated in our public institutions."[56] "If students, or other private parties, wish to speak religiously while in school or at school-related events, they may exercise their First Amendment right to do so."[57] The court noted that the school should remain neutral in matters of religion, neither commanding nor suppressing, but instead permitting religious expression.[58] The court correctly noted:

> The discriminatory suppression of student-initiated religious speech demonstrates not neutrality but hostility toward religion because the: "exclusion of religious ideas, symbols, and voices marginalizes religion. . . . Silence about a subject conveys a powerful message. When the public sphere is open to ideas and symbols representing nonreligious viewpoints, culture, and ideological commitment, to exclude all those whose basis is 'religious' would profoundly distort public culture."[59]

A school policy which allows students to deliver a message of choice, neither commanded nor censored by school officials, maintains government neutrality toward religion. In this way the student message is truly private speech, even

---

[55]*Id.* at 1261.
[56]*Id.* at 1262.
[57]*Id.* at 1264.
[58]*Id.* at 1261, 1264.
[59]*Id.* at 1261 (quoting Michael McConnell, *Religious Freedom at the Crossroads,* 59 U. CHI. L. REV. 115, 189 (1992)).

though it occurs at a school-sponsored event. The resulting message is only that of the students and cannot be attributed to the school. Such a policy is constitutional. "So long as the prayer is *genuinely student-initiated,* and not the product of any school policy which actively or surreptitiously encourages it, the speech is private and it is protected."[60]

2. Option Two—Students Selected by Religion-Neutral Criteria

Similar to option one, another option includes a valedictorian, salutatorian, president of the senior class, or any other student participant chosen, based on academic criteria or other secular standards, to be a part of the graduation ceremony. When addressing the senior class, this person could voluntarily offer a prayer or religious message. In this circumstance, the school would not place prayer on the agenda and would not select the student for the specific purpose of prayer. The school may not even know that the participant desired to pray until the participant stood up and prayed. Again, under this particular option, if the school prohibited this student participant from praying, it would violate the First Amendment Free Speech and Establishment Clauses because the school would be restricting speech based on the viewpoint of the message and showing hostility toward religion.

The Madison School District in Rexburg, Idaho, had a policy which allowed a minimum of four students selected by virtue of having the highest academic standing to deliver a message of their choice at graduation.[61] Students accepting

---

[60] *Chandler,* 230 F.3d at 1317.
[61] *See Doe v. Madison Sch. Dist. No. 321,* 147 F.3d at 832.

the invitation to speak could deliver "an address, poem, reading, song, musical presentation, prayer, or any other pronouncement."[62] School officials were not permitted to "censor any presentation or require any content." Since these students were selected using neutral criteria and were free to address any subject without censorship or influence, the policy was upheld by the court.[63]

In one case Liberty Counsel was contacted by a high school senior class president who was chosen to be the keynote speaker at graduation. The class president wanted to thank God in his speech. When he spoke to the principal, he was warned not to mention anything regarding religion. Liberty Counsel advised the student that he had the right to speak about his relationship with Jesus Christ. He was rightfully there on the platform by virtue of his position as a class officer, and while there, he had the right to speak freely so long as he did not speak libelous or defamatory remarks toward other students. When he spoke during the graduation ceremony, he acknowledged and thanked God for his accomplishments. At the end of the speech, he received a standing ovation. Afterwards, he received numerous cards from students and parents congratulating him for having the courage to speak about God. The response was so overwhelming that even the principal wrote the student a thank-you card.

In another school, the valedictorian sneezed after giving the valedictory address. The students responded in unison, "God bless you." Although this is a humorous way of

---

[62]*Id.* at 834.
[63]The decision was later vacated because the students who challenged the policy graduated, and the case became moot on appeal. However, the substantive reasoning of the case was not disturbed.

acknowledging God during a ceremony, the Constitution does not require students to resort to such tactics in order to acknowledge God. When student speakers enter the podium during a graduation ceremony, they do not shed their constitutional rights to freedom of expression, just as they do not shed this right when they enter the schoolhouse gate.[64]

3. Option Three—Outside Speaker Selected by Religion-Neutral Criteria

If a school does not place "prayer" on the agenda and does not select a clergy for the sole purpose of delivering a prayer, it avoids two of the Supreme Court's major concerns. School officials can use neutral criteria for selecting the participants. A neutral criteria is one that does not select a speaker for the sole purpose of delivering a religious message. If a school chose a speaker because of some contribution the speaker made to society and not only because the speaker is a clergy, then the school may avoid one of the concerns of the Supreme Court. In short, school officials could choose a speaker or participant because of some recognized contribution to society. A clergyman could be a participant as long as the selection was made using neutral criteria and not solely because the participant will deliver a religious message.

An individual selected using neutral criteria could then participate in the public graduation ceremony and voluntarily offer a prayer or make religious comments. In this way, the school does not intentionally select a religious person for the purpose of prayer. For the school to forbid this participant from saying a prayer may violate that person's First

---

[64]*Tinker v. Des Moines Indep. Sch. Dist.*, 393 U.S. 503, 506 (1969).

Amendment right to free expression. Furthermore, if a school prohibits such a person from saying a prayer, the school may also violate the First Amendment Establishment Clause for demonstrating hostility, rather than neutrality, toward religion. In summary, a school may select a participant using neutral or secular criteria, and that participant could voluntarily pray or offer religious comments.

4. Option Four—Privately Sponsored Graduation

Under the above options, prayer can still be conducted during public school graduation ceremonies. There may be some years when prayer is conducted and other years when the speaker may choose not to pray. In order to ensure that prayer is conducted on a consistent basis, community leaders and churches may privately sponsor graduation ceremonies. Many schools are not large enough to hold public graduation ceremonies. Such schools often use outside facilities, and many use church auditoriums. Churches throughout the community can organize public graduation ceremonies or baccalaureate services. The time, place, and manner could be organized by the churches or other community leaders, and student groups could publicize the event through their on-campus clubs. Public school students, along with teachers and staff, could be invited to participate in the ceremony designed and choreographed by private individuals.

School officials could participate in ceremonies conducted at churches as long as the school is not sponsoring the event. At such a service, there would be no prohibition against inviting a religious speaker to address the students.

If a public school allows use of its facilities by outside secular organizations, then the school must allow use of the same facilities by religious organizations for religious meetings.[65] Such a purpose can be the performance of a graduation or baccalaureate ceremony. In one case, a United Methodist Church sued a school board because it wished to rent the facilities for a graduation ceremony. The school refused, and an Alabama federal court ruled that disallowing use of the facilities by the Methodist church was a violation of the First Amendment Free Speech Clause, because the school allowed use of its facilities to other outside secular organizations.[66] Indeed, the United States Supreme Court stated that "if a State refused to let religious groups use facilities open to others, then it would demonstrate not neutrality, but hostility toward religion."[67] In another case, a group of parents and graduating senior students requested use of a high school gymnasium to conduct a baccalaureate ceremony. The baccalaureate ceremony was privately sponsored and open to the public. Participation by the students was completely voluntary. However, the school board decided not to rent the gymnasium because its use would be for a religious purpose. The school board had on other occasions allowed use of its facilities to outside secular organizations. A federal court in Wyoming ruled that refusal to rent the gymnasium to the parents and students to conduct the religious baccalaureate service was an unconstitutional violation of the First Amendment.[68] Thus, private persons or groups may

---

[65]See Good News Clubs v. Milford Central Sch. Dist., 533 U.S. 98 (2001).
[66]Verbena United Methodist Church v. Chilton County Bd. of Educ., 765 F. Supp. 704 (M.D. Ala. 1991).
[67]Mergens, 496 U.S. at 248; see also Grace Bible Fellowship, Inc. v. Maine Sch. Admin. Dist. #5, 941 F.2d 45 (1st Cir. 1991); Gregoire v. Centennial Sch. Dist., 907 F.2d 1366 (3d Cir. 1990), cert. denied, 498 U.S. 899 (1993); Concerned Women for Am. v. Lafayette County, 883 F.2d 32 (5th Cir. 1990).
[68]Shumway v. Albany County Sch. Dist. #1, 826 F. Supp. 1320 (D. Wyo.

organize a graduation or baccalaureate ceremony, and the event may be held off campus in a private facility or on the school campus if the school allows the community to use its facilities for secular meetings.

Court Prayers

A North Carolina state court judge regularly opened his court saying: "Let us pause for a moment of prayer." The judge would then bow his head and recite aloud the following prayer:

Oh Lord, our God, our Father in heaven, we pray this morning that You will place Your divine guiding hand on this courtroom and that with Your mighty outreached arm You will protect the innocent, give justice to those who have been harmed and mercy to us all. Let truth be heard and wisdom be reflected in the light of Your presence with us here today. Amen.[69]

The American Civil Liberties Union brought suit against this state court judge, and a federal court of appeals agreed that the judge violated the First Amendment Establishment Clause. The court reasoned that the prayer's primary purpose was religious and that it advanced and endorsed religion under the auspices of the state.[70]

1993); In *Pratt v. Arizona Board of Regents,* 520 P.2d 514 (Ariz. 1974), the Arizona Supreme Court ruled that the rental of the Sun Devils Stadium on a university campus to an evangelist for a religious service did not violate the First Amendment Establishment Clause.

[69]*North Carolina Civil Liberties Union Legal Found. v. Constangy,* 947 F.2d 1145 (4th Cir. 1991), *cert. denied,* 505 U.S. 1219 (1992).

[70]*Id.* at 1149–52.

Despite this court's ruling, prayers in the courtroom should be analyzed like prayers offered in legislative chambers. The United States Supreme Court has already ruled that prayer offered by a legislative chaplain is constitutional.[71] In fact, the Supreme Court observed the following:

> The opening of sessions of legislative and other deliberative public bodies with prayer is deeply embedded in the history and tradition of this country. From colonial times to the founding of the Republic and ever since, the practice of legislative prayer has coexisted with the principles of disestablishment and religious freedom. In the very courtroom in which the United States District Judge and later three Circuit Judges heard and decided this case, the proceedings opened with an announcement and concluded "God save the United States and this Honorable Court." *This same invocation occurs at all sessions of this Court.*[72]

The Supreme Court of the United States itself acknowledged that every day when it opens the Court, a paid official offers an "invocation," stating "God save the United States and this Honorable Court." If the Supreme Court of the United States acknowledges that every day it opens its sessions with an invocation, then surely a lower state court or federal court should be able to open its day with prayer. In fact, the Supreme Court not only acknowledged daily invocations within the Supreme Court building, it also acknowledged that these daily invocations occurred in federal,

---

[71]*Marsh v. Chambers*, 463 U.S. 783 (1983).
[72]*Id.* at 786 (emphasis added).

district, and appellate courtrooms. At a minimum, a moment of silence is constitutional.

Legislative Prayers

The issue of legislative prayers came before the United States Supreme Court in 1983 in its landmark decision of *Marsh v. Chambers*.[73] This case dealt with a challenge to the Nebraska legislature opening its sessions with prayer offered by a paid chaplain chosen by the Legislative Council. In finding the practice constitutional, the Court did not use its previous three-part test from the case of *Lemon v. Kurtzman*.[74] The so-called *Lemon* test requires that for a statute to be found constitutional and not a violation of the First Amendment Establishment Clause it (1) must have a secular purpose, (2) must not have a primary purpose of promoting or endorsing religion, and (3) must not foster excessive governmental entanglement with religion. This test has caused great confusion among the federal courts.[75] Instead of using this often-criticized *Lemon* test, the Court looked at the original intent of the First Amendment by overviewing history.

---

[73]463 U.S. at 783.
[74]403 U.S. 602 (1971).
[75]Justices Scalia and Thomas have been very critical of the Supreme Court's use of the so-called *Lemon* test.

> Like some ghoul in a late-night horror movie that repeatedly sits up in its grave and shuffles abroad, after being repeatedly killed and buried, *Lemon* stalks our Establishment Clause jurisprudence once again, frightening the little children and school attorneys. . . . Its most recent burial, only last Term [in *Lee v. Weisman*] was, to be sure, not fully six-feet under. . . . Over the years, however, no fewer than five of the currently sitting Justices have, in their own opinions, personally driven pencils through the creature's heart. . . .

The Court began by stating that the "opening of sessions of legislative and other deliberative public bodies with prayer is deeply imbedded in the history and tradition of this country."[76] Indeed, judicial proceedings are always begun by the announcement: "God save the United States and this Honorable Court."[77] In 1774, the Continental Congress adopted the tradition of opening its sessions with prayer offered by a paid chaplain.[78] As one of its first items of business, the First Congress "adopted the policy of selecting a chaplain to open each session with prayer."[79] In 1789, the same year that the First Amendment was drafted, the Senate appointed a committee to consider the manner of electing chaplains, and a similar committee was appointed in the House of Representatives. The first chaplain was elected in the Senate on April 25, 1789, and in the House on May 1, 1789.[80] On September 25, 1789, three days after Congress authorized the appointment of paid chaplains, a final agreement had been reached on the language of the Bill of Rights, including the

---

The secret of the *Lemon* test's survival, I think, is that it is so easy to kill. It is there to scare us (and our audience) when we wish it to do so, but we can command it to return to the tomb at will. . . . When we wish to strike down a practice it forbids, we invoke it. . . . Sometimes we take a middle ground of course, calling its three prongs "no more than helpful signposts." Such a docile and useful monster is worth keeping around, at least in a somnolent state; one never knows when one might need him.

Lamb's Chapel v. Center Moriches Union Free Sch. Dist., 508 U.S. 384, 398 (1993) (Scalia, J., concurring).
[76]*Marsh,* 463 U.S. at 786.
[77]*Id.*
[78]*Id.* at 787.
[79]*Id.* at 787–88.
[80]*Id.*

First Amendment. The Court gleaned from this early history that "the men who wrote the First Amendment Religion Clause did not view paid legislative chaplains and opening prayers as a violation of that Amendment, for the practice of opening sessions with prayer has continued without interruption ever since that early session of Congress."[81]

In reviewing the history of legislative prayers, the Court went to the heart of the First Amendment's intent by stating: "Historical evidence sheds light not only on what the draftsmen intended the Establishment Clause to mean, but also on how they thought that Clause applied to the practice authorized by the First Congress—their actions reveal their intent."[82]

The Supreme Court concluded that "legislative prayer presents no more potential for establishment than the provision of school transportation, beneficial grounds for higher education, or tax exemptions for religious organizations."[83] After reviewing more than two hundred years of unbroken history, the Court noted:

> There can be no doubt that the practice of opening legislative sessions with prayer has become part of the fabric of our society. To invoke Divine guidance on a public body entrusted with making the laws is not, in these circumstances, an "establishment" of religion or a step toward establishment; it is simply a

---

[81]*Id.* at 788.
[82]*Id.* at 790.
[83]*Id.* at 791 (citing *Everson v. Board of Educ.*, 330 U.S. 1 (1947)); *see also Tilton v. Richardson*, 403 U.S. 672 (1971); *Walz v. Tax Comm'n*, 397 U.S. 664 (1970).

tolerable acknowledgment of beliefs widely held among the people of this country. As Justice Douglas observed, "We are a religious people whose institutions presuppose a Supreme Being."[84]

The Supreme Court's analysis makes sense. Obviously those who drafted the First Amendment saw no conflict between that Amendment and the offering of a prayer in a public event.

Board Meetings

Prayers are frequently said at county, municipal, and school board meetings, as well as other meetings of public officials. In many respects, these prayers are similar to prayers preceding legislative sessions.

A federal court of appeals ruled that a resolution of the Board of St. Louis County in Minnesota, which provided for an invocation at its public meetings, was not a violation of the First Amendment Establishment Clause.[85] Under this

---

[84]*Marsh*, 463 U.S. at 792 (citing *Zorach v. Clauson*, 343 U.S. 306, 313 (1952)). A California appeals court ruled that a presidential proclamation for a national day of thanksgiving was constitutional. In an interesting turn of events, President George H. Bush declared April 5–7, 1991, as National Days of Thanksgiving following the conclusion of the Persian Gulf War. In the state of California, the educational code required community colleges to close on every day appointed by the President as a public fast, thanksgiving, or holiday. Certain school employees requested the three days off as paid holidays, but the Governing Board refused, claiming that the presidential proclamation was unconstitutional. The California appeals court ruled that the presidential proclamation was consistent with the First Amendment. *See California Sch. Employees Ass'n v. Marin Community College Dist.*, 15 Cal. App. 4th 273 (Cal. Ct. App. 1993).
[85]*Bogen v. Doty*, 598 F.2d 1110 (8th Cir. 1979).

policy, a board of commissioners invited local clergymen to offer prayers prior to the commencement of each board meeting. The chairman of the board would generally announce the following: "As is our practice, the Reverend John Doe will now give a prayer." The Court found that this practice was consistent with the First Amendment because the prayer had a "secular legislative purpose of setting a solemn tone for the transaction of governmental business" and assisted "the maintenance of order and decorum."[86] The practice of opening these board meetings with prayers was not "an establishment of religion proscribed by the Establishment Clause of the First Amendment in any pragmatic, meaningful and realistic sense of that clause."[87] Similarly, the state Supreme Court of New Hampshire ruled that inviting local ministers to open town meetings with an invocation was not prohibited by the First Amendment Establishment Clause.[88]

In a 2-to-1 decision, one federal appeals court ruled that prayer offered at the opening of a school board meeting is

---

[86]*Id.* at 1114–15. *But see, Wynne v. Town of Great Falls,* 376 F.3d: 292 (4th Cir. 2004) (finding practice of opening meetings with only Christian prayers using the name of "Jesus" unconstitutionally suggesting rotating a variety of prayers would be permissible).

[87]*Id.* at 1115.

[88]*Lincoln v. Page,* 241 A.2d 799 (N.H. 1968). Other courts have similarly ruled that prayer offered at the outset of public assemblies are constitutional. *See, e.g., Marsa v. Wernik,* 430 A.2d 888 (N.J.), *app. dismissed and cert. denied,* 454 U.S. 958 (1981) (prayer at the outset of borough council meeting constitutional); *Lincoln v. Page,* 341 A.2d 799 (N.H. 1968) (invocation at town meeting constitutional); *Colo v. Treasurer and Receiver General,* 392 N.E.2d 1195 (Mass. 1979) (salaries for legislative chaplains constitutional); *Snyder v. Murray City Corp.,* 902 F. Supp. 1444 (D. Utah 1995) (statements by a minister at outset of council meeting constitutional).

unconstitutional.[89] The Cleveland school board traditionally opened its deliberative session with prayer. Historically, the school board invited representatives of the Protestant, Roman Catholic, Jewish, and Muslim faiths. The federal district court upheld the practice, but two of the three appeals court judges voted to reverse the decision.[90]

A California federal court found that the Palo Verde Unified School District's practice of opening each meeting with prayer did not violate the Constitution.[91] In upholding the practice, the court relied on the Supreme Court's legislative prayer case in *Marsh*. The court noted that school board meetings, unlike classroom sessions, are composed primarily of adults. The "fact that at any given board meeting there may be children present in the audience, some of whom may participate in an awards session or address the board on a particular topic, does not change the nature or the function of the board meeting. A board meeting is a meeting of adults with official business and policymaking functions."[92] Clearly, prayer can still play a role in public assemblies and meetings.

---

[89]*Coles v. Cleveland Bd. of Educ.*, 171 F.3d 369 (6th Cir. 1999).
[90]*Coles v. Cleveland Bd. of Educ.*, 950 F. Supp. 1337 (N.D. Ohio 1996) (reasoning that prayers at school board meetings are no different than prayers at legislative meetings, thus finding that the Supreme Court decision in *Marsh* controls the outcome).
[91]*Bacus v. Palo Verde Unified Sch. Dist. Bd. of Educ.*, 11 F. Supp. 2d. 1192 (C.D. Cal. 1998).
[92]*Id.* at 1197.

6
PARENTAL RIGHTS TO DIRECT THE EDUCATION OF CHILDREN

PARENTAL RESPONSIBILITY REACHES ITS APEX in the duty to train and educate children. Parents form the critical link between the past and the future. History and heritage are transmitted from one generation to the next through the medium of parents. Our future depends in part upon the transmission of religious and moral values to our children. The "family is the basis of our society"[1] and the epicenter of our culture.

Constitutional Claims for Parental Rights

The right of parents to train and educate their children according to their religious and moral objectives is of paramount importance. The seminal Supreme Court case addressing

---

[1] *In re: Guardianship of Faust,* 123 So. 2d 218, 221 (Miss. 1960).

parental rights began with the 1923 decision of *Meyer v. Nebraska*.[2] In *Meyer*, an instructor at Zion Parochial School was charged with and convicted of unlawfully teaching the subject of reading in the German language to a ten-year-old student who had not yet completed the eighth grade. Nebraska law forbade instruction in a language other than English to any student who had not yet successfully passed the eighth grade. At issue was whether the Nebraska law unreasonably infringed on the liberty guaranteed by the Fourteenth Amendment which states in pertinent part: "No state . . . shall deprive any person of life, liberty or property without due process of law."[3] While the Court conceded that it had not yet attempted to define the liberty interest protected by the Fourteenth Amendment, the Court concluded:

> Without doubt, it denotes not merely freedom from bodily restraint but also the right of the individual to contract, to engage in any of the common occupations of life, to acquire useful knowledge, to marry, establish a home and bring up children, to worship God according to the dictates of his own conscience, and generally to enjoy those privileges long recognized at common law as essential to the orderly pursuit of happiness by free men.[4]

The Court stated that the liberty protected by the Fourteenth Amendment may not be interfered with by state legislative action which is arbitrary or without reasonable

---

[2] 262 U.S. 390 (1923).
[3] U.S. CONST. amend. XIV.
[4] *Meyer*, 262 U.S. at 399 (citations omitted).

relation to some legitimate state interest.[5] The Court acknowledged that parents have the "natural duty" to educate their children suitable to their situation in life.[6] The Court then concluded that state legislation which prohibits instruction in a language other than English violates the Fourteenth Amendment, because it has no reasonable relationship to any legitimate state interest.

Two years later, the Supreme Court returned to the issue of parental rights in the case of *Pierce v. Society of Sisters*.[7] *Pierce* addressed an Oregon statute that required students between eight and sixteen years of age to attend public school. The only exceptions were for children who were "not normal," who had completed the eighth grade, with parents who were private teachers residing at considerable distances from any public school, or whose parents held special permits from the county superintendent.[8] The Court pointed out the following:

> The fundamental theory of liberty upon which all governments in this Union repose excludes any general power of the state to standardize its children by forcing them to accept instruction from public teachers only. The child is not the mere creature of the state; those who nurture him and direct his destiny have the right, coupled with the high duty, to recognize and prepare him for additional obligations.[9]

---

[5]*Id.* at 399–400.
[6]*Id.*
[7]268 U.S. 510 (1925).
[8]*Id.* at 530–31.
[9]*Id.* at 535.

The Supreme Court found the Oregon law unconstitutional under the Fourteenth Amendment, because it had no reasonable relationship to any legitimate state interest. The Court concluded that the legislation "unreasonably interferes with the liberty of parents and guardians to direct the upbringing and education of their children under their control."[10]

In 1944 the Supreme Court upheld the conviction of a Jehovah's Witness who violated child labor laws by knowingly allowing her minor daughter to sell religious literature.[11] Strategically, the parent's fatal mistake was not asserting her right to free speech in her defense.[12] In upholding the conviction, the Court nevertheless recognized that "the custody, care and nurture of the child reside first in the parents, whose primary function and freedom include preparation for obligations the state can neither supply nor hinder."[13]

The next major Supreme Court decision related to parental rights to educate their children was the 1972 case of *Wisconsin v. Yoder.*[14] This case involved a Wisconsin compulsory education law that required children to attend public

---

[10]*Id.* at 534–35.

[11]*Prince v. Massachusetts,* 321 U.S. 158 (1944).

[12]The mother refused to raise the right to free speech because she thought such a claim was "secular" and thus rested her claim solely on freedom of religion and parental rights. *Id.* at 164, 172. In the term prior to the *Prince* decision, the Supreme Court declared in *Murdock v. Pennsylvania,* 319 U.S. 105 (1943) that the mere fact religious literature is sold by itinerant preachers rather than donated does not transform the transaction into commercial speech. The mother should have argued that a child selling religious literature was not engaged in a commercial transaction and, thus, was not governed by child labor laws.

[13]*Prince,* 321 U.S. at 166.

[14]406 U.S. 205 (1972).

or private school until the age of sixteen. The two children in the *Yoder* case were fourteen and fifteen years old. They were members of the Old Order Amish religion. Fundamental to the Amish belief is that salvation requires life in a church community, separate and apart from the world and any worldly influence.[15] Amish beliefs require members of the community to earn their living by farming or closely related activities. Amish objection to formal education beyond the eighth grade is a fundamental aspect of their religious faith and practice. The Court observed the following with respect to the Old Order Amish religion:

> They object to high school and higher education generally, because the values they teach are in marked variance with Amish values and the Amish way of life; they view secondary school education as an impermissible exposure of their children to a "worldly" influence in conflict with their beliefs. The high school tends to emphasize intellectual and scientific accomplishments, self-distinction, competitiveness, worldly success, and social life with other students. Amish society emphasizes informal learning-through-doing; a life of "goodness," rather than a life of intellect; wisdom, rather than technical knowledge; community welfare, rather than competition; and separation from, rather than integration with, contemporary worldly society.
>
> Formal high school education beyond the eighth grade is contrary to Amish beliefs, not only because it places Amish children in an environment hostile to Amish beliefs with increasing emphasis on competition

---

[15]*Id.* at 210.

in classwork and sports and with pressure to conform to the styles, manners, and ways of the peer group, but also because it takes them away from their community, physically and emotionally, during the crucial and formative adolescent period of life.[16]

The Amish do not object to education through the first eight grades as a general proposition, because they agree their children must have certain basic skills, but they object to education beyond the eighth grade. Testimony presented in the *Yoder* case indicated that compulsory high school attendance could not only result in great psychological harm to Amish children but would also ultimately result in the destruction of the Old Order Amish Church community as it exists in the United States.[17]

The Supreme Court began its decision by stating that the state had a high responsibility to educate its citizens and to impose reasonable regulations for the control and duration of basic education.[18] However:

> [A] State's interest in universal education, however highly we rank it, is not totally free from a balancing process when it impinges on fundamental rights and interests, such as those specifically protected by the Free Exercise Clause of the First Amendment, and the traditional interest of parents with respect to the religious upbringing of their children so long as they, in the words of *Pierce*, "prepare (them) for additional obligations."[19]

---

[16]*Id.* at 210–11.

[17]*Id.* at 212.

[18]*Id.* at 213.

[19]*Id.* at 214 (quoting *Pierce*, 268 U.S. at 535).

The Court declared that the "'additional obligations' . . . include the inculcation of moral standards, religious beliefs, and elements of good citizenship."[20] The Court noted that the *Pierce* decision "stands as a charter of the rights of parents to direct the religious upbringing of their children."[21] Although the Court pointed out that the state's compulsory education law conflicted with the twin interests of free exercise of religion and parental rights, the Court thereafter focused only on the free exercise of religion under the First Amendment. The Court stated that "only those interests of the highest order . . . can overbalance legitimate claims to the free exercise of religion."[22] The State of Wisconsin argued in favor of the legislation because it applied uniformly to all citizens and did not, on its face, discriminate against any religion or particular religious practice. However, the Court observed:

> A regulation neutral on its face may, in its application, nonetheless offend the constitutional requirement for governmental neutrality if it unduly burdens the free exercise of religion. The Court must not ignore the danger that an exception from a general obligation of citizenship on religious grounds may run afoul of the Establishment Clause, but that danger cannot be allowed to prevent any exception no matter how vital it may be to the protection of values promoted by the right of free exercise.[23]

---

[20]*Id.* at 233.
[21]*Id.*
[22]*Yoder,* 406 U.S. at 215.
[23]*Id.* at 220–21 (citations omitted).

While it appears that the *Yoder* decision is based primarily on the free exercise of religion, the Court did mention parental rights one time. The basis of the decision seemed to turn on the religious free exercise rights of the Old Order Amish religion claimed by the parents. Despite the fact that the law was a general law of neutral applicability, the Supreme Court found it nevertheless burdened a sincerely held religious belief of the Old Order Amish religion.[24]

Wisconsin argued that the state's interest in compulsory education was so compelling that even the established religious practices of the Old Order Amish must give way. The Supreme Court disagreed and ruled that the compulsory education statute as applied to the Old Order Amish religion was unconstitutional. The Court found that the intrusion into the Old Order Amish beliefs was severe. Moreover, the interest advanced by the state in educating a responsible citizenry was extremely weak as applied to the Old Order Amish, which had a history of independence and successful social functioning. The balance tipped quite favorably to the side of the Amish.

The next case dealing with parental rights is *Troxel v. Granville*[25] which dealt with grandparents' visitation rights.

---

[24]In *Employment Division v. Smith,* 494 U.S. 872 (1990), the Supreme Court ruled that any general law of neutral applicability will be upheld against a religious objection to the contrary. Despite the fact that it appears the *Smith* decision is contrary to the *Yoder* decision, the *Smith* court nevertheless did not overrule *Yoder. Smith* (unconvincingly) distinguishes *Yoder* on the basis that *Yoder* involved a free exercise and parental rights claim. Therefore, by combining parental rights with the free exercise of religion, the state must have a compelling governmental interest and achieve that interest in the least restrictive manner before the legislation will be held constitutional.

[25]530 U.S. 57 (2000).

A parent of a minor child challenged the state of Washington's statute that provided visitation rights "at any time" by "any person" if the visitation served the best interest of the child. The Court struck down the statute, noting that it was "breathtakingly broad."[26] The Court stated:

> Our constitution long ago rejected any notion that a child is a mere creature of the State and, on the contrary, asserted that parents generally have the right coupled with the high duty to recognize and prepare [their children] for additional obligations. . . . The law's concept of the family rests on a presumption that parents possess what a child lacks in maturity, experience, and capacity for judgment required for making life's difficult decisions. More important, historically it has recognized that natural bonds of affection lead parents to act in the best interests of their children.[27]

So long as the parent adequately cares for his or her children, there will normally be no reason for the state to inject itself into the private realm of the family.[28]

---

[26]*Id.* at 67.

[27]*Id.* at 68 (quoting *Parham v. J.R.*, 442 U.S. 584, 602 (1979)).

[28]*Id.* at 68–69. Justice Thomas concurred in the judgment but stated he would apply strict scrutiny to infringements of fundamental rights. *Id.* at 80 (Thomas, J., concurring). Justice Scalia dissented stating that the right of parents to direct the upbringing of their children is among the "unalienable Rights" contained within the Declaration of Independence and retained by the people under the Ninth Amendment. *Id.* at 91 (Scalia, J., dissenting). Scalia stated:

> Consequently, while I would think it entirely compatible with the commitment to representative democracy set forth in the founding documents to argue, in legislative chambers or in electoral campaigns, that the state has no power to interfere with parents' authority over the rearing of their children, I do not believe that the

In addition to the above cases, the Supreme Court in other decisions has recognized the right of parents to direct the care and control of their children.[29] In reality, parental rights are not derived from or created by the United States Constitution. Rather, parental rights derive from natural law, what the Declaration of Independence refers to as "unalienable rights" with which we are endowed by our Creator.[30]

---

power which the Constitution confers upon me as a judge entitles me to deny legal effect to laws that (in my view) infringe upon what is (in my view) that unenumerated right.

Id. Justice Scalia argued that the cases of *Meyer, Pierce,* and *Yoder* dealt with "an era rich in substantive due process" that has "since been repudiated," and therefore, he would not extend these cases. *Id.* at 92. He believes the issue of whether parental rights constitute a "liberty" interest for purposes of procedural due process is a different question not implicated in the *Troxel* case. *Id.* at 92 n.1.

[29]*See, e.g., Stanley v. Illinois,* 405 U.S. 645, 651 (1972) ("It is plain that the interest of a parent in the companionship, care, custody, and management of his or her children 'come[s] to this Court with the momentum for respect lacking when appeal is made to liberties which derive merely from shifting economic arrangements'"); *Quilloin v. Walcott,* 434 U.S. 246, 255 (1978) ("We have recognized on numerous occasions that the relationship between parent and child is constitutionally protected."); *Parham v. J. R.,* 442 U.S. 584, 602 (1979) ("Our jurisprudence historically has reflected Western civilization concepts of the family as a unit with broad parental authority over minor children. Our cases have consistently followed that course. . . . The law's concept of the family rests on a presumption that parents possess what a child lacks in maturity, experience, and capacity for judgment required for making life's difficult decisions. More important, historically it has recognized that natural bonds of affection lead parents to act in the best interests of their children."); *Santosky v. Kramer,* 455 U.S. 745, 753 (1982) (discussing "the fundamental liberty interest of natural parents in the care, custody, and management of their child"); and *Washington v. Glucksberg,* 521 U.S. 702, 720 (1997) ("In a long line of cases we have held that, in addition to the specific freedoms protected by the Bill of Rights, the 'liberty' specifically protected by the Due Process Clause includes the righ[t] . . . to direct the education and upbringing of one's children.") (citing *Meyer* and *Pierce*).

[30]Supreme Court Justice Antonin Scalia also shares this view. *See Troxel,* 530 U.S. at 91 (Scalia, J., dissenting).

Several principles can be gleaned from the Supreme Court's cases involving parental rights in education. First, the state has a recognized interest in educating its citizenry.[31] Second, parents have a constitutionally protected liberty interest under the Fourteenth Amendment to educate their children. Finally, parents have a constitutionally protected religious right under the First Amendment to educate their children.[32]

Parents may object to certain educational requirements apart from any religious objection by using the Fourteenth Amendment liberty interest. However, parents may also find that certain educational requirements directly collide with their sincerely held religious beliefs and may rely upon the First Amendment as additional protection. While challenges to an entire curriculum have not been met with much success,[33] parents may successfully challenge

---

[31]*Yoder,* 406 U.S. at 213 ("providing public schools ranks at the very apex of the function of a State").

[32]Of course, parental rights are not absolute, especially when no fundamental constitutional right is involved. *See, e.g. Ingraham v. Wright,* 430 U.S. 651 (1977) (no parental right to preapprove corporal punishment at school); *Runyon v. McCrary,* 427 U.S. 160 (1976) (no parental right to send children to segregated private schools); *Kite v. Marshall,* 661 F.2d 1027 (5th Cir. 1981) (no parental right to send children to summer camp); *Lipsman v. New York City Bd. of Educ.,* No. 98 Civ.2008(SHS), 1999 WL 498230 (S.D.N.Y. July 14, 1999) (no parental right to opt child out of wearing uniform); *Immediato v. Rye Neck Sch. Dist.,* 73 F.3d 454, (2d Cir. 1996) (no parental right to opt child out of compulsory community service requirement).

[33]In *Brown v. Woodland Joint Unified School District,* 27 F.3d 1373 (9th Cir. 1994), parents objected to portions of *Impressions,* a teaching aid, used in the first through sixth grade. The parents objected to thirty-two of the fifty-nine books used in the series, stating that the books promoted the religion of Wicca, requiring students to discuss witches or create poetic chants, pretend that they were witches and sorcerers, and to engage in role-play. The

portions of curriculum and request opt out or other alternative accommodations.[34]

---

court assumed that Wicca was a religion and analyzed the case under the Establishment Clause. The court found that an Establishment Clause violation does not occur every time a student believes a school practice either advances or disapproves of religion. The court then upheld the curriculum against the parental challenges. Note that the parents used the First Amendment Establishment Clause as the basis for their challenge. In *Fleischfresser v. Directors of School District 200*, 15 F.3d 680 (7th Cir. 1994), the Seventh Circuit Court of Appeals also upheld the *Impressions* curriculum. Similarly, in *Grove v. Meade School District No. 354*, 753 F.2d 1528 (9th Cir. 1985), the Ninth Circuit Court of Appeals rejected a challenge to *The Learning Tree* against the allegation that it advanced the religion of secular humanism. The court observed that the "Supreme Court has stated clearly that literary or historic study of the Bible is not a prohibited religious activity." *Id.* at 1534. One judge also pointed out that "'Luther's Ninety-five Theses' are hardly balanced or objective, yet their pronounced and even vehement bias does not prevent their study in a history class's exploration of the Protestant Reformation, nor is protestantism itself 'advanced' thereby." *Id.* at 1540 (Canvy, J. concurring). In *Smith v. Board of School Commissioners of Mobile County*, 827 F.2d 684 (11th Cir. 1987), the Eleventh Circuit Court of Appeals rejected a challenge brought by parents to the school's use of textbooks that they characterized as endorsing the religion of secular humanism. The court noted that while the books contained ideas consistent with the tenets of secular humanism, the textbooks did not violate the Establishment Clause because "mere consistency with religious tenets is insufficient to constitute unconstitutional advancement of religion." *Id.* at 692. The court reached a similar conclusion in *Mozert v. Hawkins County Board of Education*, 827 F.2d 1058 (6th Cir. 1987). However, in *Malnak v. Yogi*, 592 F.2d 197 (3d Cir. 1979), the Third Circuit Court of Appeals found unconstitutional student participation in a ceremonial offering to deities as part of a regularly scheduled public school course, noting that participation crossed the boundary and, therefore, violated the Establishment Clause.

[34]The Sixth Circuit Court of Appeals, rejecting a challenge to the Holt series reading curriculum, noted that if "an objecting student was *required* to participate beyond reading and discussing assigned materials, or was disciplined for disputing assigned materials" there might be a Free Exercise Clause violation. *Mozert*, 827 F.2d at 1064. Similarly, although the First Circuit Court of Appeals said there was no Establishment Clause or Free

Federal Claims for Parental Rights

Protection of Pupil Rights Amendment

A former educator and United States Senator, Samuel I. Hayakawa, warned the United States Senate in 1978 that schools have become vehicles for a "heresy that rejects the idea of education as the acquisition of knowledge and skill" and stated that schools regarded their "fundamental task in education as therapy."[35] Congress responded the same year by amending the General Education Provisions Act to include a section entitled *Protection of Pupil Rights Amendment* (hereafter PPRA).[36]

Notwithstanding the passage of the PPRA, the law was not implemented until September 6, 1984, when the Department of Education promulgated rules after conducting extensive hearings. These hearings revealed that schools were using federal funds to implement experimental testing programs to make personal inquiries into students' individual personal, sexual, family, and religious lives. The PPRA requires that all instructional material, including teacher manuals, films, tapes, or other supplementary items used in connection with any survey, analysis, or evaluation, be made available for inspection by the parents or guardians of the children involved in such program or project.[37]

Exercise Clause violation in the public high school's celebration of Earth Day, the Court implied that it might have found a Free Exercise Clause violation if attendance or participation in Earth Day ceremonies was mandatory. *Altman v. Bedford Cent. Sch. Dist.* 245 F.3d 49, 80, (2d. Cir.), *cert. denied sub nom., Dibari v. Bedford Cent. Sch. Dist.,* 534 U.S. 827 (2001).

[35]Child Abuse in the Classroom 13 (Phyllis Schlafly, ed., Pere Marquette Press, 1985).

[36]20 U.S.C. § 1232h.

[37]20 U.S.C. § 1232h(a).

The PPRA further states that without the prior consent of the student, or in the case of an unemancipated minor, without the prior written consent of the parent, no student shall be required to submit to a psychiatric examination, testing, or treatment, or psychological examination, testing, or treatment in which the primary purpose is to reveal information concerning: (1) political affiliation or beliefs of the student or the student's parent; (2) mental and psychological problems of the student or his family; (3) sexual behavior and attitudes; (4) illegal, antisocial, self-incriminating, and demeaning behavior; (5) critical appraisals of other individuals with whom respondents have close family relationships; (6) legally recognized privileged and analogous relationships, such as those of lawyers, physicians, and ministers; or (7) income (other than that required by law to determine eligibility for participation in a program or for receiving financial assistance under such program), religious practices, affiliations, or beliefs of the student or student's parent.[38]

Educational agencies and institutions are required to give students and parents notice of their rights under the PPRA. Parents and students should avail themselves of their rights to prior notice, prior consent, and to inspect instructional materials. Unfortunately, the application of the PPRA may be limited since it only applies to federally funded surveys, analyses, or evaluations.[39] Thus, the first step to applying the

---

[38]20 U.S.C. § 1232h(b).

[39]The PPRA refers to an "applicable program," which is defined in 20 U.S.C. §1221(c)(1) as "any program for which the Secretary or the Department has administrative responsibility as provided by law or by delegation of authority pursuant to law. The term includes each program for which the Secretary or the Department has administrative responsibility under the Department of Education Organization Act [20 U.S.C. §3401 *et*

PPRA is to determine whether the program or activity is federally funded.[40] Another weakness of the PPRA is its enforcement procedure. Some early cases suggested that the PPRA may provide a private right of action enforceable through judicial process, but in light of developing case law, the PPRA may be enforced primarily through filing an administrative complaint with the federal Department of Education.[41]

---

seq.] or under Federal law effective after May 4, 1980." Although the term "federally funded" does not appear anywhere in the definition of an "applicable program," the Courts that have interpreted this act require that the particular survey, analyses, or evaluations be part of a federally funded program. *See Herbert v. Reinstein,* 976 F. Supp. 331 (E.D. Pa. 1977).

[40]The Safe and Drug Free Schools Communities Act is a federal law aimed at reducing adolescent drug use to 3 percent of the population by December 31, 2003. *See* 21 U.S.C. § 1701 *et seq.* Any application for funding submitted by a school under the Safe and Drug Free Schools Communities Act must contain objective data on the prevalence of drug use and violence by youth in schools and communities. *See* 20 U.S.C. § 7112(a)(2). The PRIDE Survey is designated as one of the measurements of illicit drug use among adolescents used to affect the purpose of the Act. *See* 21 U.S.C. § 1705(a)(4)(B). However, the PRIDE Survey is not part of the Act, and some schools will argue that the PRIDE drug survey is not covered by the PPRA, because it is not part of the Safe and Drug Free Schools Communities Act. Promoting community service within the schools represents another example over which the Secretary of the Department has administrative control under the national education goals. *See* 20 U.S.C. § 5812(3)(B)(iii) (providing that all students will be involved in activities that promote and demonstrate good citizenship, good health, community service, and personal responsibility).

[41]The PPRA most likely must be enforced through the filing of an administrative complaint. Some case law does suggest that the PPRA may be enforced under 42 U.S.C. §1983. *See C. N. v. Ridgewood Bd. of Educ.,* 146 F. Supp. 2d 528 at n.7 (D.N.J. 2001); *Altman v. Bedford Cent. Sch. Dist.,* 45 F. Supp. 2d 368 (S.D.N.Y. 1999); *Herbert,* 976 F. Supp. at 339–40. However, the Supreme Court in *Gonzaga University v. Doe,* 536 U.S. 273 (2002), held that the Family Educational Records Privacy Act (FERPA), a similarly designed federal provision, does not create a private right of action and so cannot be enforced under 42 U.S.C. §1983. The PPRA will probably be treated in the same manner.

Reading the testimony received by the Department of Education in 1984 is enlightening and concerning. One parent who testified in the state of Washington stated that the guidance counseling program asked the following questions of the students:

> Do you believe in a God who answers prayer?
> Do you believe that tithing—giving one-tenth of one's earnings to the church—is one's duty to God?
> Do you pray about your problems?
> Do you read the Bible or other religious writings regularly?
> Do you love your parents?
> Do you believe God created man in His own image?
> If you ask God for forgiveness, are your sins forgiven?[42]

A parent from Oregon stated that her son was required to participate in a Magic Circle where the students would hold hands and divulge personal information about their thoughts, feelings, values, and beliefs. Students were also given a questionnaire that asked whether they drank alcohol, used drugs, lied to their parents, or believed in God.[43] The questions included: "Are you going to practice religion just like your parents?" and "What is your parents' income?" Surprisingly, a third-grade class was asked, "How many of you ever wanted to beat up your parents?"[44]

---

[42]CHILD ABUSE IN THE CLASSROOM 29–30.
[43]*Id.* at 55–56.
[44]*Id.* at 57.

In another school one course, entitled *Risk Taking,* required students to arrange themselves in small groups and roll dice to determine which category of questions they would discuss. Some of the questions in the personal and social category required seventh- through ninth-grade students to consider swimming in the nude at a private beach with friends, not telling your parents the truth about where you are going and what you will be doing, and having sexual intercourse with your boyfriend or girlfriend.[45] Another parent testified during these hearings that a values clarification handbook used by the teacher indicated that the purpose of the program was to have students "begin to realize that on most issues there are many shades of gray, and they are more likely to move away from either/or black-and-white thinking which often occurs when controversial issues are discussed in the classroom."[46]

The Department of Education received testimony from a Michigan parent where senior high schoolteachers were instructed to administer the following program:

> First ask the students to relax, feel comfortable and close their eyes. Then ask them to fantasize and design a form of birth control that they would enjoy using. If possible, they should include in their design how the contraceptive would work to prevent pregnancy, but this is not necessary.[47]

In another case, students were divided up into three groups representing eight- and nine-year-olds, twelve- and

---

[45]*Id.* at 72–73.
[46]*Id.* at 95.
[47]*Id.* at 146.

thirteen-year-olds, and young adults. They discussed abortion, teenage pregnancies, contraceptives, and a person of the opposite sex naked.[48] A vocabulary brainstorming program was conducted by dividing the class into groups of five or six to list as many synonyms as they could in three to five minutes using such words as "penis, vagina, intercourse, [or] breast."[49]

After being subjected to this kind of social behavior testing, one student testified:

> I was severely depressed. I didn't know what I believed about myself. I didn't know who I was or anything. Even things I was positive about earlier, I just didn't know. I had to learn to know myself all over again. I had to learn what I believed all over again, using all the sources that the school taught me were outdated, such as my mom and dad, my pastor, and my Bible. I had to learn to make decisions again, the hardest part of all, and one that now, four years later, I am still having problems with.[50]

Psychological and behavior modification is not new to the public school system. School administrators often act as if the PPRA does not exist. Students and parents should insist on schools abiding by the PPRA. In addition to this federal law, many states have laws requiring public schools to reveal all records, including teaching material, to parents upon request. If schools refuse this request, state laws often provide

---

[48]*Id.* at 147–48.
[49]*Id.* at 148.
[50]*Id.* at 124.

for the award of attorney's fees if a parent has to retain an attorney to obtain such documents.

The PPRA is designed to return some student and parental control over these types of intrusions into private family life. Students and parents should become familiar with the PPRA and use it when necessary.

OTHER FEDERAL LAWS

Federal grants administered pursuant to the law known as the Adolescent Family Life Demonstration Projects may cover family planning services.[51] No funds provided for demonstration projects or services may be used for the provision of family planning services (other than counseling and referral services) to adolescents unless appropriate family planning services are not otherwise available in the community.[52] Any recipient of any such federal grant must present assurances that the facility will notify the parents or guardians of any unemancipated minor requesting services and obtain the permission of parents or guardians with respect to the provision of such services.[53] However, the facility need not notify the parents or guardians or obtain consent of the minor (1) if the minor requests only pregnancy testing or testing or treatment of venereal disease; (2) if the minor is a victim of incest involving a parent; or (3) if an adult sibling of the minor or an adult aunt, uncle, or grandparent who is related to the minor by blood certifies that notification of the parents or guardians would result in physical injury to the minor, and the facility

---

[51] 42 U.S.C. § 300z–1(a)(P).
[52] 42 U.S.C. § 300z–3(b)(1).
[53] 42 U.S.C. § 300z–5(a)(22)(A)(i).

further certifies that it will not require parental consent of a pregnant minor if the parents or guardians are attempting to compel the minor to have an abortion.[54]

Pursuant to the Maternal and Child Health Services block grant, federal funds may be provided to the states in order to enable the states to provide abstinence education.[55] To obtain federal funds pursuant to the Strengthening and Improvement of Elementary and Secondary Schools Act, the school must include the health benefits of abstinence when teaching sex education or HIV prevention.[56] Thus, parents may insist that abstinence be taught under such programs.

State Claims for Parental Rights

In addition to the constitutional and federal protection of parental rights, parents in some cases may also assert parental rights based on state law. Whenever parental rights are threatened, parents should always look to at least three independent sources of protection: constitutional, federal, and state law.

In 2002 New Jersey passed a law patterned after the federal PPRA.[57] This statute uses the exact language of one section of the 1994 version of the PPRA (thus excluding protection for "religious practices, affiliations, or beliefs of the student or student's parents" added in the 2002 amendment). The New Jersey law also adds protection for the "social security number" of the student. It does not, however, include

---

[54] 42 U.S.C. § 300z–5(a)(22)(B)(i) & (C).
[55] 42 U.S.C. § 710.
[56] 20 U.S.C. § 7906.
[57] N.J. Stat. Ann. § 18A:36–34.

any provision requiring the program to be federally funded before it is protected.

Parents successfully combined both constitutional and state law protection of parental rights to prohibit the distribution of condoms throughout the New York public schools. In September 1987, the New York State Commission of Education directed that all elementary and secondary schools include, as part of health education programs, instruction concerning the Human Immunodeficiency Virus (HIV) which causes Acquired Immune Deficiency Syndrome (AIDS). In late 1990 the chancellor of the New York City Board of Education suggested enlarging the HIV/AIDS curriculum to include the distribution of condoms to high school students upon request. When complaints by parents fell on deaf ears, several parents filed suit in state court. These parents claimed that the distribution of condoms constituted health services rather than education and, therefore, violated state law which prohibited health services to minors without parental consent. Furthermore, they argued that the distribution violated the due process rights of parents to direct the upbringing of their children under the Fourteenth Amendment of the United States Constitution.[58]

The New York state court noted that at common law it was "for parents to consent or withhold their consent to the rendition of health services to their children."[59] The court pointed out that historically children are considered legal incompetents and, therefore, unable to consent to medical treatment or enter into contracts except in certain situations

---

[58]*Alfonso v. Fernandez,* 195 A.D.2d 46 (N.Y. App. Div. 1993).
[59]*Id.* at 50.

such as when children marry, are able to support themselves, are inducted into the military, or their parents abandon or fail to support them. The court agreed with the parents that condom distribution "is not merely education, but it is a health service to prevent disease by protecting against HIV infection."[60] Although there may be certain exceptions, parental consent was required for minors to receive health services, and the legislature, not the courts, could provide additional exceptions.[61]

The court correctly observed that parents have the constitutional right to rear their own children and noted the following:

> The petitioner parents are being compelled by State authority to send their children into an environment where they will be permitted, even encouraged, to obtain a contraceptive device, which the parents disfavor as a matter of private belief. Because the Constitution gives parents the right to regulate their children's sexual behavior as best they can, not only must a compelling State interest be found supporting

---

[60]*Id.* at 52.

[61]*Id.* at 54. The *Alfonso* court reviewed certain federal laws that provided federal funds for family planning programs and specifically required that adolescents be treated confidentially. The court pointed out that the Supreme Court of the United States invalidated state regulations mandating parental consent for family planning services to otherwise eligible minors. *Jones v. T. H.,* 425 U.S. 986 (1976). *See also Planned Parenthood Ass'n of Utah v. Dandoy,* 810 F.2d 984 (10th Cir. 1987); *Jane Does 1 through 4 v. State of Utah Dep't. of Health,* 776 F.2d 253 (10th Cir. 1985); *State of N.Y. v. Heckler,* 719 F.2d 1191 (2d Cir. 1983). However, the court noted that these statutes were merely legislatively enacted exceptions to the requirement of parental consent. The court then concluded, "It is for the Congress or the Legislature, not the courts—and certainly not the State

the need for the policy at issue, but the policy must be essential to serving that interest as well. We do not find the policy is essential. No matter how laudable its purpose, by excluding parental involvement, the condom availability component of the program impermissibly trespasses on the petitioners' parental rights by substituting the [school board] *in loco parentis* [in place of the parents], without a compelling necessity therefore.[62]

The court correctly noted that parents "enjoy well-recognized liberty interests in rearing and educating their children in accord with their own views. . . . Intrusion into the relationship between parent and child requires a showing of overriding necessity."[63] Although the school board contended that the provision of condoms was merely education, the court reasoned that students "are not just exposed to talk or literature on the subject of sexual behavior; the school offers the means for students to engage in sexual activity. . . ."[64] In ruling the condom distribution unlawful under both state and constitutional authority, the court observed:

In determining whether this program intrudes on parental rights in the first instance the issue is not one of purpose but one of effect. We must take great care not to be blinded by the concept that the end justifies

---

Commissioner of Education or a Board of Education—to provide the exceptions to parental consent requirements." *Alfonso,* 195 A.D.2d at 54.
[62]*Alfonso,* 195 A.D.2d at 56.
[63]*Id.*
[64]*Id.* at 57.

233

the means. In accord with the foregoing, we conclude that the policy intrudes on [the parents'] rights
by interfering with parental decisionmaking in a particularly sensitive area. Through its public schools
the City of New York has made a judgment that minors should have unrestricted access to contraceptives, a decision which is clearly within the purview
of the [parents'] constitutionally protected right to
rear their children, and then has forced that judgment on them.[65]

Despite the importance of HIV and AIDS education, the
court noted the following:

---

[65]*Id.* at 57–58. However, the federal appeals court in *Brown v. Hot, Sexy
and Safer Productions, Inc.,* 68 F.3d 525 (1st Cir. 1995), *cert. denied,* 516
U.S. 1159 (1996), distinguished the *Alfonso* case on the basis that the distribution of condoms did not constitute education but rather a health service, whereas the discussion of sexual activity was education and could not
be prevented by parents. In the case of *Hot, Sexy and Safer Productions,*
students were required to attend a mandatory, schoolwide assembly which
consisted of a ninety-minute presentation by an individual who was affiliated with *Hot, Sexy, and Safer, Inc.* During this presentation, the students
were told by the representative of *Hot, Sexy, and Safer* that they were going
to have a "group sexual experience with audience participation." The pre-
senter used profane, lewd, and lascivious language to describe body parts
and excretory functions, advocated and approved oral sex, masturbation,
homosexual activity, and condom use during promiscuous premarital sex,
simulated masturbation, characterized the loose pants worn by one minor
as "erection wear," referred to being in "deep sh—" after anal sex, had a
male minor lick an oversized condom with her, after which she had a female minor pull it over the male minor's entire head and blow it up,
encouraged a male minor to display his "orgasm face" with her for the
camera, informed a male minor that he was not having enough orgasms,
closely inspected a minor and told him that he had a "nice butt," and made

The primary purpose of the Board of Education is not to serve as a health provider. Its reason for being is education. No judicial or legislative authority directs or permits teachers and other public school educators to dispense condoms to minor, unemancipated students without the knowledge or consent of their parents. Nor do we believe that they have any inherent authority to do so.[66]

The court concluded that by excluding parental involvement, the condom availability program "impermissibly trespasses" on parental rights.[67]

The vast majority of states have specific laws that require any sex or AIDS/HIV education be abstinence based and/or require either parental consent or opt-out or both.[68] Regardless of state law, parents can assert a constitutional right to opt out of sex education that controverses their religious beliefs.

---

eighteen references to orgasms, six references to male genitals, and eight references to female genitals. Unbelievably, the federal appeals court found that the parental liberty interest to raise and direct the rearing of children did not encompass "a fundamental constitutional right to dictate the curriculum at the public school to which they had chosen to send their children." *Id.* at 533.

[66]*Alfonso*, 195 A.D.2d at 56. The Third Circuit Court of Appeals upheld a condom distribution policy in *Parents United for Better Schools, Inc. v. School District of Philadelphia Board of Education*, 148 F.3d 260 (3d Cir. 1998). The court distinguished *Alfonso* from this case, noting that the Philadelphia policy provided an opt-out provision for parents. *Id.* at 276.

[67]*Id. But see, Parents United*, 148 F.3d at 260 (condom distribution program did not violate parental rights when parents could refuse participation for their children).

[68]For a complete list, visit http://www.lc.org and search for "parental rights."

Parental Notification or Consent Regarding Abortion

The United States Supreme Court has issued several rulings regarding parental notification and parental consent statutes regarding minors seeking abortions. Parental consent statutes require that the minor obtain the consent of a parent or legal guardian, while notification statutes merely require the minor to notify the parent or legal guardian. The Court has ruled that a state statute without a judicial bypass procedure is unconstitutional.[69] A statute must contain a provision allowing the minor child to bypass the requirement of parental consent or notice if the circumstances suggest that notifying the parent might place the minor in danger, and the minor is deemed mature. Furthermore, a state statute requiring parental consent of both parents is unconstitutional even if it contains a judicial bypass provision.[70] However, a state statute requiring parental consent of one parent along with a judicial bypass provision is constitutional,[71] and a state law requiring parental notification along with a judicial bypass procedure is also constitutional.[72] The vast majority of states have laws that require parental consent or notification.

---

[69]*Bellotti v. Baird,* 443 U.S. 622 (1979).

[70]*Hodgson v. Minnesota,* 497 U.S. 417 (1990).

[71]*Planned Parenthood of Southeastern Pa. v. Casey,* 505 U.S. 833 (1992); *Lucas v. South Carolina Coastal Council,* 505 U.S. 1003 (1992); *Ohio v. Akron Ctr. for Reproductive Health,* 497 U.S. 502 (1990); *Planned Parenthood Ass'n of Kansas City, Mo., Inc. v. Ashcroft,* 462 U.S. 476 (1983); and *H.L. v. Matheson,* 450 U.S. 398 (1981).

[72]*Lambert v. Wicklund,* 520 U.S. 292 (1997).

Summary

In addition to constitutional and federal protection of parental rights, parents should always consider whether there is additional state law that affords protection for parents to train and educate their children. Sometimes state law allows parents to inspect curriculum and imposes penalties whenever an educational institution prohibits inspection. It may also require parental consent for certain educational activities. In addition, parents may find protection under their state's constitution.

Many state and federal laws require that sex or AIDS/HIV education be abstinence based. A number of states also require parental consent or allow the child to opt out of objectionable sex education programs. The vast majority of states have laws requiring parental consent or notification before a minor may obtain an abortion.

Whatever the source, parental rights must be protected. Parents, not the state, have the primary duty to train and educate their children.

7
PAROCHIAL SCHOOL STUDENTS AND PUBLIC BENEFITS

CONTROVERSY CONTINUES TO FUEL the debate regarding parochial school students receiving taxpayer-funded benefits. Not surprisingly, the Supreme Court's past precedents muddied the waters. The Supreme Court categorically altered its interpretation in this area, specifically overruled some of its prior decisions, and clarified its position on this issue.

When considering the constitutionality of parochial schools receiving public benefits, both clauses of the First Amendment should be considered. The first question to be addressed is whether the Establishment Clause[1] prohibits the government from diverting public funds to parochial schools, thereby extending public benefits to parochial school students.

---

[1]"Congress shall make no law respecting an establishment of religion." U.S. CONST. amend. I.

The second question is whether parochial school students may affirmatively claim under the Free Exercise Clause that the government must divert public funds to finance their education.[2] In this area the issue is whether a parochial school student may force an unwilling government to divert public funds.

Under current jurisprudence, the question of the Establishment Clause is settled; extending public funds to students enrolled in parochial schools and receiving neutral instruction is permissible under the Establishment Clause. Still, the question of whether a parochial school or its students may affirmatively force the government to extend funds to the parochial school has been met with mixed results. The more recent issue of whether education vouchers may be used by parents who send their children to private religious schools has now received an affirmative response from the Supreme Court.

Voucher or Scholarship Programs

The Supreme Court ruled that the voucher portion of the Ohio Pilot Scholarship Program did not violate the Establishment Clause.[3] Despite the fact that in 1995, a federal court declared a "crisis of magnitude" and placed the Cleveland City School District under state control, educational bureaucrats such as the National Education Association and its state counterpart resisted the voucher

---

[2]"Congress shall make no law respecting an establishment of religion, *or prohibiting the free exercise thereof.*" U.S. CONST. amend I (emphasis added).
[3]*Zelman v. Simmons-Harris,* 536 U.S. 639 (2002).

program.[4] The educational "gurus" wanted to conduct business as usual, even after a state auditor found that Cleveland's public schools faced a crisis "perhaps unprecedented in the history of American education."[5] The district failed to meet any of the eighteen state standards for minimal acceptable performance, as only one in ten ninth graders could pass a basic proficiency examination. More than two-thirds of high school students either dropped out or failed.

To address the dire situation, the state of Ohio passed a law that provided financial assistance to families in any Ohio school district that was or had been under federal court order requiring supervision and operational management of the district by the state superintendent. The program provided tuition aid for students to attend a participating public or private school of the parents' choice. The program also provided tutorial aid for those students who chose to remain enrolled in public school. Any private school, whether religious or nonreligious, could participate in the program so long as the school was located within the boundaries of the covered district.

During the 1999–2000 school year, fifty-six private schools participated, of which forty-six (or 82 percent) had a religious affiliation. None of the public schools adjacent to Cleveland elected to participate. More than thirty-seven hundred students elected to participate in the program, most of whom (96 percent) enrolled in religiously affiliated schools.[6]

In upholding the voucher program, the Court declared that its past cases

---

[4]*Id.* at 2463.
[5]*Id.*
[6]*Id.* at 2465.

make clear that where a government aid program is neutral with respect to religion, and provides assistance directly to a broad class of citizens who, in turn, direct government aid to religious schools wholly as a result of their own genuine and independent private choice, the program is not readily subject to challenge under the Establishment Clause. A program that shares these features permits government aid to reach religious institutions only by way of the deliberate choices of numerous individual recipients. The incidental advancement of a religious mission, or the perceived endorsement of a religious message, is reasonably attributable to the individual recipient, not to the government, whose role ends with the disbursement of benefits.[7]

In other words, if the public funds permit individual applicants to exercise private choice among a broad class of possible recipients, including religious organizations or institutions, then there is no violation of the First Amendment Establishment Clause when the religious recipients receive the funds as a result of these private choices. Although the overwhelming majority of recipients of the Ohio voucher program were religiously affiliated schools, the outcome did not change. The decision was driven by private, not government, choice, and thus there was no constitutional violation.

Although the Ohio program originated out of the dire condition of the Cleveland public schools, there is no requirement

[7]*Id.* at 2467.

that a voucher system must be limited to failing schools. Indeed, vouchers may be offered to any parent regardless of the performance of the public schools. The only requirements are that (1) the public funds must be available to a broad class of recipients which include both secular and religious schools, and (2) the school receiving the funds must be designated by the parent or guardian rather than the government. Vouchers allowing parents to make private choices about the training and education of their children have the potential to restore quality to the American educational experience.

Relying on the *Zelman* case, a federal court ruled that the state of Wisconsin may fund a faith-based, long-term alcohol and drug addiction program.[8] Another federal court using the *Zelman* decision ruled that the government may issue a tax-exempt industrial revenue bond to benefit a private, religious university where similar bonds had been issued to both religious and nonreligious institutions using neutral criteria.[9] The Supreme Court's voucher decision will have a broad impact on the payment of public funds to religious institutions.

A state that offers vouchers or scholarships may not discriminate on the basis of religion. Thus, a state may not refuse funds to students who attend religious schools or take religious classes. However, a state may refuse funds to a student who is intending to major in theology, provided that the refusal was not based on hostility toward religion.[10]

---

[8]*Freedom from Religion Found., Inc. v. McCallum*, 214 F. Supp. 905 (W.D. Wis. 2002).
[9]*Steele v. Industrial Dev. Bd. of Metro. Gov't of Nashville*, 201 F.3d 401 (6th Cir. 2002).
[10]*See Locke v. Davey*, 124 S.Ct. 1307 (2004).

Title I of the Elementary and Secondary Education Act

Congress enacted Title I of the Elementary and Secondary Education Act of 1965[11] to "provide full educational opportunity to every child regardless of economic background."[12] Title I channels federal funds through the states to "local educational agencies" (hereafter "LEAs").[13] The LEAs spend these funds to provide remedial education, guidance, and job counseling to eligible students and to provide "conflict mentoring, and other pupil services."[14]

According to Title I, an eligible student is one who resides within the attendance boundaries of a public school located in a lower income area[15] and who is failing, or is at risk of failing, the State Student Performance Standards.[16] Title I funds must remain available to all eligible children regardless of whether they attend public schools,[17] and the services provided to the children attending private schools must be "equitable in comparison to services and other benefits for public school children."[18]

Title I funds extended to students enrolled in private schools may be provided only to those private school students eligible for aid and cannot be used to provide services

---

[11]20 U.S.C. § 6301 *et seq.*
[12]S. Rep. No. 146, 89th Cong., 1st Sess. 5 (1965).
[13]20 U.S.C. §§ 6311, 6312. Title I has been reenacted in various forms over the years, most recently in the No Child Left Behind Act of 2001, 115 Stat. 1425.
[14]20 U.S.C. §§ 6315(c)(1)(A) and 6314(b)(1)(B)(i), (iv).
[15]20 U.S.C. § 6313(a)(2)(B).
[16]20 U.S.C. § 6315(b)(1)(B).
[17]20 U.S.C. § 6312(e)(1)(F).
[18]20 U.S.C. § 6321(a)(3); *see also* 20 U.S.C. § 6321(a)(1); 34 C.F.R. §§ 200.10(a), 200.11(b) (1996).

on a "school-wide" basis.[19] The LEA must retain complete control over the Title I funds, retain title of all materials used to provide Title I services, and provide those services through public employees or other persons independent of the private school and any religious institution.[20] Services provided under Title I must be Asecular, neutral, and nonideological,[21] and may supplement, but "in no case supplant, the level of services" already provided by the private school.[22]

In 1966, the year after Congress adopted Title I, the New York City School Board arranged to transport children attending sectarian schools to the public schools for after-school Title I instruction. However, this program was largely unsuccessful because attendance was poor, as it obviously made for a very long day. The School Board then altered its provision of Title I services. Under the revised plan, school board employees went directly to the sectarian schools to provide Title I instruction and counseling. Assignments to the private schools were voluntary. The school employees were given written and oral instructions emphasizing the secular purpose of Title I and outlining the rules to be followed. However, several individuals sued the school board claiming that the use of their tax money to provide Title I instruction at a sectarian school violated the Establishment Clause. In 1985 the Supreme Court in *Aguilar v. Felton*[23] "held that the Establishment Clause of the First Amendment barred the city

---

[19]*Cf.* 34 C.F.R. § 200.12(b) *with* 20 U.S.C. § 6314 (allowing "school-wide" programs at public schools).
[20]20 U.S.C. §§ 6321(c)(1), (2).
[21]20 U.S.C. § 6321(a)(2).
[22]34 C.F.R. § 200.12(a) (1996).
[23]473 U.S. 402 (1985).

of New York from sending public school teachers into parochial schools to provide remedial education to disadvantaged children pursuant to a congressionally mandated program."[24] After the Supreme Court's ruling, the New York City School Board reverted to its prior practice of providing instruction at public school sites, leased sites, and in mobile instructional units parked near the sectarian schools. In a case overruling *Aguilar,* the Supreme Court noted the financial burden of that decision:

> It is not disputed that the additional costs of complying with *Aguilar*'s mandate are significant. Since the 1986–1987 school year, the Board has spent over $100 million providing computer-aided instruction, leasing sites and mobile instructional units, and transporting students to those sites.[25]

The so-called *"Aguilar* costs" therefore reduced the amount of Title I money an LEA had available for remedial education. LEAs were forced to cut back on the number of students who received Title I benefits, with some estimates noting that the increased cost resulted in a decline of about 35 percent in the number of private school children who were served.[26]

In 1997 the United States Supreme Court overruled *Aguilar,* holding that the Establishment Clause of the First Amendment did not bar a public school from sending teachers into parochial schools to provide remedial education to

---

[24]*Agostini v. Felton,* 521 U.S. 203, 208 (1997).
[25]*Id.* at 213.
[26]*Id.* at 214.

disadvantaged children pursuant to a congressionally mandated program under Title I. The Court stated that *Aguilar* was eroded by its subsequent Establishment Clause jurisprudence.

The Court pointed out that *Aguilar* rested upon several judicial decisions and outdated constitutional presumptions. *Aguilar* relied in part upon *School District of Grand Rapids v. Ball*[27] and *Meek v. Pittenger*.[28] In *Meek,* the Court reviewed a program in which full-time public employees provided supplemental "auxiliary services" involving remedial and accelerated instruction, guidance counseling and testing, and speech and hearing services to nonpublic school children on the site of the nonpublic school. The Court found this program unconstitutional because "the teachers participating in the programs may become involved in intentionally or inadvertently inculcating particular religious tenets or beliefs."[29] According to the Court, the presence of the public school teachers on parochial school grounds created a "graphic symbol of the 'concert or union or dependency' of church and state."[30] The Supreme Court in *Mitchell v. Helms* specifically overruled *Meek.*[31]

In *Ball,* the Supreme Court evaluated a Shared Time program wherein classes were taught during regular school hours at private schools by public school teachers using materials purchased with public funds. The Shared Time courses were in subjects designed to supplement the "core curriculum" of the nonpublic schools. In *Ball,* the Court found the

---

[27]473 U.S. 373 (1985).
[28]421 U.S. 349 (1975).
[29]*Ball,* 473 U.S. at 385.
[30]*Id.* at 391 (quoting *Zorach v. Clauson,* 343 U.S. 306, 312 (1952)).
[31]530 U.S. 793, 808 (2000).

Shared Time program violated the Establishment Clause because it had the impermissible effect of advancing religion.[32]

The Supreme Court's previous conclusion that the Shared Time program in *Ball* had the impermissible effect of advancing religion rested on three assumptions: (1) a public school employee working on the premises of a sectarian school is presumed to inculcate religion; (2) the presence of a public school employee on a sectarian school campus creates a symbolic unity between church and state; and (3) any public aid that directly benefits the educational function of a sectarian school impermissibly finances religious indoctrination, even if that aid reaches the school as a consequence of the student's private decision making. Moreover, the *Aguilar* decision added a fourth assumption, namely that the Title I program necessitated an excessive governmental entanglement with religion, because public employees who teach on the premise of a religious school must be closely monitored to ensure that they do not inculcate religion.[33]

Since its 1985 *Aguilar* decision, the Supreme Court has altered its Establishment Clause jurisprudence. First, the Court "abandoned the presumption erected in *Meek* and *Ball* that the placement of public employees on parochial school grounds inevitably results in the impermissible effect of state-sponsored indoctrination or constitutes a symbolic union between government and religion."[34] Second, the Court "departed from the rule relied on in *Ball* that all government aid that directly aids the educational function of religious schools

---

[32]*Ball,* 473 U.S. at 395.
[33]*Agostini,* 521 U.S. at 219.
[34]*Id.* at 223.

is invalid."[35] In 1993 the Court decided[36] that under the Individuals with Disabilities Education Act, the Establishment Clause did not bar a state-employed sign language interpreter provided to a student enrolled in a Roman Catholic high school. The Court "refused to presume that a publicly employed interpreter would be pressured by the pervasively sectarian surroundings to inculcate religion by 'adding to [or] subtracting from' the lectures translated."[37]

Zobrest therefore expressly rejected the notion—relied on in *Ball* and *Aguilar*—that, solely because of her presence on private school property, a public employee will be presumed to inculcate religion in the students. *Zobrest* also implicitly repudiated another assumption on which *Ball* and *Aguilar* turned: that the presence of a public employee on private school property creates an impermissible "symbolic link" between government and religion.[38]

In *Agostini,* the Court noted that it has now "departed from the rule relied on in *Ball* that all government aid that directly aids the educational function of religious schools is invalid."[39] In *Witters v. Washington Department of Services for the Blind,*[40] the Supreme Court held that "the Establishment Clause did not bar a State from issuing a vocational tuition grant to a blind person who wished to use the grant to attend a Christian

---

[35]*Id.* at 225.
[36]*Zobrest v. Catalina Foothills Sch. Dist.,* 509 U.S. 1 (1993).
[37]*Agostini,* 521 U.S. at 224 (quoting *Zobrest,* 509 U.S. at 13).
[38]*Id.*
[39]*Id.* at 225.
[40]474 U.S. 481 (1986).

college and become a pastor, missionary, or youth director."[41]
Even though the parochial school student used the public
funds to obtain a religious education, the Court observed that
the grants were "made available generally without regard to
the sectarian-nonsectarian, or public-nonpublic nature of the
institution benefitted."[42] According to the Supreme Court, the
grants were distributed directly to the students and used to
pay for tuition at the educational institution of their choice. In
the Supreme Court's view, "this transaction was no different
from a State's issuing a paycheck to one of its employees,
knowing that the employee would donate part or all of the
check to a religious institution."[43]

According to the Supreme Court's *Agostini* decision, "interaction between church and state is inevitable, and we have
always tolerated some level of involvement between the
two."[44] In *Agostini,* the Court stated that the Title I program implemented by New York, in which public school employees
deliver Title I instruction on parochial campuses, did not run
afoul of the Establishment Clause or any of the three primary
criteria used to evaluate whether government aid has the effect of advancing religion. First, the Court stated that the program did not result in governmental indoctrination. Second,
the Title I program did not define its recipients by reference to
religion. Finally, the Title I program did not create an excessive entanglement with religion.[45] The Court concluded:

---

[41]*Agostini,* 521 U.S. at 225.
[42]*Witters,* 474 U.S. at 487 (quoting *Committee for Pub. Educ. & Religious
Liberty v. Nyquist,* 413 U.S. 756, 782–83, n.38 (1973)).
[43]*Agostini,* 521 U.S. at 226.
[44]*Id.* at 233 (citation omitted).
[45]*Id.* at 231–35.

We therefore hold that a federally funded program providing supplemental, remedial instruction to disadvantaged children on a neutral basis is not invalid under the Establishment Clause when such instruction is given on the premises of sectarian schools by government employees pursuant to a program containing safeguards such as those present here.[46]

In *Mitchell v. Helms,* the Supreme Court reaffirmed *Agostini,* pointing out that "nothing in the Establishment Clause requires the exclusion of pervasively sectarian schools from otherwise permissible aid programs, and other doctrines of this Court bar it."[47] *Mitchell* upheld a federal program that provided money to local agencies to lend educational materials and equipment to public and private schools. In *Mitchell,* the Court implied that any government program of aid to religious schools that did not provide religious content may be permissible, since it is not practical to draw any other line between types of aid allowed.[48] The important factor is whether the aid is appropriated on a neutral basis.[49] In order to eliminate the risk of an Establishment Clause violation in a government aid program, private choices, and not public ones, should determine which schools receive assistance.[50]

---

[46]*Id.* at 234–35.

[47]530 U.S. at 828. The plurality opinion of Justices Thomas, Rehnquist, Scalia, and Kennedy relied on *Agostini,* as did the concurring opinion of Justices O'Connor and Breyer. However, O'Connor was concerned that the plurality may be using neutrality as the only test and was not concerned enough that government aid would be diverted by the recipient to the direct use for religious indoctrination. *Id.* at 837–38 (O'Connor, J., concurring).

[48]*Id.* at 825.

[49]*Id.* at 830.

[50]*Id.* at 810.

Aid given directly to a sectarian school selected by the government for special treatment is still prohibited.[51]

Individuals with Disabilities Education Act

Under the Individuals with Disabilities Education Act (hereafter IDEA), a state receiving federal funds for the education of handicapped children must provide those children with a "free appropriate public education."[52] A "'free appropriate public education' consists of educational instruction specially designed to meet the unique needs of the handicapped child, supported by such services as are necessary to permit the child 'to benefit' from the instruction."[53] The special education must be "meaningful" and not trivial or de minimis.[54]

The centerpiece of the IDEA's education delivery system for disabled children is the Individualized Education Program (hereafter "IEP").[55] "The IEP consists of a detailed, written statement arrived at by a multi-disciplinary team summarizing a child's abilities, outlining the goals for the child's education and specifying the services a child will receive."[56] The instruction and services offered by the state "must be

---

[51]See *Zelman*, 536 U.S. at 644–45. ("Our decisions have drawn a consistent distinction between government programs that provide aid directly to religious schools . . . and programs of true private choice, in which government aid reaches religious schools only as a result of the genuine and independent choices of private individuals.")

[52]20 U.S.C. § 1412(a).

[53]*Board of Educ. v. Rowley*, 458 U.S. 176, 188–89 (1982).

[54]*Polk v. Central Susquehanna Intermediate Unit 16*, 853 F.2d 171, 184 (3d Cir. 1988), *cert. denied*, 488 U.S. 1030 (1989).

[55]*Honig v. Doe*, 484 U.S. 305, 311 (1988).

[56]*Oberti v. Board of Educ.*, 995 F.2d 1204, 1213, 1216 (3d Cir. 1993) (quoting *Polk*, 853 F.2d at 173).

provided at public expense, must meet the state's educational standards, must approximate the grade levels used in the state's regular education, and must comport with the child's IEP."[57]

Federal rules implementing IDEA funding prohibit the use of federal funds to pay for "religious worship, instruction, or proselytization."[58] In any administrative or judicial proceeding brought by a parent challenging the school's implementation of the IDEA, the school district bears the burden of proving the appropriateness of the IEP it has proposed for the child.

If a court determines that a school has offered an inappropriate education for a child, and an aggrieved parent has unilaterally chosen to place her child in an appropriate placement, appropriate relief may be ordered. Courts have often approved relief in the form of tuition reimbursement to the parent for the costs of educating her child during the period in which the school district failed to offer a free appropriate public education in accordance with its obligations under the IDEA. However, a parent who chooses to educate her child in a placement other than that offered by the school does so at her own financial risk in the event that the school's offered placement is determined to be appropriate.[59]

---

[57] *Rowley,* 458 U.S. at 203.
[58] 34 C.F.R. § 76.532(a)(1).
[59] *Christen G. v. Lower Merion Sch. Dist.,* 919 F. Supp. 793, 798–99 (E.D. Pa. 1996) (citations omitted).

In *Zobrest v. Catalina Foothills School District,*[60] the United States Supreme Court held that the Establishment Clause does not prohibit a public school from providing the services of an interpreter under the IDEA to a student attending a sectarian school.[61] The Supreme Court pointed out the following:

> We have never said that "religious institutions are disabled by the First Amendment from participating in publicly sponsored social welfare programs." For if the Establishment Clause did bar religious groups from receiving general government benefits, then a "church could not be protected by the police and fire departments, or have its public sidewalk kept in repair." Given that a contrary rule would lead to such absurd results, we have consistently held that government programs that neutrally provide benefits to a broad class of citizens defined without reference to religion are not readily subject to an Establishment Clause challenge just because sectarian institutions may also receive an attenuated financial benefit.[62]

---

[60]509 U.S. 1 (1993).

[61]Note this case was based solely on the Establishment Clause. By the time the case made its way to the United States Supreme Court, the parents had abandoned their Free Exercise claim.

[62]*Zobrest,* 509 U.S. at 8 (quoting *Bowen v. Kendrick,* 487 U.S. 589, 609 (1988) and *Widmar v. Vincent,* 454 U.S. 263, 274–75 (1981)). The Court pointed out that in *Mueller v. Allen,* 463 U.S. 388 (1983) and in *Witters,* 474 U.S. at 481, it upheld government programs offering general educational systems even though it indirectly benefited religion. In *Mueller,* the Court rejected an Establishment Clause challenge to a Minnesota law allowing taxpayers to deduct certain educational expenses in computing their state income tax, even though the vast majority of the deductions went to parents whose children attended sectarian schools. In *Witters,* the Court upheld

In *Zobrest,* the Court stated that the services provided under the IDEA were "part of a general government program that distributes benefits neutrally to any child qualifying as 'handicapped' under the IDEA, without regard to the 'sectarian-nonsectarian, or public-nonpublic nature' of the school the child attends."[63] The Court continued:

> By according parents freedom to select a school of their choice, the statute insures that a government-paid interpreter will be present in a sectarian school only as a result of the private decision of individual parents. In other words, because the IDEA creates no financial incentive for parents to choose a sectarian school, an interpreter's presence there cannot be attributed to state decisionmaking.[64]

Under the IDEA, "no funds traceable to the government ever find their way into sectarian schools' coffers."[65] According to the Court, the only economic benefit a sectarian school might receive from IDEA funding "is the handicapped child's tuition."[66]

Because the government funds flowing from the IDEA are neutrally provided benefits to a broad class of citizens defined without reference to religion, IDEA funding does not violate the Establishment Clause. Moreover, IDEA funds do not

---

against an Establishment Clause challenge to the State of Washington's extension of vocational assistance (as part of a general state program) to a blind person studying at a private Christian college to become a pastor, missionary, or youth director.

[63]*Zobrest,* 509 U.S. at 10.
[64]*Id.*
[65]*Id.*
[66]*Id.*

go directly to the sectarian school, but the funds instead go to the individual student, who freely chooses to attend either a public or a nonpublic school.

In *Zobrest*, the Court answered the question as to whether the government may extend IDEA funding to students attending sectarian schools. The Court unequivocally ruled that the First Amendment does not bar such funding. In *Goodall v. Stafford County School Board*,[67] a federal appeals court ruled that the Free Exercise Clause of the First Amendment does not *require* state funds to be provided to a student attending a sectarian school.[68] However, the issue of whether the government is required to extend benefits under the IDEA to a student attending a sectarian school under the student's free exercise of religion claim has not yet been answered by the Supreme Court.

Apart from the free exercise claim, other federal courts have ruled that by its own terms, the IDEA may require state-funded services for individuals attending sectarian schools. In each case the question is whether the public schools are able

---

[67]60 F.3d 168 (4th Cir. 1995), *cert. denied*, 516 U.S. 1046 (1996).

[68]Note an earlier case involving *Goodall v. Stafford County School Board*, 930 F.2d 363 (4th Cir. 1991), was overruled by *Zobrest*. In the 1991 *Goodall* decision, the Court ruled that the Establishment Clause prohibited the provision of funds to a student requiring a cued speech interpreter at a private religious school. After that case was overruled by *Zobrest* in 1993, the same parents brought another action claiming that the state was affirmatively required to fund the interpreter on the basis that the Free Exercise Clause compelled such funding due to the economic burden born by the parents for choosing to place their student in a religious school. The *Goodall* court in 1995 rejected that argument. In *Miller v. Benson*, 68 F.3d 163 (7th Cir. 1995), the Court was faced with a free exercise challenge similar to that brought forth in *Goodall*. However, by the time it made its way to the Seventh Circuit Court of Appeals, the free exercise challenge was moot, and therefore the court did not reach the merits of the case.

to provide a free and appropriate public education to the disabled student.[69] The amendments to the IDEA which took effect in 1997 clarify that a school district has no obligation to provide public funds to a disabled student who voluntarily chooses to enroll in a private school, where the public school is able to provide a "free appropriate public education."[70] The amendments, in part, state as follows:

> This part [of the Act] does not require a local educational agency to pay for the cost of education, including special education and related services, of a child with a disability at a private school or facility if

---

[69]See *Felter v. Cape Girardeau Sch. Dist.*, 810 F. Supp. 1062 (E.D. Mo. 1993) (student was entitled to transportation, as necessary service related to her individualized education program, from the sidewalk of her parochial school to her special education classes at a public school); *see also McNair v. Cardimone*, 676 F. Supp. 1361 (S.D. Ohio 1987) (Education of the Handicapped Act does not compel provision of transportation to and from private school for child with hearing impairments when child could have attended public school), *aff'd sub. nom. McNair v. Oak Hills Local Sch. Dist.*, 872 F.2d 153, 156–57 (6th Cir. 1989) (affirming on ground that transportation is not service required by child's disability but refusing to reach question whether EHA compelled provision of necessary services to handicapped children attending private schools); *Work v. McKenzie*, 661 F. Supp. 225 (D.D.C. 1987) (public school not required to provide transportation to private school for student who could have attended public school); *Russman v. Sobol*, 150 F.3d 219 (2d Cir. 1998) (IDEA does not require on-campus counseling and aide services that could be obtained elsewhere at public cost.); *Foley v. Special Sch. Dist. of St. Louis County*, 927 F. Supp. 1214 (E.D. Mo. 1996) (IDEA does not require school district to provide special education services at private parochial school in which the student had been unilaterally placed by her parents, so long as the services are made available at a public school.); *K.R. v. Anderson Community Sch. Corp.*, 125 F.3d 1017 (7th Cir. 1997), *cert. denied*, 523 U.S. 1046 (1998) (public school's offer of instructional assistant at public school fulfilled its duty to student who opted to attend private school).

[70]*K.R.*, 125 F.3d at 1019; *Cefalu v. East Baton Rouge Sch. Dist.*, 117 F.3d 231 (5th Cir. 1997).

that agency made a free appropriate public education available to the child and the parents elected to place the child in such private school or facility.[71]

Thus, if the public school offers a "free appropriate public education," then parents who voluntarily place their child in private school have no claim to fund the cost of the private tuition or other educational services. Whether parents would succeed in a claim that the lack of funding violates their free exercise of religion, despite the fact that the child may be educated in the public school, remains uncertain. Some courts have rejected such a claim, but the United States Supreme Court has not considered this specific issue.

Other Funding Programs

There are many other state or federally funded programs that may indirectly benefit religion other than Title I or IDEA funding. Funding schemes might include loaning textbooks and equipment[72] or providing transportation.[73]

---

[71]*K.R.,* 125 F.3d at 1019 (quoting Section 101 of the IDEA Amendments Act, 1997, Pub. L. No. 105–17, which amended §616[a][1] of the IDEA).

[72]*See, e.g., Mitchell,* 530 U.S. at 793 (Elementary and Secondary Education Act of 1965 [ESEA], which gives funds to state and local governments to lend educational material and equipment to public and private schools, does not violate Establishment Clause); *Walker v. San Francisco Unified Sch. Dist.,* 46 F.3d 1449 (9th Cir.), *reh'g denied,* 62 F.3d 300 (9th Cir. 1995) (public school loaning of instructional materials to parochial schools permissible).

[73]Many state and federal district courts have upheld the public payment for the transportation of parochial school students. *See, e.g., Helms v. Cody,* 856 F. Supp. 1102 (E.D. La. 1994). *Felter,* 810 F. Supp. at 1062 (upholding publicly funded transportation of handicapped student from parochial school to special classes at public school); *Cromwell Property Owners Ass'n v. Toffolon,* 495 F. Supp. 915 (D. Conn. 1979) (upholding state statute for transportation

Apart from any state constitutional provision, these programs will be deemed constitutional so long as the programs "neutrally provide benefits to a broad class of citizens defined without reference to religion."[74] Even if a state constitutional provision or state law provided that no state funds may be diverted to religious institutions, these provisions would conflict with the federal guarantee of equal protection and the free exercise of religion.[75]

---

of private school students); *Springfield Sch. Dist. v. Department of Educ.*, 397 A.2d 1154 (Pa.), *appeal dismissed*, 443 U.S. 901 (1979); *Americans United for Separation of Church and State v. Paire*, 359 F. Supp. 505 (D.N.H. 1973) (upholding state reimbursement of transportation fare to parochial students); *West Morris Reg'l Bd. of Educ. v. Sills*, 279 A.2d 609 (N.J.), *cert. denied*, 404 U.S. 986 (1971) (upholding state statute authorizing local districts to provide transportation for parochial school students); *Alexander v. Bartlett*, 165 N.W.2d 445 (Mich. App. 1968) (same); *Honohan v. Holt*, 244 N.E.2d 537 (Ohio Com. Pl.1968) (same); *Snyder v. Town of Newton*, 161 A.2d 770 (Conn. 1960), *appeal dismissed*, 365 U.S. 299 (1961) (same).

[74]*Zobrest*, 509 U.S. at 8. *But see, Freedom from Religion Found., Inc. v. Bugher*, 249 F.3d 606 (7th Cir. 2001) (reimbursing religious schools for the cost of Internet access violates Establishment Clause because grant had no restrictions or guidelines).

[75]If a state took the position that no public funds may go to religious institutions pursuant to the state constitutional or statutory mandate, a good argument could be made that such law violates the federal guarantee of equal protection. Even if strict scrutiny of such law were not considered, a good argument could also be made that the law fails to pass the rational basis test. In *Romer v. Evans*, 517 U.S. 620 (1996), the Supreme Court struck down a provision of the Colorado constitution on the basis that the law evinced animus toward homosexuals by precluding them from the general protections of the state and local laws. The same argument may be made if religious institutions are disabled from participating in neutral funding programs. Such an extreme position would mean that no religiously affiliated hospital could participate in Medicare programs.

8
USE OF PUBLIC FACILITIES

THE USE OF PUBLIC FACILITIES is an important aspect of religious liberty. Use of such facilities is significant because many people gather in public places. Oftentimes those charged with oversight unfortunately have the mistaken idea that religious persons or groups must be prohibited from engaging in expressive activity because they assume that to allow religious expression might violate the so-called "separation of church and state." Sometimes this misunderstanding is a result of ignorance, blatant hostility, or bigotry toward religion. Regardless of the motive, this understanding is incorrect and unconstitutional.

Traditional Public Forums

PARKS, STREETS, AND SIDEWALKS

Regarding free speech in general and religious speech in particular, public parks, streets, and sidewalks are critical areas for the discussion of public debate. According to the

United States Supreme Court, public parks, streets, and sidewalks "have immemorially been held in trust for use of the public . . . and are properly considered traditional public fora."[1] The "purpose of the public forum doctrine is to give effect to the broad command of the First Amendment to protect speech from governmental interference."[2]

Unlike a limited or designated public forum, a traditional public forum such as a park, street, or sidewalk is always open to the public and cannot be permanently closed to public use.[3] In order to restrict the discussion of certain subject matters within a traditional public forum, the government must demonstrate that it has a compelling interest and has used the least restrictive means in order to achieve that interest.[4] However, reasonable content-neutral[5] speech restrictions

---

[1]*Frisby v. Schultz,* 487 U.S. 474, 481 (1988) (public sidewalk); *see also Perry Educ. Ass'n v. Perry Local Educators' Ass'n,* 460 U.S. 37 (1983); *see also Capital Square Review and Advisory Bd. v. Pinette,* 515 U.S. 753 (1995) (public park); *Forsyth County v. The Nationalist Movement,* 505 U.S. 123 (1992) (public street); *Hague v. CIO,* 307 U.S. 496, 515 (1939).

[2]*ISKCON v. Lee,* 505 U.S. 672, 697 (1992) (Kennedy, J., concurring, in which Blackmun, Stevens and Souter joined).

[3]In an interesting case, a federal court of appeals ruled that the Naturist Society, which advocated "clothing optional" lifestyles and educated the public through writings, lectures, and public demonstrations, could use a Florida park near a public beach to distribute literature, circulate petitions, and display a sign because the park was a public forum. See *Naturist Soc'y, Inc. v. Fillyaw,* 958 F.2d 1515 (11th Cir. 1992).

[4]Restricting subject matter is often referred to as a content-based restriction. For example, a law banning the discussion of alcohol would be a content-based restriction on speech. To survive a constitutional challenge to this restriction, the government must show a compelling governmental interest in restricting the subject matter and that the restriction is the least restrictive means available to achieve the government interest.

[5]Content-neutral regulations are those "justified without reference to the content of the regulated speech." *Virginia State Bd. of Pharmacy v. Virginia Citizens Consumer Council,* 425 U.S. 748, 771 (1976).

such as a time, place, or manner restriction, may be placed upon the use of a public forum. For example, so long as the restriction has nothing to do with the content of the message, the government may allow use of a street for a parade at certain hours so as not to interfere with rush-hour traffic. Such a restriction applies to all speech irrespective of the content of the message. While reasonable, content-neutral restrictions are permissible on speech in a traditional public forum, the government cannot flatly prohibit all speech in such forums.

One case brought to Liberty Counsel's attention dealt with a public park in Texas. The park allowed use of its facilities by the general public; however, churches were required to sign a waiver that they would not offer prayer in the public park or perform baptisms. Liberty Counsel's involvement brought rapid change to the unconstitutional policy. Public parks can be used by religious groups for evangelization, drama, skits, speaking, congregating, or distributing religious literature, and streets may be used for parades or demonstrations.

Palm Beach County, Florida, learned the hard way that political and religious speech cannot be excluded from public parks. The County adopted a policy that required permission from government officials prior to engaging in political or religious speech in public parks. The ordinance also prohibited the distribution of political or religious literature. In the fall of 1994 on Labor Day weekend, Ken Connor, who was running for governor of the State of Florida, took his campaign trip through Palm Beach County. When he stopped at a public park to greet people and distribute "Connor for Governor" literature, a police officer told him that he could not enter the park without written permission. He was also informed that park policy prohibited the distribution of political or religious literature. Mr. Connor, an experienced trial attorney, was surprised when he was threatened with arrest simply for distributing political literature in a public park. Liberty Counsel filed suit against Palm Beach County on behalf of Mr. Connor. Ruling the park policy unconstitutional, the federal court ruled that public parks are traditional public forums, that political and religious speech cannot be excluded from a public park, and that requiring prior permission before engaging in political or religious speech in a public park is unconstitutional. The court also pointed out that had this policy been around during the time of Abraham Lincoln, Mr. Lincoln himself would apparently have been prohibited from standing on a nearby stump to talk about the political and social issues of his day.[6] Obviously, government may not prohibit political or religious speech in traditional public forums.

Like parks and streets, public sidewalks are traditional public forums that may be used by religious speakers. While the use of sound magnification devices may be restricted to certain levels[7] and blocking ingress or egress is not permissible, peaceful picketing on a public sidewalk is clearly protected First Amendment activity. Simply because the government disagrees with the content of a protester's message does not allow the government to restrict speech in a traditional public forum. Indeed, the government "may not prohibit the expression of an idea simply because society finds the idea itself offensive or

---

[6]*Connor v. Palm Beach County,* No. 95–8628-CIV-HURLEY, 1996 WL 438779 (S.D. Fla. May 29, 1996).
[7]*Saia v. New York,* 334 U.S. 558 (1948); *Kovacs v. Cooper,* 336 U.S. 77 (1949) (antinoise ordinances must meet the strict tests of vagueness and overbreadth); *U.S. Labor Party v. Pomerlau,* 557 F.2d 410 (4th Cir. 1977).

disagreeable."[8] The Supreme Court has also noted that its prior cases have "consistently stressed that we are often captives outside the sanctuary of the home and subject to objectionable speech."[9] Restricting speech within a public forum based upon the content of the message is repugnant to the Constitution. Stressing its disdain for content-based restrictions on speech, the United States Supreme Court stated:

> Above all else, the First Amendment means that the government has no power to restrict expression because of its message, its ideas, its subject matter or its content. . . . The essence of this forbidden censorship is content control. Any restriction on expressive activity because of its content would completely undercut the "profound national commitment to the principles that debate on public issues should be uninhibited, robust and wide open."[10]

Sidewalks within residential neighborhoods are also considered traditional public forums. Picketing within a residential neighborhood is a constitutionally protected First Amendment right. The United States Supreme Court has ruled that a person may picket within a residential neighborhood so long as the picketing is not targeted toward a specific

---

[8]*Simon & Schuster, Inc. v. Members of NY State Crime Victims Bd.*, 502 U.S. 105, 117 (1991); *see also Cohen v. California*, 403 U.S. 15 (1971) (overturning a criminal conviction based on a breach of the peace charge for wearing a T-shirt in a public forum with the words "F – the Draft").
[9]*Cohen*, 403 U.S. at 21.
[10]*Police Dep't of Chicago v. Mosley*, 408 U.S. 92, 95–96 (1972) (quoting *New York Times Co. v. Sullivan*, 376 U.S. 254, 270 [1964]).

residence.[11] In other words, so long as the picketer moves about within the residential neighborhood on the public sidewalk and does not localize the picketing activities in front of one specific residence, the picketing is permissible speech activity. Picketers should, therefore, continually move on the public sidewalk within the residential neighborhood rather than stand still in front of the same house.

Limited or Designated Public Forums

If the location in question is not a public park, street, or sidewalk, it is either considered a limited or designated public forum or a nonpublic forum.[12] This second category includes any public property which the government by policy or practice intentionally opens to the public for expressive activity. For example, facilities such as public schools, libraries, public housing, public arenas, or any other public facility other than parks, streets, or sidewalks, frequently come

---

[11]*Frisby,* 487 U.S. at 474; *see also Madsen v. Women's Health Ctr, Inc.,* 512 U.S. 753 (1994); *Carey v. Brown,* 447 U.S. 455 (1980); *Vittitow v. City of Upper Arlington,* 830 F. Supp. 1077 (S.D. Ohio 1993) (picketing near the home of a physician who performs abortions is permissible so long as the protestors move about the neighborhood and do not solely target one residence).

[12]The United States Supreme Court has used both terms, *limited* and *designated* public forums, to describe this category. *Cf. Arkansas Educ. Television Comm. v. Forbes,* 523 U.S. 666 (1998) with *Rosenberger v. Rector and Visitors of the Univ. of Va.,* 515 U.S. 819, 829 (1995); *see also ISKCON v. Lee,* 505 U.S. 672, 678 (1992) ("The second category of public forum property is the designated public forum, whether of a limited or unlimited character—property that the State has opened for expressive activity by part or all of the public."). For purposes of this chapter, the term *limited* public forum will be used to describe this second category of public property.

within the limited public forum when the public is permitted to use these facilities for expression. As mentioned earlier, parks, streets, and sidewalks are considered traditional public forums. As such, parks, streets, and sidewalks are always open to the public. On the other hand, limited public forums are governed according to the limited public forum analysis. To be a limited public forum, the public facility must be intentionally opened to the general public. This is an important key to the use of these public facilities. Thus, if a public school allows use of its facilities to outside guests after school hours as a meeting place for a Rotary club or the Boy Scouts, then the school facilities have become a limited public forum. The same holds true for a library, which frequently opens its facilities to use by the public for meetings. A public housing facility that opens its meeting rooms for residents has created a limited public forum for residents only, while a public housing facility that also allows nonresidents to use its meeting rooms has created a limited public forum for all those wishing to use its meeting rooms.

In order to determine whether a public facility is a limited public forum, one must consider who and what type of persons or groups use the facility. Once it is clear that outside persons or groups use the facilities, the public facility must not discriminate against other outside organizations, even if the organizations are religious in nature. Once open for use by the general public, the same analysis is used here as is used for public parks, streets, or sidewalks. However, unlike a traditional public forum, the government is not required to keep a limited public forum open to the public and can, therefore, close the forum, so long as the forum is closed to all outside use. While it is open for use by the public, the government can only exclude a subject matter from the forum if the exclusion is necessary to serve a compelling state interest and the exclusion is the least restrictive means to achieve that interest. As in the traditional public forum, the government may impose reasonable content-neutral speech restrictions such as time, place, and manner of the speech. Still, the government must show that there are ample alternative channels of communications available. For example, a public school can open its facilities to the public but ban any use after 10:00 p.m. Since this restriction applies to *all* speech, it is content-neutral and permissible.

PUBLIC SCHOOLS

Two landmark decisions governing use of public schools by outside organizations include the United States Supreme Court's opinion in *Lamb's Chapel v. Center Moriches Union Free School District*[13] and *Good News Club v. Milford Central School District.*[14] In *Lamb's Chapel,* New York law authorized local school boards to adopt reasonable regulations permitting the after-hours use of school property for ten specified purposes. Religious purposes were excluded from the specified purposes. In fact, the school district, while allowing use of its facilities to secular organizations, specifically prohibited use to any group for religious purposes. A pastor of an evangelical church requested to use the school facilities to show a six-part film series containing lectures by Dr. James Dobson. The content of the film series included traditional

---

[13]508 U.S. 384 (1993).
[14]533 U.S. 98 (2001).

Christian family values. Because the content was religious, the school district denied the church's request.

Since the school offered use of its facilities to outside secular organizations, the United States Supreme Court agreed that the school had become a limited public forum. The school argued that it was offering use of its facilities to religious groups in a nondiscriminatory manner, namely that it did not allow any religious group to use its facilities. Indeed, the principle that had previously emerged from Supreme Court opinions was that "the First Amendment forbids the government to regulate speech in ways that favor some viewpoints or ideas at the expense of others."[15]

The school also argued that to allow use of its facilities by religious organizations would violate the First Amendment Establishment Clause because of the appearance that the school was endorsing religion. However, the United States Supreme Court rejected this argument, stating that because the school offered use of its facilities to other secular organizations, "there would have been no realistic danger that the community would think that the District was endorsing religion or any particular creed, and any benefit to religion or to the Church would have been no more than incidental."[16] In short, the school violated the First Amendment when it offered use of its facilities to secular organizations but denied use of the same facilities to a religious organization.

The *Good News Club* case involved an adult-initiated, adult-led, after-school religious club sponsored by Child

---

[15]*Members of City Council of L.A. v. Taxpayers for Vincent,* 466 U.S. 789, 804 (1984).

[16]*Lamb's Chapel,* 508 U.S. at 395.

Evangelism Fellowship. Good News Clubs are designed for children ages five to twelve. The clubs teach morals and character development from a decidedly Christian viewpoint. The Milford Central School District allowed groups like the Boy Scouts to meet on campus after school, which also addressed such topics as morals and character development. Although the parties to the case stipulated that the school opened its facilities to the public and created a limited public forum, the Court ruled that the nature of the forum was irrelevant because the district engaged in viewpoint-based discrimination. Thus, the "exclusion of the Club on the basis of its religious viewpoint constitutes unconstitutional viewpoint discrimination."[17] In other words, since the district allowed the subject matter of moral and character development by the after-school groups, the district could not prohibit a group from addressing this subject matter from a religious viewpoint. A limitation on viewpoint of a permitted subject matter is unconstitutional, regardless of the classification of the forum.

The principle is clear that if a school opens its facilities to the "community for meetings and discussions during non-school hours, then it becomes a public forum for the community" which cannot exclude religious groups.[18] A public school cannot prohibit a religious group from using its auditorium or other facilities when the same facilities are made

---

[17]533 U.S. at 107 n.2. For more information about use of public school facilities for after-school religious meetings, see chapter 3 entitled "Students' Rights on Public School Campuses." *See also* Mathew D. Staver, *Equal Access*, available by contacting Liberty Counsel at www.lc.org or at 1-800-671-1776.

[18]*Country Hills Christian Church v. Unified Sch. Dist.*, 560 F. Supp. 1207 (D. Kan. 1983).

available to nonreligious groups.[19] Moreover, if a school is a limited public forum for outside use purposes, religious organizations like churches may request use of the school facility to conduct, for example, a public school graduation ceremony.[20]

The Supreme Court of Delaware found that the University of Delaware's ban on use of its common facilities by students for religious activities was unconstitutional.[21] The court stated:

> The University cannot support its absolute ban of all religious worship on the theory that, without such a ban, University policy allowing all student groups, including religious groups, free access to dormitory common areas would necessarily violate the Establishment Clause. The Establishment cases decided by the United States Supreme Court indicate that neutrality is the safe harbor in which to avoid First Amendment violations: "neutral accommodation" of religion is permitted, while "promotion" and "advancement" of religion are not. University policy without the worship ban could be neutral towards religion and could have the primary effect of advancing

---

[19]*Gregoire v. Centennial Sch. Dist.,* 674 F. Supp. 172 (E.D. Pa. 1987); *see also Gregoire v. Centennial Sch. Dist.,* 907 F.2d 1366 (3d Cir. 1990), *cert. denied,* 498 U.S. 899 (1990).

[20]*Verbena United Methodist Church v. Chilton County Bd. of Educ.,* 765 F. Supp. 704 (M.D. Ala. 1991); *see also Shumway v. Albany County Sch. Dist. #1,* 826 F. Supp. 1320 (D. Wyo. 1993); *see also Pratt v. Arizona Bd. of Regents,* 110 Ariz. 466, 520 P.2d 514 (Ariz. 1974) (the Arizona Board of Regents did not violate the First Amendment Establishment Clause when it rented the Sun Devil Stadium to an evangelist for an evangelistic service).

[21]*Keegan v. University of Del.,* 349 A.2d 14 (Del. 1975), *cert. denied,* 424 U.S. 934 (1976).

education by allowing students to meet together in the common room of their dormitory to exchange ideas and share mutual interests. If any religious group or religion is accommodated or benefitted thereby, such accommodation or benefit is purely incidental, and would not, in our judgment, violate the Establishment Clause.[22]

One school allowed use of its facilities, including a public auditorium, to outside groups for secular use but denied access to a Christian meeting that included religious worship. The federal court sided with the Christian organization, stating that the public school could not prohibit the Christian organization from worshipping or having other religious activities in the auditorium.[23] It is impossible to draw the line between where worship begins and ends, and to permit such line drawing is itself unconstitutional.[24]

Some schools have charged rental fees for use of their facilities by religious organizations. Other schools have allowed churches to use their facilities as places of worship only if the church had a building permit or was actively seeking another site with the intention of moving from the public school. In *Fairfax Covenant Church v. Fairfax County School Board*,[25] the school district allowed a church to use its facilities as a place of worship. In addition to allowing the church to meet for Sunday worship, an array of other community groups was also allowed to rent the facilities during

---

[22]*Id.* at 16 (citations omitted).
[23]*Gregoire,* 907 F.2d at 1366.
[24]*See Widmar v. Vincent,* 454 U.S. 263 (1981).
[25]811 F. Supp. 1137 (E.D. Va. 1993).

weeknights and weekends. However, district policy provided that for the first five rental years, churches and religious groups were permitted to rent school facilities at the same rate as all other secular groups. After five years, only churches were required to pay the higher rate. Additionally, the district policy required churches to provide "satisfactory evidence of progress towards the construction or acquisition of a church site."[26] No other rental group was required to make such a showing.

The school board argued that it must treat religious groups differently from secular groups, especially when religious groups use the facilities on a long-term basis, because to do otherwise would violate the First Amendment Establishment Clause. The court reasoned that since the school facilities were open to other community groups, the school had created a limited public forum. The court noted that "religious speech cannot be barred from a limited public forum simply because it is religious speech."[27] Indeed, a limited public forum "does not confer any imprimatur of state approval on religious sects or practices."[28] The court stated that "by creating a forum generally open for use by various groups, the Fairfax County School Board does not thereby endorse or promote any of the particular ideas aired there."[29] The court further noted that "First Covenant Church cannot be treated differently from other groups that use the forum simply because of the content of its speech."[30] The court warned that to single out a religious

---

[26]*Id.* at 1138.
[27]*Id.* at 1139.
[28]*Widmar,* 454 U.S. at 274.
[29]*Fairfax Covenant Church,* 811 F. Supp. at 1139.
[30]*Id.*

organization as opposed to a secular organization violated not only the Free Speech Clause but also the Free Exercise Clause of the First Amendment.[31] Certainly "the government may not impose special disabilities on the basis of religious views or religious status."[32] Courts must "strictly scrutinize governmental classifications based on religion."[33] Finally, the court rejected the school's argument that it must exclude the religious organization to prevent a violation of the First Amendment Establishment Clause. Since the school offered use of its facilities to other secular groups, offering such use to a religious group did not raise any church/state problems. The court rejected the idea that it was providing a monetary benefit to the school, noting that "the Supreme Court has also ruled that it does not violate the Establishment Clause for religious groups to partake of governmental financial benefits that are available for everyone."[34] The result of the *Fairfax Covenant Church* case was that the policy requiring increased rent and evidence of

---

[31]*Id.* (relying on *Employment Div. v. Smith,* 494 U.S. 872 (1990)).

[32]*Smith,* 494 U.S. at 877.

[33]*Id.* at 886 n.3.

[34]*Fairfax Covenant Church,* 811 F. Supp. at 1141 (citing *Mueller v. Allen,* 463 U.S. 388 (1983)) (upholding the Minnesota tax deduction for student expenses at all schools including parochial schools); *Witters v. Washington Dep't of Serv. for the Blind,* 474 U.S. 481 (1986) (rejecting a claim by the State of Washington that it was required to ban a blind person from a state program funding the college educations of blind people because he wanted to go to a Bible college); *Bowen v. Kendrick,* 487 U.S. 589 (1988) (upholding a federal program to teach sexual chastity to teenagers that funded many secular as well as religious groups to promote that goal); *Walz v. Tax Comm'n,* 397 U.S. 664 (1970). Another case which could be cited, but which was not because it was not decided until after *Fairfax Covenant Church,* is the United States Supreme Court decision in *Zobrest v. Catalina Foothills Sch. Dist.,* 509 U.S. 1 (1993) (providing government funds for the services of an interpreter to a student attending a religious school does not violate the Establishment Clause).

progress toward the construction or acquisition of a church site was ruled unconstitutional. Since the school had overcharged the church $287,456, the court ordered that the money be refunded.[35]

The Gideons have a long tradition of coming on public school campuses to distribute Bibles to students. Although students clearly have the right to distribute Bibles to others students, depending on the circumstances, Gideons may or may not have that same right. Students have the right to distribute literature including Bibles because students are rightfully on campus and, in fact, are commanded to be there. However, when considering the use of public school facilities by outside persons or organizations, there is no absolute right to be on campus. The same analysis used in a limited public forum must be considered with respect to Gideon distribution of Bibles. For example, if a school allows use of its facilities after school hours to any secular organization, it must also allow use of that facility to a religious organization. The difference with Gideon distribution of Bibles is that it usually occurs during school hours rather than after school. The unique aspect here is that the Gideons actually distribute the Bibles to the students. Some courts have ruled that Gideon distribution of Bibles is unconstitutional,[36] while others have

---

[35]*Fairfax Covenant Church v. Fairfax County Sch. Bd.,* 17 F.3d 703 (4th Cir. 1994). The Fourth Circuit Court of Appeals affirmed the lower court's decision that the school policy violated the Constitution. The appellate court applied the decision retroactively and thus required the school district to refund the overcharged rent.

[36]*See, e.g., Berger v. Rensselaer Cent. Sch. Corp.,* 982 F.2d 1160 (7th Cir.), *cert. denied,* 508 U.S. 911 (1993); *Bacon v. Bradley-Bourbonnais High Sch. Dist. No. 307,* 707 F. Supp. 1005 (C.D. Ill. 1989); *Goodwin v. Cross County Sch. Dist. No. 7,* 394 F. Supp. 417 (E.D. Ark. 1973).

ruled that Gideons may distribute Bibles to public school students.[37] To determine whether Gideons distributing Bibles to a public school student is constitutional, three factors must be considered. First, if the school allows other outside organizations to come on campus to distribute information to public school students, then the school has probably created a limited public forum and, therefore, cannot prohibit religious persons or groups from coming on campus to distribute their literature. Second, the place of distribution is also important. It is better to distribute the material in the hallways from a table, so that willing students may approach and those who are not interested may pass. In this manner, an announcement could be made indicating that the literature is available but that no student is required or compelled to accept the material. Distributing Bibles to all of the school students in class may be considered by some courts unconstitutional. Finally, the time of the distribution may also be important. The timing could be prior to or immediately after the official school day begins or ends.

Public Libraries

Public libraries are governed by the same analysis used above for public schools. Both are public facilities. Whenever a public library opens its facilities for use by the general public, it creates a limited public forum. When this occurs, religious organizations must receive equal treatment.

---

[37]*Meltzer v. Board of Pub. Instruction of Orange County,* 548 F.2d 559 (5th Cir. 1977), rev'd in part, aff'd in part on reh'g, 577 F.2d 311 (5th Cir. 1978) (en banc), cert. denied, 439 U.S. 1089 (1979); *Peck v. Upshur County Bd. of Educ.,* 941 F. Supp. 1465 (N.D. W.Va. 1996); *Schanou v. Lancaster County Sch. Dist. No. 160,* 863 F. Supp. 1048 (D. Neb. 1994).

Unfortunately, many libraries have unconstitutional policies that specifically prohibit use of facilities by political or religious organizations.

One library in Wisconsin had a community room which it ironically named, "The Constitution Room." The name was prominently displayed over the door entrance, and the Constitution along with the Declaration of Independence were displayed inside. However, the library policy banned religious and political viewpoints. Chris Pfeifer's application to use the room to discuss creation science was denied when the library learned he intended to open the meeting with prayer and to use the Bible during his scientific lecture. Finding the policy unconstitutional, the court observed: "It may be that the exclusion of partisan political meetings and religious services or instruction is based on the Library's desire to avoid controversy. However, the avoidance of controversy is not a valid ground for restricting speech in a public forum."[38]

Concerned Women for America came face-to-face with one of these discriminatory policies in Mississippi. The library had created a limited public forum, with its policy allowing outside persons use of its facilities for meetings of "civic, cultural or educational character." However, the policy specifically excluded use of its facilities by religious groups. The federal court rightfully found that this exclusion violated the First Amendment.[39]

---

[38]*Pfeifer v. City of West Allis,* 91 F. Supp. 2d 1253, 1267 (E.D. Wis. 2000).
[39]*Concerned Women for America v. Lafayette County,* 883 F.2d 32, 34 (5th Cir. 1989).

Public Housing Facilities

There are public housing facilities in almost every city or county. These facilities often have general meeting rooms which are used by the residents and frequently made available to the general public. Sometimes religious tenants or outside religious groups have been discriminated against when attempting to use these types of public facilities. The analysis in a public housing facility is basically the same as it is for schools and libraries. The only difference is whether the person requesting the meeting is a tenant or a nontenant. For example, it is permissible under the First Amendment for a public housing facility to exclude all nontenants, because the government may limit the intended use of the facility.

If use of the facilities is allowed for any tenant, then there must be no discrimination based upon the content of the tenant's speech. Tenants who use such a facility for religious Bible studies or religious purposes should be allowed the same use as tenants who use it for secular purposes. Likewise, if use of the facilities is offered to nontenants, a nontenant speaker should be treated equally, even if the content of the speech is religious.[40]

A tenant living in a public housing facility in Atlanta wanted to use the facility to conduct a Bible study. Although the housing authority allowed use of its facilities by tenants for secular purposes, it tried to discriminate against this tenant. Part of the reasoning was that the use of the facilities by

---

[40]In addition to the protection against discrimination afforded by the First Amendment, a tenant who is discriminated against on the basis of religion regarding use of the public facility may also rely upon the Fair Housing Act. *See* 42 U.S.C. § 3601–19.

tenants should benefit all tenants rather than just a few. After several requests, a representative of the housing authority agreed to allow use of the facilities for a Bible study on Friday evenings. However, since many of the tenants were elderly, the Friday evening time was not convenient, in that most were in their homes. Over the objection of the tenant, the housing authority would not change its position. Consequently, the tenant conducted the Bible study anyway during the day at another time. The housing authority called the police and had the tenant arrested for conducting the Bible study. The federal court of appeals ruled that the housing authority violated the First Amendment by limiting the time for the Bible study to a Friday night, when it did not equally apply this time limitation to other secular usages.[41] If the housing authority allows use of its facilities by tenants or nontenants for secular purposes, it must offer its facilities on an equal basis to tenants or non-tenants who seek to conduct religious meetings.

In another case, a Tallahassee housing authority allowed use of its facilities by tenants and nontenants for secular meetings. One day when a Christian organization was con-ducting a meeting, the director of the facility noted that the leader of the group was reading from the Bible. He inter-rupted the meeting and later told the leader that he did not want any "Jesus stuff" in his facility. Liberty Counsel worked for several months with the organization to no avail. After filing a federal lawsuit, the Tallahassee Housing Author-ity agreed to allow the tenants and nontenants equal access to its facilities. In a similar case, a nursing home in

---

[41]*Crowder v. Housing Auth. of the City of Atlanta,* 990 F.2d 586 (11th Cir. 1993).

Albuquerque, New Mexico, refused to allow a showing of the film *Jesus*. This film, prepared by Campus Crusade for Christ, has been translated into more languages than any other film in history and has been shown throughout the United States and the world. Amazingly, the nursing home refused to allow the film on the basis that it would violate the "separation of church and state." A federal court of appeals ruled that the public facility violated the Constitution by discriminating against the film solely because of its Christian content.[42]

SHOPPING MALLS

The issue of shopping malls has proven to be difficult for the United States Supreme Court. If the shopping mall is owned by a governmental entity, then the first consideration is whether the government has opened use of the shopping mall to outside persons for expressive activity. If so, those desiring access to the government-owned facility cannot be turned away simply because the content of their speech is religious.

However, most shopping malls are privately owned. As such, there is no government action in the purest sense and, therefore, no application of the First Amendment. Notwithstanding, the issue has been unclear from its inception.

The United States Supreme Court developed a doctrine known as the "public function doctrine" which should be

---

[42]*Church on the Rock v. City of Albuquerque*, 84 F.3d 1273 (10th Cir. 1996). Even after the public facility lost its battle at the federal court of appeals level, it took an emergency petition to the United States Supreme Court in a final attempt to block the film. The Supreme Court refused to hear the case. Later the film *Jesus* was shown without incident.

distinguished from the public forum doctrine discussed earlier in this chapter. One authority describes it as follows:

> It is now clear that constitutional limitations on state activities restrict the manner in which governmental functions are conducted. If private persons are engaged in the exercise of governmental functions their activities are subject to similar constitutional restrictions. The state cannot free itself from the limitations of the Constitution in the operations of its governmental functions merely by delegating certain functions to otherwise private individuals. If private actors assume the role of the state by engaging in these governmental functions then they subject themselves to the same limitations on their freedom of action as would be imposed upon the state itself.[43]

A private person who engages in activity that could be performed by a governmental entity does not transform the activity into a public function. Only "those activities or functions which are traditionally associated with sovereign governments, and which are operated almost exclusively by governmental entities . . . will be deemed public functions."[44]

---

[43]Nowak, Rotunda, & Young, CONSTITUTIONAL LAW 477–78 (5th ed., West Pub. Co., 1995).

[44]*Id.* Courts have found state action where there is a symbiotic relationship between the private actor and the state, where the state commands or encourages the private discriminatory action, where a private party carries on a traditional public function, or where the involvement of the governmental authority aggravates or contributes to unlawful conduct. *Symbiotic Relationship. See Burton v. Willimington Parking Auth.,* 365 U.S. 715 (1961) (private restaurant located within a public parking garage which leased the space from the city where improvements were tax-exempt held

In 1946 the United States Supreme Court considered a case involving a "company town" which was located on privately owned land that included residential and commercial districts. The Golf Shipbuilding Corporation owned and governed the area but had no direct connection with governmental authorities. Jehovah's Witnesses wished to distribute religious literature in the area but were prohibited from doing so. The Supreme Court found this prohibition against literature distribution a violation of the First Amendment.[45] The Court reasoned that the state allowed private ownership of land and property to such a degree as to allow the private corporation to replace all the functions and activities which would normally belong to a city. Since the area served as the equivalent to a community shopping district in a city, the First Amendment was applicable.

---

to be state actor). *State Commands or Encourages Private Discriminatory Action. See Rendell-Baker v. Kohn,* 457 U.S. 830 (1982) (state action exists where state has exercised coercive power or has provided significant encouragement to the private discriminatory conduct); *Jackson v. Metropolitan Edison Co.,* 419 U.S. 345 (1974) (initiative for the discriminatory conduct must come from the state, not the private actor) *Public Function. See Evans v. Newton,* 382 U.S. 296 (1966) (a park given by a private party to the City of Macon acting as trustee of the park which the City maintained as a public facility for whites only, was a public function); *Flagg Bros., Inc. v. Brooks,* 436 U.S. 149, 159 n.8 (1978) (limiting the holding of *Evans* because there "the transfer had not been shown to have eliminated the actual involvement of the City in the daily maintenance and care of the park"). *Government Aggravates or Contributes to Unlawful Private Conduct. See Edmonson v. Leesville Concrete Co., Inc.,* 500 U.S. 614, 624 (1991) (where the government has "elected to place it power, property and prestige behind the alleged discrimination" the court will find state action of the private conduct). *See also Shelley v. Kraemer,* 334 U.S. 1 (1948) (state action found in court enforcement of a racially restrictive covenant).
[45]*Marsh v. Alabama,* 326 U.S. 501 (1946).

The Court considered a similar issue in 1968. Logan Valley Plaza was a privately owned shopping center where striking laborers attempted to picket a store during a labor dispute. The Supreme Court ruled that the shopping center was the functional equivalent of a company town, and therefore the picketers were protected by the First Amendment.[46] The Supreme Court in *Lloyd Corporation* altered its opinion in 1972, when confronted with a group of antiwar demonstrators who desired to enter a private shopping mall to distribute literature. The High Court attempted to distinguish this case from the two previous cases on the basis that in *Logan Valley Plaza,* the labor picketing was directly related to the shopping mall, but here the antiwar literature distribution was not related to the shopping center's purpose, and consequently, the private mall could prohibit the literature distribution.[47]

Finally, in 1976 the Supreme Court ruled in *Hudgens* that the First Amendment does not apply to privately owned shopping centers. Unfortunately, the members of the Court could not agree on how they reached that decision. A majority agreed that the result in denying the application of the First Amendment to a private shopping mall was permissible in this particular case.[48] Justice Stevens did not take part in the decision. Two Justices wrote opinions concurring in the result but specifically mentioned that the prior Supreme Court decision in *Logan Valley Plaza* was not overruled, while two other Justices dissented relying upon the prior decision in *Logan Valley Plaza.*

---

[46]*Amalgamated Food Employees Union v. Logan Valley Plaza,* 391 U.S. 308 (1968).
[47]*Lloyd Corp. v. Tanner,* 407 U.S. 551 (1972).
[48]*Hudgens v. NLRB,* 424 U.S. 507 (1976).

One other case is relevant to this inquiry. In 1980 the United States Supreme Court in *Pruneyard Shopping Center* considered a case involving provisions of the California state constitution, which specifically granted access for free speech purposes to privately owned property. The private property owners argued that this state constitutional provision violated their Due Process rights under the federal Constitution. The Supreme Court ruled that the state constitutional provision did not violate Due Process or constitute the unlawful taking of property.[49] The Court noted that its 1976 ruling in *Hudgens* did not preclude a state from granting free speech protection in privately owned shopping centers.

As is clear from the analysis above, the private shopping center issue is far from settled. Clearly, if a shopping center is a governmentally owned institution, the First Amendment is applicable, and presumably literature could be distributed and placards could be held at such malls. Verbal discussion should clearly be permitted at such malls. If the shopping center is privately owned, the Supreme Court's position is somewhat murky. If the shopping mall is performing a public function, presumably the First Amendment would apply. However, if the shopping mall is solely private in nature, the most recent Supreme Court opinion holds that the First Amendment would not apply. The Supreme Court also has ruled, however, that states may grant protection to free speech and association at privately owned shopping malls. Several states currently grant free speech access to privately owned facilities.

---

[49]*Pruneyard Shopping Ctr. v. Robins,* 447 U.S. 74 (1980) (California's State Constitution prohibited the use of trespass laws by shopping center owners to exclude peaceful distribution of literature and petitions in the mall area of the shopping center).

While the federal Constitution may not afford a general right to free speech in privately owned shopping centers, courts in at least five states have found limited free speech rights under their state constitutions. These states include California,[50] Colorado,[51] Massachusetts,[52] New Jersey,[53] and Washington.[54] However, several other states that have considered this matter found no state constitutional basis for allowing expressive activity on private property. These states include Arizona,[55] Connecticut,[56] Georgia,[57] Illinois,[58] Iowa,[59] Michigan,[60] Minnesota,[61] New Mexico,[62] New York,[63] North

[50]*Robins v. Pruneyard Shopping Ctr.*, 592 P.2d 341, 347 (Cal. 1979), *aff'd*, 447 U.S. 74 (1980); *see also NLRB v. Calkins*, 187 F.3d 1080 (9th Cir. 1999), *cert. denied*, 529 U.S. 1098 (2000).

[51]*Bock v. Westminster Mall Co.*, 819 P.2d 55 (Colo. 1991).

[52]*Batchelder v. Allied Stores Int'l*, 445 N.E.2d 590, 593 (Mass. 1983).

[53]*New Jersey Coalition against War in the Middle East v. JMB Realty Corp.*, 650 A.2d 757 (N.J. 1994); *State v. Schmid*, 423 A.2d 615 (N.J. 1980), appeal dismissed sub nom. *Princeton Univ. v. Schmid*, 455 U.S. 100 (1982).

[54]*Alderwood Assoc. v. Washington Env't Council*, 635 P.2d 108 (Wash. 1981). This holding is limited to the collection of signatures for constitutional initiatives. Outside of this limited holding, there is no general right to free speech in private shopping malls in Washington. *See Southcenter Joint Venture v. National Democratic Policy Comm.*, 780 P.2d 1282 (Wash. 1989).

[55]*Fiesta Mall Venture v. Mecham Recall Comm.*, 767 P.2d 719 (Ariz. Ct. App. 1989).

[56]*United Food and Commercial Workers Union, Local 919, AFL-CIO, Crystal Mall Assoc.*, 852 A.2d 659 (Conn. 2004). *Cologne v. Westfarms Assoc.*, 469 A.2d 1201 (Conn. 1984).

[57]*Citizens for Ethical Gov't v. Gwinnett Place Assoc.*, 392 S.E.2d 8 (Ga. 1990).

[58]*Illinois v. DiGuida*, 604 N.E.2d 336 (Ill. 1992).

[59]*West Des Moines v. Engler*, 641 N.W.2d 803 (Iowa 2002).

[60]*Woodland v. Michigan Citizens Lobby*, 378 N.W.2d 337 (Mich. 1995).

[61]*Minnesota v. Wicklund*, 589 N.W.2d 793 (Minn. 1999).

[62]*Southwest Comm. Resources, Inc. v. Simon Property Group, LP*, 108 F. Supp. 2d 1239 (D. New Mexico (2000) (First Amendment of the United States Constitution does not apply to private mall).

[63]*SHAD Alliance v. Smith Haven Mall*, 488 N.E.2d 1211 (N.Y. 1985).

Carolina,[64] Ohio,[65] Oregon,[66] Pennsylvania,[67] South Carolina,[68] and Wisconsin.[69] Most of the state courts that found no constitutional right to engage in expressive activity on private property analyzed their state constitutions.[70] However, some relied primarily on federal constitutional doctrine without independently analyzing their own state constitutions.[71]

California,[72] Colorado,[73] Massachusetts,[74] New Jersey,[75] and Washington[76] have held that their citizens have a limited state constitutional right to engage in certain types of expressive conduct at privately owned malls. Of these five, only California and New Jersey found that their state constitutional right to free speech protects citizens from private action as well as state action and grants issue-oriented free speech rights at regional shopping centers. The other three states have granted limited access to private shopping centers for expressive activity. For example, Massachusetts only permits political speech in private shopping centers on the basis that

---

[64]*State v. Felmet*, 273 S.E.2d 708 (N.C. 1981).
[65]*Eastwood Mall v. Slanco*, 626 N.E.2d 59 (Ohio 1994).
[66]*Stranaham v. Fred Meyer, Inc.*, 11 P.3d 228 (Ore. 2000).
[67]*Western Pa., Socialist Workers 1982 Campaign v. Connecticut Gen. Life Ins. Co.*, 515 A.2d 1331 (Pa. 1986).
[68]*Charleston Joint Venture v. McPherson*, 417 S.E.2d 544 (S.C. 1992).
[69]*Jacobs v. Major*, 407 N.W.2d 832 (Wis. 1987).
[70]*E.g., SHAD Alliance*, 488 N.E.2d at 1211; *Eastwood Mall*, 626 N.E.2d at 59.
[71]*E.g., Southwest Comm. Resources, Inc.*, 108 F. Supp. 2d at 1239; *Citizens for Ethical Gov't*, 392 S.E.2d at 8; *Felmet*, 273 S.E.2d at 708.
[72]*Robins*, 592 P.2d at 347.
[73]*Bock*, 819 P.2d at 55.
[74]*Batchelder*, 445 N.E.2d at 590.
[75]*New Jersey Coalition*, 650 A.2d at 757.
[76]*Alderwood*, 635 P.2d at 108.

its state constitution places high priority on free elections and the right of its citizens to elect officers to public office.[77] The Massachusetts Supreme Court did not base its ruling on the state's constitutional free speech provision but instead focused on another state constitutional provision which guarantees free elections and the right to be elected. The political activity in the Massachusetts case involved a person's attempt to solicit signatures for his nomination as a congressional candidate. The Massachusetts court ruled that shopping centers must permit solicitation of signatures for ballot access because of its fundamental importance to the state's form of government. The court ruling is limited to that narrow issue. The court also stated that shopping centers may impose reasonable regulations as to time, place, and manner with respect to the solicitation of signatures.

Colorado relied upon its state constitution's free speech provision when finding that a political activist had a constitutional right to distribute literature at a privately owned mall.[78] Like the United States Supreme Court, the state of Washington has vacillated on this issue. However, it still appears that the Washington state constitution provides some right to distribute literature or solicit signatures for constitutional initiatives at private shopping malls.[79]

---

[77]*Batchelder,* 445 N.E.2d at 590.

[78]*Bock,* 819 P.2d at 55.

[79]In *Alderwood Associates,* 635 P.2d at 108, a majority of the Washington Supreme Court ruled that it was improper to issue a court order against a group seeking to collect signatures at a private shopping mall. However, a four-justice plurality, rather than a majority, concluded that the state's constitutional free speech clause did not require state action. In other words, the state's free speech provision not only applied to government actors, but to private shopping centers, thereby prohibiting private shopping centers

Although Nevada law does not afford the right to free speech in a private shopping mall, one court accorded constitutional rights in the context of what might be called a government shopping mall.[80] The Fremont Street Experience Mall in Las Vegas was created pursuant to state law and local ordinance. The Pedestrian Mall Act was designed to provide an attraction in order to compete with the Strip and bring tourists and business back to the sagging downtown casinos and businesses. The City contracted with a private entity to construct, operate, and maintain the Mall. Although downtown casinos contributed $25 million to the Mall's initial $70 million cost, the private contractor was responsible for paying the Mall's operation and maintenance expenses. The federal court found that the antileafletting ordinance had no rational basis and invalidated the restriction under the Equal Protection Clause of the Fourteenth Amendment.[81] The court then considered the "mall vending" restriction which applied

---

from excluding free speech. Later in the case of *Southcenter Joint Venture v. National Democratic Policy Committee,* 780 P.2d 1282 (Wash. 1989), the Washington Supreme Court, in a deeply divided decision, rejected the four-justice plurality position in *Alderwood* and instead held that the state's free speech provision does not protect speech on private property. Interestingly, the opinion in *Southcenter* did not disturb or reverse the remainder of the holding in *Alderwood*—that in fact there is a right to solicit signatures on private property under the state constitution's initiative provision. It appears that the Washington Supreme Court's position is that the state constitution's free speech clause does not grant a right to solicit signatures or distribute literature at private shopping malls, but the state constitution does provide a right to solicit signatures for certain political issues under its initiative provision. Thus, the right to distribute literature or solicit signatures in private shopping malls in Washington appears to be limited to ballot initiatives.
[80]*ACLU of Nevada v. City of Las Vegas,* 13 F. Supp. 2d 1064 (D. Nev. 1998), *appeal dismissed,* 168 F.3d 497 (9th Cir. 1999).
[81]*Id.* at 1078–79.

to the distribution, display, or sale of consumer goods or services from a pushcart, concession stand, kiosk, or other similar structure. The local ordinance gave the private contractor in charge of operating the mall the right to grant or deny the request but provided little guidelines for the contractor to follow. Thus, the court found that the private contractor was vested with unbridled discretion, and since there was nothing to ensure that the contractor would not engage in unlawful censorship, the law was unconstitutional under the First Amendment.[82]

Some courts have ruled that a shopping center "now performs a traditional public function by providing the functional equivalent of a town center or community business block."[83] In 1950 there were fewer than 100 privately owned shopping centers throughout the country.[84] The number of larger regional shopping malls grew to 105 by 1967. This number continued to grow to 199 in 1972 and 333 in 1978.[85] Shopping centers continued to expand to at least 1,835 by the year 1992.[86] During the twenty-year time period from 1972 to 1992, the number of regional shopping centers grew by approximately 800 percent. A New Jersey court remarked that "malls are where the people can be found today."[87] The

---

[82]*Id.* at 1081–82.

[83]*Alderwood,* 635 P.2d at 117. *But see Southcenter Joint Venture,* 780 P.2d at 1282.

[84]Steven J. Eagle, *Shopping Center Control: The Developer Besieged,* 51 J. URB. L. 585, 586 (1974).

[85]Thomas Muller, *Regional Malls and Central City Retail Sales: An Overview,* SHOPPING CENTERS: USA 180, 189 (1991).

[86]*Shopping Center World/NRB 1992 Shopping Center Census,* SHOPPING CENTER WORLD, Mar. 1993, at 38 n.8.

[87]*New Jersey Coalition,* 650 A.2d at 765.

shopping center industry frequently refers to large shopping malls as "the new downtowns."[88]

One industry expert observed, "The suburban victory in the regional retail war was epitomized by the enclosed regional mall. . . . [Regional malls] serve as the new "main streets" of the region—the dominant form of general merchandise retailing.[89] Another expert has pointed out that shopping centers have "evolved beyond the strictly retail stage to become a public square where people gather," and such malls provide "a place for exhibitions that no other space can offer."[90]

Several legal commentators have written that today's shopping malls are the functional equivalent of yesterday's downtown business districts. One commentator stated that "privately owned shopping centers are supplanting those traditional public business districts where free speech once flourished."[91] Indeed, the "privately held shopping center now serves as the public trading area for much of metropolitan America."[92] While it seems obvious that today's privately owned regional shopping malls perform the functional equivalent of yesterday's downtown business districts, not all

---

[88]Note, *Private Abridgment of Speech in the State Constitutions,* 90 YALE L.J. 165, 168 n.19 (1980) (citation omitted).

[89]James W. Hughes and George Sternlieb, *3 Rutgers Reg'l Report,* RETAILING IN REGIONAL MALLS 71 (1991).

[90]*Specialty Malls Return to the Public Square Image,* SHOPPING CENTER WORLD, Nov. 1995, at 104.

[91]James M. McCauley, *Transforming the Privately owned Shopping Center into a Public Forum: Pruneyard Shopping Center v. Robin,* 15 U. RICH. L. REV. 699, 721 (1981).

[92]Note, *Private Abridgment of Speech in the State Constitutions,* 90 YALE L.J. 168 n.19 (1980).

courts agree. In fact, one court specifically noted that shopping malls "are not the functional equivalent of towns."[93] Although privately owned regional shopping malls may have supplanted yesterday's town forums, courts have been reluctant to extend free speech rights to these facilities, primarily because of their privately owned nature. There is an inherent tension between the shrinking of the town forum with its reemergence in privately owned shopping malls and government intrusion into privately owned businesses.

In summary, five states allow some free speech activity in private shopping centers. In California and New Jersey, there are state constitutional free speech rights to distribute political and nonpolitical literature in private shopping malls. Colorado provides a state constitutional free speech right to distribute political literature in private malls. It is possible that Colorado courts might extend this right to nonpolitical literature. Massachusetts, and Washington offer a state constitutional right to distribute literature and solicit signatures regarding political elections and ballot access. This right is not based on free speech and has not yet been extended generally to all political issues or to nonpolitical issues. Overall it appears the Supreme Court is confused on this matter.

PUBLIC ARENAS

Public arenas may be considered limited public forums if the facilities are opened to certain expressive activities. If these facilities are not open to any expressive activities, they may be analyzed under a nonpublic forum analysis outlined below. Many public stadiums allow private citizens to hang

---

[93] *Fiesta Mall Venture*, 767 P.2d at 724.

banners in the seating area. We have all seen these banners during Monday night football, supporting or opposing a particular team.

In the city of Cincinnati, a baseball fan whose religious sign was confiscated by stadium security officials during a World Series game filed a lawsuit challenging the constitutionality of the team's banner policy. The banner policy permitted fans to hang signs only if they were in "good taste." A federal court found this policy unconstitutionally vague and overbroad and, therefore, ruled in favor of the religious banner.[94]

A football fan, who regularly attended RFK Stadium to watch the Washington Redskins, claimed that his constitutional rights were violated when stadium officials removed his banner.[95] This football fan hung the banner with the Scripture verse John 3:16 in the end zone area so that it would be clearly visible on television. Stadium officials removed the banner because of its religious content. Since stadium officials allowed other secular banners to be placed within the stadium by private fans, the stadium was prohibited from restricting the banner solely because of its religious message.

In Fargo, North Dakota, Martin Wishnatsky sought to distribute small pamphlet Bibles to people entering the thirty-thousand-seat Fargodome. Mr. Wishnatsky wanted to distribute these pamphlet Bibles in a public area located at the stadium's entrance. The Fargodome attracts people from three surrounding states who come for rock concerts, Christian

---

[94]*Aubrey v. City of Cincinnati,* 815 F. Supp. 1100 (S.D. Ohio 1993).
[95]*Stewart v. District of Columbia Armory Bd.,* 863 F.2d 1013 (D.C. Cir. 1988).

concerts, football games, and other public events. Fargo officials threatened to arrest Mr. Wishnatsky if he did not cease distributing Bibles. Liberty Counsel filed suit against the Fargodome Authority and the City of Fargo, claiming that Mr. Wishnatsky had a constitutional right to distribute the Bibles. After the lawsuit was filed, city officials cooperated with Liberty Counsel to draft a new policy. The first month after the policy was put into place, Mr. Wishnatsky distributed one thousand Bibles. In the second and third months after the policy was adopted, he distributed another one thousand Bibles each month for a total of three thousand Bibles in only three months. Mr. Wishnatsky continues to distribute Bibles at the Fargodome to thousands of people who attend the public events held there each year.

In summary, public arenas may be analyzed under a traditional public forum, a limited public forum, or nonpublic forum analysis. The analysis under a traditional public forum would occur on the public sidewalk area or entranceways surrounding the arena. A limited forum analysis applies in certain places that do not fall within the traditional public forum context (streets, sidewalks, or parks) but where the facility has been opened for use by the general public. A nonpublic forum analysis generally occurs if the expressive activity takes place inside the facility at a location that is not generally open to indiscriminate expressive activities. At any rate, public forums provide a unique opportunity for freedom of speech.

OTHER PUBLIC FACILITIES

Other public facilities which do not fall into the category of parks, streets, or sidewalks, or which are not specifically mentioned above, can also be considered limited public forums.[96] Such facilities can be any public place that allows use by the community. This applies to buildings or nonbuildings. For example, a court ruled that a rotunda in a state capitol was a limited public forum if expressive activities such as political, religious, or other varieties of symbolic speech had been permitted in the past.[97] When considering the nature of the forum, focus must be on the access being sought. For example, Christ's Bride Ministries sought to display posters on an advertising board within the Philadelphia transportation terminal.[98] The transportation authority argued that the facility was a nonpublic forum, but Liberty Counsel argued that the access being sought was not to the facility as a whole but to the specific advertising board. The court ruled that the advertising board had been opened to the public for advertising upon payment of the required advertising fee and was, thus, a limited public forum. The court also found that when the authority revoked the advertising contract following its determination that the message publicizing the link between breast cancer and abortion was too controversial, it violated the First Amendment. Similarly, another court found that the advertising space on the outside of public transportation

---

[96]A public fair may be an ideal location for expressive activity. *See Heffron v. ISKCON*, 452 U.S. 640 (1981). This case involved a state fair which designated a specific location for the distribution or sales of literature for both secular and religious groups. The Krishna group wanted to be in a different location, but the court upheld the place regulation because it was applied evenly to secular and religious groups.

[97]*Chabad-Lubavitch of Georgia v. Miller*, 5 F.3d 1383 (11th Cir. 1993) (*en banc*).

[98]*Christ's Bride Ministries, Inc. v. Southeastern Pennsylvania Transp. Auth.*, 148 F.3d 242 (3d Cir. 1998), *cert. denied*, 525 U.S. 1068 (1999). *See also Focus on the Family v. Pinellas Suncoast Transit Auth.*, 344 F.3d 1263 (11th Cir. 2003).

buses was a limited public forum.[99] When the transportation authority rejected a pro-union advertisement because it might be controversial, the court found that the authority violated the First Amendment.

Nonpublic Forums

AIRPORTS, METROS, RAILS, AND BUS STATIONS

Airports, metros, rail stations, and bus stations are ideal places for First Amendment expressive activity. Millions of people traverse through these public transportation facilities every year, many of them from around the country and many from around the world. Such places are ideal locations for the distribution of religious literature.

An airport does not fall into the category of a traditional public forum, which includes public parks, streets, and sidewalks. Consequently, its facilities are not automatically deemed to be open to the public. Moreover, airports, like the other forms of public transportation facilities, generally do not intentionally open their facilities for expressive activity by outside organizations and, therefore, are not usually considered limited public forums. This third type of public forum is known as a nonpublic forum. In nonpublic forums, the government regulation "need only be reasonable, as long as the regulation is not an effort to suppress the speaker's activity due to disagreement with the speaker's view."[100] Thus,

---

[99]*United Food & Commercial Workers Union, Local 1099 v. Southwest Ohio Reg'l Transit Auth.*, 163 F.3d 341 (6th Cir. 1998).

[100]*Lee*, 505 U.S. at 679; *see also Arkansas Educ. Television Comm.*, 523 U.S. at 666 (television broadcast of candidate debate was a nonpublic forum from which the broadcaster could exclude a candidate so long as the exclusion was reasonable and viewpoint-neutral).

content-neutral and content-based restrictions on speech will be upheld so long as they are reasonable. However, viewpoint-based restrictions on an otherwise permissible subject matter are still *per se* unconstitutional.[101]

A restriction on speech in a nonpublic forum is reasonable when it is consistent with the government's legitimate interest in preserving the property for the use to which it is lawfully dedicated.[102] With respect to regulating literature distribution at airport facilities or other transportation facilities, "the reasonableness inquiry . . . is not whether the restrictions on speech are 'consistent with preserving the property' for air travel, but whether they are reasonably related to maintaining the multi-purpose environment that the authority has deliberately created."[103]

The Los Angeles International Airport formerly had a policy that prohibited all First Amendment activities within any of the airport facilities. When Jews for Jesus wanted to distribute religious literature, they were unable to do so because of this restriction. The United States Supreme Court ruled that this restriction on free speech was unreasonable and consequently violated the First Amendment.[104]

---

[101]See *Good News Club*, 533 U.S. at 98; *Lamb's Chapel*, 508 U.S. 384. In *Atlanta Journal and Constitution v. City of Atlanta Department of Aviation*, 322 F.3d 1298 (11th Cir. 2003) (*en banc*), the court found that the placement of for-profit publications in the Atlanta airport should be addressed under a nonpublic forum analysis and further found that the advertising plan was viewpoint-based and thus unconstitutional.

[102]*Arkansas Educ. Television Comm.*, 523 U.S. at 678.

[103]*Id.* (quoting Perry, 460 U.S. at 50–51).

[104]*Board of Airport Comm'rs of Los Angeles v. Jews for Jesus*, 482 U.S. 569 (1987).

In a case involving the International Society for Krishna Consciousness, the United States Supreme Court ruled that the New York Airport Authority could prohibit solicitation of funds at the airport facilities but could not prohibit the distribution of literature, because to do so violated the First Amendment. The court noted:

> Leafletting does not entail the same kinds of problems presented by face-to-face solicitation. Specifically, "one need not ponder the contents of a leaflet or pamphlet in order to mechanically take it out of someone's hand. . . . 'The distribution of literature does not require that the recipient stop in order to receive the message the speaker wishes to convey; instead the recipient is free to read the message at a later time.'" With the possible exception of avoiding litter, it is difficult to point to any problems intrinsic to the act of leafleting that would make it naturally incompatible with a large, multipurpose forum such as those at issue here.[105]

In ruling that airports cannot prohibit the distribution of religious literature, the Supreme Court looked at the nature and character of the airport. Airports are often, in a sense, like small cities. Many airports have restaurants, banking facilities, retail facilities, newspapers, and some even have hotel accommodations. These airports look, act, and sound like small cities. However, the Court did not classify modern airports as traditional public forums, simply because they have not been around as long as traditional public parks, streets, or

---

[105]*ISKCON*, 505 U.S. at 690 (citing *United States v. Kokinda*, 497 U.S. 720, 734 (1990) (O'Connor, J., concurring)).

sidewalks. Yet the nature and character of these airports are similar to traditional public forums. They provide a place for many people to meet, conduct business, and make transactions. They have sidewalks around the facilities and hallways for congregating. They have benches, restroom facilities, and for all practical purposes, operate like traditional public forums.

In one case, the Orlando International Airport required that anyone seeking to distribute literature must fill out a lengthy application form and wait at least three days prior to approval. The application form also required that the person distributing literature obtain $500,000 in liability insurance, naming the City of Orlando and the Greater Orlando Aviation Authority as additional insured, and wear a name badge identifying their name, home address, height, age, weight, eye color, hair color, principal occupation, and organization affiliation. During an international conference by the Gideon Bible Society, one Gideon was unable to obtain the $500,000 liability insurance policy. After correspondence between Liberty Counsel and the airport, the liability insurance policy was dropped from $500,000 to $100,000. However, other individuals seeking to distribute literature could not obtain the required policy. On behalf of Tom and Shirley Snyder, who wanted to distribute gospel tracts, Liberty Counsel filed suit against the Orlando International Airport. After filing suit, the airport dropped these restrictive requirements. The Snyders still frequently distribute gospel tracts at the airport. In one year, Orlando International Airport transports almost thirty million people through its facilities. Many of these people are from foreign countries visiting the entertainment facilities in Central Florida. In order to understand the magnitude of this mass of people, compare the number of airport visitors to the total population of the state of Florida, which is over seventeen million. More than twice the population of the state of Florida traverses through the Orlando International Airport every year. As a result of the Snyder's lawsuit, religious literature given out in Orlando literally goes around the entire world. The same can be true for other airports and other major locations of public transportation.

The same analysis applied to airports can be applied to metro or subway systems, railway systems, and bus stations. These facilities are very similar to airport facilities. In fact, one court ruled that literature distribution could not be prohibited by the Massachusetts Bay Transportation Authority within the subway system.[106] The Authority prohibited the distribution of any printed materials for political or nonprofit purposes, prohibiting all noncommercial expressive activities from the paid areas of the subway stations and from the free areas of at least twelve stations. Within the free areas of the remaining stations, the Authority required prior authorization to engage in noncommercial speech. For many years, Jews for Jesus had distributed religious literature throughout the paid areas of the transit system. The new policy prohibited distribution in these particular areas, whereupon Jews for Jesus filed suit. The Authority argued that the ban on literature distribution was necessary for the public safety. The Authority argued that leafletting threatened public safety by disrupting passenger flow and creating litter. Litter, in turn, could cause accidents and fires or other disruptions, especially if paper

---

[106]*Jews for Jesus v. Massachusetts Bay Transp. Auth.*, 984 F.2d 1319 (1st Cir. 1993).

clogged the switching devices on the tracks. The court re-marked, "Authority thus bears a heavy burden in justifying its absolute ban on leafletting, an activity that long has enjoyed the full protection of the First Amendment."[107] Noting that the Supreme Court had previously dismissed the danger to traffic congestion as a justification to ban leafletting, the court ruled that this flat ban in the subway area was unconstitutional.[108] In another case, a federal court found that a total ban on leafletting at Chicago's Navy Pier was not reasonable and, therefore, leafletting must be permitted.[109]

Nonpublic forums such as airports, metros, rail or subway systems, and bus stations are areas where First Amendment activity can occur. These are ideal areas for distributing religious literature because of the enormous number of people passing through these transportation facilities.

Discriminatory Fee Schemes

Equal access under the First Amendment does not end with the provision of access alone. Discriminatory financial schemes also violate the principle of equal access.

In *Rosenberger v. Rector & Visitors of the University of Virginia*,[110] the Supreme Court found that the placing of a "financial burden" on speech based on viewpoint is unconstitutional.

---

[107]*Id.* at 1324 (citing *Lovell v. City of Griffin*, 303 U.S. 444, 450–52 (1938)).
[108]*Id.* at 1324–25.
[109]*Chicago Acorn, SEIU Local No. 880 v. Metropolitan Pier and Exposition Auth.*, 150 F.3d 695 (7th Cir. 1998); *see also Chicago Acorn, SEIU Local No. 880 v. Metropolitan Pier and Exposition Auth.*, No. 96C4997, 1999 WL 413480 (N.D. Ill. June 2, 1999).
[110]515 U.S. at 819.

In the realm of private speech or expression, government regulation may not favor one speaker over another. Discrimination against speech because of its message is presumed unconstitutional. These rules informed our determination that *the government offends the First Amendment when it imposes financial burdens on certain speakers based on the content of their expression.* When the government targets not the subject matter, but particular views taken by the speakers on the subject, the violation of the First Amendment is all the more blatant. Viewpoint discrimination is thus an egregious form of content discrimination. The government must abstain from regulating speech when a specific motivating ideology or the opinion or perspective of the speaker is the rationale for the restriction.[111]

The Ninth Circuit decision in *Gentala v. City of Tuscon*,[112] illustrates the impact of the United States Supreme Court's decision in *Good News Club v. Milford Central School District*.[113] Although *Gentala* focused more on the Establishment Clause than the Free Speech Clause, the underlying principles are essentially the same for purposes of this Court's inquiry. The city of Tuscon maintains a Civic Events Fund, which consists of funds appropriated from its general coffers and derived from tax revenue. Organizers of eligible civic events may apply for payment from the fund of any fees incurred for the use of city equipment or services.[114]

---

[111]*Id.* at 828–29 (citations omitted) (emphasis added).
[112]244 F.3d 1065 (9th Cir. 2001) (*en banc*).
[113]533 U.S. 98 (2001).
[114]*Gentala,* 244 F.3d at 1069.

Organizers of a National Day of Prayer applied for $340.00 from the fund to pay for lighting and sound equipment and services. Their request for reimbursement was denied on the basis that the event involved religious services and organizations. The Ninth Circuit upheld the exclusion from the fund, stating that the violation of the Establishment Clause is a sufficiently compelling reason to justify exclusion from certain private speech in a forum otherwise dedicated to community activity.[115] The *Gentala* opinion was decided on March 30, 2001. Then on June 11, 2001, the United States Supreme Court handed down the decision in *Good News Club*. On October 9, 2001, the United States Supreme Court granted a Petition for Writ of Certiorari, vacated the judgment, and remanded the case to the Ninth Circuit for further consideration in light of *Good News Club*.[116] The *Good News Club* decision clearly cut the heart out of the *Gentala* decision, and thus the Ninth Circuit remanded the case to the district court for further consideration in light of *Good News Club*.[117] The history of the *Gentala* case illustrates that discriminating against a religious viewpoint from an otherwise permissible forum may not be upheld under the Establishment Clause. Moreover, under the free speech analysis, the imposition of a discriminatory fee must also be rejected.

At issue in *Simon & Schuster, Inc. v. Members of the New York State Crime Victims Board*,[118] was the so-called "Son of Sam" law, which required that income from an accused or

---

[115]*Id.* at 1073.
[116]*See Gentala v. City of Tuscon,* 534 U.S. 946 (2001).
[117]*See Gentala v. City of Tucson,* 275 F.3d 1160 (9th Cir. 2002) (*en banc*).
[118]502 U.S. at 105.

convicted criminal's written works describing the crime be deposited in an escrow account and then made available to victims of the crime as well as creditors. The court began the constitutional analysis by stating that a "statute is presumptively inconsistent with the First Amendment if it imposes a financial burden on speakers because of the content of their speech."[119] The court further addressed its distaste for financial burdens on speech:

> In the context of financial regulation, it bears repeating, as we did in *Leathers*, that the government's ability to impose content-based burdens on speech raises the specter that the government may effectively drive certain ideas or viewpoints from the marketplace. The First Amendment presumptively places this sort of discrimination beyond the power of government.[120]

In *Arkansas Writers' Project, Inc. v. Ragland*,[121] the Supreme Court found that the imposition of a discriminatory fee on a magazine was unconstitutional. The tax imposed on the magazine was imposed upon certain magazines depending upon

---

[119]*Id.* at 115 (emphasis added). Note the court used the broader subject matter term of "content" as opposed to the narrower word "viewpoint," which is an expression on the subject matter. If a financial burden placed on a speaker's "content" is presumed unconstitutional, then how much more will a financial burden imposed on a speaker's "viewpoint" be presumed unconstitutional? See *Rosenberger*, 515 U.S. at 828–29 ("When the government targets not the subject matter, but particular views taken by the speakers on the subject, the violation of the First Amendment is all the more blatant.").

[120]*Simon & Schuster*, 502 U.S. at 116 (citing *Leathers v. Medlock*, 499 U.S. 439, 448–49 (1991)).

[121]481 U.S. 221 (1987).

their content. The Court noted that if the *Arkansas Times* devoted its discussion to subjects of religion or sports, the magazine would be exempted from the sales tax, but because the articles dealt with a variety of subjects (which sometimes included religion and sports), the tax was imposed. Arkansas state law exempted from taxation certain subject matters, such as religion and sports, but did not exempt other subject matters. The *Arkansas Times* addressed a variety of issues, and since it addressed issues outside of the exempted subjects, the magazine was taxed. "Our cases clearly established that a discriminatory tax on the press burdens rights protected by the First Amendment."[122]

In *Fairfax Covenant Church v. Fairfax County School Board*,[123] the court struck down a school board policy that imposed different fees for religious use of school facilities than were imposed for secular use. The policy at issue allowed groups like the Boy Scouts and Girl Scouts, which provided activities for school children, to use the facilities with no fee. Cultural, civic and educational groups paid a noncommercial rate. Churches were allowed to use the facilities under the noncommercial rate for the first five years, but thereafter, the Church was required to pay the higher commercial rate. After paying the higher rate for a period of time, the Church challenged the policy. The court agreed with the Church, finding the policy unconstitutional because of the discriminatory fee between religious and nonreligious uses, and further rejected the school's Establishment Clause defense.[124] In support of its

---

[122]*Arkansas Writers' Project,* 481 U.S. at 227.
[123]17 F.3d at 703.
[124]*Id.* at 707.

conclusion, the court pointed to Supreme Court precedent in *Widmar*[125] and *Lamb's Chapel*.[126] The Fourth Circuit Court of Appeals in *Fairfax Covenant Church* found that the policy imposing different fees for religious use "discriminates against religious speech in violation of the Free Speech Clause."[127]

Placing different financial burdens or schemes on religious viewpoints is clearly unconstitutional.

Summary

Equal access to public facilities is an important liberty protected by the First Amendment. The first step in any equal access consideration is to identify the nature of the forum. A traditional public forum includes parks, streets and sidewalks. Limited or designated public forums include any public property, other than a street, sidewalk or park, which the government has intentionally opened for expressive activity. A nonpublic forum is anything that does not fall within either a traditional or a limited public forum. The second step is to identify the kind of restriction placed on speech within the forum. Reasonable time, place and manner restrictions may be placed on speech in a traditional or limited public forum,

---

[125]454 U.S. at 263 (finding that a university's denial of a student religious club from use of school facilities violated the right to free speech, and rejecting the university's Establishment Clause defense).

[126]508 U.S. at 384 (denying access to a public school facility to show a film addressing an otherwise permissible subject matter of family from a religious viewpoint is unconstitutional).

[127]17 F.3d at 707. The Supreme Court has clearly stated that "religious institutions need not be quarantined from public benefits that are neutrally available to all." *Roemer v. Maryland Bd. of Pub. Works,* 426 U.S. 736, 746 (1976).

so long as they are content-neutral. If content-based, then the government must show that it has a compelling interest in the restriction and that the governmental interest has been achieved by using the least restrictive means available. If the restriction is viewpoint-based, then it will most assuredly be invalid. Prior restraints on speech are presumptively unconstitutional. However, if the speech occurs in a nonpublic forum, the restriction must meet the less strict standard of reasonableness in light of the nature of the forum, and the restriction must be viewpoint-neutral.

Equal access encompasses not only access to public property for expressive activities but also equal treatment for similarly situated meetings in terms of fee schemes. It is just as discriminatory to exclude a speaker from a forum because of the viewpoint of the message as it is to allow access only on the condition that the speaker pay a fee amount which is not required of other similarly situated speakers. The First Amendment protects against overt and subtle acts of discrimination against speech.

9
RELIGIOUS SYMBOLS ON PUBLIC PROPERTY

THE RELATIONSHIP BETWEEN RELIGION and the United States Constitution is often misunderstood. Some have assumed that the Constitution requires total separation of church and state. However, according to the United States Supreme Court, "Total separation is not possible in the absolute sense. Some relationship between government and religious organizations is inevitable."[1]

Although some have argued that there must be a "wall of separation between church and state,"[2] the Supreme Court

---

[1]*Lemon v. Kurtzman,* 403 U.S. 602, 614 (1971).

[2]The so-called "wall of separation between church and state" is not in the Constitution. This phrase came from a letter written by Thomas Jefferson to a group of Danbury Baptists. President Jefferson assured the religious group that he had no intention of creating a national religious holiday wherein he would require the individual states to adhere to a sectarian doctrine. In this

has stated that this so-called "wall" metaphor is not an "accurate description" of the relationship between church and state.[3] Accordingly, the High Court has stated that it "has never been thought either possible or desirable to enforce a regime of total separation."[4] The Constitution does not "require complete separation of church and state; it affirmatively mandates accommodation, not merely tolerance, of all religions, and forbids hostility toward any."[5] Anything less than mandating affirmative accommodation of religion would require "callous indifference," which the Constitution never intended.[6]

---

sense President Jefferson is correct. The First Amendment did prohibit the federal government from establishing a national church or requiring sectarian policy to be imposed on the individual states. However, the "wall" metaphor has been used out of context. Thomas Jefferson was not involved in drafting the First Amendment. While the First Amendment was being drafted, he was in France. Moreover, Thomas Jefferson did not take the extreme separation view promoted by some organizations. As founder of the University of Virginia and chairman of the District of Columbia School Board, he saw no conflict with the study of Bible or the use of the Watts hymnal. He also declared that to exclude religious instruction from the public schools would create a great chasm in the public education system. While the First Amendment prohibits government from controlling religion and prohibits government from requiring sectarian support, it was never intended to prohibit people of faith from influencing government or from expressing their religious convictions in the public square or through public policy. See Mathew D. Staver, TAKE BACK AMERICA 33–44 (2000) (discussing the origin of the phrase "separation of church and state" and pointing out that Thomas Jefferson never intended that this phrase be used to exclude people of faith or religious ideas from influencing and shaping government).

[3]Lynch v. Donnelly, 465 U.S. 668, 673 (1984).

[4]Committee for Pub. Educ. & Religious Liberty v. Nyquist, 413 U.S. 756, 760 (1973).

[5]Lynch, 465 U.S. at 673. See, e.g., Zorach v. Clauson, 343 U.S. 306, 314 (1952); Illinois ex rel. McCullom v. Board of Educ., 333 U.S. 203, 211 (1948).

[6]Zorach, 343 U.S. at 314; Lynch, 465 U.S. at 673.

Total separation of church and state would actually result in hostility toward religion and would bring this country into "war with our national tradition as embodied in the First Amendment's guarantee of the free exercise of religion."[7] A correct interpretation of the First Amendment must be in accord "with what history reveals was the contemporaneous understanding of its guarantees."[8] The Supreme Court recognizes "that religion has been closely identified with our history and our government."[9] The history of this country "is inseparable from the history of religion."[10] American history clearly indicates that "we are a religious people whose institutions presuppose a Supreme Being."[11]

Obviously, the First Amendment requires that the state affirmatively accommodate religion and prevents the state from showing hostility toward any religion. Examples of accommodation of religion throughout history include: legislation providing paid chaplains for the House and Senate adopted by the First Congress in 1789 when the First Amendment was framed;[12] national days of thanksgiving;[13] Executive Orders proclaiming Christmas and Thanksgiving as national holidays;[14] the national motto "In God We Trust;"[15] the term "one nation under God" as part of the Pledge of Allegiance;[16] art

---

[7]*McCullom*, 333 U.S. at 211–12.
[8]*Lynch*, 465 U.S. at 673.
[9]*School Dist. of Abington Township v. Schempp*, 374 U.S. 203, 212 (1963).
[10]*Engel v. Vitale*, 370 U.S. 421, 434 (1962).
[11]*Zorach*, 343 U.S. at 313.
[12]*Lynch*, 465 U.S. at 674.
[13]*Id.* at 675.
[14]*Id.* at 676.
[15]36 U.S.C. § 302. The national motto was also mandated for currency. 31 U.S.C. § 5112(d)(1).
[16]*Lynch*, 465 U.S. at 676.

galleries supported by public revenues displaying religious paintings of the fifteenth and sixteenth centuries, including the National Gallery in Washington maintained by government support, exhibiting masterpieces with religious messages such as the Last Supper and paintings depicting the birth of Christ, the crucifixion, and the resurrection, along with many other explicit Christian themes;[17] and the inscription of Moses with the Ten Commandments etched in stone in the Supreme Court of the United States of America.[18] These are just a few of many examples. "Our history is pervaded by expressions of religious beliefs."[19] Consequently, government would do well to "respect the religious nature of our people."[20]

The Judeo-Christian history of this country is evident when considering religious symbols on public property. These symbols include crosses perched atop water towers, crosses within city seals, the Ten Commandments on public buildings, Scripture verses etched in stone, nativity scenes, and many other symbols. One cannot walk through our nation's capitol without realizing the impact of Christianity on this country. Indeed, in the United States Supreme Court, inscribed directly above the seat of the Chief Justice, is Moses with the Ten Commandments. The centrality of the Ten Commandments within the United States Supreme Court symbolizes that all other laws throughout history are based upon and derived from the Ten Commandments. Each day the

---

[17]*Id.* at 677. The National Gallery regularly exhibits more than two hundred similar religious paintings. *Id.* at 677 n.4.

[18]*Id.* at 677.

[19]*Id.*

[20]*Zorach,* 343 U.S. at 314; *see also Lynch,* 465 U.S. at 678.

court is in session, the justices sit below the Ten Commandments purportedly to apply its principles.[21]

Religious symbols within the public sector have come under attack. The battle over nativity scenes greatly contributed to pushing my career from ministry to law. Every year as I read about one nativity scene falling after another, I became frustrated. After entering law school I began to realize that nativity scenes are still constitutional when displayed in the proper context.

Nativity scenes on public property and religious Christmas carols in the public schools are rapidly disappearing from American culture. Displays of the Ten Commandments have also come under fierce attack. The loss of religious consensus and the "separation of church and state" myth have contributed toward the demise of America's Christian heritage.

In the 1970s the American Civil Liberties Union (hereinafter "ACLU") was initially successful in removing nativity scenes from public property. However, the United States Supreme Court later issued several important opinions regarding nativity scenes.[22] The Court has never ruled that all nativity scenes on public property are unconstitutional. To the

---

[21]While one of Liberty Counsel's attorneys was taking a guided tour of the Supreme Court building in 2002, the guide told the group that the several depictions of the Ten Commandments in the Court chambers were actually the first ten amendments to the United States Constitution. This, of course, is outrageous. The Supreme Court itself has acknowledged the inscriptions of the Ten Commandments. See *Lynch*, 465 U.S. at 677–78. Moreover, the first ten amendments, also known as the Bill of Rights, have never been depicted using Roman numerals, and finally, the drafters of the ten amendments did not wear full length Middle Eastern robes.

[22]*County of Allegheny v. American Civil Liberties Union*, 492 U.S. 573 (1989); *Lynch*, 465 U.S. at 673; *Lemon*, 403 U.S. at 602.

contrary, nativity scenes are constitutional if properly displayed, as well as public displays of the Ten Commandments. Unfortunately, the ACLU has used smoke and mirrors to intimidate public officials into removing nativity scenes and Christmas carols from the public square. Similar tactics have been directed at the Ten Commandments and other religious symbols. More unfortunate is that many public leaders cower to these threats without ever considering whether the ACLU is right.

Publicly and Privately Sponsored Symbols

The display of nativity scenes and religious symbols takes on two forms: publicly sponsored and privately sponsored, both of which can be displayed on public property. A publicly sponsored scene is one that is erected and maintained by public officials. A privately sponsored scene is one that is erected and maintained by private citizens. Both are constitutional, and both can be displayed on public property. The main difference is that a publicly sponsored scene should have some form of secular display in the same context, while a privately sponsored scene need not have any secular symbols. The private display should probably have a sign indicating the display is privately sponsored.

PUBLICLY SPONSORED SYMBOLS

An example of a publicly sponsored religious symbol is one that is erected and maintained by city officials on public property. The key to the constitutionality of a publicly sponsored display is the presence of a secular symbol or symbols within the same context. The display of a publicly sponsored religious symbol standing by itself may be unconstitutional.[23] However, if secular symbols are displayed within the same context of the religious symbol, the Supreme Court would consider the display constitutional. Therefore, a publicly sponsored display containing a religious symbol should generally include secular symbols.[24]

The proximity of the secular symbols to the religious display is also important. The secular and religious symbols should be within the same parameter of view. When viewing the scene, one should also be able to view the secular display in close proximity to the religious symbol. For example, a nativity scene could be displayed with Mary and Joseph looking into the manger at Baby Jesus, and Santa Claus could be standing near the manger; his reindeer could be parked somewhere nearby with a Christmas tree in the same general area. In most cases there should be a combination of both secular and religious symbols because the publicly sponsored display of religious symbols standing alone is more likely to be found unconstitutional.

PRIVATELY SPONSORED SYMBOLS

A privately sponsored religious symbol can also be displayed on public property. The main difference is that the display is erected and maintained by private citizens instead of public officials. Privately sponsored scenes are more common in public parks where citizens are allowed to

---

[23]*Id.*

[24]The absence of a secular symbol does not automatically mean the religious symbol is unconstitutional. One must consider the overall context of the display to determine whether the display has a secular purpose and whether the primary purpose is to endorse religion.

engage in expressive activity.[25] In most public parks, citizens are allowed to hold gatherings and erect displays. To prohibit religious expression in a public park where other expressive activity is permitted violates the Constitution. Public officials cannot discriminate against a religious viewpoint by allowing secular expression while censoring religious expression.

In a privately sponsored scene, there is no need for secular symbols to be displayed within the same context of the religious symbol. A privately sponsored scene can stand alone without secular symbols. However, in order to designate clearly that the display is privately sponsored, a sign should be erected similar to the following example: "This display is privately sponsored by XYZ Company."[26] However, such a sign is not mandatory because the Supreme Court has held that an observer of the display is assumed to know the history and background of the display.[27]

Nativity Scenes and Other Holiday Symbols

Publicly Sponsored

Some have the mistaken idea that publicly sponsored nativity scenes on public property maintained by public entities are unconstitutional. This is clearly not the law. In the famous

---

[25]See *Capitol Square Review and Advisory Bd. v. Pinette,* 515 U.S. 753 (1995); *Doe v. Small,* 964 F.2d 611 (7th Cir. 1992) (*en banc*).

[26]A disclaimer on a privately sponsored religious scene on public property is not necessary but may be helpful to alert the public that the display is in fact privately sponsored.

[27]*Capitol Square Review,* 515 U.S. at 753.

case of *Lynch v. Donnelly*,[28] the United States Supreme Court ruled that the city of Pawtucket, Rhode Island, could continue to display its Christmas scene that included a crèche which it had displayed for the previous forty years.

When considering the constitutionality of the nativity scene, the Court addressed the following three questions: (1) whether the display had a secular purpose; (2) whether the display had the primary effect of advancing religion; and (3) whether the display fostered excessive governmental entanglement.[29]

1. Whether There Is a Secular Purpose

In addressing this first question, the Court stated that the focus must be on the entire Christmas display, not simply on the crèche or nativity scene. Under this inquiry, the entire display must have a secular purpose. There certainly may be a religious purpose to parts of the display, but when looking at the entire display, if at least some secular aspect exists, then there is a secular purpose. Thus, a nativity scene by itself may only have a religious purpose, but when placed in the context of other secular symbols of Christmas such as Santa Claus, a Christmas tree, or reindeer, the entire display may be said to have at least a secular purpose, although the display

---

[28]465 U.S. 668 (1984).

[29]This three-part test is referred to as the *Lemon* test, named after the Supreme Court decision known as *Lemon v. Kurtzman*. This three-part test has often been modified by the High Court by using a two-part test known as the endorsement test. *See County of Allegheny*, 492 U.S. at 573. The Court formally adopted this refinement of the *Lemon* test so that the test now asks (1) whether the government has a secular purpose for the action and (2) whether the primary effect of the action is to endorse religion. *Id.* at 593–94. These essentially are the first and second prongs of the *Lemon* test.

may still also have a religious purpose. In fact, the Supreme Court has declared that a nativity scene sponsored by the government, on government property, accompanied by other secular symbols, serves "legitimate secular purposes."[30]

2. Whether the Primary Effect Is to Advance Religion

The second consideration is whether the *primary* effect of the display as a whole advances religion. To answer this question, the entire context should be viewed as a whole, not in isolation. If one were to focus solely on the nativity scene in isolation from the Christmas tree, then the impression might be that the primary effect is to advance religion. However, the Supreme Court has indicated that the display as a whole must be considered.[31] Although the nativity scene by itself may be said to advance religion, when viewed in the entire context of

---

[30]*Lynch,* 465 U.S. at 681.

[31]Similarly, if an outsider walked into a public school auditorium to hear a Christmas program, and the first song heard was "Silent Night," the impression this person might receive is that the school is promoting the Christian religion. However, if this same person stayed for the entire program and later heard secular songs, such as "Here Comes Santa Claus," this person would then understand the school was acknowledging both the sacred and secular aspects of the holiday. Courts refers to this person as a "reasonable observer," meaning the person is informed of the context including the history surrounding the event. Such a person is informed of what went on before and what will take place later. If this were not the standard, then every religious display would be called into question by an "Ignoramus veto." *See Capitol Square Review,* 515 U.S. at 753; *Chabad-Lubavitch of Ga. v. Miller,* 5 F.3d 1383, 1392 (11th Cir. 1993) (*en banc*) ("The reasonable observer knows that other speakers have used the [forum] before, and will do so again. Instead of concluding that religious zealots have stormed the gates with the city's endorsement, the reasonable observer recognizes this display as yet another example of free speech.") (quoting *Americans United for Separation of Church and State v. City of Grand Rapids,* 980 F.2d 1538, 1549 (6th Cir. 1992) (*en banc*)).

the surrounding secular symbols, it cannot be said that the *primary* purpose is to advance religion. In making this decision, the *Lynch* Court cited other examples of governmental aid to religion which did not have the primary effect of advancing religion, namely expenditures of large sums of public money for textbooks supplied throughout the country to students attending church-sponsored schools,[32] expenditure of public funds for transportation of students to church-sponsored schools,[33] federal grants for college buildings of church-sponsored institutions of higher education combining secular and religious education,[34] noncategorical grants to church-sponsored colleges and universities,[35] tax exemptions for church properties,[36] Sunday labor laws,[37] release time programs for religious training during public school hours,[38] and legislative prayers.[39] Since the Supreme Court has in the past found all of these activities to be consistent with the Constitution, the mere placement of a nativity scene within a Christmas display provides no greater aid to religion and clearly would not violate the Constitution. In fact, the Court noted that not every law which confers an indirect, remote, or incidental benefit upon religion is, for that reason alone, constitutionally invalid.[40]

Lynch specifically noted that the "display of the crèche is no more an advancement or endorsement of religion than the

---

[32]*Board of Educ. v. Allen,* 392 U.S. 236, 244 (1968).

[33]*Everson v. Board of Educ.,* 330 U.S. 1, 17 (1947).

[34]*Tilton v. Richardson,* 403 U.S. 672 (1971).

[35]*Roemer v. Maryland Bd. of Pub. Works,* 426 U.S. 736 (1976).

[36]*Walz v. Tax Commissioner,* 397 U.S. 664 (1970).

[37]*McGowan v. Maryland,* 366 U.S. 420 (1961).

[38]*Zorach,* 343 U.S. at 306.

[39]*Marsh v. Chambers,* 463 U.S. 783 (1983).

[40]*Lynch,* 465 U.S. at 683 (*citing Nyquist,* 413 U.S. at 771).

Congressional and Executive recognition of the origins of the Holiday as 'Christ's Mass,' or the exhibition of literally hundreds of religious paintings in governmentally sponsored museums."[41]

3. Whether There Is Excessive Governmental Entanglement

The Supreme Court in *Lynch* found that there was no excessive governmental entanglement when a public entity displays a nativity scene during Christmas, because there is no excessive administrative entanglement between the state and church concerning the content, the design of the exhibit, or upkeep. The monetary expense is also minimal. In fact, the display required far less ongoing, day-to-day interaction between church and state than religious paintings in public galleries.[42]

As the above shows, the context of the nativity scene is most important. In one case, the Supreme Court ruled that the prominent placement of a nativity scene without other secular symbols nearby made it unconstitutional, while a Jewish menorah was constitutional because of its proximity to a Christmas tree.[43] In the *County of Allegheny* case, the Court considered two recurring holiday displays located on public property in downtown Pittsburgh. The first display was a crèche depicting the Christian nativity scene, which was placed on the grand staircase of the Allegheny County courthouse. This was apparently the most beautiful and most public part of the courthouse. The crèche was donated by the

---

[41]*Lynch,* 465 U.S. at 683.
[42]*Id.* at 684.
[43]*County of Allegheny v. ACLU,* 492 U.S. at 573.

Holy Name Society, a Roman Catholic group, and bore a sign to that effect. The second holiday display was an eighteen-foot Hanukkah menorah, or candelabrum, which was placed just outside the city-county building next to the city's forty-five-foot decorated Christmas tree. The menorah was owned by Chabad, a Jewish group, but was stored and erected each year by the city.

Splitting hairs in this case, the Supreme Court ruled that the nativity scene violated the First Amendment Establishment Clause, but the menorah did not. The nativity scene was at the main entrance to the courthouse and was not surrounded by any secular symbols of Christmas. However, the menorah was not at the main entrance and was surrounded by secular symbols of Christmas. Presumably, the nativity scene would have been constitutional had the menorah and the Christmas tree been at the main entrance or had the nativity scene been adjacent to the menorah and the Christmas tree. However, because the nativity scene did not have any corresponding secular symbols of Christmas, the court ruled that the nativity display was unconstitutional and had the primary effect of endorsing religion.

The *County of Allegheny* case demonstrates that a publicly sponsored nativity must be within close proximity to some other secular symbol of Christmas. A number of federal courts applying this reasoning have upheld publicly sponsored religious holiday displays.[44] Unfortunately, some city

---

[44]*See, e.g., ACLU of N. J. v. Township of Wall,* 246 F.3d 258 (3d Cir. 2001) (finding that plaintiffs lacked standing to challenge display); *Wells v. City and County of Denver,* 257 F.3d 1132 (10th Cir. 2001), *cert. denied,* 534 U.S. 997 (2001) (upholding a crèche display that also included tin soldiers, Christmas trees, snowmen, reindeer and other animals, a sled, and Santa

officials have become frustrated or confused and have jettisoned the whole idea of nativity scenes. Such drastic measures are not required by the Constitution.

PRIVATELY SPONSORED

The main difference between a publicly sponsored and a privately sponsored religious symbol, aside from the sponsorship, is that while the former may require a secular symbol be mixed in the context, the latter does not. The Supreme Court has unequivocally ruled that the private display of a religious symbol in a public park is constitutional.[45] In an unusual case, the Ku Klux Klan sought to erect a Latin (Christian) cross during the Christmas season in the statehouse plaza in Columbus, Ohio. An application was required for all groups requesting use of the public square for temporarily erected, unattended symbols. Historically the City of

---

Claus); *ACLU of N. J. v. Schundler,* 168 F.3d 92 (3d Cir. 1999) (upholding city's modified nativity scene display which added *Kwanza* symbols, sled, Frosty the Snowman and Santa Claus); *ACLU v. City of Florissant,* 186 F.3d 1095 (9th Cir. 1999) (upholding a crèche in a seasonal display at a city civil center); *Elewski v. City of Syracuse,* 123 F.3d 51 (2d Cir. 1997), *cert. denied,* 523 U.S. 1004 (1998) (upholding crèche and religious banner in the context of a decorated evergreen tree, sawhorse containing names of mayor and municipal agency and a menorah display in a nearby park); *Sechler v. State College Area Sch. Dist.,* 121 F. Supp. 2d 439 (M.D. Pa. 2000) (upholding holiday display sponsored by public elementary school where the display was set up at the entrance to the school building and which included a menorah, a *Kwanza* candelabra, along with books about Hanukkah and *Kwanza*); *Grutzmacher v. County of Clark,* 33 F. Supp. 2d 896 (D. Nev. 1999) (upholding display in an airport which included a menorah, a Christmas tree, and a "Happy Hanukkah" sign); *Amancio v. Town of Somerset,* 28 F. Supp. 2d 677 (D. Mass. 1998) (upholding nativity scene in the context of holiday lights, wreath, Christmas tree, and Santa Claus).

[45]*Capitol Square Review,* 515 U.S. at 753.

Columbus allowed a broad range of speakers and events in what was known as Capitol Square. In the past, the city permitted a variety of unattended displays including a state-sponsored Christmas tree, a privately sponsored menorah, and a display showing the progress of a United Way fundraising campaign. Booths, exhibits, and art festivals were periodically on the public grounds. However, when the Ku Klux Klan sought to erect the Latin cross, Columbus officials who opposed the message of hate and bigotry promoted by the KKK declined the request. When the KKK filed suit, the city of Columbus took the position that the Constitution required the city to censor religious displays because the casual observer would assume that the religious display was endorsed by the city. City officials maintained that allowing the cross on public property would violate the Constitution.

The Supreme Court rejected the city's arguments. The Court found that the KKK's Latin cross was private expression. The Court's prior

> precedent establishes that private religious speech, far from being a First Amendment orphan, is as fully protected under the Free Speech Clause as secular private expression. Indeed, in Anglo-American history, at least, government suppression of speech has so commonly been directed precisely at religious speech that a free-speech clause without religion would be Hamlet without the prince.[46]

The Court stated that its prior cases "[had] not excluded from free-speech protections religious proselytizing [or] . . .

---

[46]*Id.* at 760 (citations omitted).

even acts of worship."[47] The Court also reasoned that there was no Establishment Clause violation because the Latin cross was private rather than public speech. The Court also rejected the argument that the cross should be excluded because the cross on public property might lead some to conclude the government endorsed Christianity. The Court noted the following:

> We find it peculiar to say that government "promotes" or "favors" a religious display by giving it the same access to a public forum that all other displays enjoy. And as a matter of Establishment Clause jurisprudence, we have consistently held that it is no violation for government to enact neutral policies that happen to benefit religion.[48]

In finding a private display of a cross in a public park constitutional, the Court poignantly noted:

> It will be a sad day when this Court casts piety in with pornography, and finds the First Amendment more hospitable to private expletives . . . than to private prayers. This would be merely bizarre were religious speech simply as protected by the Constitution as other forms of private speech; but it is outright perverse when one considers that private religious expression receives preferential treatment under the Free Exercise Clause. It is no answer to say that the Establishment Clause tempers religious speech. By its terms that Clause applies only to the words and acts

---

[47]*Id.* (citations omitted).
[48]*Id.* at 764.

of government. It was never meant, and has never been read by this Court, to serve as an impediment to purely private religious speech connected to the State only through its occurrence in a public forum.[49]

Justice Scalia concluded: "Religious expression cannot violate the Establishment Clause where it (1) is purely private, and (2) occurs in a traditional or designated public forum, publicly announced and open to all on equal terms."[50]

Similarly, an Illinois federal appeals court ruled that privately displayed nativity pictures in a public park were constitutional. In 1956 the Ottawa Retail Merchants Association, a private organization, commissioned the painting of sixteen canvases depicting scenes from the life of Christ in an effort to "put Christ back in Christmas."[51] These paintings were displayed in Washington Park, located in the center of the city of Ottawa, Illinois, during the Christmas seasons from 1957 to 1969. These paintings were again displayed from 1980 through 1988. Except for the years 1964 through 1967, when the city arranged for the erection of the paintings, the display was exhibited by private parties. However, these paintings were not displayed during the 1970s, as they were stored in an old grandstand structure and apparently forgotten. A newspaper article in 1980 discussed the paintings, prompting a local chapter of the Junior Chamber of Commerce (Jaycees), a national service-oriented organization, to contact the city and volunteer to take charge of the paintings.

---

[49]*Id.* at 767 (plurality) (citations omitted).
[50]*Id.* at 770.
[51]*Doe,* 964 F.2d at 611.

When these private paintings were displayed in the city park, they occupied less than one-half of the west side of Washington Park. These paintings were accompanied by a sign that read: "This Display Has Been Erected and Maintained Solely by the Ottawa Jaycees, a Private Organization, without the Use of Public Funds."[52] In considering this situation, the court of appeals found that the park was a traditional public forum, and it was, therefore, obviously open to the public. Space had always been allocated on a first-come, first-served basis. Since this was a public park and the displays were owned and maintained privately with a sign indicating private ownership, the federal court ruled that the display was constitutional. To remove these paintings would violate the First Amendment Free Speech Clause. Since this display was privately sponsored on public property, the court need not even consider the Establishment Clause. The Establishment Clause does not apply to private speech; it only applies to government speech.[53] Merely because a religious display occurs on public property does not transform private speech into government speech. Similar to the Seventh Circuit Court of Appeals, the Fourth, Sixth, Ninth, and Eleventh Circuit Courts of Appeals have also ruled that private holiday displays of religious symbols on public property are permissible under the Free Speech Clause.[54]

---

[52]*Id.* at 612.

[53]The Supreme Court observed that "there is a crucial difference between *government* speech endorsing religion, which the Establishment Clause forbids, and *private* speech endorsing religion, which the Free Speech and Free Exercise Clauses protect." *Board of Educ. of Westside Comm. Schs. v. Mergens,* 496 U.S. 226, 250 (1990).

[54]See, e.g., Warren v. Fairfax County, 196 F.3d 186 (4th Cir. 1999) (county's refusal to allow a private display of a religious holiday display violated the

Since 1964 the city of Grand Rapids had granted Chabad House of Western Michigan a permit to display a twenty-foot-high steel menorah during the eight days of the Jewish holiday of Hanukkah. The menorah was purchased entirely with private funds and was owned by Chabad House, a private organization. The city had no role in the planning, erecting, removal, maintenance, or storage of the menorah. Except for a small cost for providing electricity, all the display costs were privately funded.

The display was located in Calder Plaza, the principal plaza in the center of downtown Grand Rapids. The city

---

right to free speech); Kreisner v. City of San Diego, 1 F.3d 775 (9th Cir. 1993) (the private sponsorship in a public park of a display of life-size statuaries depicting biblical scenes from the life of Christ having a disclaimer sign indicating that the display was privately sponsored is constitutional and is protected free expression); Americans United, 980 F.2d at 1538 (upholding privately funded menorah display in public park). In another case the City of Cincinnati enacted an ordinance which stated, "The proposed use including presence of any display, exhibit, or structure, will not occur in Fountain Square between the hours of 10:00 p.m. and 6:00 a.m." However, this limitation on the use of the public square exempted "agencies, political subdivisions and instrumentalities of governments of the United States, the State of Ohio, the County of Hamilton, the City of Cincinnati, and the Board of Education of the City of Cincinnati." The Congregation Lubavitch wished to display its eighteen-foot-high menorah during Hanukkah. It had displayed this menorah in the past. The assembly and disassembly of this structure took approximately six hours. The new city ordinance requiring that no use of Fountain Square could occur between 10:00 p.m. and 6:00 a.m. would have required the dismantling of this menorah every day. Congregation Lubavitch sued the city of Cincinnati claiming that the ordinance was not content-neutral because, as applied to them, it violated their First Amendment right to free speech. Unlike other outside organizations, Congregation Lubavitch would not be able to adequately use Fountain Square with this limitation. A federal court of appeals agreed stating that the ordinance was not content-neutral and therefore violated the Constitution. See Congregation Lubavitch v. City of Cincinnati, 997 F.2d 1160 (6th Cir. 1993). See also Chabad-Lubavitch of Ga., 5 F.3d at

required that the menorah be accompanied by two illuminated signs measuring two-feet by three-feet that read as follows:

HAPPY HANUKKAH TO ALL

This menorah display has been erected by Chabad House, a private organization. Its presence does not constitute an endorsement by the city of Grand Rapids of the organization or the display.[55]

Since the city made the plaza available to the public for all forms of speech and assembly, the plaza became a traditional public forum. As a traditional public forum accessible by other members of the public for expressive activities, the plaza must be open to the Jewish organization for display of the menorah. To prohibit display of the menorah would be content-based censorship and would violate the First Amendment Free Speech Clause.[56]

The Eleventh Circuit Court of Appeals also found that the private display of a Jewish menorah in a public park was constitutional.[57] This case has great significance because it was decided by the entire panel of the court of appeals rather than the usual three-judge panel. The court found that the public entity allowed secular speech and therefore had created a

1383 (ruling that a state could not deny permission to a private Jewish organization to display in a designated or limited public forum its fifteen-foot-tall menorah in the state capitol rotunda, because not being accompanied by other secular symbols and without a disclaimer of private sponsorship, the display would violate the First Amendment Establishment Clause).

[55]City of Grand Rapids, 980 F.2d at 1540.
[56]See id. at 1553.
[57]Chabad-Lubavitch of Ga., 5 F.3d at 1383.

limited public forum. Consequently, the public entity could not exclude religious speech from this forum. The court stated that private speech in a public forum does not violate the Establishment Clause. "The speech that takes place in a public forum belongs and can be attributed to the private speaker only; neither approbation nor condemnation of the private speaker's message may be imputed to the State."[58] "Any perceived endorsement of religion is simply misperception; the Establishment Clause is not, in fact, violated."[59] The court concluded as follows:

> Giving full effect to the public forum doctrine does not elevate the Free Speech Clause above the Establishment Clause. . . . In the public forum, . . . the speech of private parties does not enjoy the State's imprimatur. There is no Establishment Clause violation in the first instance to weigh against . . . the Free Speech Clause. Courts that have found otherwise, . . . simply misunderstood the principals they sought to apply.[60]

Commenting on the Establishment Clause and private speech, one court observed:

> The Establishment Clause is a limitation on the power of government: it is not a restriction on the rights of individuals acting in their private lives. The threshold question in any Establishment Clause case is whether there is sufficient governmental action to invoke the

---

[58]*Id.* at 1392.
[59]*Id.* at 1393.
[60]*Id.* at 1393–94 n.17.

prohibition. . . . It is clear that the mere fact that [private] speech occurs on [public] property fails to make it government supported.[61]

When private speech occurs on public property, "the Establishment Clause simply is inapplicable."[62] Public officials cannot argue that religious speech must be censored because it may be divisive or offensive. One federal court of appeals was correct when it observed:

> The potency of religious speech is not a constitutional infirmity; the most fervently devotional and blatantly sectarian speech is protected when it is private speech in a public forum. Zealots have First Amendment rights too.[63]

In summary, publicly sponsored religious symbols are constitutional so long as there is at least a secular purpose within the overall context. A secular purpose can be achieved by the presence of secular symbols. Privately sponsored religious scenes are also constitutional. There is no requirement that secular symbols be within the same context of the display. However, a sign connoting the private sponsorship is a wise addition to such a display.

Unfortunately some public officials mistakenly believe that censoring religion from the public square is the safest approach. Under this mistaken assumption, city officials have removed religious symbols from display and school

---

[61]*Rivera v. Board of Regents,* 721 F. Supp. 1189, 1195 (D. Col. 1989).
[62]*Id.*
[63]*Capitol Square Review and Advisory Bd. v. Pinette,* 30 F.3d 675, 680 (6th Cir. 1994), *aff'd,* 515 U.S. 753 (1995).

principals have prohibited the singing of religious carols. However, rather than avoiding a constitutional violation by removing religion, these officials actually create a constitutional violation by censoring religion. Indeed, the display of religious symbols on public property and the singing of religious Christmas carols in public schools are protected by the constitutional guarantee to freedom of speech and freedom of religion. Censoring religion violates the core of our constitutional freedoms.

Ten Commandments

The law regarding public displays of the Ten Commandments follows the same reasoning as the display of religious symbols.[64] Since private displays on public property are clearly constitutional, this section will focus only on publicly sponsored displays. While a nativity scene is a seasonal display, a Ten Commandments display is not limited to any particular season. A publicly sponsored nativity scene accompanied by other secular seasonal displays is constitutional. However, since the Ten Commandments is not seasonal, secular symbols are appropriate within a publicly sponsored display. The best secular symbols for Ten Commandments displays are secular laws or lawgivers. Displays of a purely historical nature or religious history displays are also appropriate.

---

[64]On October 12, 2004, the United States Supreme Court agreed to hear two cases involving the Ten Commandments—*McCreary County v. ACLU of Kentucky,* 125 S. Ct. 310 (2004) and *Van Orden v. Perry,* 125 S. Ct. 346 (2004). Liberty Counsel represents the two county courthouses in the *McCeary County* case.

A Ten Commandments display will be invalidated under the purpose prong, of the *Lemon* or endorsement test only if the action by the government is "entirely motivated by a purpose to advance religion."[65] Governmental action may satisfy *Lemon's* first prong, even if it is "motivated in part by a religious purpose."[66] "Unless it seems to be a sham, . . . the government's assertion of a legitimate secular purpose is entitled to deference."[67] Courts must be "deferential to a [government's] articulation of a secular purpose."[68]

If the reason for the display includes an educational or historical purpose, then the display should pass the first test. In order to determine whether the display passes the second test, sometimes referred to as the "effects" test, one must consider what a reasonable observer would conclude. The relevant determination is "whether an objective observer, acquainted with the text, legislative history, and implementation of the statute, would perceive it as state endorsement."[69]

The objective observer is "deemed aware of the history and context of the community and forum in which the religious display appears."[70] However,

> the endorsement inquiry is not about the perceptions of particular individuals or saving isolated

---

[65]*Wallace v. Jaffree*, 472 U.S. 38, 56 (1985); *see also Bowen v. Kendrick*, 487 U.S. 589, 602 (1988).
[66]*Wallace*, 472 U.S. at 56.
[67]*ACLU v. Capitol Square Review and Advisory Bd.*, 243 F.3d 289, 307 (6th Cir. 2001) (*en banc*) (quoting *Brooks v. City of Oak Ridge*, 222 F.3d 259, 265 (6th Cir. 2000)).
[68]*Edwards v. Aguillard*, 482 U.S. 578, 586 (1987).
[69]*Capitol Square Review*, 243 F.3d at 302 (quoting *Wallace*, 472 U.S. at 76 [O'Connor, J. concurring]).
[70]*Pinette*, 515 U.S. at 779–80 (O'Connor, J., concurring).

nonadherents from . . . discomfort. . . . It is for this reason that the reasonable observer in the endorsement inquiry must be deemed aware of the history and context of the community and forum in which the religious display appears.[71]

It should be remembered that while the Ten Commandments is a religious document, it also has secular aspects irrespective of its context. While the first four commands deal with our relationship to God, the remaining six address our relationship to one another.[72] Additionally, the Ten Commandments has a rich history in America. Each of the Ten Commandments has played some significant role in the foundation of our system of law and government. Twelve of the thirteen original colonies adopted the entire Decalogue into their civil and criminal laws. In this respect, the Supreme Court has observed that when a governmental practice has been "deeply embedded in the history and tradition of this country," such a practice will not violate the Establishment Clause because the practice has become part of the "fabric of our society."[73]

Relying upon history and tradition, the High Court upheld legislative prayers even when the chaplain is paid by the

---

[71]*Id.; see also Good News Clubs v. Milford Cent. Sch. Dist.,* 533 U.S. 98, 119 (2001) (same).

[72]Commandments 1–4 address worshipping God alone, prohibition against making idols, taking God's name in vain, and worshipping on the Sabbath. Commandments 5–10 address honoring parents, murder, adultery, stealing, bearing false witness or perjury and covetousness. *See* Exodus 20:2–17. Some printed versions of the Ten Commandments combine Commandments 1 and 2 and split 10 in two. The same substance is contained except the numbering is different. Of course, the original Hebrew text did not contain numbered sentences.

[73]*Marsh,* 463 U.S. at 786.

government to deliver a prayer at the highest seat of government, namely the chambers where laws are made.[74] The reason legislative prayers are upheld is that such prayers predated the First Amendment. Indeed, the first act of those who drafted the First Amendment was to vote to authorize legislative prayers. In the same way, the use and display of the Ten Commandments predates the First Amendment and finds its roots in the colonial era and the founding of America. The Supreme Court has often recognized the Ten Commandments' impact on our system of law and government.[75] Commenting on the religious and secular mix, one Supreme Court justice stated:

> A carving of Moses holding the Ten Commandments, if that is the only adornment on a courtroom wall, conveys an equivocal message, perhaps of respect for Judaism, for religion in general, or for law. The addition of carvings depicting Confucius and Mohammed may honor religion, or particular

---

[74]*Id.*

[75]*See Griswold v. Connecticut,* 381 U.S. 479, 529 n.2 (1965) (Stewart, J., dissenting) (most criminal prohibitions coincide with the prohibitions contained in the Ten Commandments); *McGowan,* 366 U.S. at 459 (Frankfurter, J., concurring) ("Innumerable civil regulations enforce conduct which harmonizes with religious canons. State prohibitions of murder, theft, and adultery reinforce commands of the decalogue."); *Stone v. Graham,* 449 U.S. 39, 45 (1980) (Rehnquist, J., dissenting) ("It is equally undeniable . . . that the Ten Commandments have had a significant impact on the development of secular legal codes of the Western World."); *Lynch,* 465 U.S. at 677–78 (describing the depiction of Moses with the Ten Commandments on the wall of the Supreme Court chamber and stating that such acknowledgments of religion demonstrate that "our history is pervaded by expressions of religious beliefs"); *Edwards,* 482 U.S. at 593–94 (acknowledging that the Ten Commandments did not play an exclusively religious role in the history of Western civilization).

religions, to an extent that the First Amendment does not tolerate any more than it does "the permanent erection of a large Latin cross on the roof of city hall." Placement of secular figures such as Caesar Augustus, William Blackstone, Napoleon Bonaparte, and John Marshall alongside these three religious figures, however, signals respect not for great proselytizers but for great lawgivers. It would be absurd to exclude such a fitting message from a courtroom, as it would to exclude religious paintings by Italian Renaissance masters from a public museum.[76]

Some cases addressing the Ten Commandments involved stand-alone displays while others were in the context of secular displays. As in the nativity scene context, stand-alone religious symbols face a tougher challenge in satisfying the secular purpose and effects test.[77] The Supreme Court first briefly addressed the Ten Commandments posted alone on a

---

[76]*County of Allegheny,* 492 U.S. at 652 (Stevens, J., concurring in part and dissenting in part) (citations and footnote omitted). In *Washegesic v. Bloomingdale Pub. Schs.,* 33 F.3d 679 (6th Cir. 1994), a federal court found the portrait of Jesus standing alone unconstitutional. It is likely that the portrait of Jesus hanging in the public school hallway in Bloomingdale, Michigan, would have been considered constitutional had there been other portraits of secular leaders hanging in the same hallway.

[77]*See, e.g., Indiana Civil Liberties Union v. O'Bannon,* 259 F.3d 766 (7th Cir. 2001), *cert. denied,* 534 U.S. 1162 (2002) (striking down stand-alone display); *Adland v. Russ,* 307 F.3d 471 (6th Cir. 2002); *Books v. City of Elkart,* 235 F.3d 292, 303–04 (7th Cir. 2000) (striking down display but acknowledging that the Ten Commandments can be properly displayed, and recognizing "the historical and cultural significance of the Ten Commandments"), *cert. denied,* 532 U.S. 1058 (2001); *ACLU of Tenn. v. Hamilton County,* 2002 F. Supp. 2d 757 (E.D. Tenn. 2002) (striking down stand-alone display); *ACLU Neb. Found. v. City of Plattsmouth,* 186 F. Supp. 2d 1024 (D. Neb. 2002) (same).

classroom bulletin board in a Kentucky school.[78] In summary fashion, the court struck down the stand-alone display stating that it did not have a secular purpose.[79] However, in so ruling, the Court made clear that the Ten Commandments may even be taught in public school in the proper context.

Upholding a publicly sponsored display of the Ten Commandments, one federal appeals court declared that the Commandments are "historically important . . . with *both* secular and sectarian effects."[80] Rutherford County, Tennessee, erected a display entitled the "Foundations of American Law and Government." The display contained (1) an explanation of each document, (2) the Mayflower Compact, (3) the Declaration of Independence, (4) the Ten Commandments, (5) the Magna Carta, (6) the lyrics of "The Star-Spangled Banner," (7) the Preamble of the Tennessee Constitution, (8) the Bill of Rights, and (9) a picture of Lady Justice.[81] Although the court struck down the display under the purpose prong test, the court found the actual display itself constitutional under the effects test. Under the first test, the court considered the governmental purpose in posting the display. In this respect, the judge relied on a 1999 county resolution in which the county sought to post a stand-alone display "in consideration of our great Biblical history."[82]

---

[78]*See Stone*, 449 U.S. at 39.

[79]The decision was pure judicial activism, and its precedential value is questionable. The case was never briefed nor argued on the merits.

[80]*Anderson v. Salt Lake City Corp.*, 475 F.2d 28, 34 (10th Cir.), *cert. denied*, 414 U.S. 879 (1973).

[81]*ACLU of Tenn. v. Rutherford County*, 209 F. Supp. 2d 799 (M.D. Tenn. 2002).

[82]*Id.* at 801–2. In *ACLU of Ohio v. Ashbrook*, 211 F. Supp. 2d 873 (N.D. Ohio 2002), the court struck down the Ten Commandments hung in a

However, the court pointed out that "a display of documents, including the Ten Commandments, may be constitutional if properly selected, exhibited, and posted with a true educational motive."[83] "Like the crèche in *Lynch* and the menorah in *Allegheny*, the Ten Commandments plaque at issue in the instant case stands not alone, but as part of a larger display."[84] The court then concluded that "the display as a whole does not have the primary effect of advancing or endorsing religion."[85] Thus, if the government acted with the intent to educate rather than indoctrinate, the county could have posted the same exact display.

In another case, a Kentucky federal court upheld the identical display, at issue in Rutherford County, Tennessee.[86] Here Mercer County officials posted the same "Foundations of Law and Government" display, but the resolution authorizing the display indicated that the purpose of the documents

---

courtroom where the judge stated the purpose of the display was religious. In contrast, a North Carolina federal court found the display of the Ten Commandments in a courtroom was constitutional. *See Suhre v. Haywood County*, 55 F. Supp. 2d 384 (W.D.N.C. 1999); *see also State v. Freedom from Religion Found., Inc.*, 898 P.2d 1013 (Colo. 1995) (upholding monument on state capital grounds). For cases focusing on the lack of a secular purpose, see *Freethought Society v. Chester County*, 191 F. Supp. 2d 589 (E.D. Penn. 2002) (religious ceremony dedicating plaque is evidence of religious purpose); *Kimbley v. Lawrence County*, 119 F. Supp. 2d 856 (S.D. Ind. 2000); *ACLU of Kentucky v. Pulaski County*, 96 F. Supp. 2d 691 (E.D. Ky. 2000); *Doe v. Harlan County School Board*, 96 F. Supp. 2d 667 (E.D. Ky. 2000); *Harvey v. Cobb County*, 811 F. Supp. 669 (N.D. Ga. 1993), *aff'd*, 15 F.3d 1097 (11th Cir. 1994); *Ring v. Grand Forks Public School District No. 1*, 483 F. Supp. 272 (D.N.D. 1980).

[83]*Id.* at 810.
[84]*Id.* at 811.
[85]*Id.* at 812.
[86]*See ACLU of Ky. v. Mercer County*, 219 F. Supp. 2d 777 (E.D. Ky. 2002).

was to educate the community about the historical foundations of American law and government. The court found that
the "stated purpose of acknowledging the historical influence
of the Commandments on our law is a sufficient secular purpose. . . . The historical evidence . . . overwhelming[ly] holds
that the Ten Commandments are not exclusively religious and
can be included in government displays in the proper context."[87] The court also found that a reasonable observer under
the effects test would not conclude that the display as a
whole had the primary effect of endorsing religion.[88]

In summary, the Ten Commandments can be displayed by
a private person or group on public property. Publicly sponsored displays of the Ten Commandments are also permitted,
especially in the context of secular laws or lawgivers and
where the governmental purpose in the display is historical or
educational.

Other Symbols

There has been a great deal of litigation regarding the
display of crosses on public property. Many crosses have
been removed from water towers and from city seals.

In the city of St. Cloud, Florida, the city owned and maintained a water tower on top of which was a lighted cross. This

---

[87] *Id.* at 788.

[88] *Id.* at 789–97. The court correctly adopted the reasoning of the
Rutherford County case regarding the display itself and rejected the flawed
decision of *ACLU of Kentucky v. Grayson County,* No. 4:01CV-202-M,
2002 WL 1558688 (W.D. Kentucky May 13, 2002), which had adopted the
holding of *ACLU of Kentucky v. McCreary County,* 145 F. Supp. 2d 845
(E.D. Ky. 2001).

cross was not surrounded by any other object and was plainly visible throughout the entire city. A federal court ruled that this stand-alone display of a Latin cross on top of a city water tower was unconstitutional.[89] Similarly, a federal court ruled that a Latin cross in a county seal was unconstitutional.[90]

Two Illinois towns, the cities of Zion and Rolling Hills, both displayed Latin crosses in their city seals. The federal court of appeals ruled that the display of these Latin crosses in the city seals violated the First Amendment Establishment Clause.[91] However, in response to this court's ruling, the city of Zion removed the Latin cross and replaced the cross with the national motto, "In God We Trust." The city seal, therefore, carried the words of the national motto. The Society of Separationists, which sued the city to remove the Latin cross, again sued the city to remove the national motto. However, this time the federal court ruled that the national motto, "In God We Trust," was constitutional.[92] Indeed, there are more than sixty federal cases indicating that the national motto is constitutional.[93]

---

[89]*Mendelsohn v. City of St. Cloud,* 719 F. Supp. 1065 (M.D. Fla. 1989).

[90]*Friedman v. Board of County Comm'rs of Beralillo County,* 781 F.2d 777 (10th Cir. 1985); *see also ACLU of Ohio, Inc. v. City of Stow,* 29 F. Supp. 2d 845 (N.D. Ohio 1998) (finding that a city seal containing a Christian cross violated the Establishment Clause).

[91]*Harris v. City of Zion,* 927 F.2d 1401 (7th Cir. 1991).

[92]*Harris v. City of Zion,* No. 87-C-7204 (N.D. Ill. 1992).

[93]*County of Allegheny v. ACLU,* 492 U.S. 573 (1989); *Regan v. Time, Inc.,* 468 U.S. 641 (1984); *Lynch,* 465 U.S. at 668; *Marsh,* 463 U.S. at 783; *Stone,* 449 U.S. at 39; *Wooley v. Maynard,* 430 U.S. 705 (1977); *Schempp,* 374 U.S. at 203; *Engel,* 370 U.S. at 421; *Sherman v. Community Consol. Sch. Dist.,* 980 F.2d 437 (7th Cir. 1992), *cert. denied,* 508 U.S. 590 (1993); *City of Grand Rapids,* 980 F.2d at 1538; *Murray v. City of Austin,* 947 F.2d 147 (5th Cir. 1991), *cert. denied,* 505 U.S. 1219 (1992); *North Carolina Civil Liberties Union Legal Found. v. Constangy,* 947 F.2d 1145 (4th Cir.

Eternal Vigilance

There has been no definitive decision regarding whether
Latin crosses may be displayed on public property. A federal
appeals court in Texas ruled that the display of a Latin cross

---

1991), cert. denied, 505 U.S. 1219 (1992); Society of Separationists, Inc. v.
Herman, 939 F.2d 1207 (5th Cir. 1991), on reh'g, 959 F.2d 1283 (5th Cir.
1992) (en banc), cert. denied, 506 U.S. 866 (1992); Jones v. Clear Creek
Indep. Sch. Dist., 930 F.2d 416 (5th Cir. 1991), on reh'g, 977 F.2d 963 (5th
Cir. 1992), cert. denied, 505 U.S. 967 (1993); Harris v. City of Zion, 927
F.2d at 1401; Doe v. Village of Crestwood, 917 F.2d 1476 (7th Cir. 1990);
Mather v. Village of Mundelein, 864 F.2d 1291 (7th Cir. 1989); Jager v.
Douglas County Sch. Dist., 862 F.2d 824 (11th Cir. 1989), cert. denied, 490
U.S. 1090 (1989); American Jewish Congress v. City of Chicago, 827 F.2d
120 (7th Cir. 1987); Stein v. Plainwell Community Schs., 822 F.2d 1406 (6th
Cir. 1987); ACLU v. City of Birmingham, 791 F.2d 1561 (6th Cir. 1986);
ACLU of Ill. v. City of St. Charles, 794 F.2d 265 (7th Cir. 1986); United
States v. Covelli, 738 F.2d 847 (7th Cir. 1984), cert. denied, 469 U.S. 867
(1984); Chambers v. Marsh, 675 F.2d 228 (8th Cir. 1982); Hall v. Bradshaw,
630 F.2d 1018 (4th Cir. 1980), cert. denied, 450 U.S. 965 (1981); Florey v.
Sioux Falls Sch. Dist. 49-5, 619 F.2d 1311 (8th Cir. 1980), cert. denied, 449
U.S. 987 (1980); O'Hair v. Murray, 588 F.2d 1144 (5th Cir. 1979), cert. denied sub nom., O'Hair v. Blumenthal, 442 U.S. 930 (1979); United States
v. Nabrit, 554 F.2d 247 (5th Cir. 1977); Tollett v. United States, 485 F.2d
1087 (8th Cir. 1973); Aronow v. United States, 432 F.2d 242 (9th Cir.
1970); Buono v. Norton, 212 F. Supp. 2d 212 (C.D. Cal. 2002), Aff'd, 371
F.3d 543 (9th Cir. 2004); Stevens v. Summerfield, 257 F.2d 205 (D.C. Cir.
1958); Schmidt v. Cline, 127 F. Supp.2d 1169 (D. Kan. 2000) (upholding
the national motto displayed on the wall in the county treasurer's office and
requiring the ACLU to pay the treasurer's attorney's fees for the frivolous
suit); Doe v. La. Supreme Court, No. 91–1635, 1992 WL 373566 (E.D. La.
Dec. 8, 1992); Carpenter v. City and County of San Francisco, 803 F. Supp.
337 (N.D. Cal. 1992); Sherman v. Community Consol. Sch. Dist. 21 of
Wheeling Township, 758 F. Supp. 1244 (N.D. Ill. 1991); North Carolina
Civil Liberties Union v. Constangy, 751 F. Supp. 552 (W.D.N.C. 1990);
Memorandum Opinion and Standing Rule for Courtroom of William M.
Acker, Jr., 1990 WL 126265 (N.D. Ala. Aug. 22, 1990); Allen v.
Consolidated City of Jacksonville, 719 F. Supp. 1532 (M.D. Fla.), aff'd, 880
F.2d 420 (11th Cir. 1989); Sherman v. Community Consol. Sch. Dist., 714
F. Supp. 932 (N.D. Ill. 1989); Horn & Hardart Co. v. Pillsbury Co., 703 F.
Supp. 1062 (S.D.N.Y.), judgment aff'd, 888 F.2d 8 (2d Cir. 1989); Smith v.
Lindstrom, 699 F. Supp. 549 (W.D. Va. 1988); Jewish War Veterans of

within a city seal was constitutional.[94] In Austin, Texas, the home of atheist Madalyn Murray O'Hair, Jon Murray, her son, brought suit against the city of Austin claiming that the Latin cross within the city seal was unconstitutional. However, the

United States v. United States, 695 F. Supp. 3 (D.D.C. 1988); _Berlin by Berlin v. Okaloosa County Sch. Dist._, No. PCA87-30450-RV, 1988 WL 85937 (N.D. Fla. Mar. 1, 1988); _Shomon v. Pott_, No. 84C10583, 1988 WL 4960 (N.D. Ill. Jan. 19, 1988); _ben Miriamv. Office of Personnel Management_, 647 F. Supp. 84 (M.D.N.C. 1986); _American Jewish Congress v. City of Chicago_, No. 85C9471, 1986 WL 20750 (N.D. Ill. Nov. 5, 1986); _Libin v. Town of Greenwich_, 625 F. Supp. 393 (D. Conn. 1985); _Greater Houston Chapter of ACLU v. Eckels_, 589 F. Supp. 222 (S.D. Tex. 1984); _Time, Inc. v. Regan_, 539 F. Supp. 1371 (S.D.N.Y. 1982), aff'd in part, rev'd in part, 468 U.S. 641 (1984); _Citizens Concerned for Separation of Church and State v. City and County of Denver_, 526 F. Supp. 1310 (D. Colo. 1981), cert. denied, 452 U.S. 963 (1981); _Voswinkel v. City of Charlotte_, 495 F. Supp. 588 (W.D.N.C. 1980); _McRae v. Califano_, 491 F. Supp. 630 (E.D.N.Y. 1980), rev'd sub nom., _Harris v. McRae_, 448 U.S. 297 (1980); _Citizens Concerned for Separation of Church and State v. City and County of Denver_, 481 F. Supp. 522 (D. Colo. 1979); _Gavin v. Peoples Natural Gas Co._, 464 F. Supp. 622 (W.D. Pa. 1979), vacated, 613 F.2d 482 (3d Cir. 1980); _O'Hair v. Blumenthal_, 462 F. Supp. 19 (W.D. Tex. 1978); _United States v. Handler_, 383 F. Supp. 1267 (D. Md. 1974); _Reed v. Van Hoven_, 237 F. Supp. 48 (W.D. Mich. 1965); _Crown Kosher Super Market of Mass., Inc. v. Gallagher_, 176 F. Supp. 466 (D. Mass. 1959), rev'd, 366 U.S. 617 (1961); _Stevens v. Summerfield_, 151 F. Supp. 343 (D.D.C. 1957); _Petition of Plywacki_, 107 F. Supp. 593 (D. Haw. 1952), rev'd, _Plywacki v. United States_, 205 F.2d 423 (9th Cir. 1953). For a well-reasoned opinion upholding the Ohio motto, "With God all things are possible," see _Capitol Square Review_, 243 F.3d at 289.

[94]The Supreme Court recently recognized that this issue had not yet been settled, although some of the circuit appellate courts have disagreed on the constitutionality of crosses or religious symbols within city seals. In the _City of Edmond_ case, the city lost its battle to maintain its religious symbol. The city petitioned the United States Supreme Court to review the case. Though the Supreme Court refused to review the case, Justices Rehnquist, Scalia, and Thomas filed a dissent, stating that the Court should have accepted the case for review to resolve the split within the circuit courts. _City of Edmond v. Robinson_, 517 U.S. 1201 (1996). The Court noted that the decisions in _City of Edmond v. Robinson_, 68 F.3d 1226 (10th Cir. 1995) and in _Harris v._

federal court ruled that the display of the Latin cross within the context of that particular city seal did not violate the First Amendment Establishment Clause.[95]

In 1959, the city of Marshfield, Wisconsin, accepted a statue of Jesus as a gift from a local citizen. The fifteen-foot-tall statue depicted Jesus standing on top of the world, which rested on a base bearing an inscription using twelve-inch lettering, "Christ Guide Us on Our Way."[96] The city placed the statue in what was later developed as a public park in downtown Marshfield. After a local resident filed suit in 1998, a newly formed private organization offered to purchase the 0.15 acres of land on which the statue was located. The bid process met all the state requirements, and the bid was the highest price the city had received for the sale of land ($3.30 per square foot). A federal court of appeals upheld the sale of the property but ordered that the city take some steps to make clear that the land was privately owned, since the surrounding property remained a prominent public park. In response, the city erected a four-foot-high, wrought–iron, gated fence, along with a sign indicating the property was privately owned.[97] Although the property is now privately owned, the

---

City of Zion, 927 F.2d at 1401, conflicted with *Murray v. City of Austin*, 947 F.2d at 147. Thus, the Court pointed out that while the Seventh and Tenth Circuit Courts of Appeal found the display of religious symbols in a public seal unconstitutional, the Fifth Circuit found such a display constitutional.
[95]*Murray v. City of Austin*, 947 F.2d 147 (5th Cir. 1991), *cert. denied*, 505 U.S. 1219 (1992).
[96]*See Freedom from Religion Found., Inc. v. City of Marshfield*, 203 F.3d 487 (7th Cir. 2000).
[97]*See Freedom from Religion Found., Inc. v. City of Marshfield*, No. 98-C-270-S, 2000 WL 767376 (W.D. Wis. May 9, 2000). In 1913 private citizens erected a cross on Mt. Soledad in San Diego. Vandals destroyed it in 1924.

statue of Jesus has not moved and is as visible now as it was prior to the lawsuit.

In summary, religious symbols may be displayed on public property with some constitutional limitations. Courts are split on whether Latin crosses may be displayed on public property. There are several ways to display religious symbols, nativity scenes, and the Ten Commandments on public property. First, the government may convey land to private entities which are under no constitutional restrictions. Second, the government may create a public forum by allowing private displays on public property. Third, the government may place both religious and secular symbols or materials in a publicly sponsored display. This final approach is the most common and time-tested way to create a constitutional display.

In 1934 someone replaced it with a cross made of wood and stucco. A windstorm destroyed that cross in 1952. The San Diego City Council then granted permission to a private group to dedicate a new cross to the veterans of World War I, World War II, and the Korean War. After a lawsuit challenged the cross, the city sold the property to a private group with a deed restriction that required the group to maintain the cross. A federal court later invalidated the sale as a sham because the city did not follow proper procedures in putting the property out for public bid. *See Paulson v. City of San Diego,* 294 F.3d 1124 (9th Cir. 2002).

10
THE RIGHT TO DISPLAY SIGNS ON PRIVATE PROPERTY

THE DISPLAY OF SIGNS on private property is an important constitutional right that frequently comes under attack.[1] In a Wisconsin case, Liberty Counsel worked with an individual who wanted to display four thousand crosses on his private property as a memorial to the number of babies aborted each day in America. Local city officials argued that the display of crosses was not permitted by the sign ordinance and was, therefore, unlawful. This allegation was clearly incorrect.

---

[1]Although this chapter focuses on signs displayed on private property, the same arguments apply to residents living in government housing who want to display signs on their units. In addition to all the arguments described in favor of displaying signs on private property, a person who lives in a government housing facility can also rely upon the public forum cases discussed in chapter 8 entitled "Use of Public Facilities."

Another instance brought to Liberty Counsel's attention involved a church sign. This sign included crosses on the church property in memory of unborn children who lost their lives through abortion. In the middle of the crosses, the church erected a sign explaining the reason for the memorial. City officials found that the crosses complied with the sign ordinance but wanted to remove the sign displayed with the crosses. The church argued that without the sign in the midst of the crosses, passersby would not know the meaning of the multiple crosses. In response, city officials determined that in order to prohibit the display of the explanatory sign, the city would pass an ordinance prohibiting the display of all religious signs. Liberty Counsel attorneys attended a city council meeting and warned the city such action was unconstitutional. At the city's request, Liberty Counsel assisted the city in drafting a new sign ordinance.

In another Liberty Counsel case, a person erected a sign on his private property with a pro-life message. One day he noticed that the sign was gone. He then erected another sign at the same location. To his surprise, he observed a crew of people dismantling the sign, and when he approached them, he realized they were city officials. Although other commercial signs were allowed in the area, city officials attempted to remove his sign because it displayed a pro-life message.

Political or cause-related messages on private property are a frequent source of controversy. Some sign ordinances restrict the duration a political sign may be erected. Other ordinances restrict cause-related messages by either banning them or requiring a permit. Such ordinances may violate the First Amendment.

When considering whether government can restrict the display of a religious, pro-life, political or any other cause-related sign, several factors must be considered, including the location of the display, the size of the display, the number and kind of exemptions, and whether the ordinance gives more protection to commercial than to noncommercial signs.

Signs on private property "are a form of expression protected by the Free Speech Clause."[2] "Communication by signs and posters is virtually pure speech."[3] Even "a minor burden on speech is sufficient to trigger a First Amendment analysis."[4] While governments may regulate the physical characteristics of signs and to some extent even their location, governments are restrained in regulating the content of signs, the duration of signs and certainly cannot ban political, religious, or issue-oriented signs.

The usual starting place in analyzing a sign restriction is first to determine whether the ordinance imposes a content-based or a content-neutral restriction on signs. However, as will be discussed, in 1994 the United States Supreme Court somewhat altered this typical approach and instead placed more importance on the right to post signs on private property.

Content-Based Versus Content-Neutral Restrictions

Using the longstanding approach to sign ordinances, consideration must be given to whether the law imposes a

---

[2]*City of Ladue v. Gilleo*, 512 U.S. 43, 48 (1994).
[3]*Arlington County Republican Comm. v. Arlington County*, 983 F.2d 587, 593 (4th Cir. 1993) (quoting *Baldwin v. Redwood*, 540 F.2d 1360, 1366 (9th Cir. 1976), *cert. denied sub nom., Leipzig v. Baldwin*, 431 U.S. 913 (1977)).
[4]*American Legion Post 7 of Durham, NC v. City of Durham*, 239 F.3d 601, 606 (4th Cir. 2001).

content-based or content-neutral restriction. "With rare exceptions, content-based discrimination in regulations of the speech of private citizens on private property or in a traditional public forum is presumptively impermissible, and this presumption is a very strong one."[5] Content-neutral restrictions are subject to a lower standard. Such restrictions are permissible if the government can prove it has a substantial interest in the regulation, and if the restriction is a reasonable time, place, and manner restriction which leaves open ample alternative channels of communication.[6] Thus, determining that the sign restriction is content-based will likely be the deathblow to the regulation.

The following cases illustrate how to determine whether a sign ordinance is content-based. These examples include restrictions where ordinances limit certain types of messages (such as political, campaign, religious, holiday, etc.), create categories of exemptions or distinguish between commercial and noncommercial speech.

POLITICAL, RELIGIOUS, OR ISSUE-ORIENTED SIGNS

To determine whether the ordinance operates as a content-based restriction on speech, the first task is to read the text to determine what kinds of signs are regulated. A typical ordinance might place a specific restriction on political or campaign signs.[7] Such restrictions are usually duration limitations

---

[5]*Ladue,* 512 U.S. at 59 (O'Connor, J., concurring) (citing *Simon & Shuster, Inc. v. Members of NY State Crime Victims Bd.,* 502 U.S. 105, 115–16 (1991)).

[6]*See, e.g., Burson v. Freeman,* 504 U.S. 191, 197 (1992).

[7]A law affecting a property owner's right to erect a political sign affects both the owner and the candidate's First Amendment rights. *See Craig v. Boren,* 429 U.S. 190, 194–97 (1976).

that restrict how long signs may be erected before and after an election. If other types of signs do not have duration limitations, or if the duration differs from political signs, then the ordinance is content-based. A "durational restriction on political campaign signs is content-based because 'determining whether a sign may stay up or must come down requires consideration of the message it conveys.'"[8] Thus, most courts have found that durational restrictions on political or campaign signs are unconstitutional.[9] A content-based restriction cannot be upheld merely to promote aesthetics. "No court has ever held that [interests in aesthetics and traffic safety] form a

---

[8]*Outdoor Systems, Inc. v. City of Lenexa,* 67 F. Supp. 2d 1231, 1240 (D. Kan. 1999) (quoting *Ackerly Communications v. City of Cambridge,* 88 F.3d 33, 36 n.7 (1st Cir. 1996) (following *City of Cincinnati v. Discovery Network, Inc.,* 507 U.S. 410, 427–31 [1993]); *see also Consolidated Edison Co. v. Public Serv. Comm'n,* 447 U.S. 530, 537 (1980) ("The First Amendment's hostility to content-based regulation extends not only to restrictions on particular viewpoints, but also to prohibition of public discussion of an entire topic."); *Whitton v. City of Gladstone,* 54 F.3d 1400, 1403–4 (8th Cir. 1995) ("The Supreme Court has held that a restriction on speech is content-based when the message conveyed determines whether the message is subject to the restriction.")

[9]*See, e.g., Whitton,* 54 F.3d at 1404; *Curry v. Prince George's County,* 33 F. Supp. 2d 447 (D. Md.1999) (striking down law which limited political signs to forty-five days before and seven days after election); *Outdoor Systems, Inc.,* 67 F. Supp. 2d at 1240 (striking down ordinance that required political signs be removed within seven days after an election); *Orazio v. Town of North Hempstead,* 426 F. Supp. 1144, 1149 (E.D.N.Y. 1977) (striking down ordinance containing pre-election time limit); *Dimas v. City of Warren,* 939 F. Supp 554, 556–57 (E.D. Mich. 1996) (striking down ordinance that prohibited temporary signs forty-five days before election); *Antioch v. Candidates' Outdoor Graphic Serv.,* 557 F. Supp. 52, 58 (N.D. Cal. 1983) (striking down ordinance limiting posting of outdoor political signs to sixty days prior to election); *Collier v. City of Tacoma,* 854 P.2d 1046, 1053 (Wash. 1993) (*en banc*) (ordinance limiting posting of political signs to sixty days before election is content-based).

compelling justification for a content-based restriction of political speech."[10] The same reasoning applies to duration restrictions on religious, holiday, or issue-oriented signs.

CATEGORICAL EXEMPTIONS

An ordinance also imposes content-based restrictions if the regulation exempts certain categories of signs. For example, a New York federal court found a city ordinance to be content-based when it did not require a permit for eighteen classes of signs.[11] Among others, the ordinance allowed traffic control signs, flags, memorial plagues, and signs of public information without a permit. In order to determine whether the sign required a permit, the city obviously considered the content of the message on the sign. Categorical exemptions raise the specter of content-based restrictions, which, as previously noted, are presumptively invalid.

COMMERCIAL VERSUS NONCOMMERCIAL MESSAGES

The Supreme Court has stated that noncommercial speech is afforded more First Amendment protection than commercial speech.[12] An ordinance providing more rights for commercial signs and fewer rights to noncommercial signs

---

[10]McCormack v. Township of Clinton, 872 F. Supp. 1320, 1325 n.2 (D.N.J. 1994); see also Whitton, 832 F. Supp. at 335. ("Traffic safety and aesthetics are significant interests . . . but they are not compelling interests, especially given the nature of the First Amendment rights at stake.")

[11]Knoeffler v. Town of Mamakating, 87 F. Supp. 2d 322, 330 (S.D.N.Y. 2000).

[12]Metromedia, Inc. v. City of San Diego, 453 U.S. 490 (1981); Matthews v. Town of Needham, 764 F.2d 58, 61 (1st Cir. 1985) (noncommercial speech is afforded more protection than commercial speech). In Discovery Network, 507 U.S. at 410, the Supreme Court seems to have narrowed the distinction between commercial and noncommercial speech.

would clearly be a content-based regulation and, therefore, presumptively invalid.[13] Therefore, it is impermissible to allow commercial signs while disallowing noncommercial signs.[14] Courts have ruled that an ordinance permitting commercial and other signs but banning political or issue-related messages violates the First Amendment.[15]

A city cannot allow commercial signs while restricting noncommercial signs.[16] The Supreme Court has noted the following in this regard:

> The fact that the city may value commercial messages relating to on-site goods and services more than it values commercial messages relating to off-site goods and services does not justify prohibiting an occupant from displaying its own ideas or those of others. . . . Insofar as the city tolerates [signs] at all, it cannot choose to limit their contents to commercial messages; the city may not conclude that the communication of commercial information concerning goods and services connected with a particular site is of greater value than the communication of noncommercial messages.[17]

---

[13]RAV v. City of St. Paul, 505 U.S. 377, 382 (1992).

[14]Runyon v. Fasi, 762 F. Supp. 280, 284 (D. Haw. 1991).

[15]Gilleo, 512 U.S. at 43; Tauber v. Town of Longmeadow, 695 F. Supp. 1358, 1362 (D. Mass. 1988) (city bylaws banning posting of political signs but allowing others constituted impermissible, content-based restriction on speech).

[16]Messer v. City of Douglasville, 975 F.2d 1505 (11th Cir. 1992), cert. denied, 508 U.S. 930 (1993).

[17]Metromedia, 453 U.S. at 513; see also John Donnelly & Sons v. Campbell, 639 F.2d 6 (1st Cir. 1980).

Noncommercial speech enjoys greater First Amendment protection than commercial speech. Thus, the government entity cannot grant more protection to commercial signs than to noncommercial signs.

Of course, the government can impose *content-neutral* restrictions on signs in the interest of aesthetics and traffic safety.[18] However, "aesthetic judgments are necessarily subjective, defying objective evaluation, and for that reason must be carefully scrutinized to determine if they are only a public rationalization of an impermissible purpose."[19] Moreover, aesthetic interests are never "sufficiently compelling to justify a content-based restriction on . . . freedom of expression."[20] In other words, in the interest of aesthetics, a government may not place differing restrictions on noncommercial and commercial signs. Such distinctions would be content-based and, therefore, invalid. Restrictions on the basis of aesthetics must be equally applied to all signs. However, simply because there is equal treatment between one message and another does not necessarily mean that all aesthetic restrictions are constitutional. Government may not, under the guise of aesthetics, prohibit free speech.

Another interest that a government entity may have in regulating signs is traffic safety. Sometimes aesthetics and traffic safety may combine in terms of limiting the size of signs. However, when considering "the universe of distractions that

---

[18]*Messer,* 975 F.2d at 1505; *Citizens United for Free Speech II v. Long Beach Township Bd. of Comm'rs,* 802 F. Supp. 1223 (D.N.J. 1992).
[19]*Metromedia,* 453 U.S. at 510.
[20]*Loftus v. Township of Lawrence Park,* 764 F. Supp. 354 (W.D. Pa. 1991); see also *Signs, Inc. v. Orange County,* 592 F. Supp. 693, 697 (M.D. Fla. 1983).

face motorists" on city streets, noncommercial signs "are not sufficiently significant to justify so serious a restriction upon expression."[21]

The constitutional protection of noncommercial signs is crucial to the ability of individuals to communicate this message. If individuals were not allowed to display signs, then some people may not be able to communicate at all to the general public. One court noted that other options of speaking through television and radio "involve substantially more cost and less autonomy and reach a significant number of nonlocal persons who [may] likely not have the interest or inclination to receive or act on such information."[22] Indeed, many citizens cannot afford to spend large sums of money to exercise their First Amendment rights.[23] In this regard, one court noted:

> Many messages advocating religious, social, or political views are greatly restricted from dissemination if they must primarily or solely rely upon costly print and electronic means for exposure; the expense and ineffectiveness in using either of these two forms of communication is often prohibitive, and signage remains an important alternative.[24]

---

[21]*Arlington County Republican Comm. v. Arlington County,* 790 F. Supp. 618, 624 (E.D. Va. 1992), *aff'd in part, rev'd in part, vacated in part,* 983 F.2d 587 (4th Cir. 1993).

[22]*Burkhart Advertising, Inc. v. City of Auburn,* 786 F. Supp. 721, 733 (N.D. Ind. 1991).

[23]*Arlington County Republican Comm.,* 790 F. Supp. at 627 (*citing Martin v. City of Struthers,* 319 U.S. 141, 146 (1943) ("Door-to-door distribution of circulars is essential to the poorly financed causes of little people.")).

[24]*Burkhart Advertising,* 786 F. Supp. at 733.

Indeed, a long-standing principle of constitutional law is that "one is not to have the exercise of his liberty of expression in appropriate places abridged on the plea that it may be exercised in some other place."[25] Therefore, it is insufficient to restrict the usage of signs simply because there might be alternative means of disseminating the message.

Although not often encountered, it is clearly impermissible to require the daily removal of signs or displays, because such a requirement would result in the denial of free speech. In one such case, the city of Cincinnati passed an ordinance prohibiting the presence of any display, exhibit, or structure in Fountain Square between the hours of 10:00 p.m. and 6:00 a.m. The case involved the Congregation of Lubavitch, which had regularly displayed an eighteen-foot menorah in Fountain Square in preceding years. The requirement of having no displays between certain specified hours appeared to be content-neutral, but in reality it would have required the Jewish organization to dismantle its menorah every day. It took approximately six hours to assemble and disassemble the structure. This unreasonable burden would have prohibited the display of the menorah. In this context, a federal appeals court rightfully struck down the ordinance as unconstitutional.[26] Although that case did not involve a sign ordinance, the constitutional principles apply to any ordinance, including those targeting signs. Since "communication by

---

[25]*Schneider v. New Jersey,* 308 U.S. 147, 163 (1939).
[26]*Congregation Lubavitch v. City of Cincinnati,* 997 F.2d 1160 (6th Cir. 1993). This case dealt with private speech on public property, but the principle applies with greater force when private speech occurs on private property.

signs and posters is virtually pure speech,"[27] the government may not easily restrict this form of expression.

Ordinances Lacking Objective Standards

A common problem with many ordinances is the lack of objective standards or the vagueness of the language contained therein. An ordinance containing vague words or language or which lacks objective standards is as unconstitutional as one imposing a content-based restriction. An ordinance is unconstitutionally vague if it "either forbids or requires the doing of an act in terms so vague that [persons] of common intelligence must necessarily guess at its meaning and differ as to its application."[28] The vagueness doctrine ensures that "all be informed as to what the state commands or forbids"[29] and is often applied in First Amendment cases.[30] Vague laws "may trap the innocent by not providing fair warning," "provide for arbitrary and discriminatory enforcement," impermissibly delegate policy matters to enforcement officials on an "ad hoc and subjective basis," and consequently chill free expression.[31] An ordinance might be vague if key words are not defined. For example, the meaning of the word *political* to some might connote signs promoting a candidate for elective office but to others might encompass the broad spectrum of governmental affairs or social debate.[32]

---

[27]*Baldwin*, 540 F.2d at 1366.

[28]*Connally v. General Constr. Co.*, 269 U.S. 385, 391 (1926).

[29]*Lanzetta v. New Jersey*, 306 U.S. 451, 453 (1939).

[30]*See Waterman v. Farmer*, 183 F.3d 208, 212 n.5 (3d Cir. 1999).

[31]*Grayned v. City of Rockford*, 408 U.S. 104, 108–9 (1972).

[32]*Curry*, 33 F. Supp. 2d at 454.

Words like *cause, issue, personal expression, holiday, memorial, plaque,* or even *religious* are not specific enough without definitional clarification.[33]

An ordinance that is vague, often by virtue of its vagueness, lacks objective standards and thereby vests unbridled discretion in some government official to grant or deny the sign. Such an ordinance may be challenged, even if the regulation has not been adversely applied. Challenging a law under the First Amendment when there has been no adverse application of the law is called a "facial" challenge. A "facial challenge lies whenever a licensing law gives a government official or agency substantial power to discriminate based on the content or viewpoint of speech by suppressing disfavored speech or disliked speakers."[34]

An Illinois federal court was confronted with a facial challenge to a sign ordinance that banned the placement of signs on private or public property without the consent of the owner or occupant.[35] The court observed that "although the ordinance does not require a 'permit' or 'license,' it does

---

[33]The term *religious* is exceptionally broad. The Supreme Court has ruled that religion may include both theistic and nontheistic beliefs so long as they are functionally equivalent to theistic religious belief. *See United States v. Seeder,* 380 U.S. 163 (1965) (conscientious objector status applies to nontheistic beliefs so long as such beliefs are the functional equivalent to theistic religious beliefs); *Torcaso v. Watkins,* 367 U.S. 488 n.3 (1961) (defining religion to include both theistic and nontheistic beliefs such as secular humanism). Constitutional scholars have also acknowledged the difficulty in defining religion. *See, e.g.,* Bower, *Delimiting Religion in the Constitution: A Classification Problem,* 11 VAL. U. L. REV. 163 (1977); A. Stephen Boyan Jr., *Defining Religion in Operational and Institutional Terms,* 116 U. PA. L. REV. 479 (1968).

[34]*City of Lakewood v. Plain Dealer Publishing Co.,* 486 U.S. 750, 759 (1988).

[35]*See Lawson v. City of Kankakee,* 81 F. Supp. 2d 930 (C.D. Ill. 2000).

require consent from the City, which owns the property on which the Plaintiff seeks to post his sign."[36] The court found that the ordinance granted "unnamed City officials unbridled discretion to allow some signs to remain while authorizing the removal of others" and, thus, violated the First Amendment.[37]

Heightened Protection for Displaying Signs on Private Property

As previously stated, the long-standing approach to sign ordinances is to determine whether the regulation is content-based or content-neutral. However, in 1994 the Supreme Court struck down a sign ordinance without following the traditional approach. The Court seemed to elevate the right to place signs on private property to a level never before articulated. The apparent reason for this is twofold: (1) in the same way the home is one's castle, the home is the preferred place to engage in personal expression; and (2) if the right to speak on private property could be eliminated by the government banning all categories of speech, the right to speak would easily be placed in grave danger.[38]

---

[36]*Id.* at 935.
[37]*Id.*
[38]See *Gilleo,* 512 U.S. at 43. One court recognized the significance of the Supreme Court's ruling in 1994 by observing, "In *City of Ladue,* the Supreme Court took a different tack." *Curry,* 33 F. Supp. 2d at 453. "The Court long has recognized that by limiting the availability of particular means of communication, content-neutral restrictions can significantly impair the ability of individuals to communicate their views to others. . . . To ensure 'the widest possible dissemination of information' (*Associated Press v. United States,* 326 U.S. 1, 20 (1945)), and the 'unfettered interchange of ideas,' (*Roth v. United States,* 354 U.S. 476, 484 (1957)) the first

The case arose because of a sign ordinance enacted by the City of Ladue, Missouri, which prohibited homeowners from displaying any sign on their property unless the sign fell among one of ten exemptions, including "residence identification" signs, "for sale" signs, signs warning of safety hazards, signs for churches, religious institutions or schools, commercial signs in commercial or industrial zones and on-site gasoline filling station advertising signs.[39] Margaret Gilleo, owner of a single-family home, placed an eight- by eleven-inch sign in the second-story window of her home stating, "For Peace in the Gulf." Since Ms. Gilleo's sign was not included as a permitted exemption, it was banned from display. Obviously, such an ordinance is content-based. In fact, both the trial and appellate courts found the ordinance unconstitutional because it was content-based. However, instead of deciding the case on this basis, the Court set that question aside and launched into a discussion about the broad right to display signs on private property.[40] The Court cited two reasons for avoiding a content-based analysis. First, if the decision rested solely on whether the ordinance was content-based, then the city could amend its ordinance to prohibit all signs. Second, the Court noted that Ms. Gilleo was not concerned about the scope of the exemptions available in other locations, but rather she asserted her "constitutional

---

amendment prohibits not only content-based restrictions that censor particular points of view but also content-neutral restrictions that unduly constrict the opportunities for free expression." *Gilleo*, 512 U.S. at 55 n.13 (quoting Geoffrey R. Stone, *Content-Neutral Restrictions*, 54 U. CHI. L. REV. 46, 57–58 [1987]).
[39]*See Gilleo*, 512 U.S. at 45.
[40]*Id.* at 53.

right to display an antiwar sign at her own home."[41] Thus, the Court paved the way for discussing the broad right of free speech on private residential property.

The Court pointed out that a prohibition on speech is not unconstitutional "merely because it applies to a sizeable category of speech."[42] For example, a law banning the posting of any flyers on public utility poles may be a valid regulation.[43] Such a restriction may be upheld because the location of the intended speech (public utility poles) is "not a 'uniquely valuable or important mode of communication,'" especially when there is no evidence that the "ability to communicate effectively is threatened by ever-increasing restrictions on expression."[44] The Court then stated:

> Here, in contrast, Ladue has almost completely foreclosed a venerable means of communication that is both unique and important. It has totally foreclosed that medium to political, religious, or personal messages. Signs that react to a local happening or express a view on a controversial issue both reflect and animate change in the life of a community. Often placed on lawns or in windows, residential signs play an important part in political campaigns, during which they are displayed to signal the resident's support for particular candidates, parties, or causes. They may not afford the same opportunities for conveying complex

---

[41]*Id.*
[42]*Id.* at 54.
[43]*Id.* (citing *Members of City Council of L.A. v. Taxpayers for Vincent,* 466 U.S. 789 (1984) (upholding law banning posting of signs on public utility poles).
[44]*Gilleo,* 512 U.S. at 54 (quoting *Taxpayers for Vincent,* 466 U.S. at 812).

ideas as do other media, but residential signs have long been an important and distinct medium of expression.[45]

The Court stressed that the home is a unique place in which to communicate and that the impact of certain messages is magnified in this setting. The Court was also concerned that government would overreach to restrict this unique form of communication.[46] The court declared:

> Our prior decisions have voiced particular concern with laws that foreclose an entire medium of expression. Thus, we have held invalid ordinances that completely banned the distribution of pamphlets within the municipality,[47] handbills on the public streets,[48] the door-to-door distribution of literature,[49] and live entertainment.[50] Although prohibitions foreclosing entire media may be completely free of content or viewpoint discrimination, the danger they pose to the freedom of speech is readily apparent—

[45]*Gilleo*, 512 U.S. at 54–55 (footnote omitted).

[46]"The elimination of a cheap and handy medium of expression is especially apt to deter *individuals* from communicating their views to the public, for unlike businesses (and even political organizations) individuals generally realize few tangible benefits from such communication." *Id.* at 56 n.15.

[47]*Lovell v. City of Griffin*, 303 U.S. 444, 451–52 (1938).

[48]*Jamison v. Texas*, 318 U.S. 413, 416 (1943).

[49]*Martin*, 319 U.S. at 145–49; *Schneider v. State of N.J.*, 308 U.S. 147, 164–65 (1939).

[50]*Schad v. Borough of Mount Ephraim*, 452 U.S. 61, 75–76 (1981); *see also Frisby v. Schultz*, 487 U.S. 474, 486 (1988) (picketing focused on individual residence is "fundamentally different from more generally directed means of communication that may not be completely banned in residential areas").

by eliminating a common means of speaking, such measures can suppress too much speech.[51]

Indeed, the home is one's castle, and any homeowner would certainly expect to have the right to engage in free expression on residential property. The court stressed this important location of speech in its opinion as follows:

> Displaying a sign from one's own residence often carries a message quite distinct from placing the same sign someplace else, or conveying the same text or picture by other means. Precisely because of their location, such signs provide information about the identity of the "speaker." As an early and eminent student of rhetoric observed, the identity of the speaker is an important component of many attempts to persuade. A sign advocating "Peace in the Gulf" in the front lawn of a retired general or decorated war veteran may provoke a different reaction than the same sign in a 10-year-old child's bedroom window or the same message on a bumper sticker of a passing automobile. An espousal of socialism may carry different implications when displayed on the grounds of a stately mansion than when pasted on a factory wall or an ambulatory sandwich board.
>
> Residential signs are an unusually cheap and convenient form of communication. Especially for persons of modest means or limited mobility, a yard or window sign may have no practical substitute.[52] Even

---

[51]*Gilleo*, 512 U.S. at 55.

[52]*Cf. Taxpayers for Vincent*, 466 U.S. at 812–13 n.30; *Anderson v. Celebrezze*, 460 U.S. 780, 793–94 (1983); *Martin*, 319 U.S. at 146; *Milk Wagon Drivers v. Meadowmoor Dairies, Inc.*, 312 U.S. 287, 293 (1941).

for the affluent, the added costs in money or time of taking out a newspaper advertisement, handing out leaflets on the street, or standing in front of one's house with a handheld sign may make the difference between participating and not participating in some public debate. Furthermore, a person who puts up a sign at her residence often intends to reach neighbors, an audience that could not be reached nearly as well by other means.

A special respect for individual liberty in the home has long been part of our culture and our law,[53]; that principle has special resonance when the government seeks to constrain a person's ability to speak there.[54] Most Americans would be understandably dismayed, given that tradition, to learn that it was illegal to display from their window an eight- by eleven-inch sign expressing their political views. Whereas the government's need to mediate among various competing uses, including expressive ones, for public streets and facilities is constant and unavoidable,[55] its need to regulate temperate speech from the home is surely much less pressing.[56]

Our decision that Ladue's ban on almost all residential signs violates the First Amendment by no means leaves the City powerless to address the ills that may be associated with residential signs. It bears

---

[53]See, e.g. Payton v. New York, 445 U.S. 573, 596–97, and nn.44–45 (1980).

[54]See Spence v. Washington, 418 U.S. 405, 406 (1974) (per curiam).

[55]See Cox v. New Hampshire, 312 U.S. 569, 574, 576 (1941); see also Widmar v. Vincent, 454 U.S. 263, 278 (1981) (Stevens, J., concurring in judgment).

[56]See Spence, 418 U.S. at 409.

mentioning that individual residents themselves have strong incentives to keep their own property values up and to prevent "visual clutter" in their own yards and neighborhoods—incentives markedly different from those of persons who erect signs on others' land, in others' neighborhoods, or on public property. Residents' self-interest diminishes the danger of the "unlimited" proliferation of residential signs that concerns the City of Ladue. We are confident that more temperate measures could in large part satisfy Ladue's stated regulatory needs without harm to the First Amendment rights of its citizens. As currently framed, however, the ordinance abridges those rights.[57]

Thus, the High Court struck down Ladue's ordinance under the First Amendment without determining whether the regulation was content-based. This case, therefore, elevates the right to speech on private residential property to a new level of superiority.

In summary, the display of religious, political, pro-life, or any other issue-oriented sign is constitutionally protected speech. Government regulations which restrict speech based on the content of the message proclaimed will rarely survive a constitutional challenge. Content-based restrictions are found in regulations that discriminate based on categories of speech or subject matter. Categorical exemptions in sign ordinances raise the specter of content-based restrictions. Clearly, if the government allows commercial signs, then it may not restrict the presence of noncommercial signs. Most residential neighborhoods allow commercial speech in the

---

[57]*Gilleo,* 512 U.S. at 56–59 (footnotes omitted).

form of real estate signs. As such, religious, political, pro-life, and other issue-oriented signs may also be displayed on residential property. Certain restrictions may be placed on the display of signs for aesthetic purposes or traffic control, but these restrictions will never justify a content-based sign ordinance. Additionally, if the ordinance is so vague as to leave one guessing its meaning, or if it vests unbridled discretion in some government official to grant or deny a request to post a sign, the regulation will not pass constitutional muster. Finally, even if the sign ordinance applies to all speech, it may not be so restrictive as to essentially prohibit First Amendment activity. The home is a unique place from which to communicate, and thus the government has little valid interest in regulating the private display of signs on private property.

11
DOOR-TO-DOOR WITNESSING

THE RIGHT TO WITNESS, canvass, or distribute literature going door-to-door in private residential neighborhoods is an important right protected by the Constitution. Ever since the 1930s when the United States Supreme Court first confronted this issue, "the Court has invalidated restrictions on door-to-door canvassing and pamphleteering."[1] This chapter will focus on the right to go door-to-door in private neighborhoods to engage in noncommercial religious or secular speech or canvassing either verbally or through distribution of literature.[2]

---

[1]*Watchtower Bible and Tract Society of New York, Inc. v. Village of Stratton,* 536 U.S. 150, 159 (2002). *See, e.g., Hynes v. Mayor and Council of Oradell,* 425 U.S. 610 (1976); *Martin v. City of Struthers,* 319 U.S. 141 (1943); *Murdock v. Pennsylvania,* 319 U.S. 105 (1943); *Jamison v. Texas,* 318 U.S. 413 (1943); *Cantwell v. Connecticut,* 310 U.S. 296 (1940); *Schneider v. State of N.J.,* 308 U.S. 147 (1939); *Lovell v. City of Griffin,* 303 U.S. 444 (1938).

[2]If the purpose of going door-to-door is for commercial sales or for the solicitation of funds, then the government may have a greater interest in placing restrictions on such activity that would otherwise be impermissible if

Most of the door-to-door witnessing cases have involved Jehovah's Witnesses.[3] The most recent Supreme Court case arose in the Village of Stratton, Ohio. The Village ordinance prohibited "canvassers" and others from "going in and upon" private residential property for the purpose of promoting any "cause" without first having obtained a permit from the mayor.[4] A group of Jehovah's Witnesses challenged the ordinance, claiming they were following the example of the apostle Paul, who taught publicly from house to house. They also claimed they were mandated by the Scriptures to go into all the world and preach the gospel.[5]

In striking down the ordinance, the High Court stressed several factors. First, the Court emphasized the value of the speech involved. The Court noted:

> Hand distribution of religious tracts is an age-old form of missionary evangelism—as old as the history of printing presses. It has been a potent force in various religious movements down through the years. . . . This form of religious activity occupies the same high estate under the First Amendment as do worship in

---

placed on noncommercial speech. However, this does not mean that the government may place burdensome restrictions on commercial speech. *See Village of Stratton,* 536 U.S. at 150, 168–69.

[3]The terms *witnessing* and *witness* in this chapter are often used to describe the particular activity in a given case. However, these terms may also be used when addressing the right to go door-to-door to engage in either religious or secular speech. This is done to avoid repeating the all-encompassing phrase, "witness, canvass or distribute literature." From a First Amendment Free Speech standpoint, there is no constitutional difference between these forms of expression. If the speech is religious, there may be the added right of Free Exercise of Religion.

[4]*Village of Stratton,* 536 U.S. at 153.

[5]*See id.* at 160; *see also* Acts 20:20; Mark 16:15.

the churches and preaching from the pulpits. It has the same claim to protection as the more orthodox and conventional exercises of religion. It also has the same claim as the others to the guarantees of freedom of speech and freedom of the press.[6]

Second, the Supreme Court underscored "the historical importance of door-to-door canvassing and pamphleteering as vehicles for the dissemination of ideas."[7] In this respect, the Court noted:

Pamphlets have proved most effective instruments in the dissemination of opinion. And perhaps the most effective way of bringing them to the notice of individuals is their distribution at the homes of the people. On this method of communication the ordinance imposes censorship, abuse of which engendered the struggle in England which eventuated in the establishment of the doctrine of the freedom of the press embodied in our Constitution. To require a censorship through license which makes impossible the *free and unhampered* distribution of pamphlets strikes at the very heart of the constitutional guarantees.[8]

Finally, the Court noted that the struggle of the Jehovah's Witnesses has not been a struggle for their rights alone. The importance of going door-to-door is broader than one group

---

[6]*Village of Stratton,* 536 U.S. at 161–62 (quoting *Murdock,* 319 U.S. at 109).

[7]*Id.* at 151.

[8]*Id.* at 162 (quoting *Schneider,* 308 U.S. at 164) (emphasis added by *Village of Stratton*).

or one cause. Many people rely on this method of communication. "Door-to-door distribution of circulars is essential to the poorly financed causes of little people."[9] Because of the importance of door-to-door speech, the Court expressed its disdain for laws requiring prior registration for such speech as follows:

> As a matter of principle a requirement of registration in order to make a public speech would seem generally incompatible with an exercise of the rights of free speech and free assembly. . . . If the exercise of the rights of free speech and free assembly cannot be made a crime, we do not think this can be accomplished by the device of requiring previous registration as a condition for exercising them and making such a condition the foundation for restraining in advance their exercise and for imposing a penalty for violating such a restraining order. So long as no more is involved than exercise of the rights of free speech and free assembly, it is immune to such a restriction. If one who solicits support for the cause of labor may be required to register as a condition to the exercise of his right to make a public speech, so may he who seeks to rally support for any social, business, religious or political cause. We think a requirement that one must register before he undertakes to make a public speech to enlist support for a lawful movement

---

[9]*Village of Stratton,* 536 U.S. at 163 (quoting *Martin,* 319 U.S. at 144–46); *see also Schaumburg v. Citizens for a Better Environment,* 444 U.S. 620 (1980); *Hynes,* 425 U.S. at 610; *Thomas v. Collins,* 323 U.S. 516 (1945).

is quite incompatible with the requirements of the First Amendment.[10]

The Court rejected the Village's argument that the permit process placed a minor burden on speech. "Even if the issuance of permits by the mayor's office is a ministerial task that is performed promptly and at no cost to the applicant, a law requiring a permit to engage in such speech constitutes a dramatic departure from our national heritage and constitutional tradition."[11] The Supreme Court cited three reasons for striking down this law that required a permit to engage in door-to-door speech.

First, obtaining a permit to speak interferes with those who want to speak anonymously.[12] "The decision to favor anonymity may be motivated by fear of economic or official retaliation, by concern about social ostracism, or merely by a desire to preserve as much of one's privacy as possible."[13] "The requirement that a canvasser must be identified in a permit application filed in the mayor's office and available for public inspection necessarily results in a surrender of that anonymity."[14]

Second, "requiring a permit as a prior condition on the exercise of the right to speak imposes an objective burden on

---

[10]*Village of Stratton*, 536 U.S. at 164 (quoting *Thomas*, 323 U.S. at 539–40).

[11]*Village of Stratton*, 536 U.S. at 166.

[12]*See id.; see also McIntyre v. Ohio Elections Comm'n*, 514 U.S. 334 (1995).

[13]*Village of Stratton*, 536 U.S. at 166 (quoting *McIntyre*, 514 U.S. at 341–42).

[14]*Id.* at 151; *see also Buckley v. American Constitutional Law Found., Inc.*, 525 U.S. 182 (1999) (striking down a badge requirement for those distributing petition circulars).

some speech of citizens holding religious or patriotic views."[15] A number of people object to applying for a permit based on religious principle. There are also some patriotic citizens "who have such firm convictions about their constitutional right to engage in uninhibited debate in the context of door-to-door advocacy, that they would prefer silence to speech licensed by a petty official."[16]

Third, a permit requirement chills spontaneous speech. "A person who made a decision on a holiday or a weekend to take an active part in a political campaign could not begin to pass out handbills until after he or she obtained the required permit. Even a spontaneous decision to go across the street and urge a neighbor to vote against the mayor could not lawfully be implemented without first obtaining the mayor's permission."[17] The High Court pointed out that any interest the government may have in protecting a homeowner's privacy or in preventing crime can be accomplished by an individual citizen posting a "No Solicitation" sign on the property.[18]

The Supreme Court's decision in *Village of Stratton* drew from a rich history of cases which had similarly struck down laws restricting door-to-door speech. In one of those cases, a city attempted to impose a licensing scheme essentially banning Jehovah's Witnesses from witnessing door-to-door in predominantly Roman Catholic neighborhoods. The Jehovah's Witnesses played records through loud speakers attacking the Roman Catholic church as an "enemy" and

---

[15]*Village of Stratton,* 536 U.S. at 167.
[16]*Id.*
[17]*Id.*
[18]*See id.* at 167–68.

stating that the church was of the devil. This licensing scheme attempted to prohibit the door-to-door witnessing activities of the Jehovah's Witnesses, but the United States Supreme Court ruled the scheme unconstitutional.[19] The regulation at issue allowed the city officials to determine who would be permitted to engage in solicitation or distribution of literature based on the content of the message.

The United States Supreme Court also ruled unconstitutional a municipal "license tax" that was imposed upon door-to-door solicitation and witnessing by Jehovah's Witnesses. The Court noted:

> Those who can tax the privilege of engaging in this form of missionary evangelism can close its doors to all those who do not have a full purse. Spreading religious beliefs in this ancient and honorable manner would thus be denied the needy. Those who can deprive religious groups of their colporteurs can take from them a part of the vital power of the press which has survived from the Reformation.[20]

In one case, the Supreme Court considered the constitutionality of a city ordinance that made it unlawful for any person distributing literature "to ring the doorbell, sound the door knocker, or otherwise summon the inmate or inmates of any residence to the door for the purpose of receiving" such literature. The United State Supreme Court ruled this type of ordinance unconstitutional stating:

---

[19]See Cantwell, 310 U.S. at 296; Tally, 362 U.S. at 60.
[20]Murdock, 319 U.S. at 112; see also Grosjean v. American Press Co., 297 U.S. 233 (1936) (striking down a circulation licensing tax).

Freedom to distribute information to every citizen wherever he desires to receive it is so clearly vital to the preservation of a free society that, putting aside reasonable police and health regulations of time and manner of distribution, it must be fully preserved.[21]

Interestingly named, the town of Babylon had an ordinance requiring a resident's consent before a speaker could approach a home. A federal district court in New York ruled that to require the "consent of householders before approaching their homes constitutes, in effect, an indirect unconstitutional imposition of a licensing fee; it generates costs which burden the exercise of first amendment rights in direct proportion to the number of persons the speaker wants to reach."[22]

Numerous other federal courts have ruled that cities may not prohibit door-to-door witnessing.[23] In the city of Ocoee, Florida, Pamela Jones and Marcia Muller sought to distribute political and religious literature in residential neighborhoods, but the city had a policy requiring a permit prior to distributing any literature. This permit had to be filled out on a specified form which was then reviewed by the chief of police. The applicant was required to identify various physical features including any bodily scars or markings. Prior to the issuance

---

[21]*Martin,* 319 U.S. at 146–67.

[22]*Troyer v. Town of Babylon,* 483 F. Supp. 1135, 1139 (E.D.N.Y.), *aff'd,* 628 F.2d 1346 (2d Cir.), *aff'd,* 449 U.S. 998 (1980).

[23]*See, e.g. Largent v. Texas,* 318 U.S. 418 (1943); *Jamison,* 318 U.S. at 413; *Weissman v. City of Alamogordo,* 472 F. Supp. 425 (D.N.M. 1979); *McMurdie v. Doutt,* 468 F. Supp. 766 (N.D. Ohio 1979); *Levers v. City of Tullahoma,* 446 F. Supp. 884 (E.D. Tenn. 1978); *Murdock v. City of Jacksonville,* 361 F. Supp. 1083 (M.D. Fla. 1973).

of the permit, the chief of police was required to determine that the applicant was a person of "good moral character." After Liberty Counsel filed suit, the city changed the policy and no longer requires prior permission to distribute literature door-to-door.

Reviewing an attempt by a municipality to regulate neighborhood activities like canvassing and soliciting, the United States Supreme Court stated that any regulation in this area must not "intrude upon the rights of free speech and free assembly."[24] Other courts have recognized the value in literature distribution.

> From the time of the founding of our nation, the distribution of written material has been an essential weapon in the defense of liberty. Throughout the years, the leaflet has retained its vitality as an effective and inexpensive means of disseminating religious and political thought. Today when selective access to the channels of mass communication limits the expression of diverse opinion, the handbill remains important to the promise of full and free discussion of public issues. For those of moderate means, but deep conviction, freedom to circulate flyers implicates fundamental liberties.[25]

Indeed, the freedom to speak and circulate flyers, especially in your neighborhood, implicates fundamental constitutional liberties.

---

[24]*Thomas,* 323 U.S. at 540–41.
[25]*Paulsen v. County of Nassau,* 925 F.2d 65, 66 (2d Cir. 1991).

Because of their vital role for people who lack access to more elaborate (and more costly) channels of communication, certain public places have special status under the First Amendment. . . . The doctrine of the public forum achieves a central purpose of the freedom of the speech—the role of equality of communicative opportunities—by opening avenues of expression for the "poorly financed causes of little people." . . . As our court has articulated the theme of the public forum cases, regulation of free expression in the public areas . . . affects most frequently those who advocate unpopular causes. It is those who seek to change the status quo who have historically taken to the streets or other public places to promote their causes. Those who are satisfied with our society as it is, normally use other forums.[26]

The Supreme Court ruled unconstitutional a city ordinance that made it a crime for a solicitor or canvasser to knock on the front door of a resident's home or ring the doorbell.[27] The ordinance was too broad and impinged upon constitutional freedoms by substituting "the judgment of the community for the judgment of the individual householder."[28] The Supreme Court has also invalidated an ordinance that prohibited the distribution of "literature of any kind . . . without first obtaining written permission from the city manager."[29]

---

[26]*Carreras v. City of Anaheim*, 768 F.2d 1039, 1043 (9th Cir. 1985) (quoting *Martin*, 319 U.S. at 146) (citations omitted).
[27]*See Martin*, 319 U.S. at 141; *see also Staub v. City of Baxley*, 355 U.S. 313 (1958).
[28]*Martin*, 319 U.S. at 144.
[29]*Lovell*, 303 U.S. at 447.

The Court ruled unconstitutional a city policy that required persons to obtain a permit, which would not be issued if the chief of police decided that the "canvasser is not of good character or is canvassing for a project not free from fraud."[30] The Court found the ordinance unconstitutional because the canvasser's "liberty to communicate with residents of the town at their homes depends upon the exercise of the officer's discretion."[31] In another case, the High Court ruled unconstitutional a municipal ordinance which required that advance written notice be given to the local police department by any person desiring to canvas, solicit, or call from house to house for a recognized charitable cause, or for a federal, state, county, or municipal political campaign or cause.[32]

The right to freedom of speech is a precious liberty. It is important that this liberty be vigilantly guarded within residential neighborhoods, because it is important to allow free communication in these areas. Whether the issue is door-to-door canvassing, picketing on a public sidewalk, or carrying on expressive activity in a public park, any policy that contains a prior licensing scheme is constitutionally suspect. Generally the government has no business monitoring the speech activities of its citizens. An individual resident can avoid intrusion to their dwelling by posting a sign indicating that solicitors, canvassers, or leafleteers are not welcome. However, this decision is best left to the individual resident and not to the government.

---

[30]*Schneider,* 308 U.S. at 147.
[31]*Id.* at 158.
[32]*See Hynes,* 425 U.S. at 610.

In addition to door-to-door witnessing, picketing in residential neighborhoods is also constitutionally protected.[33] Most residential neighborhoods have public sidewalks, and these public sidewalks are considered traditional public forums.[34] As the Supreme Court has noted, public sidewalks "have immemorially been held in trust for the use of the public."[35] Notwithstanding the fact that the public sidewalks are in residential neighborhoods, they still are classified as traditional public forums and, therefore, are open to expressive activity by the public.

One difference between residential and business areas containing public sidewalks is that in residential areas, the government has an interest in protecting "the well-being, tranquility, and privacy of the home."[36] In this regard, the Supreme Court has stated that the home is the "last citadel of the tired, the weary, and the sick."[37] In order to protect residential privacy, a city may pass an ordinance that restricts targeted picketing of a single residential address. Focused "picketing taking place solely in front of a particular residence" may be prohibited, but the government may not ban the general "marching through residential neighborhoods, or even walking around in front of an entire block of houses."[38]

---

[33]For a more in-depth discussion of picketing, see chapter 12 entitled, "The Right to Picket, Demonstrate, and Parade."

[34]See Frisby v. Schultz, 487 U.S. 474, 481 (1988); see also Perry Educ. Ass'n v. Perry Local Educators' Ass'n, 460 U.S. 37 (1983); Hague v. CIO, 307 U.S. 496, 515 (1939).

[35]Frisby, 487 U.S. at 481 (quoting Hague, 307 U.S. at 515).

[36]Frisby, 487 U.S. at 484.

[37]Id.

[38]Frisby, 487 U.S. at 477, 483; see also Madsen v. Women's Health Ctr., Inc., 512 U.S. 753, 775–76 (1994).

In other words, while the government may prohibit picketing targeted at a single residential address, it may not prohibit general picketing throughout a neighborhood. Individuals may protest a particular residence but must do so by marching on the public sidewalk throughout the neighborhood. Congregating solely in front of a single residential home can be restricted, but marching generally throughout the neighborhood protesting an individual location is constitutionally protected.

In summary, the right to go door-to-door in private neighborhoods to engage in noncommercial religious or secular speech or canvassing, either verbally or through distribution of literature, has long been protected by the First Amendment. Laws which restrict this right or which require a permit to engage in such noncommercial speech are unconstitutional.

12
THE RIGHT TO PICKET, DEMONSTRATE, AND PARADE

THE ABILITY OF CITIZENS to gather peacefully and demonstrate for a particular cause is an important component of liberty. The First Amendment prohibits the government from "abridging the freedom of speech" and from prohibiting "the right of the people peacefully to assemble."[1] The Supreme Court has noted:

> Public places are of necessity the locus for discussion of public issues, as well as protest against arbitrary government action. At the heart of our jurisprudence lies the principle that in a free nation citizens must have the right to gather and speak with other persons in public places.[2]

---

[1] *See* U.S. Const. amend. I.
[2] *ISKCON v. Lee,* 505 U.S. 672, 696 (1992) (Kennedy, J., concurring, joined by Blackmun, Stevens and Souter).

Picketing is expressive activity protected by the First Amendment Free Speech Clause. The right to picket or demonstrate is, in part, dependent on the location. Picketing in traditional public forums such as parks, streets, and sidewalks is clearly protected speech. Picketing may also occur outside of these areas in limited or designated public forums or in nonpublic forums.[3] When considering picketing, it is also important to determine whether the property site is privately or publicly owned, and there may be certain noise-level restrictions.

Some courts have placed buffer zones around areas frequented by picketers to protect private business interests. Because some pickets have turned violent, courts have attempted to restrain this violence. However, nonviolent picketing and demonstrating predate the Constitution and are clearly protected by the First Amendment.

The act of picketing may encompass several factors, including carrying picket signs, wearing inscribed messages on clothing, speaking, distributing literature, or merely congregating. The Supreme Court has noted that direct one-on-one communication is probably "the most effective, fundamental, and perhaps economical avenue of political discourse."[4] The First Amendment protects the speaker's right "not only to advocate their cause but also to select what they believe to be the most effective means for doing so."[5]

The First Amendment limits the government's ability to restrict picketing because of the content of the speech. The

---

[3]See chapter 8 for a discussion about public forums.
[4]*Meyer v. Grant*, 486 U.S. 414, 424 (1988).
[5]*Id.*

Court stated:

> The First Amendment means that the government has no power to restrict expression because of its message, its ideas, its subject matter, or its content. . . . Any restriction on expressive activity because of its content would completely undercut the "profound national commitment to the principle that debate on public issues should be uninhibited, robust, and wide-open."[6]

Indeed, "regulations which permit the government to discriminate on the basis of the content of the message cannot be tolerated under the First Amendment."[7] Any "content-based restriction on political speech in a public forum . . . must be subjected to the most exacting scrutiny."[8] Restricting picketing or demonstrating based on the content of the speech constitutes "censorship in a most odious form," which in most cases violates the First Amendment.[9] Rather than restricting speech, the government should continue to offer other avenues of speech. Speech should be combated with more speech rather than censorship. Education is the proper and preferable alternative.[10]

A correlative of individual picketing and demonstration is the constitutional right to engage in such activity with others of similar beliefs. The "freedom to associate applies to the

---

[6]*Police Dep't of Chicago v. Mosley,* 408 U.S. 92, 95–96 (1972) (quoting *New York Times Co. v. Sullivan,* 376 U.S. 254, 270 [1963]).

[7]*Simon & Schuster v. New York Crime Victims Bd.,* 502 U.S. 105, 116 (1991).

[8]*Boos v. Barry,* 485 U.S. 312, 321 (1988).

[9]*Cox v. Louisiana,* 379 U.S. 536, 581 (1965).

[10]*See Whitney v. California,* 274 U.S. 357 (1927).

beliefs we share, and to those we consider reprehensible. It tends to produce the diversity of opinion that oils the machinery of democratic government and insures peaceful, orderly change."[11] Although the term "freedom of association" is not specifically used in the First Amendment, "it has long been held to be implicit in the freedoms of speech, assembly, and petition."[12] The Supreme Court has declared that the "freedom to speak, to worship, and to petition the Government for the redress of grievances could not be vigorously protected from interference by the State [if] a correlative freedom to engage in group effort toward those ends were not also guaranteed."[13]

Whether picketing is done individually or in a group, there is "no conceivable government interest" that justifies a complete ban on this protected First Amendment activity.[14] Although some courts have attempted to restrict peaceful literature distribution, "a complete ban on handbilling would be substantially broader" than any necessary government interest.[15] Indeed, peaceful literature distribution cannot be prohibited under the concern that to allow such might block the flow of traffic on a public sidewalk, because one "need not ponder the contents of a leaflet or pamphlet in order to mechanically take it out of someone's hand."[16]

---

[11]*Gilmore v. City of Montgomery,* 417 U.S. 556, 575 (1974).
[12]*Healy v. James,* 408 U.S. 169, 181 (1972).
[13]*Roberts v. United States Jaycees,* 468 U.S. 609, 622 (1984).
[14]See *Board of Airport Comm'rs of Los Angeles v. Jews for Jesus,* 482 U.S. 569, 575 (1987).
[15]*Ward v. Rock Against Racism,* 491 U.S. 781, 799 n.7 (1989).
[16]*Lee,* 505 U.S. at 690 (citing *United States v. Kokinda,* 497 U.S. 720, 734 (1990)).

The Right to Picket, Demonstrate, and Parade

Collective First Amendment expression may take the form of a picket, a parade, or an assembly. While it may be reasonable to require a parade permit, it may not be permissible to require a permit to picket or assemble. Parades are fundamentally different from pickets or assemblies. Generally, pickets occur on public sidewalks or other public property. Rarely do they occur on public roads. Obviously, a parade cannot be conducted in the midst of traffic. Therefore, it is reasonable to require a parade permit which places time, place, and manner restrictions on the parade. Such a restriction would designate a time, place, and route of the parade. So long as the permit does not regulate the content of speech, includes specific neutral guidelines which limit an official's individual discretion, and provides for a quick resolution of the application, a parade permit will generally be upheld.

Since a parade is a collective expressive activity, it is protected by the First Amendment. If a public entity were to put on a parade, it could not restrict a participant from the parade based on disagreement with the participant's message. However, if private citizens organize their own parade, the private group can exclude participants with which the group disagrees.

City officials in Boston attempted to force the South Boston Allied War Veterans Council to allow a homosexual activist group in its privately organized parade by refusing to grant their parade permit. The Veterans Council sued, and in a unanimous opinion, the United States Supreme Court held that a privately organized parade may restrict participants which tend to dilute or contradict the purpose of the private parade.[17] The Court noted:

---

[17] See *Hurley v. Irish-American Gay, Lesbian and Bisexual Group of Boston,* 515 U.S. 557 (1995).

Since all speech inherently involves choices of what to say and what to leave unsaid, one important manifestation of the principle of free speech is that one who chooses to speak may also decide what not to say. Although the State may at times prescribe what shall be orthodox in commercial advertising by requiring the dissemination of purely factual and uncontroversial information, outside that context it may not compel affirmance of a belief with which the speaker disagrees. Indeed this general rule, that the speaker has the right to tailor the speech, applies not only to expressions of value, opinion, or endorsement, but equally to statements of fact the speaker would rather avoid, subject, perhaps, to the permissive law of defamation. Nor is the rule's benefit restricted to the press, being enjoyed by business corporations generally and by ordinary people engaged in unsophisticated expression as well as by professional publishers. Its point is simply the point of all speech protection, which is to shield just those choices of content that in someone's eyes are misguided, or even hurtful.[18]

In fact, the High Court compared a private organizer of a parade to a composer selecting "the expressive units of the parade from potential participants."[19] Inherent in the right to free speech is the right to choose what not to say. The Supreme Court clearly declared this principle: "Disapproval of a private speaker's statement does not legitimize use of the

---

[18]*Id.* at 575 (quotations and citations omitted).
[19]*Id.*

[state's] power to compel the speaker to alter the message by including one more acceptable to others."[20]

While the government may not exclude participants from a government-sponsored parade based upon disagreement with the content of the participant's message, a private group organizing a privately sponsored parade may discriminate on the content of speech. The remedy for being excluded from a privately sponsored parade is simply to organize another parade espousing the desired message. There is no constitutional harm in not being invited to another person's party.

Frequently Encountered Unconstitutional Roadblocks

Permit or Licensing Schemes

Some governmental bodies have required picketers or demonstrators to notify public officials prior to the conducted activity. While this may be reasonable for a parade in terms of logistics and traffic control, it is likely not permissible for a peaceful demonstration on a public sidewalk. The requirement of giving advance notice to the government of one's intent to speak inherently inhibits free speech.[21] The "delay inherent in advance notice requirements inhibits free speech by outlawing spontaneous expression."[22] It is clear that "when an event occurs, it is often necessary to have one's voice heard promptly, if it is to be considered at all."[23]

---

[20]*Id.* at 581.
[21]*See NAACP v. City of Richmond,* 743 F.2d 1346 (9th Cir. 1984).
[22]*NAACP v. City of Richmond,* 743 F.2d at 1355.
[23]*Shuttlesworth v. City of Birmingham,* 394 U.S. 147, 163 (1969).

A law requiring permission prior to engaging in speech is a prior restraint on speech.[24] "A prior restraint on the exercise of First Amendment rights comes to Court bearing a heavy presumption against its constitutional validity."[25] The heavy presumption is justified because "prior restraints on speech . . . are the most serious and the least tolerable infringements on First Amendment rights."[26] The presumption against prior restraints is heavier, and the degree of protection is broader than that against limits on expression imposed by criminal statutes. This is so because society "prefers to punish the few who abuse rights of speech *after* they break the law rather than throttle them and all others beforehand."[27]

"In determining the extent of the constitutional protection, it has been generally, if not universally, considered that it is the chief purpose of the [First Amendment] to prevent previous restraints."[28] Indeed, "the prevention of [prior restraints] was a leading purpose in the adoption of the [First Amendment]."[29] The problem with a prior restraint on speech is that it "suppresses the precise freedom which the First Amendment sought to protect against abridgement."[30]

Striking down a prior permit law, one federal court declared:

---

[24]"A prior restraint on expression exists when the government can deny access to a forum for expression before the expression occurs." *United States v. Frandsen*, 212 F.3d 1231, 1236 (11th Cir. 2000).

[25]*Vance v. Universal Amusement Co., Inc.*, 445 U.S. 308, 317 (1980); *see also Bantam Books, Inc. v. Sullivan*, 372 U.S. 58, 70 (1963).

[26]*Nebraska Press Ass'n v. Stuart*, 427 U.S. 539, 559 (1975).

[27]*Southeastern Promotions, Ltd. v. Conrad*, 420 U.S. 546, 559–60 (1975).

[28]*Near v. Minnesota*, 283 U.S. 697, 713 (1931).

[29]*Lovell*, 303 U.S. at 451.

[30]*Carroll v. Presidents and Comm'rs of Princess Anne*, 393 U.S. 175, 181 (1968).

We find the requirement of advanced registration as a condition to peaceful pamphleteering, picketing, or communicating with the public to be unconstitutional. The United States Supreme Court has held [long] ago that persons desiring to exercise their free speech rights may not be required to give advanced notice to the state.[31]

Another court struck down a permit policy as an unconstitutional prior restraint on free speech and assembly, stating that the delay inherent in such a scheme was unconstitutional.[32] Any prior permission policy may create unreasonable delays on the expression of free speech. "When an event occurs, it is often necessary to have one's voice heard promptly, if it is to be considered at all."[33] Indeed, the Supreme Court has indicated that a prior notification requirement is "quite incompatible with the requirements of the First Amendment."[34] "The simple knowledge that one must inform the government of his desire to speak and must fill out appropriate forms and comply with applicable regulation discourages citizens from speaking freely."[35] The Court has traditionally condemned licensing schemes as prior restraints without regard to content restrictions.[36]

---

[31] *Rosen,* 641 F.2d at 1247 (citing *Thomas,* 323 U.S. at 523).
[32] *See Grossman v. City of Portland,* 33 F.3d 1200 (9th Cir. 1994).
[33] *Shuttlesworth,* 394 U.S. at 163.
[34] *Thomas,* 323 U.S. at 540.
[35] *NAACP v. City of Richmond,* 743 F.2d at 1455.
[36] *See Forsyth County v. Nationalist Movement,* 505 U.S. 123 (1992) (parade permits); *Shuttlesworth,* 394 U.S. at 147 (public demonstration permits); *Lovell,* 303 U.S. at 444 (literature distribution permit).

At a minimum, a prior restraint will be found unconstitutional when such a scheme places unbridled discretion in the hands of a government official to grant or deny the permit or when the scheme places no time limit within which the decision must be rendered.[37] A prior restraint which regulates the content of the message must have at least three procedural safeguards. These include: (1) any restraint prior to judicial review can be imposed only for a specified brief time; (2) expeditious judicial review of that decision must be available; and (3) the censor must bear the burden of initiating judicial proceedings and must bear the burden of proof once in court to justify the censorship.[38] A content-neutral prior restraint must have at least the latter two procedural safeguards.[39]

In the rare circumstance where a permit scheme may be permissible, it must contain (1) a specific short time in which the public official must grant or deny the request and (2) specific criteria which the official must follow in rendering the decision. The former is required to ensure the official cannot censor the speech merely through inaction or delay.[40]

---

[37]See FW/PBS, Inc. v. Dallas, 493 U.S. 215, 225–26 (1990).

[38]See Thomas v. Chicago Park Dist., 534 U.S. 316, 321 (2002); FW/PBS, 493 U.S. at 227; Freedman v. Maryland, 308 U.S. 51, 58 (1965).

[39]See id. An example of a content-neutral prior restraint would be a permit requirement that applies to anyone desiring to conduct a parade on a public street.

[40]See Artistic Entertainment, Inc. v. City of Warner Robins, 223 F.3d 1306 (11th Cir. 2000); Redner v. Dean, 29 F.3d 1495 (11th Cir. 1994) (striking down license scheme that contained a time limit but which did not provide that the application is automatically approved if no decision was rendered within the time frame); see also Frandesen, 212 F.3d at 1231 (discussing case law which holds a prior restraint facial challenge is an exception to the rule in United States v. Salerno, 481 U.S. 739 (1987) that facial challenges must establish that no set of circumstances exist under which the law would be valid).

In addition to the inherent delay in a prior permit policy, licensing schemes are often unconstitutionally vague and vest excessive authority in administrative officials to grant or deny the permit.[41] Vesting a public official with discretionary authority to suppress speech violates the First Amendment. "It is not merely the sporadic abuse of power by the censor but the pervasive threat inherent in its very existence that constitutes a danger to freedom of discussion."[42] One court pointed out the following in this regard:

> Vesting [government authorities] with this discretion permits the government to control the viewpoints that will be expressed. Whether the city council or the police exercise this power, we believe that it runs afoul of the basic principle that "forbids the government from regulating speech in ways that favor some viewpoints or ideas at the expense of others."[43]

As a matter of due process, "no one may be required at peril of life, liberty or property to speculate as to the meaning of penal statutes. All are entitled to be informed as to what the State commands or forbids."[44] The general test for vagueness applies with particular force in review of laws dealing with speech. "Stricter standards of permissible statutory vagueness may be applied to a statute having a potentially

---

[41]See, e.g., Forsyth County, 595 U.S. at 130–34; see also Lakewood v. Plain Dealer Publishing Co., 486 U.S. 750 (1988).

[42]See Thornhill v. Alabama, 310 U.S. 88, 97 (1940).

[43]Association of Community Org. v. Municipality of Golden, Colo., 744 F.2d 739, 747 (10th Cir. 1984) (quoting Members of City Council of L.A. v. Taxpayers for Vincent, 466 U.S. 789, 804 (1984)).

[44]Lanzetta v. New Jersey, 306 U.S. 451, 453 (1939).

inhibiting effect on speech; a man may the less be required to act at his peril here, because the free dissemination of ideas may be the loser."[45] A regulation is considered unconstitutionally vague if it "either forbids or requires the doing of an act in terms so vague that [persons] of common intelligence must necessarily guess at its meaning and differ as to its application."[46] The prohibition against overly vague laws protects citizens from voluntarily having to curtail their First Amendment activities because of fear that those activities could be characterized as illegal.[47] "Precision of regulation" is the touchstone of the First and Fourteenth Amendments.[48]

Vague laws "may trap the innocent by not providing fair warning," "provide for arbitrary and discriminatory enforcement," impermissibly delegate policy matters to enforcement officials on an "ad hoc and subjective basis," and consequently chill free expression.[49] Promises by government officials not to apply unconstitutionally a vague law will not save the law. "Well-intentioned prosecutors and judicial safeguards do not neutralize the vice of a vague law."[50] The

---

[45]*Smith v. California,* 361 U.S. 147, 151 (1959); *see also Buckley v. Valeo,* 424 U.S. 1, 76–82 (1976); *Broadrick v. Oklahoma,* 413 U.S. 601, 611–12 (1973).

[46]*Connally v. General Constr. Co.,* 269 U.S. 385, 391 (1926).

[47]*See Grayned v. City of Rockford,* 408 U.S. 104, 109 (1972).

[48]*See NAACP v. Button,* 371 U.S. 415, 435 (1963). Vague laws violate both free speech and due process. *Cf. Grayned,* 408 U.S. at 108–9 (noise ordinance); *Papachristou v. City of Jacksonville,* 405 U.S. 156 (1972) (loitering law); and *Coates v. City of Cincinnati,* 402 U.S. 611 (1971) (ordinance prohibiting three or more persons from assembling in an annoying manner void for vagueness).

[49]*Grayned,* 408 U.S. at 108–9; *see also Baggett v. Bullitt,* 377 U.S. 360, 374 (1964).

[50]*Baggett,* 377 U.S. at 374.

Supreme Court has noted that it must apply strict scrutiny to any policy infringing on speech if it is vague, because such a policy has an "inhibiting effect on speech."[51] When free speech is at stake, "precision of drafting and clarity of purpose are essential."[52]

FINANCIAL BURDENS

In addition to prior notice or permit requirements, some governmental authorities have attempted to place financial burdens on free speech. Certainly the government may impose minimal financial burdens on the exercise of free speech such as permit fees, but these burdens are permitted only when the amount is reasonable and directly related to the accomplishment of legitimate governmental purposes.[53] However, the government cannot make the financial cost of obtaining a permit so unreasonable as to restrict free speech activities. One federal court struck down an ordinance requiring groups to obtain liability insurance in the amount of at least $300,000 and property damage insurance in the amount of at least $50,000. The court ruled that these requirements were unconstitutional since the activity involved free speech.[54] If a parade permit is necessary to picket or demonstrate on a public street, the cost should be minimal, and the standards for requiring the permit must be objective

---

[51]*Hynes,* 425 U.S. at 620; *see also Smith,* 361 U.S. at 151.

[52]*Erznoznik v. City of Jacksonville,* 422 U.S. 205, 212–13 (1975).

[53]*See Collin v. Smith,* 447 F. Supp. 676, 684 (N.D. Ill.), *cert. denied,* 439 U.S. 916 (1978); *see also Cox v. New Hampshire,* 312 U.S. 569, 575–77 (1941); *Lubin v. Panish,* 415 U.S. 709 (1974); *Bullock v. Carter,* 405 U.S. 134 (1972); *United States Labor Party v. Codd,* 527 F.2d 118 (2d Cir. 1975).

[54]*See Collin,* 447 F. Supp. at 676.

and applied equally.[55] In the context of literature distribution, Liberty Counsel filed suit against the Orlando International Airport's requirement of obtaining $100,000 of liability insurance prior to the distribution of literature. After filing suit, the airport eliminated the financial requirement.

The Supreme Court found that placing a "financial burden" on speech violates the First Amendment when it stated:

> In the realm of private speech or expression, government regulation may not favor one speaker over another. Discrimination against speech because of its message is presumed to be unconstitutional. These rules informed our determination that the government offends the First Amendment when it imposes *financial burdens* on certain speakers based on the content of their expression.[56]

ANONYMITY

Some government entities have attempted to limit picketing and demonstrating by restricting the distribution of literature or by requiring the picketer to be publicly identified. Courts have

---

[55]*See Forsyth County,* 505 U.S. at 123.

[56]*Rosenberger v. Rector & Visitors of the Univ. of Va.,* 515 U.S. 819, 828–29 (1995) (citations omitted) (emphasis added). *See also Simon & Schuster,* 502 U.S. at 105 (striking down New York's "Son of Sam" law that required income from an accused or convicted criminal's written works describing the crime be deposited in an escrow account and then made available to victims of the crime as well as creditors); *Arkansas Writers' Project, Inc. v. Ragland,* 481 U.S. 221, 227 (1987) ("Our cases clearly established that a discriminatory tax on the press burdens rights protected by the First Amendment."); *Keenan v. Superior Court of L.A. County,* 40 P.3d 718 (Cal. 2002) (invalidating California's "Son of Sam" law, finding that the financial burden imposed upon free speech violated both the First Amendment of the United States Constitution as well as the Liberty of Speech Clause of the California Constitution). For more information about discriminatory fee

routinely struck down these restrictions. A regulation banning literature distribution while picketing actually suppresses "a great quantity of speech that does not cause the evils that it seeks to eliminate, whether they be fraud, crime, litter, traffic congestion or noise."[57] Neither the picketer nor the organization represented need be identified in the material used during the picket. The Supreme Court has consistently stated that "anonymous pamphlets, leaflets, brochures and even books have played an important role in the progress of mankind."[58] Anonymity is an important part of First Amendment rights.[59]

Anonymity when expressing ideas has a long and respectable history in America and Great Britain. The Supreme Court resoundingly upheld this tradition in the context of distribution of political literature.[60] Authors like Benjamin Franklin, Charles Dickens, and Samuel Clemmons (Mark Twain) shielded their identities when publishing.[61] The tradition of anonymity extends beyond literature to political advocacy; even the Federalists Papers were published under fictitious names.[62] The Court recognized:

An advocate may believe her ideas will be more persuasive if her readers are unaware of her identity.

---

schemes, see chapter 8 entitled "Use of Public Facilities." *See also* Mathew D. Saver, *Equal Access*, available on www.lc.org or at 1-800-671-1776.
[57]*Ward,* 491 U.S. at 799 n.7 (citation omitted).
[58]*Talley v. California,* 362 U.S. 60, 64 (1960).
[59]*See McIntyre v. Ohio Elections Comm'n,* 514 U.S. 334, 342 (1995); *see also Buckley v. American Constitutional Law Found.,* 525 U.S. 182 (1999) (striking down requirement that initiative-petition circulators wear an identification badge).
[60]*See id.; see also Watchtower Bible and Tract Soc'y of N.Y., Inc. v. Village of Stratton,* 536 U.S. 150, 165–67 (2002).
[61]*See McIntyre,* 514 U.S. at 341 n.4.
[62]*See id.* at 342.

Anonymity thereby provides a way for a writer who may be personally unpopular to ensure that readers will not prejudice her message simply because they do not like its proponent.[63]

The occasional need for anonymity goes to the heart of free speech:

Anonymity is a shield from the tyranny of the majority. . . . It thus exemplifies the purpose behind the Bill of Rights, and of the First Amendment in particular; to protect unpopular individuals from retaliation—and their ideas from suppression—at the hand of an intolerant society.[64]

Moreover, the government may not compel members of groups involved in picketing to be publicly identified.[65] Any identification requirement "would tend to restrict freedom to distribute information and thereby freedom of expression."[66] Requiring public identification is repugnant to the Constitution. The Supreme Court declared:

Persecuted groups and sects from time to time throughout history have been able to criticize oppressive practices and laws either anonymously or not at all. The obnoxious press licensing law of England, which was also enforced on the Colonies was due in part to the knowledge that exposure of the names of

---

[63]*Id.*
[64]*Id.* at 357.
[65]See *Bates v. City of Little Rock,* 361 U.S. 412 (1960); *NAACP v. Alabama ex. rel. Patterson,* 357 U.S. 449 (1957).
[66]*Talley,* 362 U.S. at 64.

printers, writers and distributors would lessen the circulation of literature critical of the government. The
old seditious libel cases in England show the lengths
to which government had to go to find out who was
responsible for books that were obnoxious to the
rulers. . . . Before the Revolutionary War colonial pa-
triots frequently had to conceal their authorship or
distribution of literature that easily could have
brought down on them prosecutions. . . . Even the
Federalist Papers, written in favor of adoption of our
Constitution, were published under fictitious names.
It is plain that anonymity has sometimes been assumed for the most constructive purposes. . . .
Identification and [its concomitant] fear of reprisal
might deter perfectly peaceful discussions of public
matters of importance.[67]

Some government officials have attempted to obtain
membership lists of organizations actively engaged in picketing or protest activities. Such action is clearly unconstitutional. Requiring organizations to identify their members may
cause fear and thus prevent them from association with the
organization. Consequently, anonymity of those engaged in
First Amendment speech and those associated with groups
participating in such activities is constitutionally protected.[68]

---

[67]*Id.* at 64–65.
[68]In *Bates,* the Court noted the chilling effect that would result from identification and disclosure requirements. "For example, a witness testified:
'Well, the people are afraid to join, afraid to join because the people they
don't want their names exposed and they are afraid their names will be exposed. . . . They will be intimidated and they are afraid to join.'" *Bates,* 361
U.S. at 416 n.6. The Court also highlighted the following testimony: "Well,

The government cannot prohibit speech or expressive conduct "because of disapproval of the ideas expressed."[69] Courts cannot restrict picketing or demonstrating "simply because society finds the idea itself offensive or disagreeable."[70] Indeed, "the mere presumed presence of unwitting listeners or viewers does not serve automatically to justify curtailing all speech capable of giving offense."[71] The Supreme Court has noted, "We are often captives outside the sanctuary of the home and subject to objectionable speech."[72] Merely because the speech is unwelcome "does not deprive it of protection."[73]

Picketing and demonstrating often create confrontation of opposing views. However, even hostile audience reactions cannot justify the suppression of speech.[74] One federal court struck down a ban on "persisting in talking to or communicating in any manner with" a person or persons "against his, her or their will" in order to persuade that person to quit or refrain from seeking certain employment.[75] The First

---

. . . we were not able to rest at night or day for quite awhile. We had to have our phone number changed because they called at day and night. . . . I would tell them who is talking and they have throwed [sic] stones at my home. . . . I got a I received a letter threatening my life and they threatened my life over the telephone." *Id.* at 416 n.7. *See also Buckley,* 525 U.S. at 182 (striking down requirement that proponents of an initiative report names and addresses of all paid circulators).

[69]*RAV v. City of St. Paul,* 505 U.S. 377, 382 (1992).
[70]*Simon & Schuster,* 502 U.S. at 119. *See also Cohen v. California,* 403 U.S. 15 (1971).
[71]*Cohen,* 403 U.S. at 21.
[72]*Id.*
[73]*United Food and Commercial Workers Int'l Union v. IBP, Inc.,* 857 F.2d 422, 432 (8th Cir. 1988) (listing cases).
[74]*See Forsyth County,* 505 U.S. at 136 (and cases cited).
[75]*United Food,* 857 F.2d at 425 n.4, 435.

Amendment was meant to permit disputatious speech, speech that "may start an argument or cause a disturbance."[76] The Supreme Court stated:

> Free speech is not a right that is given only to be so circumscribed that it exists in principle but not in fact. Freedom of expression would not truly exist if the right could be exercised only in an area that a benevolent government has provided as a safe haven for crackpots.[77]

The First Amendment, which prohibits government from abridging free speech, "means what it says."[78] Like it or not, the First Amendment is strong medicine to those seeking to suppress speech. "The fact that society may find speech offensive is not a sufficient reason for suppressing it. Indeed, if it is the speaker's opinion that gives offense, that consequence is a reason for according it constitutional protection."[79]

Private Versus Public Property

The site of the picket or demonstration activity is important to determining its constitutionality. As stated in a previous chapter, the First Amendment protects individuals against government action seeking to restrict free speech.[80] The First

---

[76]*Tinker v. Des Moines Indep. Sch. Dist.*, 393 U.S. 503, 508 (1969).
[77]*Id.* at 513.
[78]*Id.*
[79]*FCC v. Pacifica Found.*, 438 U.S. 726, 745 (1978) (quoted in *Hustler Magazine, Inc. v. Falwell*, 485 U.S. 46, 55 (1988)).
[80]For an in-depth discussion on the application of the First Amendment, see chapters 2 and 8.

Amendment restrains only government action, not private action. An individual has no right to picket on private property, since the First Amendment does not restrain the private property owner. However, since the Constitution restrains government activity, a citizen does have the right to picket within a traditional public forum or, in some situations, within a designated, limited, or nonpublic forum.

Traditional public forums include streets, sidewalks, and parks. Access to traditional public forums or other similar public places "for the purpose of exercising First Amendment rights cannot constitutionally be denied broadly."[81] Public parks, streets, and sidewalks "have immemorially been held in trust for the use of the public."[82] "In [these] quintessential public forums, the government may not prohibit all communicative activity."[83]

Some protesters at abortion clinics have been arrested for trespassing on private property. These arrests generally arise out of situations involving picketers blocking ingress to or egress from an abortion clinic or being physically on private rather than public property. Sometimes pro-life demonstrators have

---

[81]*Grayned,* 408 U.S. at 117.

[82]*Frisby v. Schultz,* 487 U.S. 474, 481 (1988) (quoting *Hague v. CIO,* 307 U.S. 496, 515 (1939)); *see also Perry Educ. Ass'n v. Perry Local Educators' Ass'n,* 460 U.S. 37 (1983).

[83]*Frisby,* 487 U.S. at 481 (quoting *Perry Educ. Ass'n,* 460 U.S. at 45); *see also Heffron v. ISKCON,* 452 U.S. 640 (1981); *United States v. Grace,* 461 U.S. 169, 176 (1983); *Carey v. Brown,* 447 U.S. 455, 460 (1980); *Gregory v. Chicago,* 394 U.S. 111, 112 (1969); *Jamison v. Texas,* 318 U.S. 413 (1943); *Thornhill,* 310 U.S. at 88; *Schneider v. New Jersey,* 308 U.S. 147 (1939); *Faustin v. City and County of Denver,* 268 F.3d 942 (10th Cir. 2001) (finding that a highway overpass is a sidewalk and therefore a traditional public forum); *Lytle v. Brewer,* 77 F. Supp. 2d 730 (E.D. Va. 1999), *rev'd on other grounds sub. nom. Lytle v. Griffth,* 240 F.3d 404 (4th Cir. 2001) (same).

used what is known as the "necessity defense" to justify breaking the trespass laws. The so-called necessity defense was defined in the early 1900s. The defense involves the necessity of one person trespassing on the private property of another person in order either to avoid serious personal harm or to save the life of another. This defense grew out of a case known as *Ploof v. Putnam*[84] which involved a boat dock on Lake Champlain. While sailing, a violent tempest arose. In order to avoid personal injury and property damage to the sailing vessel, the owner of the vessel moored the sloop to a private dock. When the dock owner noticed the sloop moored to his dock, he untied the sloop, and it was destroyed in the storm. The court ruled that the defense of necessity applied with special force to the preservation of human life and that one may sacrifice the personal property of another in order to save either his life or those lives around him. In another case known as *Vincent v. Lake Erie Transportation Company*,[85] a state court ruled that, because of necessity, it was lawful for a ship to maintain its tie to a dock, even though the waves forcing the ship up and down destroyed the dock. The court also indicated that the ship owner was responsible for repairing the dock.

Based on the defense of necessity, pro-life picketers have argued that it is permissible to break the law of trespass in order to save the life of an unborn child by blocking access to, or trespassing upon, the private property of an abortion clinic. So far this defense has had little success in relieving picketers from trespass laws.[86]

---

[84]71 A. 188 (Vt. 1908).

[85]124 N.W. 221 (Minn. 1910).

[86]*See City of Wichita v. Tilson*, 855 P.2d 911 (Kan. 1993) (ruling that when the objective sought is to prevent by criminal activity a lawful, constitutional

Residential picketing involves both public and private issues. Residences are certainly privately owned, but the sidewalks in front of residential areas are public sidewalks and therefore traditional public forums. As stated in a previous chapter, the Supreme Court has ruled that peaceful picketing within a residential area is constitutionally protected, so long as the picketing activities move throughout the neighborhood on the sidewalk and are not directly localized at one particular residential address.[87] Picketing in a residential area is permissible so long as the protesters move about on public sidewalks within the neighborhood. For example, courts have ruled that pro-life demonstrators may picket in a residential neighborhood where a physician who performs abortions resides, so long as the protesters move about in the neighborhood and do not solely target one residential address.[88]

Buffer Zones

A buffer zone is a parameter set by either a court or legislative body around a particular facility where pickets frequently take place. These buffer zones have restricted the amount of picketers and the activity of picketing within a

---

right of abortion, the defense of necessity is inapplicable and evidence of when life begins is irrelevant and should not be admitted at trial).

[87]*See Frisby,* 487 U.S. at 479; *see also* chapter 11 entitled "Door-to-Door Witnessing."

[88]*See, e.g., Veneklase v. City of Fargo,* 248 F.3d 738 (8th Cir. 2001) (upholding a statute that allows residential picketing but which prohibits targeted picketing of a single home); *Olmer v. City of Lincoln,* 192 F.3d 1176 (8th Cir. 1999) (striking down law that prohibited targeted picketing of churches outside a residential area, noting that the home is different); *Vittitow v. City of Arlington,* 830 F. Supp. 1077 (S.D. Ohio 1993); *see also Madsen v. Women's Health Ctr., Inc.,* 512 U.S. 753, 775 (1994).

certain parameter. In light of the escalating activity around abortion clinics, some courts have placed buffer zones around clinics. Legislative attempts to create buffer zones around abortion clinics and other medical facilities have also occurred. These buffer zones are clearly a threat to free speech activities.

POLLING PLACES

The concept of buffer zones may be traced back to voter intimidation around polling booths. The Supreme Court ruled that the state of Tennessee could place a one hundred-foot buffer zone around a polling place within which no literature distribution or display of campaign posters, signs, or other campaign material may occur on the day of elections.[89] In reaching this conclusion, the Court recognized that "the First Amendment 'has its fullest and most urgent application' to speech uttered during a campaign for political office."[90] The Court also noted that First Amendment expression around the polling place in question occurred in a public forum where people were invited to be present. The Court further noted that the specific regulation on speech was content-based because only political speech was prohibited, whereas other speech was not. Consequently, the Court ruled that such a buffer zone must be subjected to "exacting scrutiny" and could only survive constitutional challenge if a state had a "compelling interest" for the buffer zone.

---

[89]See Burson v. Freeman, 504 U.S. 191 (1992).
[90]Id. at 196, (quoting UEU v. San Francisco Democratic Comm'n, 489 U.S. 214, 223 (1989)).

To reach its conclusion, the Court reviewed extensive history. States clearly have a compelling interest to protect the rights of citizens to vote freely in an election conducted with integrity and reliability.[91] "No right is more precious in a free country than that of having a voice in the election of those who make the laws under which, as good citizens, we must live. Other rights, even the most basic, are illusory if the right to vote is undermined."[92]

Although a content-based regulation of speech in a public forum "rarely survives such scrutiny," based on the history involved, the Tennessee buffer zone was upheld.[93] This voting history dates back to the colonial period when many government officials were elected *viva voce*, or by the showing of hands. Voting was not a private affair but, in fact, "an open, public decision witnessed by all and improperly influenced by some."[94] Approximately twenty years after the formation of the Union, most states had incorporated a paper ballot in the electoral process. The various political parties wishing to gain influence then began producing their own paper ballots in flamboyant colors. Persons taking these paper ballots to polling places were frequently met by "ticket peddlers" who tried to convince individuals to vote for a particular party ticket. These discussions often became heated and influenced the outcome of votes. This situation was not a "pleasant spectacle."[95]

---

[91] *Burson,* 504 U.S. at 199. The Court noted that the "right to vote freely for the candidate of one's choice is the essence of a democratic society." *Reynolds v. Sims,* 377 U.S. 533, 555 (1964).
[92] *Wesberry v. Sanders,* 376 U.S. 1, 17 (1964).
[93] *See Burson,* 504 U.S. at 199.
[94] *Id.*
[95] *Id.*

Australia adopted an official ballot encompassing every candidate on the same ticket. The Australian system then incorporated the erection of polling booths. This system appeared to be a vast improvement and was eventually adopted in England in 1872. The polling booth concept failed after several attempts but eventually began in Louisville, Kentucky, and then moved to Massachusetts and the state of New York in 1888. The city of Louisville "prohibited all but voters, candidates or their agents, and electors from coming within 50 feet of the voting room enclosure."[96] The Massachusetts and New York laws placed a guardrail around the booths and excluded the general public from mingling within the guardrail areas. New York eventually adopted a one hundred-foot buffer zone around any polling place, and consequently, much of the intimidation and fraud encountered in earlier years had been cured. One commentator remarked, "We have secured secrecy; and intimidation by employers, party bosses, police officers, saloon keepers and others has come to an end."[97]

Today all fifty states limit access to areas in and around polling places. Even the National Labor Relations Board limits activities at or near its polling places during union elections. After reviewing this history, the Court concluded by stating the following:

> In sum, an examination of the history of election regulation in this country reveals a persistent battle against two evils: voter intimidation and election fraud. After an unsuccessful experiment with an unofficial ballot system, all 50 States, together with

---

[96]*Id.* at 203.
[97]*Id.*

numerous other Western democracies, settled on the same solution: a secret ballot secured in part by a restricted zone around the voting compartments. We find that this wide-spread and time-tested consensus demonstrates that some restricted zone is necessary in order to serve the States' compelling interest in preventing voter intimidation and election fraud.[98]

Although buffer zones originally arose out of elections and polling booths, the significant history is important. It is improper to take buffer zones arising out of the election process and, in turn, place buffer zones around other facilities. Buffer zones will rarely survive the First Amendment. The only reason buffer zones in the election process survived a First Amendment analysis is due to the fundamental right to vote, which is one of the most important rights of an American citizen. Moreover, buffer zone restrictions around polling places are deeply imbedded in American history.

CHURCHES

Albeit somewhat rare, one city in the state of Kansas passed an ordinance creating a type of buffer zone around churches. An individual sought to picket around the church carrying a pro-life sign. Even though he was aware of the no-picketing buffer zone ordinance around the church, he picketed anyway and was arrested. The Kansas Supreme Court ruled that the picketer did not violate the buffer zone, because the ordinance could be interpreted as prohibiting only targeted picketing of churches.[99] A federal court struck

---

[98]*Id.*
[99]*City of Prairie Village v. Hogan,* 855 P.2d 949 (Kan. 1993).

down a similar ordinance in Lincoln, Nebraska, that prohibited picketing targeted at churches.[100]

PUBLIC SCHOOLS

An ordinance placing a 150-foot buffer zone around public schools while exempting labor disputes was struck down by the United States Supreme Court.[101] The Court primarily found this buffer zone unconstitutional because it discriminated based on the content of speech.

ABORTION CLINICS

Abortion clinics have been the primary focus of controversy concerning buffer zones.[102] Court-ordered buffer zones

---

[100]*See Olmer,* 192 F.3d at 1176.

[101]*See Grayned,* 408 U.S. at 104; *Mosley,* 408 U.S. at 92.

[102]Although not a buffer zone case, the U.S. Supreme Court ruled in *Bray v. Alexandria Women's Health Clinic,* 506 U.S. 263 (1993), that 42 U.S.C. § 1985(3), the so-called Ku Klux Klan Act, could not be used to restrict picketing of abortion clinics. The Court ruled that abortion does not qualify as an individiously discriminatory animus directed toward women in general, that the incidental effect of abortion clinic demonstrations on some women's right to interstate travel was not sufficient to show a conspiracy to deprive those women of their protected interstate travel right and that the deprivation of the right to an abortion could not serve as the basis for a purely private conspiracy. The Supreme Court ruled that the first part of section 1985(3), known as the "deprivation" clause, does not provide a federal cause of action against persons obstructing access to abortion clinics. However, the Court left open the possibility that the second part of section 1985(3), known as the "hindrance" clause, may provide a federal cause of action. The Tenth Circuit Court of Appeals picked up on this idea and suggested that the "hindrance" clause may be used against abortion protestors. *See National Abortion Fed'n v. Operation Rescue,* 8 F.3d 680 (9th Cir. 1993); *see also* Nina Pillard, *Litigating* § *1985(3) Claims after Bray v. Alexandria Women's Health Clinic,* in 9 CIVIL RIGHTS LITIGATION AND ATTORNEY FEES ANNUAL HANDBOOK 325 (Steve Saltzman & Barbara M. Wolvovitz eds., 1993).

surfaced during the Civil Rights era. In one case, a state court crafted a three hundred-foot buffer zone around white-owned businesses due to civil rights protesting activities. A federal court later invalidated the state court injunction, ruling that the buffer zone violated free speech.[103]

One court noted that pro-life advocates must "be permitted to articulate their belief that abortion should not be permitted because it involves the taking of human life."[104] One court correctly recognized that "although the words 'killings' or 'murder' are certainly emotionally charged, it is difficult to conceive of a forceful presentation of the anti-abortion viewpoint which would not assert that abortion is the taking of human life."[105] Abortion speech is certainly political speech and therefore should receive the highest protection under the First Amendment. "Indeed, abortion may be the political issue of the last twenty years."[106]

Some have reasoned that buffer zones are permissible because they do not prohibit all speech, and pro-lifers may exercise their right to speak in another locale. However, one "is not to have the exercise of his liberty of expression in appropriate places abridged on the plea that it may be exercised in some other place."[107] The mere fact that demonstrators "remain free to employ other means to disseminate their ideas does not take their speech . . . outside the bounds of First Amendment protection."[108]

---

[103]See Machesky v. Bizzell, 414 F.2d 283 (5th Cir. 1969).

[104]Planned Parenthood Shasta-Diablo v. Williams, 16 Cal. Rptr. 2d 540, 549 (1993).

[105]Cannon v. City and County of Denver, 998 F.2d 867 (10th Cir. 1993).

[106]Planned Parenthood Shasta-Diablo, 16 Cal. Rptr. at 549.

[107]Schneider, 308 U.S. at 163.

[108]Meyer v. Grant, 468 U.S. at 424.

The Right to Picket, Demonstrate, and Parade

The first case to reach the Supreme Court involving abortion clinic buffer zones was *Madsen v. Women's Health Center, Inc.*[109] This case arose in Melbourne, Florida, when a

---

[109]512 U.S. at 753; *see also Schenck v. Pro-Choice Network of Western New York,* 519 U.S. 357 (1997) (moving bubble zones are unconstitutional). Prior to *Madsen,* some courts upheld and some struck down buffer zones. *See, e.g., Cheffer v. McGregor,* 6 F.3d 705 (11th Cir. 1993), *vacated and remanded,* 41 F.3d 1422 (11th Cir. 1994) (a 36-foot and 300-foot buffer zone and a ban on images violates free speech); *Cannon,* 998 F.2d at 867 (ruling that arrest of abortion protestors violated the constitutional right to picket on a public sidewalk in front of an abortion clinic and that words such as "murder" or "The Killing Place" were not fighting words and could not be proscribed); *Mississippi Women's Medical Clinic v. McMillan,* 866 F.2d 788 (5th Cir. 1989) (ruling a 500-foot buffer zone around an abortion clinic unconstitutional); *United Food,* 857 F.2d at 430–32 (same); *Howard Gault Co. v. Texas Rural Legal Aid, Inc.,* 848 F.2d 544, 548–61 (5th Cir. 1988) (ruling unconstitutional a ban on more than two picketers within 50 feet of each other); *Davis v. Francois,* 395 F.2d 730 (5th Cir. 1968) (ban on more than two picketers at a building "patently unconstitutional"); *Town of West Hartford v. Operation Rescue,* 792 F. Supp. 161 (D. Conn. 1992) (order upheld prohibiting blocking of clinic but not prohibiting other free speech or association activities), *vacated in part,* 991 F.2d 1039 (2d Cir. 1993); *Jackson v. City of Markham,* 773 F. Supp. 105 (N.D. Ill. 1991) (granting an injunction to protect the right to picket on a sidewalk outside of a roller rink); *Thomason v. Jernigan,* 770 F. Supp. 1195 (E.D. Mich. 1991) (ruling it unconstitutional to prohibit pro-life individuals in a public right of way); *Northeast Women's Ctr., Inc. v. McMonagle,* 939 F.2d 57 (3d Cir. 1991) (A buffer zone allowing six protestors within a buffer zone was permissible, but a 500-foot buffer zone in a residential area was unconstitutional.); *Southwestern Medical Clinics, Inc. v. Operation Rescue,* 744 F. Supp. 230 (D. Nev. 1989) (order prohibiting blockading of clinic but allowing other free speech or free association activities upheld); *National Org. for Women v. Operation Rescue,* 726 F. Supp. 1483 (E.D. Va. 1989) (A restriction on activities tending to intimidate, harass, or disturb patients by expression of views on the issue of abortion was ruled unconstitutionally overbroad.), *aff'd,* 914 F.2d 582 (4th Cir. 1990), *rev'd in part, vacated in part sub nom., Bray v. Alexandria Women's Health Clinic,* 506 U.S. 263 (1993); *National Org. for Women v. Operation Rescue,* 726 F. Supp. 300 (D.C. District 1989) (upholding an order blockading a clinic but not prohibiting or restricting other free speech activities); *Fargo Women's Health*

state court judge entered an injunction placing a thirty-six-foot buffer zone around three sides of an abortion clinic. Within this zone was a public highway and a public sidewalk. The injunction also contained a noise restriction and prohibited the display of any "images observable" from within the clinic. Additionally, a three hundred-foot buffer zone was placed around the clinic and around the private residential homes of any owner, employee, staff member, or agent of the clinic. Pro-life speech could occur within the

---

Org., Inc. v. Lambs of Christ, 488 N.W.2d 401 (N.D. 1992) (a buffer zone allowing only two protestors within 100 feet, prohibiting literature distribution, and prohibiting speaking to abortion clinic staff was unconstitutional, but the noise restriction was upheld); *Hirsch v. City of Atlanta,* 401 S.E.2d 530 (Ga.), *cert. denied,* 502 U.S. 818 (1991) (upholding a restriction allowing only twenty protestors to use a sidewalk at any one given time within a 50-foot buffer zone); *Planned Parenthood v. Maki,* 478 N.W.2d 637 (Iowa 1991) (a prohibition against one individual from blocking entrance to and trespassing upon clinic property upheld because no other protestor's right to free speech was restricted); *Dayton Women's Health Ctr. v. Enix,* 68 Ohio App. 3d 579, 589 N.E.2d 121 (Ohio App. 2d 1991); *Planned Parenthood v. Project Jericho,* 52 Ohio St. 3d 56, 556 N.E.2d 157 (Ohio 1990) (a buffer zone permitting picketing and literature distribution within reasonable limits for the purpose of expression of opinion upheld); *Planned Parenthood v. Operation Rescue,* 550 N.E.2d 1361 (Mass. 1990) (upholding a restriction blocking a clinic while allowing the right to pray, sing, and peacefully picket on public sidewalks); *Cousins v. Terry,* 721 F. Supp. 426 (N.D.N.Y. 1989) (prohibiting blocking access to an abortion clinic); *Zimmerman v. DCA at Welleby, Inc.,* 505 So. 2d 1371 (Fla. 4th DCA 1987) (overturning an injunction against peaceful picketing at sales office of condominium project); *Bering v. Share,* 106 Wash. 2d 212, 721 P.2d 918 (Wash. 1986), *cert. dismissed,* 479 U.S. 1060 (1987) (upholding a buffer zone restriction which did not prohibit picketing on a public sidewalk); *Planned Parenthood v. Cannizzaro,* 499 A.2d 535 (N.J. Super. Ct. Ch. Div. 1985) (a restriction allowing picketing in sidewalks or streets abutting the clinic but requiring five-feet distance between picketers upheld); *Parkmed Company v. Pro-Life Counseling, Inc.,* 442 N.Y.S. 396 (N.Y. App. Div. 1981) (injunction on demonstrating in public areas outside an abortion business unconstitutional).

three hundred-foot buffer zone only upon the consent of the listener. Violations of these buffer zones resulted in criminal prosecution.[110]

Stating that an injunction may not "burden more speech than necessary," the United States Supreme Court ruled that the three hundred-foot buffer zone around the clinic and the residential property violated the First Amendment.[111] The Court also stated that the injunction's requirement that pro-life picketers receive consent from those persons seeking access to the clinic was unconstitutional, as was the ban on all images observable and two sides of the thirty-six-foot speech buffer around the clinic.[112] The *Madsen* Court upheld a ban on excessive noise which could be heard within the clinic and part of the thirty-six-foot zone at the clinic entrance.

Before an injunction may be sought to ban picketing, there generally must be a showing that (1) the picketers have violated, or imminently will violate, some provision of statutory or common law, and (2) there is a cognizable danger of recurrent violation.[113] The *Madsen* test can be summarized as follows:

Injunctive relief affecting speech is permissible only upon a showing that: (1) the defendant has violated, or imminently will violate, some provision of statutory or common law;[114] (2) there is a cognizable

---

[110]*See Cheffer v. McGregor,* 6 F.3d at 705 (ruling that the buffer zone as applied to a person not a party to the state court action was unconstitutional).
[111]*See Madsen,* U.S. at 774.
[112]*See id.* at 771–72.
[113]*See id.* at 765 n.3; *see also* Mathew D. Staver, *Injunctive Relief and the Madsen Test* 14:2 St. Louis U. Pub. L. Rev. 456–94 (1995).
[114]*See Madsen,* 512 U.S. at 765 n.3.

danger of recurrent violation;[115] and (3) a subsequent speech-restrictive injunction may not burden more speech than necessary to serve a significant government interest.[116]

The first two prongs of the above test are applicable to any injunction, since injunctive relief is an equitable remedy.[117] Thus, prongs one and two must be met before the entry of any injunction, whether the injunction restricts speech or conduct. After prongs one and two are met, a court should first attempt to restore law and order by a nonspeech-restrictive injunction, and once that injunction proves to be ineffective, a subsequent speech-restrictive injunction may be issued, but that injunction cannot burden more speech than necessary to serve a significant government interest.[118] As a result of the *Madsen* decision, most buffer zones around abortion clinics will be considered unconstitutional.[119]

---

[115]*See id.*

[116]*See id.* at 767.

[117]*See Madsen,* 512 U.S. at 765 n.3.

[118]The *Madsen* Court relied heavily on the assumption that the pro-life protestors repeatedly violated a nonspeech-restrictive injunction, and it is based on this reliance that the Court upheld a portion of the thirty-six-foot buffer zone involving the speech-restrictive section of the second injunction. The *Madsen* Court suggested that individuals may have restrictions placed on their right to free speech if they repeatedly engage in illegal conduct. *See National Soc'y of Professional Eng'rs v. United States,* 435 U.S. 679, 697–98 (1978).

[119]*See, e.g., Schenck,* 519 U.S. at 381; *Spitzer v. Operation Rescue Nat'l,* 273 F.3d 184 (2d Cir. 2001). Below is a diagram of the clinic and surrounding geography which was part of the record before the United States Supreme Court:

In upholding the portion of the thirty-six-foot zone at the clinic entrance and driveway, the Court focused on two factors: (1) an assumption that the protestors had violated a prior nonspeech-restrictive injunction which was

Relying on the *Madsen* case, the Supreme Court later ruled that a floating bubble zone that moved with the person or vehicle was unconstitutional.[120] Such a bubble zone would essentially ban all literature distribution. Thus the Court, in striking down the bubble zones, stated:

> Leafletting and commenting on matters of public concern are classic forms of speech that lie at the heart of the First Amendment, and speech in public areas is at its most protected [sic] on public sidewalks, a prototypical example of a traditional public forum.[121]

Picketing on matters of public concern, including picketing in and around abortion clinics, must be a highly guarded right under the First Amendment. The Supreme Court acknowledged this much when it stated:

> We have indicated that in public debate our own citizens must tolerate insulting, and even outrageous, speech in order to provide adequate breathing space to the freedoms protected by the First Amendment.[122]

---

ineffective in maintaining free ingress and egress; and (2) the narrow confines of the clinic which included a strip of sidewalk approximately four feet wide and thirty-seven feet long that connected the two parking lots. The road directly in front of the clinic, Dixie Way, was only twenty-one feet four inches wide. Other than the narrow strip of sidewalk directly in front of the clinic, no other sidewalks existed in the residential area along Dixie Way or U.S. Highway 1. Clearly, if the first factor was absent, the Court would not have upheld the thirty-six-foot zone at the clinic entrance and driveway.

[120]*Schenck,* 519 U.S. at 357.
[121]*Id.*
[122]*Schenck,* 519 U.S. at 373 (*quoting Madsen,* 512 U.S. at 773).

Certainly "there is no right to be free of unwelcome speech on the public streets while seeking entrance to or exit from abortion clinics."[123]

In a poorly reasoned case, the Supreme Court upheld a Colorado statute that regulated conduct within one hundred feet of the entrance to any health-care facility.[124] The statute made it a crime for any person to "knowingly approach" within eight feet of another person without that person's consent for the purpose of distributing a leaflet, displaying a sign, or engaging in oral protest. The Court pointed out that the statute would not prohibit a protestor from standing still while another approached.[125]

In 1994 Congress passed the Freedom of Access to Clinic Entrances Act (hereinafter "FACE").[126] FACE applies to "reproductive health services" (a euphemism for abortion clinics)[127] and "places of religious worship."[128] FACE prohibits anyone who "by force or a threat of force or by physical obstruction, intentionally injures, intimidates, or interferes" with (1) another person obtaining or providing reproductive health services or (2) a person lawfully exercising or seeking to exercise their First Amendment right of religious freedom at a place of religious worship. FACE also applies to anyone who intentionally damages or destroys the property of any

---

[123]*Schenck,* 512 U.S. at 386 (Scalia, J. dissenting).

[124]*See Hill v. Colorado,* 530 U.S. 703 (2000).

[125]Prior to this ruling a federal court struck down a similar law. *See Sabelko v. City of Phoenix,* 68 F.3d 1169 (9th Cir. 1995), *vacated,* 519 U.S. 1144 (1997).

[126]*See* 18 U.S.C. § 248.

[127]18 U.S.C. § 248(a)(1).

[128]18 U.S.C. § 248(a)(2).

facility that provides "reproductive health services" or the property of a "place of religious worship."[129] One federal court correctly recognized that FACE is only applicable against acts of "physical" force.[130] FACE does not, and cannot, restrict peaceful, nonviolent speech, no matter how offensive, so long as acts of physical force are not used to convey the message.[131]

---

[129]18 U.S.C. § 248(a)(3).

[130]*Cheffer,* 55 F.3d at 1517.

[131]Courts have found that Congress had the authority to pass FACE. *See, e.g., United States v. Bird,* 124 F.3d 667 (5th Cir. 1997), *cert. denied,* 523 U.S. 1006 (1998); *Hoffman v. Hunt,* 126 F.3d 575 (4th Cir. 1997); *Terry v. Reno,* 101 F.3d 1412 (D.C. Cir. 1996), *cert. denied,* 520 U.S. 1264 (1999); *United States v. Unterburger,* 97 F.3d 1413 (11th Cir.), *cert. denied,* 97 U.S. 1413 (1996); *United States v. Soderna,* 82 F.3d 1370 (7th Cir. Wis.), *cert. denied, sub. nom., Hatch v. United States,* 519 U.S. 1006 (1996); *Cook v. Reno,* 74 F.3d 97 (5th Cir. 1996); *United States v. Dinwiddie,* 76 F.3d 913 (8th Cir.), *cert. denied,* 519 U.S. 1043 (1996); *United States v. Wilson,* 73 F.3d 675 (7th Cir. 1995); *Cheffer v. Reno,* 55 F.3d 1517 (11th Cir. 1995); *American Life League, Inc. v. Reno,* 47 F.3d 642 (4th Cir.), *cert. denied,* 519 U.S. 809 (1995); *United States v. Weslin,* 964 F. Supp. 83 (W.D.N.Y. 1997), 156 F.3d 292 (2d Cir. 1998), *cert. denied,* 525 U.S. 1071 (1999); *United States v. Scott,* 958 F. Supp. 761 (D. Conn. 1997); *Planned Parenthood Ass'n of Southeastern Pa., Inc. v. Walton,* 949 F. Supp. 290 (E.D. Pa. 1996); *United States v. Roach,* 947 F. Supp. 872 (E.D. Pa. 1996); *Planned Parenthood of Columbia/Williamette, Inc. v. American Coalition of Life Activists,* 945 F. Supp. 1355 (D. Or. 1996); *United States v. McMillan,* 946 F. Supp. 1254 (S.D. Miss. 1995); *United States v. Scott,* 919 F. Supp. 76 (D. Conn. 1996), *aff'd and remanded, sub. nom., United States v. Vazquez,* 145 F.3d 74 (2d Cir. 1998); *United States v. White,* 893 F. Supp. 1423 (C.D. Cal. 1995); *United States v. Lucero,* 895 F. Supp. 1421 (Dist. Kan. 1995); *United States v. Lindgren,* 883 F. Supp. 1321 (D.N.D. 1995); *United States v. Hill,* 893 F. Supp. 1034 (N.D. Fla. 1994); *United States v. Brock,* 863 F. Supp. 851 (E.D. Wis. 1994); *Riely v. Reno,* 860 F. Supp. 693 (D. Ariz. 1994); *Council for Life v. Reno,* 856 F. Supp. 1422 (S.D. Cal. 1994).

Racketeer Influenced and Corrupt Organizations Act

The Racketeer Influenced and Corrupt Organizations Act (hereinafter "RICO")[132] is a federal law designed originally to target organized crime, as its name obviously suggests. However, RICO has long since been applied to a much broader audience. RICO is not a law in and of itself that a person may violate. Rather, RICO is a law which enhances the penalties for breaking certain other specified laws. In order for RICO to apply, an offender must commit some "predicate" act, which is to say an offender must violate one or more of certain laws enumerated by RICO more than once during a specified period of time. One such law is extortion, which is prohibited under the federal statute known as the Hobbs Act.[133]

In a landmark case, the Supreme Court ruled that picketers or demonstrators do not commit extortion when the targeted business loses money or may even cease operations as a result of the protest.[134] Abortion clinics have tried to use RICO as a sledgehammer against pro-lifers. However, the High Court's decision ended this assault. The definition of extortion involves obtaining property from another with his consent by force, threat of force, or under color of an official right. The abortion clinics had argued that abortion protestors committed extortion when the protests resulted in financial loss to the clinics by driving away patients. The Court noted that even though the protestors actually deprived the clinics

---

[132]18 U.S.C. § 1964.
[133]18 U.S.C. § 1951.
[134]*See Scheidler v. National Org. for Women,* 537 U.S. 393 (2003).

of their so-called property rights, "they did not acquire any such property" and therefore did not commit extortion.[135] Thus, since protests or boycotts may financially damage a business but do not result in the protestors obtaining the property of the damaged business, the crime of extortion cannot be committed in that manner. In the absence of this predicate act, RICO does not apply.[136]

Noise Levels

Noise levels, with or without sound amplification, have often become an issue for pickets or demonstrations. Noise ordinances must be precise and sometimes have been ruled unconstitutional, either because they are vague or overbroad.[137]

A noise ordinance is unconstitutional if it "either forbids or requires the doing of an act in terms so vague that men of common intelligence must necessarily guess at its meaning and differ as to its application."[138] Certainly those expected to obey a noise ordinance must "be informed as to what the state commands or forbids."[139]

Ordinances which contain decibel levels are more specific than those which simply prohibit "loud" noises. Oftentimes noise ordinances which do not have decibel levels require specific case-by-case evaluation to determine

---

[135]*Id.* at 402.

[136]There are a number of other predicate acts listed within the RICO law. However, the predicate act generally relied upon by the abortion clinics has been the crime of extortion.

[137]*See Grayned,* 408 U.S. at 108–09 (citations omitted).

[138]*Connally,* 269 U.S. at 391.

[139]*Lanzetta,* 306 U.S. at 453.

whether the protester willfully created a noise level incompatible with the area.[140]

Noise ordinances must be specific because "annoyance at ideas can be cloaked in annoyance at sound."[141] In one case, the Supreme Court overturned a city ordinance that prohibited use of sound amplification devices without permission of the police chief. In doing so, the Court noted that "noise can be regulated by regulating decibels. The hours and place of public discussion can be controlled. But to allow the police to bar the use of loudspeakers because their use can be abused is like barring radio receivers because they make too much noise."[142]

The Supreme Court struck down several noise ordinances in *Kaplan v. City of Cincinnati*.[143] The invalid Cincinnati ordinance prohibited people from conducting themselves "in a noisy, boisterous, rude, insulting or other disorderly manner."[144] The ordinance was unconstitutional because it prohibited more speech than just words that "inflict injury or tend to incite an immediate breach of the peace."[145] One of the laws struck down prohibited disturbing the peace by "loud or unusual noise, or by tumultuous or offensive conduct" or by using "vulgar, profane or indecent language . . . in a loud and boisterous manner."[146] The Court also invalidated an ordinance that forbade words or actions of "a noisy,

---

[140]*See Kovacs v. Cooper,* 336 U.S. 77 (1949).
[141]*Saia v. New York,* 334 U.S. 558, 562 (1948).
[142]*Id.* at 562.
[143]416 U.S. 924 (1974); *see also Lewis v. City of New Orleans,* 415 U.S. 130 (1974).
[144]*Id.* at 929 (Douglas, J., dissenting).
[145]*Id.*
[146]*Id.* at 931.

boisterous or other disorderly manner . . . which disturb the good order and quiet of the Municipality."[147] One may challenge an overbroad regulation "without demonstrating that his own conduct could not be regulated by a more precisely drawn act."[148]

Violent Mixed with Nonviolent Activity

While courts have a right to restrict violent activity, which is not protected by the First Amendment, any restriction on picketing or protesting must be precise so as to separate the violent from the nonviolent activity. Indeed, a "free society prefers to punish the few who abuse rights of speech *after* they break the law than to throttle them and all others beforehand."[149]

The classic case involving violent activity mixed with nonviolent activity is *NAACP v. Claiborne Hardware*.[150] The facts of *Claiborne Hardware* are quite interesting. In March 1966, several hundred black demonstrators implemented a boycott of white merchants following racial abuses in Claiborne County, Mississippi. The business merchants sued for an injunction against the demonstrators and Charles

---

[147]*Id.* at 930.
[148]*Id.* at 931 (citing *Gooding v. Wilson,* 405 U.S. 518, 520–21 (1972)). To the extent an ordinance seeks to define and regulate conduct that is the legitimate object of government regulation, it must not do so "by means which sweep unnecessarily broadly and thereby invade the area of protected freedoms." *NAACP v. Alabama,* 377 U.S. 288, 307 (1964); *see also City of Beaufort v. Baker,* 432 S.E.2d 470 (S.C. 1993) (upholding noise ordinance which grew out of a long history of loud and boisterous protests).
[149]*Southeastern Promotions,* 420 U.S. at 559.
[150]458 U.S. 886 (1982).

Evers, a leader of the movement who "sought to persuade others to join the boycott through pressure and the 'threat' of social ostracism."[151] Mr. Evers and other active participants of the boycott furthered their cause by seeking to embarrass nonparticipants and "coerce them into action" and conformity.[152]

Some of the demonstrators, acting for all others, became involved in "acts of physical force and violence" against potential customers and used "intimidation, threats, social ostracism, vilification, and traduction" in order to achieve their desired results.[153] "Enforcers" known as "black hats" were stationed in the vicinity of the white-owned business to record the names of the boycott violators. Those violators were later disclosed in a pamphlet entitled the *Black Times,* which was published by the organization.[154] "In two cases, shots were fired at a house; in a third, a brick was thrown through a windshield; . . . and a group of young blacks apparently pulled down the overalls of an elderly black mason known as 'Preacher White' and spanked him for not observing the boycott."[155] The boycott gained momentum following the assassination of Dr. Martin Luther King Jr., on April 4, 1968, and "tension in the community neared a breaking point." On April 18, 1969, a local civil rights leader was shot and killed.[156] Mr. Evers was quoted as saying: "If we catch any of you going into any of them racist stores, we're going to

---

[151]*Id.* at 909–10.
[152]*Id.* at 910.
[153]*Id.* at 894.
[154]*See id.* at 904–05.
[155]*Id.* at 904–5.
[156]*See id.* at 901–02.

break your damn neck."[157] Nevertheless, coinciding with the escalation in activities was the continuous "uniformly peaceful and orderly" picketing of the white-owned businesses, which often involved small children and occurred "primarily on weekends."[158]

After hearing all of the above evidence, the Mississippi Supreme Court entered a permanent injunction restricting the demonstrators from stationing "store watches" at the merchants' business premises, from "persuading" any person to withhold his patronage from the merchants and from "using demeaning and obscene language to or about any person," and finally, from "picketing or patrolling" the premises of any of the merchants.[159] However, the United States Supreme Court overruled the decision, stating that every element of the boycott was "a form of speech or conduct that is ordinarily entitled to protection under the First and Fourteenth Amendments."[160] The Supreme Court also stated that when restricting free speech activities, there must be "precision of regulation" when "conduct occurs in the context of constitutionally protected activity."[161] The Court further noted that "only unlawful conduct and the persons responsible for conduct of that character" may be restrained.[162]

In another case, a court ruled that it is improper to lump together protected peaceful activity with violent unprotected activity and to prohibit both forms of activity because one is

---

[157]*Id.* at 902.
[158]*Id.* at 903.
[159]*See id.* at 893.
[160]*Id.* at 907.
[161]*Id.* at 916.
[162]*Id.* at 927 n.67.

unlawful.[163] In a similar but unrelated situation, the United States Supreme Court ruled that a university could not prohibit the presence of a student group simply because its parent or national affiliate organization had displayed violent and disruptive behavior.[164] It is, therefore, impermissible to use violent activities to justify prohibiting all peaceful picketing activities. There must be a distinction between the violent and nonviolent activities. While violent activities can be prohibited, lawful demonstration cannot. Moreover, simply the fact that an individual is a member of an organization known for its violent activities is not a sufficient reason to restrict that individual's speech.

It is unconstitutional for one person to lose First Amendment free-speech rights because someone else acted unseemly. There might be rights of other persons to consider in picketing cases, but "the Supreme Court's First Amendment jurisprudence tilts the scale assessing threatened harm decisively in favor of the protesters."[165] Certainly the "First Amendment retains a primacy in our jurisprudence because it represents the foundation of a democracy—informed public discourse."[166]

The "right to associate does not lose constitutional protection merely because some members of the group may have participated in conduct or advocated doctrine that itself is not protected."[167] The Supreme Court has firmly held that

---

[163]See Machesky, 414 F.2d at 283.

[164]See Healy, 408 U.S. at 169.

[165]McMillan, 866 F.2d at 795.

[166]Id. at 796.

[167]Claiborne Hardware, 458 U.S. at 908; see also Citizens against Rent Control/Coalition for Fair Housing v. City of Berkeley, 454 U.S. 290, 294 (1981) (The "practice of persons sharing common views banding together to achieve a common end is deeply embedded in the American political process."); Scales v. United States, 367 U.S. 203, 229 (1961) (A "'blanket

"peaceful assembly for lawful discussion cannot be made a crime."[168] If "absolute assurance of tranquility is required, we may as well forget about speech."[169] While dissidents elsewhere face legal sanctions for their views, in the United States the right to free speech belongs to the politically correct and incorrect, the disaffected as well as the loyal, the obnoxious as well as the sensitive, the vociferous as well as the meek.[170]

---

prohibition of association with a group having both legal and illegal aims' would present 'a real danger that legitimate political expression or association would be impaired.'"); *NAACP v. Alabama ex. rel. Patterson,* 357 U.S. at 460 ("Effective advocacy of both public and private points of view, particularly controversial ones, is undeniably enhanced by group association."); *Thornhill,* 310 U.S. at 88.

[168]*De Jonge v. Oregon,* 299 U.S. 353, 365 (1937).

[169]*See City of Houston v. Hill,* 482 U.S. 451, 462 n.11 (1987) (quoting *Spence v. Washington,* 418 U.S. 405, 416 (1974) (editing remarks and citations omitted)).

[170]*See, e.g., Forsyth County,* 505 U.S. at 123 (racist march); *Texas v. Johnson,* 491 U.S. 397 (1989) (flag burning); *Falwell,* 485 U.S. at 46 (lewd parody); *Claiborne Hardware,* 458 U.S. at 886 (aggressive boycott enforced with threats of ostracism).

13
BREAKING DOWN THE ZONING BARRIER

RELIGIOUS ASSEMBLIES AND INSTITUTIONS, particularly houses of worship, frequently encounter discrimination by local zoning authorities. The typical motivating reasons for such discrimination include opposition to the religious institutions (1) because they are nonprofit entities, and thus they will not produce property tax revenue for the taxing authorities, and (2) because of the religious mission. Eventually, every church, synagogue, or religious institution will come face-to-face with zoning laws. This will occur either during the initial building phase or at some time in the history of the organization when the ministry seeks to expand its facilities or its mission.

Zoning controversies are not limited to religious institutions. Liberty Counsel has represented individual homeowners who received "cease and desist" orders from zoning authorities for merely conducting a small Bible study or prayer meeting in their homes. In such instances, the zoning citation will state that the private homeowner is conducting worship in the home and therefore must apply for a zoning permit to operate a "church" in a residential neighborhood.

Whatever the circumstance may be, the fact remains that religious worship, whether conducted in the home or corporately in a house of worship, is protected by the United States Constitution and by various federal laws. Although there are several federal laws that may protect religious institutions,[1] this chapter will focus on the Fourteenth Amendment Equal Protection Clause, the First Amendment Free Exercise Clause and the federal law known as the Religious Land Use and Institutionalized Persons Act.[2]

Understanding a few terms will be helpful before addressing the legal issues. Zoning involves land use in which a zoning authority divides up the land under its jurisdiction into sectors to which are ascribed initials. These designations vary from one zoning law to the next. An example of one such designation might be R for "residential" and the number 1 for single family. Thus, land zoned residential for single family might be denominated R-1. Within each sector, the zoning authorities list the kinds of uses, and these uses typically fall into three categories: (1) permitted as of right, (2) special exception, or (3) not permitted. For example, if

---

[1] Some of these laws include the Fair Housing Act, 42 U.S.C. § 3601 *et seq.*, the Rehabilitation Act, 29 U.S.C. §701 *et seq.*, and the Americans with Disabilities Act, 42 U.S.C. §12101 *et seq.* The Fair Housing Act is an important law that covers discrimination based on, among other things, religion and disability. Disability discrimination may occur when the ministry operates a program for the physically or mentally challenged or a drug rehabilitation program. Similarly, the Rehabilitation Act and the Americans with Disabilities Act may be used to protect such ministry programs.
[2] *See* 42 U.S.C. §2000cc *et seq.*

you want to build a single family residential home in the R-1 district, you do not need to obtain zoning approval because your use is "as of right."[3]

Continuing with the above example, the zoning code will list those uses "as of right" in this hypothetical R-1 district and will also list other uses permitted by "special exception." If the use you seek in the district is not listed as permitted, look at the categories permitted by "special exception." A "special exception" means the zoning authorities have determined that such uses are compatible with the area but may only be allowed by specific approval of the zoning board. Such uses that may be permitted by special exception in a residential area include schools, churches, and in some cases, filling stations, grocery stores, shopping malls, and professional offices.

If the use you seek is neither permitted "as of right" nor by "special exception," then, assuming the restriction is constitutional, you may have to seek a rezoning of the property. This often occurs in growing regions where property formerly zoned agricultural is rezoned to commercial. In a "special exception," the burden on the applicant is less than in a rezoning. A "special exception" assumes that the use you seek is compatible with the surrounding area. A rezoning request assumes that the use is not compatible.

The typical zoning problems churches face occur when there are permitted "as of right" uses of various types, yet churches are not permitted "as of right" *anywhere* within the

---

[3]Zoning should not be confused with building. In the example given here, the applicant would not need zoning approval but would still be required to obtain a building permit.

city or county. Another problem occurs when a church is denied a special exception, but other secular uses that have similar impact in the area are permitted "as of right" or have received a "special exception." Examples of similar uses to a church include, but are not limited to, theaters, private clubs, civic centers, and shopping malls. If these uses are permitted "as of right" or by "special exception," then most likely churches should also be permitted.

Equal Protection—Religious Assemblies Deserve Equal Treatment

Quoting the U.S. Constitution, the Supreme Court in *City of Cleburne v. Cleburne Living Center* has declared: "The Equal Protection Clause of the Fourteenth Amendment commands that no State shall 'deny to any person within its jurisdiction the equal protection of the laws,' which is essentially a direction that all persons similarly situated should be treated alike."[4] Although the facts involved a city government discriminating against a home for the mentally challenged, the principles set forth in the *Cleburne* case apply with equal force to religious assemblies. The Court observed the following:

> The city does not require a special use permit . . . for apartment houses, multiple dwellings, boarding and lodging houses, fraternity or sorority houses, dormitories, apartment hotels, hospitals, sanitariums, nursing homes for convalescents or the aged . . . , private clubs or fraternal orders, and other specified uses. It does,

---

[4]473 U.S. 432, 439 (1985). *See also* U.S. Const. amend. XIV.

however, insist on a special permit for the Featherston home, . . . a facility for the mentally retarded.[5]

The Court ruled that the city had no rational basis for treating the mentally challenged differently, stating, "If the potential residents of the Featherston Street home were not mentally retarded, but the home was the same in all other respects, its use would be permitted under the city's zoning ordinance."[6] The Court found the ordinance unconstitutional and concluded that requiring a special exception permit for a mental home but not for other similarly situated and intensive uses bore no rational relation to any legitimate interest of the city.[7] The city's asserted interests, such as the negative attitude of the neighboring property owners, students at a nearby school, and the property being located on a five-hundred-year flood plain, as well as the size of the home, concentration of population and congestion of the streets, were not advanced equally but rather were only applied against homes for the mentally challenged.[8] The court noted that these "concerns obviously fail to explain why apartment houses, fraternity and sorority houses, hospitals and the like may freely locate in the area without a permit. . . . The short of it is that requiring the permit in this case appears to us to rest on an irrational prejudice against the mentally retarded."[9]

The City of Evanston, Illinois, enacted a zoning ordinance which did not permit churches anywhere within the city

---

[5]*Cleburne,* 473 U.S. at 447–48.
[6]*Id.* at 449.
[7]*Id.* at 448, 450.
[8]*Id.* at 448–50.
[9]*Id.* at 450.

limits, with the exception of the residential or business/commercial districts, provided they obtained special use permits.[10] In this case, the court contrasted the situation of the churches in Evanston with meeting halls, theaters, schools, funeral parlors, community centers, and not-for-profit recreational buildings which were permitted as of right in some zoning districts. "From the face of the ordinance, we conclude that Evanston gave secular assembly users preference over substantially similar religious assembly users in possible violation of the Equal Protection Clause. . . . Unequal treatment among similarly situated individuals, no matter how subtle, is anathema under the Equal Protection Clause."[11] Looking at the zoning ordinance as a whole, the court stated:

> If all land uses similarly situated to churches must obtain special use permits, then Evanston's argument that the classification is not based on religion may have some merit. . . . We note that contrary to Evanston's reading of its ordinance, community centers (and not-for-profit recreation buildings) are permitted in residential zones 6 and 7. Schools are also permitted in those zones. It appears, then, that Evanston, by its own admission, treats churches differently than these uses.[12]

Because the ordinance classified on the basis of religion, the court held the ordinance violated the Equal Protection

---

[10]See Love Church v. City of Evanston, 671 F. Supp. 515, 516 (N.D. Ill. 1987), vacated on other grounds, 896 F.2d 1082 (7th Cir. 1990).
[11]Id. at 517.
[12]Id. at 518.

Clause.[13] The government's asserted interests could not justify discrimination on the basis of religion.[14]

Failing to learn its lesson, the City of Evanston passed another discriminatory ordinance which a court again struck down.[15] The ordinance allowed cultural facilities and membership organizations as permitted uses in the O1 zoning district. However, the ordinance required religious institutions to obtain a special exception. The court found that the ordinance classified on the basis of religion because "the major difference between the permitted and special use organizations on the one hand, and Vineyard on the other, is that Vineyard wishes to conduct worship services at its property."[16] The court found the ordinance unconstitutional under the Equal Protection Clause because it was not rational to "treat worship services differently than, for example, a meeting of the Masons."[17]

Free Exercise of Religion— Removing Substantial Burdens

The Free Exercise Clause of the First Amendment to the United States Constitution mandates that if an exemption is

[13]*Id.* at 521.

[14]*See also Open Homes Fellowship, Inc. v. Orange County,* 325 F. Supp. 2d 1349 (M.D. Fla. 2004) (finding in favor of a church which also operated a drug rehabilitation program by ruling that the zoning regulations violated equal protection).

[15]*See Vineyard Christian Fellowship of Evanston v. City of Evanston,* 250 F. Supp. 2d 961 (N.D. Ill. 2003).

[16]*Id.* at 976.

[17]*Id.* at 979; *see also Sullivan v. City of Pittsburgh,* 620 F. Supp. 935 (W.D. Pa. 1985) (holding zoning code as applied to deny conditional use permit

given for secular reasons from a neutral, generally applicable requirement, then an exemption must also be given for religious reasons. The United States Supreme Court stated:

> Our cases establish the general proposition that a law that is neutral and of general applicability need not be justified by a compelling governmental interest even if the law has the incidental effect of burdening a particular religious practice. . . . A law failing to satisfy these requirements [of neutrality and general applicability] must be justified by a compelling governmental interest and must be narrowly tailored to advance that interest.[18]

The Court in *Smith* stated that where "a system of individualized exemptions" is in place, the government "may not refuse to extend that system to cases of religious hardship without compelling reason."[19] The Court noted:

> At a minimum, the protections of the Free Exercise Clause pertain if the law issue discriminates against some or all religious beliefs or regulates or prohibits conduct because it is undertaken for religious reasons. . . . If the object of a law is to infringe

---

for drug and alcohol recovery center was unconstitutional because it singled out drug and alcohol addicts for disfavored treatment). This case can be used in combination with the above-listed cases whenever a religious institution provides drug and alcohol rehabilitation.

[18]*Church of the Lukumi Babalu Aye, Inc. v. City of Hialeah*, 508 U.S. 520, 531–32 (1993) (citing *Employment Div. v. Smith*, 494 U.S. 872 (1990)). The compelling interest test is based on several prior Supreme Court cases. *See Thomas v. Review Bd. of Ind. Employment Sec. Div.*, 450 U.S. 707 (1981); *Sherbert v. Verner*, 374 U.S. 398 (1963).

[19]*Id.* at 884.

upon or restrict practices because of their religious motivation, the law is not neutral. . . . To determine the object of a law, we must begin with its text, for the minimum requirement of neutrality is that a law not discriminate on its face.[20]

"Where government restricts only conduct protected by the First Amendment and fails to enact feasible measures to restrict other conduct producing substantial harm or alleged harm of the same sort, the interest given in justification of the restriction is not compelling."[21] Restricting religious expression or activity while not restricting similar secular activity evinces either that the restriction is unnecessary or that the restriction is discriminatory toward religion. In either case, the restriction is unconstitutional.

A scheme that creates a system of individualized exemptions from a law or policy that is otherwise generally applicable is by nature discriminatory and therefore suspect to a constitutional challenge. Although not a case about zoning, a religious freedom case involving the Newark, New Jersey's Police Department's uniform policy illustrates the First Amendment principle of individualized exemptions.[22] The policy, which required that all officers be clean shaven, made

---

[20]*Lukumi,* 508 U.S. at 532–33.

[21]*Id.* at 546. In *Cornerstone Bible Church v. City of Hastings,* 948 F.2d 464 (8th Cir. 1991), the court noted that a city's exclusion of churches from the central business district violated the congregation's right to free speech, because the ordinance was not narrowly tailored. *Id.* at 468–70. The city "may not regulate expression in such a manner that a substantial portion of the burden on speech does not serve to advance its goals." *Id.* at 469.

[22]*See Fraternal Order of Police Newark Lodge No. 12 v. City of Newark,* 170 F.3d 359 (3d Cir. 1999).

exemptions for medical reasons (typically because of a skin condition called pseudo folliculitis barbae), but made no exemptions for officers whose religious beliefs prohibit them from shaving their beards. The court ruled that since the "Department makes exemptions from its policy for secular reasons and has not offered any substantial justification for refusing to provide similar treatment for officers who are required to wear beards for religious reasons, we conclude that the Department's policy violates the First Amendment."[23]

Zoning laws are classic examples of individualized exemptions. Zoning laws are not usually neutral or generally applicable.[24] The laws typically allow certain uses as of right, uses by special exception, and completely prohibit certain uses. Almost always, the applicant must be individually scrutinized to determine whether the use is permissible under the zoning scheme. To succeed under the Free Exercise Clause, the religious institution must show that the intended land use stems from (1) a sincerely held religious belief (2) on which the zoning law places a substantial burden. If this is proven, then the burden shifts to the government to prove that the law is supported by (1) a compelling governmental interest, and (2) the infringement on the religious exercise is the least restrictive means available to achieve this interest.

---

[23]*Id.* at 360.
[24]*See* Mathew D. Staver & Anita L. Staver, *Disestablishmentarianism Collides with the First Amendment: The Ghost of Thomas Jefferson Still Haunts Churches,* 33 Cumb. L. Rev. 43, 71–75 (2003).

The Religious Land Use Law

The Religious Land Use and Institutionalized Persons Act ("RLUIPA")[25] prohibits government from imposing or implementing a land-use regulation that imposes a substantial burden on the religious exercise of any person, religious assembly or institution, unless the government can demonstrate that the burden (1) is in furtherance of a compelling governmental interest and (2) is the lease restrictive means of furthering that interest. For purposes of this chapter, RLUIPA typically applies to governmental actions involving zoning and historical landmarking.[26]

When bringing a claim under the First Amendment Free Exercise Clause, the person, religious assembly, or institution must first contend that the activity in question arises out of a sincerely held religious belief. RLUIPA *presumes* that land

---

[25]42 U.S.C. § 2000cc *et seq.*

[26]RLUIPA sets forth the scope of the law to three primary applications. These include where a substantial burden (1) is imposed in a program or activity that receives federal financial assistance, (2) affects, or the removal of the substantial burden would affect, commerce with foreign nations, among the states, or with Indian tribes, or (3) is imposed in the implementation of a land use regulation or system of land use regulations, under which the government makes, or has in place formal or informal procedures or practices that permit the government to make, individualized assessments of the proposed uses for the property involved. *See* 42 U.S.C. § 2000cc(a)(2)(A)-(C). In addition to land use, RLUIPA also applies to protect the religious exercise of prisoners. Prisons that receive federal funding are covered by the first application noted above. Government activity involving land use is covered by number one above if government receives federal funding, number two above if the activity of the religious assembly affects interstate or international commerce or commerce with an Indian tribe (broadcast information, sales, contributions or attendees crossing state or international borders, or an Indian reservation affect commerce), or number three above in the typical zoning context where the government makes individualized assessments.

use by a religious assembly or institution is a religious exercise.[27] Therefore, in a RLUIPA claim, the applicant need not prove that the activity is motivated by a sincerely held religious belief.[28] Under RLUIPA, the government may not (1) implement or impose a land use regulation in a manner that treats a religious assembly or institution on less than equal terms with a nonreligious assembly or institution, (2) discriminate against any assembly or institution on the basis of religion or religious denomination, or (3) totally exclude religious assemblies from a jurisdiction or unreasonably limit religious assemblies, institutions, or structures within a jurisdiction.[29]

Unequal Treatment, Discrimination, and Exclusion Are Prohibited

RLUIPA makes it unlawful for a government to "impose or implement a land use regulation in a manner that treats a religious assembly or institution on less than equal terms with a nonreligious assembly or institution."[30] Courts have recognized that the equal treatment section codifies existing Equal

---

[27]RLUIPA defines religious exercise as, "The use, building, or conversion of real property for the purpose of religious exercise." 42 U.S.C. §2000cc-5(7)(B).

[28]Although it is unnecessary to show that the land use is motivated by a sincerely held religious belief, it is nevertheless recommended that the applicant do so anyway.

[29]42 U.S.C. § 2000cc(b)(1)-(3).

[30]42 U.S.C. § 2000cc(b)(1). RLUIPA defines a "land use regulation" as, "a zoning or landmarking law, or the application of such a law, that limits or restricts a claimant's use or development of land (including a structure affixed to land), if the claimant has an ownership, leasehold, easement, servitude, or other property interest in the regulated land or a contract or option to acquire such an interest." 42 U.S.C. §200cc-5(5).

Protection case law.[31] Because this section codifies existing
Equal Protection case law, the Supreme Court's decision in the
City of Cleburne case applies with equal force here.[32] In a similar way that RLUIPA codifies the Fourteenth Amendment
Equal Protection Clause in the unequal treatment section, it
also codifies the First Amendment Free Exercise Clause case
law regarding discriminatory individualized assessments.[33]
Unequal treatment is generally proven by comparing the kinds
of uses permitted in the zoning area with the intended use by
the religious assembly. For example, if the zoning district permits a movie theater but prohibits a church, this distinction
may indicate unequal treatment. Movie theaters, clubs, or
other assembly-type uses have a similar impact on the zoning

---

[31]*See Ventura County Christian High Sch. v. City of San Buenaventura*, 233
F. Supp. 2d 1241, 1246 (C.D. Cal. 2002); *see also Freedom Baptist Church
of Del. County v. Township of Middleton*, 204 F. Supp. 2d 857, 869 (E.D.
Pa. 2002).

[32]*See also Vineyard Christian Fellowship*, 250 F. Supp. 2d at 975–79 (striking down zoning ordinance that required churches to obtain a special exception but did not require the same of similarly situated groups); *Love
Church*, 671 F. Supp. at 515 (same).

[33]"RLUIPA's limitations and proscriptions explicitly codify firmly established Supreme Court rights under its Free Exercise and Equal Protection jurisprudence." *Freedom Baptist Church*, 204 F. Supp. 2d at 874; *Ventura
County Christian High Sch.*, 233 F. Supp. 2d at 1246 (noting that the unequal treatment section codifies existing Supreme Court decisions under
the Free Exercise and Establishment Clauses of the First Amendment as well
as under the Equal Protection Clause of the Fourteenth Amendment). The
legislative history states that §2000cc(b)(3) "enforces the Free Speech
Clause as interpreted in *Schad v. Borough of Mount Ephraim*, 425 U.S. 61
(1981), which held that a municipality cannot entirely exclude a category
of first amendment activity," and "enforces the right to assemble for
worship or other religious exercise under the Free Speech Clause, and the
hybrid free speech and free exercise right to assemble for worship or other
religious exercise under *Schad* and *Smith*." 146 Cong. Rec. S7776 (2000)
(Joint Statement of Sens. Hatch and Kennedy).

district in terms of traffic and people as houses of worship. The point here is to compare the kinds of uses of the religious assembly to the permitted uses. This is a powerful section of RLUIPA. Unequal treatment between secular and religious land uses is forbidden under this section of the federal law.

RLUIPA prohibits the government from implementing or imposing a land use regulation that discriminates against a religious assembly or institution on the basis of religion.[34] This section can be used where the use is permitted but the government places additional requirements on the religious assembly and not on the secular assemblies. For example, if the government required the religious assembly to pay additional impact fees or make additional improvements to the area which are not required of secular uses, then it may be argued that the land use regulation is discriminatory.

RLUIPA also prohibits the government from (1) totally excluding religious assemblies from a jurisdiction or (2) unreasonably limiting religious assemblies, institutions, or structures within a jurisdiction.[35] Some governments have attempted totally to exclude religious assemblies from locating within the city limits. Total exclusion may occur in several ways. First, the zoning law may completely prohibit religious assemblies. Second, the zoning scheme may permit religious assemblies *only* by special exception while permitting many other similar secular uses as of right. Either way, such exclusion violates RLUIPA.[36] However, RLUIPA prohibits more

---

[34]42 U.S.C. § 2000cc(b)(2).

[35]42 U.S.C. § 2000cc(b)(3).

[36]See *Midrash Sephardi, Inc. v. Town of Surfside,* 366 F.3d 1214 (11th Cir. 2004). (Town's zoning ordinance, which prohibited religious assemblies within the city, violated RLUIPA.)

than total exclusion under this section. If the government does not totally exclude religious assemblies but still places unreasonable limitations on them or upon religious structures, then RLUIPA is also violated.

SUBSTANTIAL BURDEN

RLUIPA prohibits government from placing a substantial burden on the religious exercise of any person, religious assembly, or institution unless the burden is in furtherance of a compelling governmental interest and it is achieved in the least restrictive means available.[37] A burden on religious

---

[37] 42 U.S.C. §2000cc(a)(1). RLUIPA codifies Supreme Court precedent interpreting the Free Exercise Clause regarding the individualized exemptions analysis in *Smith*, 494 U.S. at 872 and in *Lukumi*, 508 U.S. at 520. *See Cottonwood Christian Ctr. v. Cypress Redev. Agency*, 218 F. Supp. 2d 1203, 1221 (C.D. Cal. 2002) (stating that RLUIPA "merely codifies numerous precedents holding that systems of individualized assessments, as opposed to generally applicable laws, are subject to strict scrutiny."); *Freedom Baptist Church*, 204 F. Supp. 2d at 868 ("What Congress manifestly has done in this subsection is to codify the individualized assessments jurisprudence in Free Exercise cases that originated with the Supreme Court's decision in *Sherbert v. Verner*, 374 U.S. 398 (1963)."); *Grace United Methodist Church v. City of Cheyenne*, 235 F. Supp. 2d 1186, 1192 n.2 (D. Wy. 2002) (same). "RLUIPA does not erroneously review or revise a specific ruling of the Supreme Court because the statute does not overturn the Court's constitutional interpretation in *Smith*." *Mayweathers v. Newland*, 314 F.3d 1062, 1069 (9th Cir. 2002). "Rather, RLUIPA provides additional protection for religious worship, respecting that *Smith* set only a constitutional floor—not a ceiling—for the protection of personal liberty. *Smith* explicitly left heightened legislative protection for religious worship to the political branches." *Id.* (citing *Smith*, 494 U.S. at 890); *see also Goodman v. Snyder*, No. 00 C 0948, 2003 WL 22765047 (N.D. Ill. Nov. 20, 2003) (rejecting a separation of powers challenge to RLUIPA); *Grace United Methodist Church*, 235 F. Supp. 2d at 1192 n.3 (RLUIPA codifies "the individualized assessments analysis for Free Exercise Clause jurisprudence."). *See Smith*, 494 U.S. at 884; *Fraternal Order of Police*, 170 F.3d at 359; *Rader v. Johnston*, 924 F. Supp. 1540 (D. Neb. 1996). RLUIPA does

exercise is substantial if it "results in the choice to the individual of either abandoning his religious principle or facing criminal prosecution"[38] or "put[s] substantial pressure on an adherent to modify his behavior and to violate his beliefs."[39] "[I]n general, if an exercise of religion is prohibited, penalized, discriminated against, or made the basis for a loss of entitlements, courts should find a substantial burden."[40]

In a case where a homeowner was given a cease and desist order to stop prayer meetings in his home, a federal court held that the order substantially burdened the homeowner.[41] "Foregoing or modifying the practice of one's religion because of governmental interference or fear of punishment by the government is precisely the type of 'substantial burden' Congress intended to trigger the RLUIPA's protections; indeed, it is the concern which impelled adoption of the First Amendment."[42]

---

not substantively change the interpretation of the Free Exercise Clause. Congress noted that this section of RLUIPA "codifies parts of the Supreme Court's constitutional tests as applied to land use regulation." 146 Cong. Rec. E1563 (daily ed. Sep. 22, 2000). The legislative history notes that this section corresponds to "§§ 3(b)(1)(B) and 3(b)(1)(C) of H.R. 1691." *Id.* These sections were part of a previous version of RLUIPA known as the Religious Liberty Protection Act. During the hearings on the identical language, testimony confirmed that RLUIPA codified existing constitutional precedent. *See Religious Liberty Protection Act of 1999: Hearing on H.R. 1691 before the Subcommittee on the Constitution of the Committee on the Judiciary, House of Representatives,* 106th Cong., 1st Sess. 214 (1999) (statement of Douglas Laycock).

[38]*Braunfeld v. Brown,* 366 U.S. 599, 605 (1961).

[39]*Thomas,* 450 U.S. at 718.

[40]Douglas Laycock, *Interpreting the Religious Freedom Restoration Act,* 73 Tex. L. Rev. 209, 229 (1994) (citing Ira C. Lupu, *Where Rights Begin: The Problem of Burdens on the Free Exercise of Religion,* 102 Harv. L. Rev. 933 (1989)).

[41]*See Murphy v. Zoning Comm'n of Town of New Milford,* 148 F. Supp. 2d 173, 188–89 (D. Conn. 2001).

[42]*Id.* at 189.

Denying an application to build a church may constitute a substantial burden, because "preventing a church from building a worship site fundamentally inhibits its ability to practice its religion."[43]

A compelling interest is "an interest of the highest order."[44] "It is basic that no showing merely of a rational relationship to some colorable state interest would suffice; in this highly sensitive constitutional area, '(o)nly the gravest abuses, endangering paramount interest, give occasion for permissible limitation.'"[45] "Moreover, if 'compelling interest' really means what it says (and watering it down here would subvert its rigor in the other fields where it is applied), many laws will not meet the test."[46] "Where government restricts only conduct protected by the First Amendment and fails to enact feasible measures to restrict other conduct producing substantial harm or alleged harm of the same sort, the interest given in justification of the restriction is not compelling."[47] Where the government claims to have a compelling interest but does not advance that interest uniformly against all dangers to that interest, the interest is not compelling.

Even if the government has a compelling interest, it must be advanced in the least restrictive means available. In other words, if there are five ways the government can further its compelling interest with one being the most restrictive and five being the least restrictive, the government will prevail only if it

---

[43]*Cottonwood Christian Ctr.,* 218 F. Supp. 2d at 1226–27.
[44]*Wisconsin v. Yoder,* 406 U.S. 205, 215 (1972).
[45]*Sherbert,* 374 U.S. at 406 (citing *Thomas v. Collins,* 323 U.S. 516, 530 (1945)).
[46]*Smith,* 494 U.S. at 888.
[47]*Lukumi,* 508 U.S. at 546–47.

chooses number five. The law must be "narrowly tailored in pursuit of those interests."[48] Consider a situation where the government balks at a religious institution's proposed construction of a school because the increased traffic will cause overuse of an already busy street. The peak traffic time on this road is from 7:30 to 8:30 a.m. Instead of denying the use (most restrictive means), assume the government's interest could be achieved if the school built a turn lane to remove traffic from the two-lane highway (less restrictive means) or moved the start time to 8:45 a.m. (least restrictive means). If the government chooses any alternative except moving the start time back to 8:45 a.m., the government loses.

Summary

Zoning is essentially a government license to use property. While zoning laws have their place, improper use of these laws can have a profound impact on the free exercise of religion. At some time or another, virtually every person of religious faith will be affected by zoning laws. Zoning laws applied to home worship, leasing space to conduct worship, constructing a house of worship, or expanding the religious mission of an ongoing entity often raise serious constitutional and statutory issues. The First Amendment Free Exercise Clause, the Fourteenth Amendment Equal Protection Clause and RLUIPA, among other laws, are powerful weapons designed to protect freedom of religion when the government oversteps its authority.

---

[48]*Id.* at 546.

14
RELIGIOUS RIGHTS IN THE WORKPLACE

THREE CHRISTIANS EMPLOYED with the Minnesota Department of Corrections faced a dilemma when their employer published a training session agenda regarding a mandatory seminar for all employees entitled "Gays and Lesbians in the Workplace." Thomas Altman, one of the employees, sent an e-mail objecting to the mandatory training, stating that the session was designed to "raise deviate sexual behavior for staff to a level of acceptance and respectability."[1] The supervisor responded by stating that the program was part of the employer's commitment to create a work environment where employees treated one another with respect and confirmed that all employees must attend.

Immediately prior to the session, these three employees met and decided to read their Bibles during the seminar as a

---

[1]See *Altman v. Minnesota Dept. of Corrections,* 251 F.3d 1199, 1201 (8th Cir. 2001).

silent protest. They read their Bibles, copied Scripture, participated to a limited extent and were not disruptive. After the seminar, and following an internal investigation of the incident, the employees were reprimanded. These reprimands precluded the employees from promotion for two years. The employees filed suit and were eventually awarded damages for their employer's behavior.

More and more frequently, employers' policies and practices are colliding with the religious beliefs of employees. Mandatory diversity training programs designed to promote homosexuality under the rubic of "diversity training" present obvious conflicts. Hospital personnel or pharmacists are often conflicted between their pro-life beliefs and employer practices that facilitate or promote abortion. Sometimes employees are told to leave their faith at home, refrain from religious expression, remove religious jewelry, take down religious pictures, or stop meeting for Bible studies during authorized breaks. An employee may want to attend worship, but the work hours established by the employer prohibit attendance. Whenever employment practices or policies collide with an employee's religious beliefs, the employee must understand the steps to take to alleviate the conflict.

Federal law, commonly referred to Title VII[2] of the Civil Rights Act of 1964, prohibits most employers[3] and unions[4] from discriminating against their employees on the basis of religion.[5] Title VII applies to any employer having fifteen or

---

[2]42 U.S.C. §2000e et seq.

[3]42 U.S.C. §2000e-2(a)(1)&(2).

[4]42 U.S.C. §2000e-2(c)(1),(2)&(3).

[5]Religious organizations are exempt from Title VII's religious discrimination requirement. Thus, a religious organization, such as a church, may

more employees for each working day in each of the twenty preceding calendar weeks in the current or preceding calendar year.[6] Other state or local laws may also prevent discrimination on the basis of religion, and such laws may apply to employers with fewer than fifteen employees.[7]

The relevant text of Title VII regarding the protected employment categories states as follows:

It shall be an unlawful employment practice for an employer—

(1) To fail or refuse to hire or to discharge any individual, or otherwise to discriminate against any individual with respect to his compensation, terms, conditions, or privileges of employment, because of such individual's race, color, religion, sex, or national origin; or

---

discriminate on the basis of religion. A Baptist church may hire only Baptists, and a Catholic church may hire only Catholics. See *Corporation of Presiding Bishop of The Church of Jesus Christ of Latter-day Saints v. Amos,* 483 U.S. 327 (1987). Title VII does not apply to the United States and corporations owned by the United States, Indian tribes, or certain employees of the District of Columbia, and furthermore does not apply to tax-exempt private clubs.

[6]42 U.S.C. §2000e-2. Part-time employees may be counted as constituting the fifteen employees. See *Pedreya v. Cornell Prescription Pharmacies, Inc.,* 465 F. Supp. 936 (D. Colo. 1979); *but see Richardson v. Bedford Place Housing Phase I Assoc.,* 855 F. Supp. 366 (N.D. Ga. 1994); *see also Bonomo v. Nat'l. Duck Pin Bowling Congress, Inc.,* 465 F. Supp. 936 (D. Colo. 1979.) (Federal courts are without jurisdiction to consider a Title VII claim if the employer has fewer than fifteen employees.)

[7]The discussion herein pertains to Title VII which is applicable to private and government employers. Additional rights may be afforded to employees who work with the state or federal government. The *Guidelines on Religious Exercise and Religious Expression in the Federal Workplace* provide an excellent discussion on this topic. To obtain a copy of the document, visit www.lc.org and search for "Guidelines on Religious Exercise." Although the *Guidelines* are specifically applicable to the federal workplace, the principles clearly apply to both private and state employers.

(2) To limit, segregate, or classify his employees or applicants for employment in any way which would deprive or tend to deprive any individual of employment opportunities or otherwise adversely affect his status as an employee, because of such individual's race, color, religion, sex, or national origin.[8]

Title VII then defines "religion" to include all aspects of religious observance and practice, as well as belief, unless an employer demonstrates that he is unable reasonably to accommodate an employee's or prospective employee's religious observance or practice without undue hardship on the conduct of the employer's business.[9]

There are several important exemptions to Title VII. Religious educational institutions are exempt under Title VII as follows:

It shall not be an unlawful employment practice for a school, college, university, or other educational institution or institution of learning to hire and employ employees of a particular religion if such school, college, university, or other educational institution or institution of learning is, in whole or in substantial part, owned, supported, controlled, or managed by a particular religion or by a particular religious corporation, association, or society, or if the curriculum of such school, college, university, or other educational institution or institution of learning is directed toward the propagation of a particular religion.[10]

---

[8]42 U.S.C. §2000e-2(a)(1)&(2).
[9]42 U.S.C. §2000e(j).
[10]42 U.S.C. § 2000e-2(e)(2).

It should be noted that the exemption for religious educational institutions is an exemption from *religious* discrimination, not from the other forms of discrimination. Another exemption is the "bona fide occupational qualification." This exemption is as follows:

> Notwithstanding any other provision of this subchapter . . . it shall not be an unlawful employment practice for an employer to hire and employ employees . . . on the basis of his religion, sex, or national origin in those certain instances where religion, sex, or national origin is a bona fide occupational qualification reasonably necessary to the normal operation of that particular business or enterprise.[11]

This exemption applies to religion, sex, or national origin. For example, the Moroccan Pavilion at Disney's EPCOT Center may hire only those of Moroccan descent, because of the necessity to create a Moroccan atmosphere. Finally, religious organizations are exempt from the religious discrimination requirement as follows:

> This subchapter shall not apply to . . . a religious corporation, association, educational institution, or society with respect to the employment of individuals of a particular religion to perform work connected with the carrying on by such corporation, association, educational institution, or society of its activities.[12]

---

[11]42 U.S.C. § 2000e-2(e).
[12]42 U.S.C. § 2000e-1.

In 1972 Congress amended Title VII to enable religious organizations to discriminate on the basis of religion in all employment decisions. Therefore, a Baptist church may hire all Baptists, and a Catholic church may hire all Catholics.[13] For other employers who are covered by Title VII, the employer is restricted from discriminating on the basis of religion. The employee must first have a sincerely held religious belief that is negatively impacted or burdened by a particular employment practice. The employee has the obligation to notify the employer of the belief and of the negative impact on that belief. The burden then shifts to the employer to provide reasonable accommodation to that belief, unless doing so would result in an undue hardship to the employer. Liberty Counsel became involved in the case of a Seventh-day Adventist who had a sincerely held religious belief that Saturday is the Sabbath, upon which no work should be conducted. This employee was a salesperson who had worked for the same employer for some time. During the week, the employer required a sales meeting to be conducted. For an unexplained reason, the employer began requiring the sales meeting to be conducted on Saturday. In this case, the employer already knew of the salesperson's religious belief. The employee brought his belief to the attention of the employer again and requested that the sales meeting be held on some other day or possibly even Sunday. The employer did not accommodate this religious belief, even though accommodation was clearly possible. In this situation, the employer discriminated on the basis of religion.

---

[13]*Amos,* 483 U.S. at 327.

Three Aspects of a Title VII Claim

The three aspects of a Title VII claim involve the employee's sincerely held religious belief, the employer's accommodation of that belief, and the employer's defense that it cannot accommodate the belief because the accommodation would result in an undue hardship.

SINCERELY HELD RELIGIOUS BELIEF

Title VII prohibits discrimination based on an employee's religious belief. This discrimination applies not only to hiring and firing but to all terms, conditions, and privileges of employment. Under Title VII, the term "religion" is broadly defined to include "all aspects such as religious observance and practice, as well as belief."[14] The Equal Employment Opportunity Commission ("EEOC") defines religious practice to include "moral or ethical beliefs as to what is right and wrong which are sincerely held with the strength of traditional religious views. . . . The fact that no religious group establishes such beliefs or the fact that the religious group to which the individual professes to belong may not set the beliefs, will not determine whether the belief is a religious belief of the employee."[15] Title VII protects individual religious practices, even though the practice is not mandated by the religious institution to which the employee belongs.[16]

---

[14] 42 U.S.C. §2000z(j). The courts and the EEOC have interpreted this provision liberally. Donald P. Kramer, *Validity, Construction, and Application of the Provisions of Title VII of the Civil Rights Act of 1964 (42 U.S.C. § 2000z et seq.) and Implementing Regulations, Making Religious Discrimination in Employment Unlawful,* 22 A.L.R. FED. 580, 602 (1975).

[15] *Guidelines on Discrimination Because of Religion,* 29 C.F.R. §1605.1.

[16] *Heller v. EBB Co.,* F.3d 1433, 1438–39 (9th Cir. 1993); *see also Redmond v. GAF Corp.,* 574 F.2d 897 (7th Cir. 1998); 22 A.L.R. FED. at 601–03.

The employee should apprize the employer of this sincerely held religious belief. For example, if the employer requires the employee to work on the Sabbath or Sunday, and if the employee has a sincerely held religious belief to attend church and worship with fellow believers on that day, then the employee should advise the employer of this belief. The employee should state the belief both verbally and in writing and should refer to any biblical or religious-based references that form the basis of this belief. The employee should also advise the employer as to why this belief conflicts with the employer's practice. An employee cannot claim religious discrimination if the employer is unaware that the belief is or will be violated.

ACCOMMODATION

Once the employee advises the employer of the sincerely held religious belief, the burden shifts to the employer to accommodate that belief. The employee should suggest accommodation alternatives. In the example of working on the Sabbath or Sunday noted above, the employee can offer to work on an alternative day or suggest other employees who may work the Sabbath or Sunday shift.

The EEOC brought suit in federal court against Dillard Department Stores because of its so-called "no excuses" policy.[17] This national department store chain apparently had a policy wherein it would accept no excuse from any employee for not working at least one Sunday per month. One employee objected to working on Sunday because of sincerely

---

[17] *EEOC v. Dillard Dep't Stores,* No. 4:93-CV-1771 CAS., 1994 WL 738971 (E.D. Mo. Nov. 2, 1994).

held religious beliefs, but the store would not accept the excuse and, therefore, terminated the employee. The employee filed a complaint with the EEOC and, after reviewing the case, the EEOC itself filed suit against the department store. This policy has now been changed. This was a blatant violation of federal law prohibiting discrimination based on religion. An employer must at least attempt accommodation of the employee's sincerely held religious belief, but this department store refused to accept any excuses.

The employer must undertake reasonable efforts to accommodate the employee's religious belief. An employer cannot establish a zero tolerance policy against accommodating religious belief and practice; it must take seriously its obligation to accommodate the belief.

UNDUE HARDSHIP

Once apprized of the employee's sincerely held religious belief, an employer is required to accommodate the belief, unless to do so would cause an undue hardship on the employer's business. An undue hardship means more than mere inconvenience. An employer cannot claim that employee morale, as a result of the accommodation, is itself undue hardship. Minimal expense is not undue hardship. Undue hardship is determined case by case. The employer must undertake serious attempts to accommodate the employee's belief.

When to File a Title VII Claim

If an employer fails or refuses to accommodate an employee's sincerely held religious belief, the employee may file a Title VII religious discrimination claim with the local EEOC office. Suit may not be brought under Title VII unless the employee first files an administrative claim with the EEOC.[18] In most states an employee must file a claim within three hundred days of the discrimination.[19] However, a few states provide that the claim must be filed within one hundred eighty days.[20]

Filing the Complaint

A Title VII claim is initiated by filing a complaint form with the nearest EEOC office. The nearest office can be located by calling (800) 669-EEOC (800-669-3362). In the complaint, the employee should describe the religious belief along with some basis for the belief, the employer practice which burdened or discriminated against the belief, and identify those in supervisory authority who have the power to accommodate the belief but failed or refused to do so. The employee should list the names, addresses, and phone numbers of any supervisory personnel who were informed of the belief and who failed or refused to accommodate the belief or who are capable of taking action to make an accommodation. The employee should then deliver the complaint to the nearest EEOC office.

---

[18]*Love v. Pullman Co.,* 404 U.S. 522 (1972).
[19]The time period is extended to three hundred days in states where a state or local agency has its own separate authority to grant or seek relief with regard to religious discrimination, separate and apart from the federal law. *See* 29 C.F.R. §1601.74. All states except Alabama, Arkansas, and Mississippi have state laws prohibiting religious discrimination. Mississippi has a state law prohibiting religious discrimination against public employees. *See* BNA's FAIR EMPLOYMENT PRACTICES MANUAL 451:103.
[20]42 U.S.C. §2000e-5(e)(1).

EEOC intake personnel are not necessarily well versed in religious discrimination claims. Some may discourage an employee from presenting a claim or ask the employee to change the category of discrimination from religion to something else. The employee should insist that the intake personnel accept the complaint. The employee may refer the intake personnel to the *EEOC Compliance Manual,* which states that "if the charging party insists on filing a charge the charge should be taken."[21]

If the state or local agency has a law or ordinance that also addresses religious discrimination, the employee may be required to file a charge with the state or local agency in addition to the EEOC.[22] Although the EEOC is supposed to file a copy of your charge with the appropriate state or local agency,[23] the employee should either file a duplicate copy or get the name of the local or state agency and follow up to see if the EEOC, in fact, filed a duplicate copy.[24]

The EEOC Proceeding

The EEOC proceeding is an administrative matter and not a court hearing. However, the EEOC may require the parties to appear before an EEOC investigator. The EEOC may take one of several steps. First, the EEOC may issue a "Right to Sue" letter, which allows you the right to file suit in a court of law. An employee has ninety days in which to file a suit after a Right to Sue letter is issued.[25] An employee may request a

---

[21]EEOC COMPLIANCE MANUAL, FIELD NOTES 112–1(1.7) (issued 1/88).

[22]42 U.S.C. §2000e-5(c).

[23]29 C.F.R. §1601.13(a)(4)(i).

[24]Either deliver a copy of the complaint personally to the state or local agency or send it by registered mail, return receipt required.

[25]42 U.S.C. §2000e-5(f)(1).

Right to Sue letter if the charge has been pending before the EEOC more than 180 days.

Second, the EEOC may issue a "No Cause" letter. Generally, the EEOC will advise the employee in advance that a No Cause letter will be issued. In this situation, an employee should request that the EEOC instead issue a Right to Sue letter, so that if the employee decides to later file suit, the court will not have any knowledge of the EEOC's reasoning behind the No Cause letter.

Finally, the EEOC may find in the employee's favor and issue a "Show Cause" letter. Instead of being a mediator at this stage, the EEOC takes the side of the employee and requests the employer to accommodate the religious belief. However, the EEOC has no power to act on its own. If the employer refuses to accommodate the employee's belief, the EEOC can either discontinue any further efforts or file suit in its own name against the employer. If the EEOC files suit against the employer in its own name, the employee has the right to obtain separate counsel and intervene as a co-plaintiff against the employer. If an employee obtains counsel and is successful against the employer in a court action, the employer may have to pay the employee's attorney's fees and costs.[26]

Summary of a Title VII Claim

Employees do not have to leave their faith at home. Work is not a religion-free zone. Federal law prohibits employers and unions with fifteen or more employees for each working

---

[26]42 U.S.C. §2000e-5(k).

day in each of the twenty preceding calendar weeks in the current or preceding calendar year from discriminating against an employee's sincerely held religious belief. An employee should apprize the employer of the sincerely held religious belief that collides with an employment practice or policy. An employer is required to accommodate the employee's sincerely held religious belief, unless to do so would result in an undue hardship on the employer's business.

15
DEFUNDING IDEOLOGICALLY DRIVEN UNIONS

UNIONS FREQUENTLY BECOME INVOLVED in partisan politics, world affairs, and social controversies such as abortion and other divisive issues that have nothing to do with the benefits of employment. It is an anathema to compel a pro-life employee to contribute hard-earned income which the employee knows will be used by the union to promote abortion. Compulsory acceptance of an ideological belief is repugnant to our historical liberty.

In one case a pro-life Roman Catholic professor employed at the University of Detroit supported the local union but objected to joining the National Education Association and the Michigan Education Association because they both campaigned to promote abortion. He offered to pay an amount equal to his entire agency fee to a charity or to remit that portion of his fee which was allocated solely to the union's local responsibilities and to pay the balance to a charitable organization.[1] In his refusal the teacher declared: "Since I believe that abortion is absolutely wrong I must choose the course that minimizes the support of it. The gravity of this issue is so great that I must consider my job expendable."[2] However, the University terminated the professor for failure to pay the agency fees. The court stated that in order "to invoke the employer's duty to offer a reasonable accommodation, it is sufficient that the employee establishes that he holds a sincere religious belief that conflicts with an employment requirement."[3] The court also pointed out that "one reasonable accommodation may be for [the teacher] to pay all of the agency fee, including the amount normally forwarded to the EMA and the NEA, to the union to be used solely for local collective bargaining purposes."[4] The court ruled against the University because it did not attempt to reasonably accommodate the teacher's sincerely held religious belief. It concluded that the University could have used alternative ways at least to attempt to accommodate these beliefs and ordered the University to do so.

Union membership, or compelling the payment of union fees, unquestionably implicates the religious rights of many private and public sector employees.[5] Oftentimes unions engage

---

[1] *EEOC v. University of Detroit*, 904 F.2d 331 (6th Cir. 1990).
[2] *Id.* at 333.
[3] *Id.* at 335.
[4] *Id.* at 335.
[5] Union membership clearly has First Amendment implications for public sector employees. *See Abood v. Detroit Bd. of Educ.*, 341 U.S. 209, 222 (1977). The same is true for those governed by the Railway Labor Act ("RLA"). *See Ellis v. Brotherhood of Railway, Airline and Steamship Clerks*, 466 U.S. 435 (1984). However, the extent of First Amendment rights enjoyed by union members in the private sector governed by the National Labor Relations Board ("NLRB") remains unresolved by the United States

in activities which are not directly related to negotiating labor agreements. Unions publish their views, lobby, litigate, and undertake public relations campaigns on political, moral, and religious issues. Whenever unions engage in these peripheral activities, the employee's religious rights may be implicated. To require a member to pay for activities to which the member is either politically or religiously opposed may violate constitutional freedoms or other federally protected rights.[6] To better understand the rights of employees in the union context, it is important to overview briefly certain federal laws affecting labor unions.

Background

In the early twentieth century, two major labor federations emerged to address concerns regarding the labor market: the American Federation of Labor ("AFL") and the Congress of Industrial Organizations ("CIO"). The AFL organized workers by craft, which meant that one company might have multiple small-craft unions working in the same factory. The CIO organized labor on an industry-wide basis. Rather

---

Supreme Court. *See Communications Workers v. Beck,* 487 U.S. 735, 761–62 (1988). The federal circuit courts of appeal remain divided on this issue. *Cf. Linscott v. Millers Falls,* 440 F.2d 14 (1st Cir. 1971) (Private-sector religious objectors may not rely upon the First Amendment.) *with Kolinske v. Lubbers,* 712 F.2d 471 (D.C.Cir.1983) (Religious objectors may rely upon the First Amendment.) and *Price v. International Union, United Auto. Aerospace and Agric. Implement Workers of America,* 927 F.2d 88 (2d Cir. 1991) (same).

[6]Title VII of the Civil Rights Act may protect employees in situations where the constitutional claim is in doubt. *See Nottelson v. A. O. Smith Corp.,* 423 F. Supp. 1345, *aff'd,* 643 F.2d 445 (7th Cir), *cert. denied,* 454 U.S. 1046 (1981).

than dealing with the individual crafts within a single employer, the CIO treated multiple employers as one unit. One example of this structure is the United Auto Workers.

The AFL eventually adopted an industry-wide union concept similar to the CIO, but when the CIO became infiltrated by communist influences and began losing membership, the two federations merged in 1955 under the leadership of George Meany to form what is now known as the AFL-CIO.

National Labor Relations Act

In 1935 Congress passed the National Labor Relations Act (NLRA).[7] Originally, certain unions had a closed shop. A closed shop involved a contract between labor and management whereby management agreed not to hire employees who were not already members of the union. It essentially made the union the hiring agent. Therefore, in order to work for the employer, the worker had to be a member of the union. In 1947 Congress passed the Taft-Hartley Act in response to criticisms of unfair labor practices carried on by organized labor following the passage of the NLRA. The Taft-Hartley Act, also known as the Labor-Management Relations Act ("LMRA")[8] instituted several major changes to labor unions.[9] Though President Lyndon B. Johnson attempted to repeal the Act in 1965, that attempt failed, and it is still a part of the

---

[7] 29 U.S.C. § 151 *et seq.*

[8] 29 U.S.C. § 141 *et seq.*

[9] The Labor Management Reporting and Disclosure Act (LMRDA), also known as the Landrum-Griffin Act, was passed by Congress in 1949. This law further amended the NLRA by creating what was known as the union members' "Bill of Rights." The LMRDA defines certain unfair labor practices

NLRA. Except for employment in the railway or airline industries, private employment relations involving unions is governed by the NLRA. The following summarizes some of the significant areas of labor law that affect religious liberty.

Closed, Agency, and Union Shops

The closed-shop concept was abolished by the passage of the LMRA in 1947. No longer is it lawful for a contract to be entered into between labor and management whereby management agrees not to hire employees who are not already members of the union. Unions may set up an Agency Shop whereby the union acts as the agent for the employee, even though the employee is not a member of the union. There is typically a security clause that requires all Agency Shop employees to pay a service fee to the union.[10] An agency shop is most often found in the public employment sector. In addition to the agency shop, the union shop replaced the closed shop after the passage of the LMRA. Under the union shop, after a brief period on the job, employees may be required to pay initiation fees and dues to the union. The requirement to "join" has been modified by court challenges, so that the payment of the fees may be all that the union is allowed to require.[11] In practice, the union shop is now similar to an

---

with respect to secondary boycotts and picketing. For example, a union having a grievance with a certain employer may not picket another employer not having direct relationship with the employer against whom the grievance is alleged.

[10]See *Chicago Teachers Union v. Hudson,* 475 U.S. 292 (1986).

[11]"Under a union-shop agreement, an employee must become a member of the union within a specified period of time after hire, and must as a

agency shop.[12] Unions may no longer require nonmembers to pay "dues."

Right to Work

Under the LMRA passed by Congress in 1947, the NLRA was revised to allow state exemption from the union shop provision by adopting right-to-work laws under section 14(b) of the NLRA.[13] Many states have adopted such right-to-work

---

member pay whatever union dues and fees are uniformly required." *Abood,* 431 U.S. at 217 n.10. Under both the National Labor Relations Act and the Railway Labor Act, "it is permissible to condition employment upon membership, but membership, insofar as it has significance to employment rights, may in turn be conditioned only upon payment of fees and dues." *NLRB v. General Motors,* 373 U.S. 734, 732 (1963). In the absence of a union security provision, Congress recognized that many employees who share in the fruits of union benefits through collective bargaining would refuse to pay their share of the union costs. *Id.* at 740–41. After the abolition of the closed shop, Congress enacted legislation allowing "employers to enter into agreements requiring all the employees in a given bargaining unit to become members 30 days after being hired as long as such membership is available to all workers on a nondiscriminatory basis," and employers were prohibited from mandatory discharge of employees expelled from the unit for any reason other than failure to pay initiation fees or dues. *Beck,* 487 U.S. at 749. The "legislative history clearly indicates that Congress intended to prevent utilization of Union security agreements for any purpose other than to compel payment of union dues and fees." *Id.* Although employees may not be required to join a union or participate in union activity, employees may be required to pay the union dues or fees. *See* 29 U.S.C. § 158(a)(3); *see also Beck,* 487 U.S. at 749.

[12]Although "a union shop denies an employee the option of not formally becoming a union member, under federal law it is the single 'practical equivalent' of an agency shop." *General Motors,* 373 U.S. at 373. *See also Lathrop v. Donohue,* 367 U.S. 820, 828 (1961).

[13]"Unlike section 14(b) of the National Labor Relations Act ("NLRA"), 29 U.S.C. § 164(b), the Railway Labor Act preempts any attempt by the State to prohibit a union-shop agreement." *Abood,* 431 U.S. at 118 n.12.

laws, and in those states unions have less power.[14] In a right-to-work state, it is unlawful to require someone to join a union in order to work with a specific employer. Additionally, in right-to-work states, most employees cannot be forced to pay initiation fees or dues to the union.[15]

Freedom of Speech and Association

The United States Supreme Court has recognized that compulsory union membership implicates important First Amendment rights for many public sector employees. An employee may have ideological objections to a wide variety of activities undertaken by the union in its role as exclusive representative. Positions taken by unions on social or political matters are usually unnecessary to negotiate a medical benefit

---

[14]The following states have right-to-work laws: ALA. CODE § 25-7-30-25-7-35; ARIZ. CONST. art. XXV; ARK. CONST. amend. 34; FLA. CONST. art.1, § 6; GA. CODE ANN. §§ 34-6-20-34-6-28; GUAM CODE ANN., Title 22, Div. 1, Ch. 4 (22 G.C.A. §§ 4101 et seq.); IDAHO CODE §§ 44-2001 to 44-2009; IOWA CODE ANN. §§ 731.1 to 731.8; KAN. CONST. art. 15, § 12; LA. REV. STAT. ANN. §§ 23:981-87; MISS. CONST. art. 7 § 198-A; NEB. CONST. art. XV, §§ 13, 14, 15; NEV. REV. STAT. §§ 613.230, 613.250-613.300; N.C. GEN. STAT. §§ 95-78-84; N.D. CENT. CODE §§ 34.01.14-14.1; OKLA. CONST. art. XXIII; S.C. CODE ANN. §§ 41-7-10-90; S.D. CONST. art. VI, § 2; TENN. CODE ANN. §§ 50-1-201-204; TEXAS CODE ANN. Title 3 §§ 101.003, 004, 052, 053, 102, 111, 121, 122, 124; UTAH CODE ANN. §§ 34-34-1-34-17; VA. CODE ANN. §§ 40.1-58 t-40.1-69; WYO. STAT. ANN. §§ 27-7-108-115.
[15]For private (Beck, 487 U.S. at 735; Ellis, 466 U.S. at 435) and public (Hudson, 475 U.S. 292 [1986]; Abood, 431 U.S. at 207; Lehnert, 500 U.S. at 507) sector employees outside of a right-to-work state, union dues may be required of an objecting employee, but no part of that employee's dues or assessment may be used for activities not germane or directly related to the union's duties as the collective bargaining representative. However, employees working under the Railway Labor Act or on certain federal jobs may still be required to pay agency fees in right-to-work states.

plan, wages, or other employee benefits. To be required to finance the union as a collective bargaining agent might well interfere with an employee's freedom to associate for the advancement of ideas or to refrain from doing so, as the employee sees fit.[16]

Indeed, the "right of freedom of thought protected by the First Amendment against state action includes both the right to speak freely and the right to refrain from speaking at all."[17] However, the United States Supreme Court has allowed some interference with First Amendment freedoms in the context of union membership because of the "governmental interest in industrial peace."[18] The "government may not require an individual to relinquish rights guaranteed him by the First Amendment as a condition of public employment."[19] "For at the heart of the First Amendment is the notion that an individual should be free to believe as he will, and that in a free society one's belief should be shaped by his mind and his conscience rather than coerced by the State."

Religious Freedom

RELIGIOUS DISCRIMINATION AND FREE EXERCISE OF RELIGION

An employee whose religious beliefs collide with union practices may raise an objection based upon freedom of religion protected under federal antidiscrimination laws and public sector employees may also rely upon the First Amendment.

---

[16]*Abood,* 431 U.S. at 222.

[17]*Wooley v. Maynard,* 430 U.S. 705, 714 (1977).

[18]*Ellis,* 466 U.S. at 455–56. *See also Abood,* 431 U.S. at 222–23.

[19]*Abood,* 431 U.S. at 234. *See also Elrod v. Burns,* 427 U.S. 347 (1976).

The federal law known as Title VII restricts employment discrimination based on religion and defines *religion* as "all aspects of religious observance and practice, as well as belief."[20] A private or public sector employee who has a sincerely held religious belief "opposing unions could be relieved from paying dues under Title VII, even if he or she was not a member of an organized religious group that opposes unions."[21]

In addition to Title VII, a public sector employee may use the First Amendment Free Exercise Clause.[22] Under the First Amendment, an employee who has a sincerely held religious belief must apprize the employer of that belief and point out

---

[20]42 U.S.C. § 2000e(j).

[21]*International Ass'n of Machinists v. Boeing Co.*, 833 F.2d 165, 169 (9th Cir. 1987), *cert. denied*, 485 U.S. 1014 (1988). *See also* 29 C.F.R. § 1605(1). Title VII was designed to supplement, rather than supplant, existing laws relating to employment discrimination. *See Alexander v. Gardner-Denver Co.*, 415 U.S. 36 (1974). "Congress did not intend section 19 of the NLRA to supersede section 701(j) of Title VII. The House report accompanying H.R. 4774 expressly stated that 'the bill would accommodate the religious beliefs of these persons and thereby reconcile the National Labor Relations Act with section 701(j) of the Equal Employment Opportunity Act.'" *International Ass'n of Machinists*, 833 F.2d at 17 (quoting H.R. REP. No. 496, 96th Cong., 1st Sess., at 2 (1980), *reprinted in* 1980 U.S.C.C.A.N. 7158–59).

[22]A public sector employee may raise a free exercise objection under the First Amendment to the United States Constitution and combine this claim with a free speech or free association claim under the First Amendment. Combining both constitutional rights would result in the so-called hybrid claim recognized under *Employment Division v. Smith*, 494 U.S. 872 (1990). In other words, when combining a free exercise claim with some other recognized constitutional right (in this case free speech or free association), the employee may argue that the rule or regulation must be necessary to further a compelling interest. If the employee can show (1) a sincerely held religious belief that (2) is burdened by some government rule or regulation or government-backed rule or regulation, as would be the case under NLRA or RLA, then (3) the government must show that it has a compelling governmental interest in the rule or regulation has achieved

what employment practice impinges on that belief. An employment arrangement that requires an employee to pay union dues may impinge upon a sincerely held religious belief, and the employer must attempt to accommodate that belief. Accommodation may require that a portion of the union dues be deducted so as not to support objectionable activities, that the dues be used only for local collective bargaining arrangements, or that the employee be allowed to pay the equivalent of the dues to a nonreligious, nonunion charitable organization recognized as a nonprofit, tax-exempt organization under 501(c)(3) of the Internal Revenue Code.

CONSCIENCE CLAUSE

On December 24, 1980, President Jimmy Carter signed into law section 19 of the NLRA, which is sometimes referred

---

its interest in the least restrictive means available. Pursuant to the analysis in *Smith,* combining free exercise of religion with some other federally recognized individual right such as free speech brings the standard of protection to its highest level. *See Smith,* U.S. at 872; *see also Hobbie v. Unemployment Appeals Comm'n of Fla.,* 480 U.S. 136 (1987) (unemployment benefits); *Thomas v. Review Bd., Indiana Employment Sec. Div.,* 450 U.S. 707 (1981) (unemployment benefits); *Wooley,* 430 U.S. at 705 (invalidating compelled display of a license plate slogan that offended individual religious beliefs); *Wisconsin v. Yoder,* 406 U.S. 205, (1972) (invalidating compulsory school attendance laws as applied to Amish parents who refused on religious grounds to send their children to public school); *Sherbert v. Verner,* 375 U.S. 398 (1963) (unemployment benefits); *Follett v. McCormick,* 321 U.S. 573 (1944) (same); *Murdock v. Pennsylvania,* 319 U.S. 105 (1943) (invalidating a flat tax on solicitation as applied to the dissemination of religious ideas); *West Virginia Bd. of Educ. v. Barnette,* 319 U.S. 624 (1943) (invalidating compulsory flag salute statute challenged by religious objectors); *Cantwell v. Connecticut,* 310 U.S. 296 (1940) (invalidating a licensing system for religious and charitable solicitations under which the administrator had discretion to deny a license to any cause he deemed nonreligious); *Pierce v. Society of Sisters,* 268 U.S. 510 (1925) (directing the education of children).

to as the "Conscience Clause." Section 19 provides in pertinent part:

> Any employee who is a member of and adheres to established and traditional tenets or teachings of a bona fide religion, body, or sect which has historically held conscientious objections to joining or financially supporting labor organizations shall not be required to join or financially support any labor organization as a condition of employment; except that such employee may be required . . . to pay sums equal to such dues and initiation fees to a nonreligious, nonlabor charitable fund.[23]

Under the Conscience Clause, certain employees with sincerely held religious convictions against joining or financially supporting labor unions may, instead of paying their dues and initiation fees to the union, pay the equivalent amount to a nonreligious, nonunion charity recognized as a 501(c)(3) organization by the Internal Revenue Service. The Conscience Clause is extremely limited because it applies only to employees who are members of a religious institution which has a long and established tradition against unions, and one court has ruled it unconstitutional because it discriminates between religious faiths.[24] Employees should be aware that a union representative may hand them a copy of the Conscience Clause statute and erroneously insist that since the employee does not belong to a religious faith with a long history of objecting to

---

[23]29 U.S.C. § 169.
[24]Seventh-day Adventists and Amish Mennonites are examples of churches having a long-established religious objection to unions. In *Wilson v. NLRB,*

unions the employee has no recourse. If faced with this situation, the employee should respond by pointing out that (1) other federal statutory (Title VII for private and public employees) and constitutional law (for public employees) protects the employee, and (2) the Conscience Clause has been found unconstitutional by a federal court because it gives preferential treatment to one religion over another.

Private, Public, Railway, and Airline Industry Employees

PRIVATE EMPLOYEES

The National Labor Relations Act governs private employees. Private sector employees cannot be required to be a member of

---

920 F.2d 1282 (6th Cir. 1990), *cert. denied,* 505 U.S. 1218 (1992), a federal appeals court found that section 19 of the NLRA violated the Establishment Clause of the First Amendment precisely because it is limited only to members of a bona fide religious organization having a long history opposing union membership. In other words, the court found that section 19 of the NLRA actually discriminates among religions. An employee who has a sincerely held religious belief opposing union membership, but who does not belong to a church having a long history or tradition in opposition to unions, may not utilize section 19. However, an employee with the same religious belief who happens to be a member of such a church having historical beliefs in opposition to union membership may utilize section 19. Consequently, the application of section 19 gives preferential treatment to some denominations but not others. For those governed by the Railway Labor Act, passed by Congress in 1926, upheld by the United States Supreme Court in 1930, and amended in 1935, there is no similar Conscience Clause. The RLA is completely separate from the NLRA and provides the framework for collective bargaining by the railroad and airline industry. The Conscience Clause in the NLRA does not apply to workers who are governed by the RLA. However, an employee governed by the RLA may still utilize Title VII, which prohibits discrimination in the workplace based upon religion, or may alternatively utilize the First Amendment Free Exercise Clause.

a union or pay the dues or fees unless the collective bargaining agreement between the employer and the union requires all employees either to join the union or to pay union fees. Even with such a provision, private sector employees do not have to join the union, may resign membership at any time, and thus may only be required to pay an "agency fee."[25] Nonmembers are still entitled to all of the employee benefits under the collective bargaining agreement, and the union is obligated to represent such employees.[26] Nonmembers may also be able to vote, attend meetings, or become involved in other union activity.

RAILWAY OR AIRLINE EMPLOYEES

The Railway Labor Act governs employees of the railway and airline industry. Such employees are not required to join a union but may be required to pay union fees and are not protected by state right-to-work laws. The union must establish certain procedures to safeguard an employee's right to pay only a limited agency fee to the union. Like the private sector employees under the NRLA, railway and airline employees who are not members of the union are still fully covered by the collective bargaining agreement and may participate in union activities.[27]

---

[25]See *Pattern Makers v. NLRB,* 473 U.S. 95 (1985) (employees may resign from the union at any time). See *Beck,* 487 U.S. at 735 (nonmembers may not be required to pay union dues but may be required to pay an agency fee that equals the employee's share of the union cost of collective bargaining, contract administration, and grievance adjustment). The agency fee does not equal the dues amount except in extraordinary cases.

[26]These benefits include, but may not be limited to, wages, seniority, vacation and sick pay, pension, and insurance. Unions may offer minor benefits reserved only for members.

[27]See *Ellis,* 466 U.S. at 435.

STATE AND LOCAL GOVERNMENT EMPLOYEES

Employees of state or local government are not required to join a union but, like the employees already mentioned, may be required to pay an agency fee. The union must set forth procedures to safeguard the employee from paying more than a limited agency fee. Nonmembers are also entitled to receive the benefits of the collective bargaining agreement and may participate in union activities.

FEDERAL EMPLOYEES

Those employed by the federal government[28] or the Postal Service[29] are not required to join a union, nor are they required to pay union dues or fees. Nonmembers are nevertheless fully covered by the benefits of the collective bargaining agreement and may participate in union activities.

Union Expenditures

A union may "spend funds for the expression of political views, on behalf of political candidates, or toward the advancement of other ideological causes" which are *germane* to its duties as a collective bargaining representative.[30] However, such expenditures *not germane* to the union's duties as a collective bargaining representative may not be financed from charges, dues, or assessments paid by employees who object to advancing those ideas. Objecting employees may not be coerced into being charged against their will by threat of loss

---

[28]5 U.S.C. § 7102.
[29]39 U.S.C. § 1209(c).
[30]*Id.* Social costs are chargeable only when *de minimis*.

of employment.[31] According to the Supreme Court, any expenditures by the union must (1) be "germane" to collective bargaining activity; (2) be justified by the government's vital policy interest in avoiding "free riders" and maintaining labor peace; and (3) not significantly add to the burden of free speech that is inherent in the allowance of an agency or union shop.[32] It is not an adequate remedy to limit the use of the actual dollars collected from dissenting employees to collective bargaining purposes.[33] A union may not exact dues from an objecting employee and then later rebate a portion of the dues. The difficulty in a rebate system, whereby the employee first pays membership dues, objects to portions of the dues being used for advocacy unrelated to the collective bargaining representative's duty, and then obtains a refund, means that the employee is actually advancing an interest-free loan to the union. The union "should not be permitted to exact a service fee from nonmembers without first establishing a procedure which will avoid the risk that their funds will be used, even temporarily, to finance ideological activities unrelated to collective bargaining."[34]

An employee may request that the union provide audited statements which document how the union spends its money and which expenses the union contends are chargeable to the employee. The union must present information documenting expenditures, and in some cases, showing the percentages of the expenses used toward the objectionable

---

[31]*Id.* at 236.
[32]*Lehnert,* 500 U.S. at 522.
[33]*Abood,* 431 U.S. at 237 n.35.
[34]*Hudson,* 475 U.S. at 305 (quoting *Abood,* 431 U.S. at 244).

activities.[35] The burden of the objecting employee is simply to make the objection known.[36] Once the objection is made, the union must identify the expenditures for collective bargaining and contract administration as well as those expenditures used for purposes that do not benefit the dissenting nonmember.[37] The pertinent procedures include: (1) presenting audited financial statements, (2) escrowing the contested funds, and (3) providing a hearing in which the union has the burden to prove the propriety of its fee.[38]

---

[35]*Hudson,* 475 U.S. at 306. "Since the unions possess the facts and records from which the portion of political to total union expenditures can reasonably be calculated, basic considerations of fairness compel that they, not the individual employees, bear the burden of proving such proportion." *Abood,* 431 U.S. at 239–40 n.40 (quoting *Railway Clerks v. Allen,* 373 U.S. 113, 122 (1963)).

[36]*Machinists v. Street,* 367 U.S. 740, 774 (1961).

[37]Although public sector unions are not subject to the disclosure requirements of the Labor Management Reporting and Disclosure Act located at 29 U.S.C. § 402(e), "the fact that private sector unions have a duty of disclosure suggests that a limited notice requirement does not impose an undue burden on the union." *Hudson* 475 U.S. at 306 n.17.

[38]The agency fee is not usually equal to union dues. Every union is supposed to have a so-called "Hudson procedure" for nonmembers. For public employees the Hudson procedure requires that employees be provided with information supporting the union's financial breakdown of forced dues, that those figures be verified by independent audit, and that employees have an opportunity for a prompt, impartial review of the union's forced-dues calculations. The court in *Abrams v. Communications Workers,* 59 F.3d 1373 (D.C. Cir. 1995) ruled that private sector unions under the NLRA must also comply with the Hudson procedure. However, the National Labor Relations Board (NLRB), which enforces the NLRA, ruled that only some of the requirements of the Hudson procedure apply under the NLRA. *See California Saw and Knife Works,* 320 NLRB 224 (1995), *enforced,* 133 F.3d 1012 (7th Cir. 1998). In order to ensure that the employee is not required to pay more than an agency fee, the NLRB only requires unions to: (1) inform employees of the right not to join the union, (2) inform nonmembers of the right to object to paying for union

The Supreme Court has indicated that the Railway Labor Act[39] does not permit a union, over the objection of non-members, to expend compelled agency fees on political causes.[40] The Supreme Court has also ruled that employees governed by the National Labor Relations Act[41] are not required to fund objectionable political causes of the authorized union.[42] Indeed, the NLRA and the RLA authorize "the exaction of only those fees and dues necessary to 'performing the duties of an exclusive representative of the employee in dealing with the employer on labor-management issues.'"[43]

In light of the above, unions (1) may not exact a service fee from nonmembers without first establishing a procedure which will avoid the risk that their funds will be used, even temporarily, to finance ideological or political activities unrelated to collective bargaining; (2) have the burden to provide adequate justification for the advance reduction of dues by detailing the amount of dues used for administrative activity directly related to the collective bargaining representative;

---

activities not germane to the collective bargaining and to obtain a reduction in fees for those activities, (3) provide procedures for filing objections, and (4) advise the employee of the percentage of the reduction, the basis for the calculation, and inform the employee of the right to object to these calculations. An employee may challenge the union calculation of the amount of agency fee. Within six months of the union conduct, an employee may file suit in federal court or file an unfair labor practice claim with the NLRB regional office claiming breach of the union's duty to provide fair representation. The NLRB refers to the above procedures as the "Beck procedures," which derive from the Supreme Court's decision in *Beck*.

[39]45 U.S.C. § 151.
[40]*Ellis*, 466. U.S. at 435.
[41]29 U.S.C. § 158(a)(3).
[42]*Beck*, 487 U.S. at 761–63.
[43]*Id.* (quoting *Ellis*, 466 U.S. at 448).

and (3) must offer a reasonably prompt decision by an impartial decision maker to resolve the objections raised by the employee. While unions are not required to put 100 percent of the funds into escrow pending final resolution, a union may, at the minimum, be required to put a sufficient amount of the funds into an interest-bearing escrow account until the objection has been resolved.[44]

Unions may subsidize lobbying and other political activities with fees from the objecting employee so long as those activities are pertinent to the duties of the union as a bargaining representative.[45] However, when lobbying activities do not relate to the ratification or implementation of an objecting employee's collective bargaining agreement but rather relate to the financial support of the employee's profession or of public employees generally, the connection to the union's function as a bargaining representative is too attenuated to justify compelled support by objecting employees.[46] In other words, an employee may not be compelled "to subsidize legislative lobbying or other political union activities outside the limited context of contract ratification or implementation."[47] In the public sector context, "a local bargaining representative may charge objecting employees for their pro rata share of the costs associated with otherwise chargeable activities of its state and national affiliates, even

---

[44]*Hudson,* 475 U.S. at 310.

[45]*Lehnert,* 500 U.S. at 519, 521–22.

[46]*Id.* at 521. In *Lehnert* the Court ruled that a state teachers education union may not use fees from an objecting employee to lobby state government to finance education because that activity is not directly related to the collective bargaining agreement.

[47]*Id.* at 522.

if those activities were not performed for the direct benefit of the objecting employees' bargaining unit."[48] However, the union may not charge objecting employees for a direct donation or interest-free loan to an unrelated bargaining unit for the purpose of promoting employee rights or unionism generally. A "contribution by a local union to its parent that is not part of the local's responsibility as an affiliate but is in the nature of a charitable donation would not be chargeable to dissenters."[49]

A union may use an objecting member's dues to help defray the cost of conventions.[50] While social activities are not central to bargaining, they may be charged to an objecting employee so long as they are minimal.[51] Union publications directly related to the union's collective bargaining duties may be chargeable to an objecting employee, but publications that promote political causes that are not directly related to the collective bargaining duties may not be charged to an objecting employee.[52] Funds expended to organize the union to increase membership or make the union stronger may not be charged to an objecting employee.[53] The expenses of litigation incident to negotiating and administering the contract or to settling grievances and disputes arising in the bargaining unit are chargeable to an objecting employee, but expenses of litigation having no such connection with the bargaining unit are not chargeable to the objecting

---

[48]*Id.* at 524.
[49]*Id.*
[50]*Ellis,* 466 U.S. at 449.
[51]*Id.* at 449–50.
[52]*Id.* at 450–51.
[53]*Id.* at 451–53.

employee.[54] As noted above, funds may not be used in the public employment context to lobby governmental branches in order to secure funds for public employees.[55] Similarly, public relations campaigns designed to enhance the reputation of the teaching profession or any other profession associated with the union may not be chargeable to an objecting employee.[56] Finally, money expended toward an illegal strike may not be chargeable to an objecting employee.[57]

All of the monies which may not be chargeable to an objecting employee must be deducted pro rata from the employee's dues or fees. Not to allow such a deduction violates not only the First Amendment right to freedom of speech but also the right to free association.

Summary

Employees who object to union membership are not required to join, but they may be required to pay an agency fee. If an employee objects to having any of the agency fee used by the union to support ideological positions with which the employee disagrees, the objection should be made in writing to the union. The letter should state that the employee objects to the collection and expenditure by the union of any funds for any purpose other than for the employee's pro rata share of the union's cost of collective bargaining, contract administration,

---

[54]*Id.* at 453. Since unrelated litigation expenses may not be chargeable to the objecting employee, writing about such litigation in a union publication may not be charged to an objecting employee. *Id.* at 1894.
[55]*Lehnert,* 500 U.S. at 527.
[56]*Id.* at 528–29.
[57]*Id.* at 531.

and grievance adjustment. The employee should also request a copy of the union's procedural rights and should demand that the union (1) reduce the fees to an amount that includes only lawfully chargeable costs associated with collective bargaining, contract administration, and grievance adjustment, (2) provide notice of the calculation of that amount which must be verified by an independent certified public accountant, and (3) provide notice of the procedure that the union has adopted to hold your fees in an interest-bearing escrow account. The employee has the right to challenge the union's calculation and to have the union's decision reviewed by an impartial decision maker.

Compulsory union membership is prohibited, and although a union may collect an agency fee in some cases, it may not compel the employee to pay union dues. Even the agency fee can be restricted from going to support political and ideological causes with which the employee disagrees. Thus, as noted above, the agency fee can be limited to the cost of collective bargaining, contract administration, and grievance adjustment.

Although the employee does not have to join and may resign after joining, nonmembers are still entitled to all of the employee benefits under the collective bargaining agreement, and the union is obligated to represent such employees. Nonmembers may also vote, attend meetings, or become involved in other union activity. Employees, therefore, are still entitled to the collective bargaining benefits of a union, while not having to support repugnant causes.

16
POLITICAL ACTIVITY OF NONPROFIT ORGANIZATIONS

THE EXTENT TO WHICH churches and nonprofit organizations may engage in lobbying and political campaigns is illusive and often misunderstood.[1] Pastors and leaders of nonprofit corporations are frequently leery about becoming too vocal on political matters for fear of jeopardizing the organization's nonprofit status. Unnecessarily paralyzed by this fear, many leaders refuse to address political issues. It is, therefore, important to know the parameters imposed on nonprofit corporations.[2] Only when these parameters are known can the

---

[1]Since churches are exempt from federal income tax, they are treated as nonprofit organizations exempt from income tax under the Internal Revenue Code 26 U.S.C. § 501(c)(3).

[2]When referring to nonprofit organizations, reference is being made to 501(c) organizations, and where necessary, the distinction will be made between 501(c)(3) and 501(c)(4) organizations. The discussion regarding 501(c)(4) nonprofit organizations is applicable to other 501(c) nonprofit

organization truly be free to communicate without jeopardizing its tax structure.

Prior to 1934, there were no lobbying limitations imposed upon nonprofit organizations by the Internal Revenue Code. However, without benefit of Congressional hearings, an amendment was added to the Revenue Act of 1934, which was designed to prohibit federal tax exemption for organizations that attempt to influence legislation.[3] In 1954, then Senator Lyndon B. Johnson proposed an amendment to what later became the Internal Revenue Code of 1954. This amendment specifically prohibited nonprofit organizations from endorsing or opposing a candidate for public office.[4] Senator Johnson, who later became President Johnson, apparently proposed this amendment to counteract a nonprofit organization which opposed his candidacy for the U.S. Senate.

The information presented in this chapter can be summarized as follows:

1. A 501(c)(3) nonprofit organization (including a church) is permitted to engage in lobbying activities so long as no substantial part of their overall activities are directed toward lobbying, but is prohibited from endorsing or opposing a candidate for public office.

2. A 501(c)(4) nonprofit organization is permitted to engage in lobbying activities without any limitation,

---

organizations other than a 501(c)(3) organization. Other nonprofit organizations such as 527 organizations are not addressed herein since different campaign finance rules are applicable to them. *See McConnell v. Federal Election Comm'n,* 540 U.S. 93 (2003); 2 U.S.C. § 431 *et seq.*

[3]Bruce Hopkins, THE LAW OF TAX-EXEMPT ORGANIZATIONS, 1991 Cum. Supp. at 14–15 (5th ed. 1987); Douglas Kirk, *Cases and Materials on Nonprofit Tax-exempt Organizations,* 1992 § 5–10.

[4]Bruce Hopkins, THE LAW OF TAX-EXEMPT ORGANIZATIONS, at 281.

but is prohibited from endorsing or opposing a political candidate for public office.

3. A 501(h) organization is permitted to engage in lobbying activities without limitation if the activities are performed by unpaid volunteers and without organizational expenditures, or may engage in limited lobbying activities if organizational expenditures are directed toward lobbying activities, but such an organization is prohibited from endorsing or opposing a candidate for public office.

4. A political action committee may engage in lobbying activities without limitation and may endorse or oppose a candidate for public office, with the only limitation being that which is imposed by state or federal law pertaining to the amount of contributions permissible per candidate and reporting requirements.

5. As long as a clergy or representative of the nonprofit organization is not purporting to speak for the organization, but is, instead, expressing views as an individual citizen, there are no lobbying limitations, and the only political limitations would be the amount of money allowed by state or federal law regarding individual contributions to a political candidate.

To determine the extent of political activity of a nonprofit organization, an important distinction must be made between (1) legislative or lobbying activities and (2) intervention in a political campaign. Nonprofit organizations are permitted to engage in legislative or lobbying activities but are prohibited from endorsing or opposing a candidate for public office. An organization will be regarded as attempting to influence legislation if the organization (a) contacts, or urges the public to contact, members of the legislative body for the purpose of proposing, supporting, or opposing legislation or (b) advocates the adoption or rejection of legislation.[5] The term *legislation* includes any action by Congress, any state legislature, any local council or similar governing body, or by the public in a referendum, initiative, constitutional amendment, or similar procedure. A 501(c)(3) tax-exempt organization may attempt to influence legislation so long as it devotes only an insubstantial part of its activities to the adoption or rejection of such legislation. A 501(c)(4) organization can engage in lobbying without any limitation. Neither organization may endorse or oppose a candidate for *elective* office. However, supporting or opposing a person to an *appointed* office is not considered to be supporting or opposing a candidate. Therefore, nonprofit organizations may support or oppose cabinet or judicial nominees who are appointed to office. Consistent with this distinction, the following guidelines will be divided between legislative activity and political campaigns.[6] The ban against engaging in a political campaign on behalf of any candidate for public office "is an

---

[5] 26 C.F.R. § 1.501(c)(3)-1(c)(3)(ii); Treas. Reg. § 1.501(c)(3)-1(c)(3)(ii).

[6] 26 C.F.R. § 1.501(c)(3)-1(c)(3)(ii)(b); Treas. Reg. § 1.501(c)(3)-1(c)(3)(ii)(b). An organization cannot be tax-exempt if it has the following characteristics: (a) its main or primary objective(s) (as distinguished from its incidental or secondary objectives), may be obtained only by legislation or a defeat of proposed legislation; and (b) it advocates, or campaigns for, the obtainment of such main or primary objective(s) as distinguished from engaging in a nonpartisan analysis, study, or research and making the results thereof available to the public. 26 C.F.R. § 1.501(c)(3)-1(c)(3)(iii); Treas. Reg. § 1.501(c)(3)-1(c)(3)(iii). *See also Cammarano v. United States*, 358 U.S. 498 (1959); *Christian Echoes Nat. Ministry, Inc. v. United States*, 470 F.2d 849 (10th Cir. 1972), *cert. denied*, 414 U.S. 864 (1973).

absolute prohibition. There is no requirement that political campaigning be substantial."[7]

Organizational Structures

501(c)(3) ORGANIZATIONS

A nonprofit organization that elects 501(c)(3) status under the Internal Revenue Code is afforded (1) federal tax-exempt status and (2) tax deductibility on behalf of the donors who contribute to the organization. One of the main advantages of a 501(c)(3) is that the donors can claim a federal tax deduction on their contributions under § 170 of the Internal Revenue Code.

Churches organized exclusively for religious or charitable purposes are automatically exempt from federal taxes. A church may apply for exemption but is not required to do so.[8] However, other nonprofit organizations seeking federal tax-exempt status must apply for exemption, using Internal Revenue Service (IRS) Form 1023. The advantage of being

---

[7]INTERNAL REVENUE MANUAL § 3(10)1. *See also United States v. Dykema,* 666 F.2d 1096, 1101 (7th Cir. 1981), *cert. denied,* 456 U.S. 983 (1982); *Hutchinson Baseball Enterprises, Inc. v. Commissioner,* 696 F.2d 757, 760 (10th Cir. 1982); *Association of the Bar of the City of New York v. Commissioner,* 858 F.2d 876 (2d Cir. 1988).

[8]Although churches may voluntarily apply to receive a 501(c)(3) letter ruling from the IRS, it is not necessary or recommended that they do so. If a church has such a letter ruling, it is not necessary to revoke it, but if the church is ever challenged by the IRS, the church should understand that loss of the letter ruling does not mean loss of tax-exempt status so long as the church continues operating as a church. Churches, unlike any other nonprofit organization, are automatically tax exempt even without an IRS letter ruling.

recognized as a 501(c)(3) organization is obvious, but there are some restrictions. A 501(c)(3) organization is described as one in which "no substantial part of the activities . . . is carrying on propaganda, or otherwise attempting, to influence legislation . . . and which does not participate in or intervene in (including the publishing or distributing of statements), any political campaign on behalf of any candidate for public office."[9]

The "substantial part" wording was enacted by Congress in 1934. The IRS has stated that an organization will be regarded as attempting to influence legislation if the organization (1) contacts or urges the public to contact members of the legislative body for the purpose of proposing, supporting, or opposing legislation or (2) advocates the adoption or rejection of legislation.[10]

The IRS has further noted that an organization may not be considered exempt if (1) its primary objective may be obtained only by legislation or defeat of proposed legislation, and (2) it advocates or campaigns for the attainment of such primary objective instead of engaging in nonpartisan analysis, study, or research, and making the results thereof available to the public.[11] Furthermore, the IRS has stated that attempts to influence legislation are not limited to direct appeals to members of the legislature but may include indirect appeals to legislators through the electorate or the general public.[12]

---

[9]INTERNAL REVENUE MANUAL § 3(10)1. *See also United States v. Dykema,* 666 F.2d at 1101; *Hutchinson Baseball Enterprises, Inc.,* 696 F.2d at 760; *Association of the Bar of the City of New York,* 858 F.2d at 876.

[10]26 C.F.R. § 1.501(c)(3)-1(c)(3)(ii); Treas. Reg. § 1.501(c)(3)-1(c)(3)(ii).

[11]26 C.F.R. § 1.503(c)(3)-1(c)(3)(iii); Treas. Reg. § 1.503(c)(3)-1(c)(3)(iii).

[12]INTERNAL REVENUE MANUAL §§ 392–94.

The *Internal Revenue Manual*[13] recognizes that "there is no simple rule" as to what constitutes a "substantial" portion of the total activities of the organization and has further recognized that the determination is a "factual one."[14] In one case a court found that legislative activity is not substantial if it does not exceed 5 percent of the organization's total activities.[15] Other cases suggest that up to 15 percent of the organization's activities could be spent on lobbying.[16] Since the so-called substantial part test looks at the organization's overall activities, one federal court of appeals indicated that in addition to time spent "writing, telegraphing, or telephoning" legislators and testifying before legislative committees, the time spent within the organization "formulating, discussing and agreeing upon the positions" which are to be advocated must be taken into account in order to determine substantiality.[17] While the so-called "5 to 15 percent" test is still used by some as the benchmark, the IRS has rejected that test and instead indicated that the determination is a factual one and is "more often one of characterizing the various activities as attempts to influence legislation."[18]

Even if you were to assume that the 5 percent level is the maximum amount of permissible overall activity for a

---

[13]*Id.*

[14]*Id.*

[15]*Seasongood v. Comm'r,* 227 F.2d 907 (6th Cir. 1955). The organization in this case was neither a church nor a religious organization.

[16]*World Family Corp. v. Commissioner,* 81 T.C. 958 (1983) (up to 10 percent is permissible); *Haswell v. United States,* 500 F.2d 1133 (Ct. Cl. 1974) (between 16 and 20 percent is impermissible).

[17]*Kuper v. Comm'r,* 332 F.2d 562 (3d Cir. 1964), *cert. denied,* 379 U.S. 920 (1964). *See also League of Women Voters of United States v. United States,* 180 F. Supp. 379 (Ct. Cl. 1960).

[18]INTERNAL REVENUE MANUAL §§ 392–94 (1989).

tax-exempt organization to devote to lobbying, this is still a considerable amount of activity. Take, for example, a church that opens its doors on Sunday morning for worship from the hours of 9:00 a.m. to 12:00 p.m., and then again on Wednesday evening for a mid-week service from 7:00 to 8:30 p.m. Assume that the church engages in absolutely no other activity. Thus, the church engages in worship and teaching activities for only 4½ hours per week and does nothing else. Four and a half hours amounts to 270 minutes, and 5 percent amounts to 13½ minutes. A church that only operates 4½ hours per week could devote at lease 13½ minutes each Sunday to lobbying activities. Every Sunday this church could urge its congregation to contact elected officials to vote in favor of or against any local, state or national law, including state and federal constitutional amendments.

As you can see, when you consider all of the activities a church engages in throughout the week, it will certainly be more than 4½ hours. To determine this amount, you would need to calculate the time of all the volunteer and paid staff throughout the entire year. The substantial part test is not determined by merely looking at a particular event in isolation of others, but in conjunction with the church's overall activities. Thus, a church could devote a significant amount of time to lobbying activities during part of the year and a small amount of time during the remainder of the year. And this is only at the 5 percent level. The 5 percent amount is only the minimum, not the maximum amount of time 501(c)(3) tax-exempt organizations can devote to lobbying. Finally, remember that no church has ever lost its tax-exempt status or IRS letter ruling for engaging in too much lobbying.

Generally speaking, a 501(c)(3) organization may (1) educate on social issues which have political ramifications, (2) urge the general public to become involved in the democratic political process, so long as it is nonpartisan, (3) publish neutral voting records of political candidates so long as there is no endorsement, (4) provide education about the political process, (5) lobby, if the legislation directly affects the tax-exempt status of the organization or directly impacts the operation of the organization, and (6) influence legislation so long as such activity does not constitute more than a "substantial" part of the organization's total activities.[19]

A 501(c)(3) organization is prohibited from engaging in any political campaign on behalf of any candidate for public office.

In the only case of its kind involving a church which directly engaged in a political campaign, a federal court of appeals for the District of Columbia sided with the IRS's decision to revoke a tax-exempt *letter ruling* from the Church at Pierce Creek located in Binghamton, New York. However, the Court's opinion reveals that the IRS has little authority over churches.[20] The ruling underscores the fact that churches do not need to fear the loss of their tax-exempt status. While the church's tax exempt *letter* was revoked, its tax exempt *status* was unaffected.

---

[19]The 501(c)(3) ministry in *Christian Echoes Nat. Ministry Inc. v. United States,* 470 F.2d at 849, *cert. denied,* 414 U.S. 864 (1973), ran into trouble because the ministry became a political machine by devoting most of its resources to political machine by devoting most of its resources to political activities. It is worth emphasizing that Christ Echoes was not a church. Another 501(c)(3) organization, also not a church, engaged in too much lobbying activity by devoting nearly 76 percent of its total budget to legislative activity. *See* Gen. Couns. Mem. 39811 (Feb. 20, 1990).

[20]*See Branch Ministries v. Rossotti,* 211 F.3d 137 (D.C. Cir. 2000).

On October 30, 1992, four days before the presidential election, the Church at Pierce Creek in New York placed full-page advertisements in *USA Today* and *The Washington Times*, opposing then-governor Bill Clinton for the office of President. Each ad bore the headline "Christians Beware" and warned that Clinton had extreme views regarding abortion and homosexuality. The advertisement clearly noted that it was sponsored by the church and its pastor and furthermore solicited "tax deductible donations" for the advertisement. The ads also stated the church's address, and as a result, the church received hundreds of contributions.

On November 20, 1992, the IRS notified the church that it intended to conduct an inquiry as to whether the church was operating as a tax-exempt organization. After negotiations failed, the IRS revoked the church's tax-exempt letter ruling, and the church filed suit. The Court pointed out that under the Internal Revenue Code, churches are the only institutions not required to apply for tax-exempt status. Churches, by their very nature, are tax-exempt.[21] While churches may ask the IRS for an advance letter ruling, they are not required to do so. If a church does not seek a letter ruling, a donor's contributions are still tax deductible. In the event of an audit, the donor must prove that the church is operating as a tax-exempt organization and following the requirements of Internal Revenue Code 501(c)(3), which includes a prohibition on endorsing or opposing a candidate for political office. If a letter ruling is in place, the donor simply points to the letter ruling on file with the IRS.

---

[21]*Id.* at 139.

The Church at Pierce Creek had applied for and received a letter ruling. The IRS simply revoked the letter ruling, and the church sued to get it back. The Court noted that "because of the unique treatment churches receive under the Internal Revenue Code, the impact of the revocation is likely to be more symbolic than substantial."[22] Indeed, the tax-exempt letter revocation is only symbolic and not substantive. During the oral argument, counsel for the IRS confirmed that if the church chose not to intervene in future political campaigns, it may hold itself out as a 501(c)(3) organization and receive all of the benefits of that status. The Court wrote: "All that will have been lost is the advance assurance of deductibility in the event a donor should be audited."[23]

The Court also pointed out that revocation of the letter ruling does not make the church liable for the payment of taxes.[24] The IRS conceded during oral argument that "the revocation of the exemption does not convert bona fide donations into income taxable to the Church."[25] The Court also noted that it knew of no authority preventing "the Church from reapplying for a prospective determination of its tax-exempt status and regaining the advance assurance of deductibility—provided, of course, that it renounces future involvement in political campaigns."[26]

The church lost only its tax-exempt *letter* but did not lose its tax-exempt *status*. Contributions given before and after the revocation of the IRS letter remain tax-deductible to the

---

[22]*Id.* at 143.
[23]*Id.* at 142–43.
[24]*Id.* at 142.
[25]*Id.*
[26]*Id.* at 143.

contributor and are not taxable income to the church. After the letter ruling was revoked, the church could continue as a church, continue receiving donations, and donors could continue to claim deductions on their income tax return provided that the church did not *continue* to endorse or oppose candidates. If the church wants an advance letter ruling at some point in the future, it is free to ask for another one. Obviously in the case of the presidential election, the church could easily have ceased endorsing or opposing a candidate since the election had transpired.

Either the church was naive, or, more likely, it sought to pick a fight with the IRS.[27] The case included several hundred pages of newspaper articles where other churches had invited candidates to speak in services where the IRS did nothing. The Church at Pierce Creek sought to make headlines when it took out full-page ads in *USA Today* and *The Washington Times*. The church identified itself and requested contributions. This is the first and only case in history where a church has ever lost its tax-exempt letter ruling for endorsing or opposing a political candidate. It is the worst set of facts from an IRS perspective, because the full-page ads essentially painted a target on the church.

However, even with these facts, the case shows that the IRS poses very little threat to churches. A church can give up the tax-exempt letter ruling and remain tax-exempt so long as it does not *continue* to endorse or oppose a candidate. If the church does not endorse or oppose a political candidate

---

[27]At the time, activist Randall Terry attended this church. Based on the posture of the case, it is more likely that the church wanted to confront the IRS.

today (even if it did so as recently as yesterday), the church remains tax-exempt. If the church's letter ruling is ever revoked, it may again apply for another letter ruling. However, unlike every other nonprofit organization, churches are unique in that they do not need an IRS letter ruling to be exempt from federal income taxes.

The IRS regulations are clear that, while churches may not endorse or oppose a candidate for political office, churches may educate about the candidates' viewpoints. Education can take the form of sermons, forums, debates, or voter guides. The church may educate about its doctrinal positions that are relevant to the political races. Education is perfectly permissible for a 501(c)(3) organization. Moreover, a church can engage in lobbying for or against legislation so long as it does not devote more than a substantial part of its overall activity to lobbying. Referenda, constitutional amendments, ballot propositions, and voter initiatives are classified as lobbying activities.[28] No church has ever lost its tax-exempt status for engaging in too much lobbying.

501(H) ORGANIZATIONS

In 1976 Congress provided a new option for 501(c)(3) organizations desiring to engage in lobbying activity. The Internal Revenue Code created a 501(h) election for 501(c)(3) organizations. Instead of using the "substantial part" test of a 501(c)(3) organization, a 501(h) organization uses an "expenditure" test.

---

[28]Treas. Reg. § 1.501(c)(3)-1(c)(3)(ii). Public charities and houses of worship are permitted to engage in lobbying activity so long as it does not constitute a substantial amount of the overall organizational activity. *See* 26 U.S.C. § 501(c)(3).

The 501(h) election is not available for all 501(c)(3) organizations. Churches, integrated auxiliaries of churches, conventions, associations of churches, private foundations, and governmental units may not elect 501(h) status.[29]

Eligible 501(c)(3) organizations may elect 501(h) status, and the election is made on Form 5768 ("Elections/ Revocation of Election by Eligible § 501(c)(3) Organization to Make Expenditures to Influence Legislation.") If an eligible organization elects the expenditure test of sections 501(h) and 4911, specific statutory dollar limits on the organization's lobbying expenditures apply. In contrast to the substantial part test, the expenditure test imposes no limit on lobbying that does not require expenditures, such as certain unreimbursed lobbying activities conducted by *bona fide* volunteers.[30]

Under the 501(h) election, the measuring factor is not the *activities* but the *expenditures* of the organization directed toward lobbying. There are two types of lobbying: (1) grassroots expenditures, which include attempts to influence public attitudes or to encourage the public to contact their legislators regarding legislation; and (2) direct lobbying, which involves any attempt to influence legislation through communication with a member or employee of the legislative body or any government official or employee. A grassroots

---

[29]Several major religious denominations lobbied Congress to prohibit churches from having the option of electing 501(h) status. The philosophical reasoning behind this unusual request was that churches should not be subject to any lobbying limitations at all. To concede that the churches needed a 501(h) status would be, in a sense, to concede that the lobbying limitations imposed in the first place were legitimate. Unfortunately, therefore, churches may not elect 501(h) status.

[30]26 C.F.R. § 1.501(h)-1 *et seq.*; Treas. Reg. § 1.501(h)-1 *et seq.*; 26 C.F.R. § 56.4911–0 *et seq.*; Treas. Reg. § 56.4911–0 *et seq.*

communication is a lobbying communication only if it refers to a specific piece of legislation, advocates a view on such legislation, or encourages the recipient of the communication to take action on the legislation. A direct lobbying communication is only considered a lobbying communication if it refers to a specific piece of legislation and advocates a view on that legislation.

The limitation on direct lobbying expenditures is based on the following: (1) 20 percent of the first $500,000 of the organization's exempt expenditures, plus (2) 15 percent of the second $500,000, plus (3) 10 percent of the third $500,000, plus (4) 5 percent of any additional exempt purpose expenditures. The expenditures may not exceed $1,000,000 for any one-year period.

Grassroots lobbying expenditures may not exceed 25 percent of the above figures. For example, if an organization has $500,000 in exempt purpose expenditures, it may spend up to $100,000 in direct lobbying (20 percent of $500,000 = $100,000). The organization may spend either the entire $100,000 toward direct lobbying, or it may spend up to 25 percent of that amount for grassroots lobbying, resulting in $75,000 for direct lobbying and $25,000 for grassroots lobbying. A $17,000,000 organization may spend up to $1,000,000 on direct lobbying expenditures (20 percent of the first $500,000; 15 percent of the second $500,000; 10 percent of the third $500,000; and 5 percent of the remaining $15,500,000 of which $750,000 may go toward direct lobbying and $250,000 may go toward grassroots lobbying).

Volunteer activities are not considered expenditures if there are no funds expended on such activities. For a 501(c)(3) organization that has not made the 501(h) election, volunteer activities are considered part of the total activities of said organization, but a 501(h) organization is only concerned with actual money spent on lobbying activities.

If a 501(h) organization exceeds the expenditure limitation, there is a penalty excise tax imposed equal to 25 percent of the amount of the excess lobbying expenditures. If the organization's lobbying expenditures normally exceed the limits by 50 percent, then the organization will jeopardize its tax-exempt status, but this is based on a four-year cycle. Thus, an organization may exceed its expenditure limit in one year by more than 50 percent without problem, so long as it remains in compliance over a four-year cycle. However, if the average of the four years is more than 50 percent of the expenditure limits, the organization may have to pay an excise tax or may lose its tax-exempt status for the years in which the limits were exceeded. Therefore, a 501(h) has more flexibility to engage in lobbying activities but is still prohibited from directly endorsing or opposing a political candidate for public office. Like a 501(c)(3) organization, a 501(h) organization may educate the public and its members about issues of concern to the organization and about the positions of the political candidates.

501(C)(4) ORGANIZATIONS

The Internal Revenue Code also recognizes a third type of organization known as a 501(c)(4) organization, sometimes referred to as a social welfare organization. A 501(c)(4) organization is afforded tax-exempt status, but unlike a 501(c)(3) or 501(h), it does not have the advantage of tax-deductible contributions. Because it does not allow donors to deduct contributions from federal income tax, 501(c)(4) organizations may devote all their efforts to influence legislation. In *Regan v. Taxation with Representation*,[31] the United States Supreme Court recognized that a 501(c)(3) organization could establish a separate organization under 501(c)(4) for the purpose of lobbying activities. The court noted that "the IRS apparently requires only that the two groups be separately incorporated and keep records adequate to show that tax deductible contributions are not used to pay for lobbying."[32]

A 501(c)(4) organization may, therefore, directly lobby either by volunteer activity or by expenditures. A 501(c)(4) is prohibited from directly opposing or supporting a political candidate for public office. However, like a 501(c)(3) and a 501(h) organization, a 501(c)(4) organization may educate its members and the community about the viewpoints of political candidates.

SUMMARY OF ORGANIZATIONS

In summary, a 501(c)(3) organization is tax-exempt, and contributions are tax-deductible. Such an organization is prohibited from expending more than a "substantial" part of its overall activities toward lobbying, including volunteer and expenditure activities. A 501(c)(3) organization which is not a church, integrated auxiliary of a church, association or convention of churches, private foundation or government unit is allowed to elect a 501(h) status and thus use an expenditure test. Under an expenditure test, only money spent toward lobbying is considered. A nonprofit organization may incorporate as a 501(c)(3) and separately incorporate as a

---

[31]461 U.S. 540 (1983).
[32]*Id.* at 544 n.6.

501(c)(4) organization. There are no lobbying limitations on 501(c)(4) organizations.

Neither a 501(c)(3), a 501(h) election, nor a 501(c)(4) may directly oppose or support a political candidate for public office, but they may educate their members and the general public about the viewpoints of political candidates. Supporting or opposing a person to an *appointed* office is not considered to be supporting or opposing a candidate. Therefore, nonprofit organizations may support or oppose cabinet or judicial appointments. To directly oppose or support a candidate for public office, a state or federal political action committee (PAC) must be established. Although PACs are governed by strict reporting requirements, the advantage is that PACs can directly support or oppose a candidate for public office. Contributions to a PAC are not tax-deductible.

Pastors and Representatives of Nonprofit Organizations

In January 1992 the IRS published a statement regarding Jimmy Swaggart Ministries. Jimmy Swaggart Ministries endorsed Pat Robertson for president in 1988. Jimmy Swaggart stated at a worship service that he would lend his support to Pat Robertson, who was soon to announce his candidacy. He also wrote an article entitled "From Me to You" in the church's official magazine, *The Evangelist,* in which he stated, "We are supporting Pat Robertson for the office of President of the United States," and, "We are going to support him prayerfully and put forth every effort we can muster in his behalf." The magazine indicated on its masthead that it was "The Voice of Jimmy Swaggart Ministries." According to the IRS, "When a minister of a religious organization endorses a candidate for public office at an official function of the organization, or when an official publication of a religious organization contains an endorsement of a candidate for public office by the organization's minister, the endorsement will be considered an endorsement of the organization since the acts and statements of a religious organization's minister at official functions of the organization and its official publications are the principal means by which a religious organization communicates its official views to its members and supporters."[33]

Although the publicized IRS statement may be an exaggeration and may not be supportable if challenged in court, it is nonetheless the IRS's view that when a minister speaks at an official church function, the expression of that minister may be considered the expression of the church. Prior to this news release, most assumed that a minister could state his personal views during a worship service so long as a disclaimer was made that the church was not endorsing or opposing those views. The IRS has taken a different position on this matter. A minister should be able to express personal views *outside* of an official church function so long as a disclaimer is made that the church is not endorsing or opposing a specific candidate for public office.

The IRS has issued further clarification about permissible political activity, stating that the prohibition from endorsing or opposing political candidates by nonprofit organizations "is not intended to restrict free expression on political matters by leaders of churches or religious organizations speaking for

---

[33]Richard Hammar, *Political Activities by Churches,* Church, L.& Tax Rep., Sept.–Oct. 1992, at 7–8.

themselves, as *individuals*. Nor are leaders prohibited from speaking about important issues of public policy."[34] The representative of the organization may state that the views expressed are personal. The IRS has given several examples on this matter.

Example 1

Minister A is the minister of Church J and is well known in the community. With their permission Candidate T publishes a full-page ad in the local newspaper listing five prominent ministers who have personally endorsed Candidate T, including Minister A. Minister A is identified in the ad as the minister of Church J. The ad states, "Titles and affiliations of each individual are provided for identification purposes only." The ad is paid for by Candidate T's campaign committee. Since the ad was not paid for by Church J, the ad is not in an official publication of Church J, and the endorsement is made by Minister A in a personal capacity, the ad does not constitute campaign intervention by Church J.

Example 2

Minister B is the minister of Church K. Church K publishes a monthly church newsletter that is distributed to all church members. In each issue Minister B has a column titled "My Views." The month before the election, Minister B states in the "My Views" column, "It is my personal opinion that Candidate U should be reelected." For that one issue, Minister B pays from his personal funds the portion of the cost of the newsletter attributable to the "My Views" column.

---

[34]IRS Publication 1828, at 7.

Even though he paid part of the cost of the newsletter, the newsletter is an official publication of the church. Since the endorsement appeared in an official publication of Church K, it constitutes campaign intervention attributed to Church K.

Example 3

Minister C is the minister of Church L and is well-known in the community. Three weeks before the election, he attends a press conference at Candidate V's campaign headquarters and states that Candidate V should be reelected. Minister C does not say he is speaking on behalf of his church. His endorsement is reported on the front page of the local newspaper, and he is identified in the article as the minister of Church L. Since Minister C did not make the endorsement at an official church function, in an official church publication, or otherwise use the church's assets, and did not state that he was speaking as a representative of Church L, his actions did not constitute campaign intervention attributable to Church L.

Example 4

Minister D is the minister of Church M. During regular services of Church M shortly before the election, Minister D preached on a number of issues, including the importance of voting in the upcoming election, and concluded by stating, "It is important that you all do your duty in the election and vote for Candidate W." Since Minister D's remarks indicating support for Candidate W were made during an official church service, they constitute political campaign intervention attributable to Church M.[35]

---

[35]*Id.* at 7–8.

When considering the above examples, leaders of non-profit organizations have a great deal of latitude in expressing their personal views about political candidates. Moreover, with respect to churches or other houses of worship, it should be remembered that only one church has ever lost its tax-exempt letter ruling for endorsing or opposing a political candidate, but even that church never lost its tax-exempt status.

In summary, nonprofit organizations may educate their members and the general public about the viewpoints of the various political candidates. These permissible activities include voter registration and "get out the vote" drives,[36] distribution of objective voter guides,[37] candidate forums and debates,[38] and most importantly, addressing social and political issues.[39]

Restrictions on Political Speech Immediately Prior to an Election

In 2002 the United States Congress amended the Federal Election Campaign Act by passing the Bipartisan Campaign Reform Act of 2002 (hereinafter "BCRA").[40] In addition to the Internal Revenue Code, this law also applies in part to certain activities of nonprofit organizations in regard to political campaigns. The law prohibits in some situations "electioneering communications" regarding (1) a *federal* candidate (2) by means of any broadcast, cable, or satellite communication,

---

[36]INTERNAL REVENUE MANUAL § 7.25.3.7.11.5.
[37]REV. RUL. 78–248, 1978–1 C.B. 154; REV. RUL. 80–282, 1980–2 C.B. 178.
[38]REV. RUL. 86–95, 1986–2 C.B. 73.
[39]*Walz v. Tax Comm'n,* 397 U.S. 664, 670 (1969). *See also Girard Trust Co. v. Commissioner,* 122 F.2d 108,110 (3d Cir. 1969) ("The step from acceptance by the believer to his seeking to influence others in the same direction is a perfectly natural one and is found in countless religious groups.").
[40]2 U.S.C. § 431 *et seq.*

(3) within sixty days of a general or runoff election or thirty days before a primary (4) that is targeted to the relevant electorate of the candidate.

While this law applies to nonprofit organizations, its application to churches and most nonprofit organizations is limited and will not apply in most cases because of the express exceptions stated in the law. Electioneering communications do not include any communication that (1) is publicly disseminated through a means of communication other than broadcast, cable, or satellite television or radio station,[41] (2) appears in a news story, commentary, or editorial distributed through the facilities of any broadcast, cable, or satellite television or radio station, unless such facilities are owned or controlled by any political party, political committee, or candidate,[42] (3) constitutes certain expenditures that are required to be reported under the law or by the Federal Election Commission, (4) constitutes a candidate debate or forum, (5) is not made by a national committee of a political party and is paid for by the candidate for state or local office in connection with a state or local election, or (6) is paid for by a 501(c)(3) organization.[43] In light of the above, the BCRA imposes few restrictions on speech by nonprofit organizations or their representatives.

---

[41]The following media is not included and thus not covered by the law: print media, including a newspaper, magazine, handbill, brochure, bumper sticker, yard sign, poster, billboard, and other written materials, including mailings; communications over the Internet, including electronic mail; or telephone communications.

[42]A news story distributed through a broadcast, cable, or satellite television or radio station owned or controlled by any political party, political committee, or candidate is exempt if the news story represents a bona fide news account and is part of a general pattern of campaign-related news coverage. *See* 2 U.S.C. § 100.29(c)(2) and 2 U.S.C. § 100.132.

[43]2 U.S.C. § 100.29(c)(1)-(6).

Comparative Overview of Permissible Activities

Having set forth the general rules governing the various organizations, the following chart is designed to compare the permissible activities of nonprofit groups and political action committees.

Clergy	(or representative)
501(c)(3)	(or church; tax-exempt and tax-deductible)
501(h)	(tax-exempt and tax-deductible)
501(c)(4)	(tax-exempt but not tax-deductible)
PAC	(not tax-exempt and not tax-deductible)

Legislative or Lobbying Activity

	Clergy	501(c)(3)	501(h)	501(c)(4)	PAC
1. Lobbying on issues unrelated to the organization's function or tax-exempt status.	Y	Y*	Y**	Y	Y

*Except that the lobbying activities cannot exceed a substantial part of the overall activities of the organization.

**If the lobbying activity is done through volunteer services; otherwise, an expenditure test must be used.

	Clergy	501(c)(3)	501(h)	501(c)(4)	PAC
2. Lobbying on issues directly related to the existence, powers and duties, exempt status, or the deductibility of contributions to the organizations.	Y	Y	Y	Y	Y

3. Educating the members of the organization orally or through written communication regarding the status of legislation in a non-partisan, objective manner without advocating a specific view on such legislation.[44]	Y	Y	Y	Y	Y

4. Educating the members of the organization orally or through written communication regarding the status of legislation and advocating a specific view on such legislation.

      Y[45]   Y*   Y**   Y   Y

*Except that such activities cannot exceed a substantial part of the organization's overall activities.

**If done by volunteer services; otherwise the expenditure test must be used.

---

[44]The IRS has indicated that an organization which objectively studies legislation in a nonpartisan manner and which compiles this information for distribution to the general public but neither proposes specific legislation nor advocates the passage or defeat of any pending legislation is not attempting to influence legislation. REV. RUL. 64–195, 1964–2 C.B. 138.

[45]See the above section on pastors and representatives of nonprofit organizations.

	Clergy	501(c)(3)	501(h)	501(c)(4)	PAC
5. Provide education regarding the political process and encourage members in a nonpartisan manner to become involved in the political process.	Y	Y	Y	Y	Y

*Except that such activities cannot exceed a substantial part of the organization's overall activities.

**If done by volunteer services; otherwise the expenditure test must be used.

	Clergy	501(c)(3)	501(h)	501(c)(4)	PAC
6. Petition drives.	Y	Y*	Y**	Y	Y

*Except that such activity should not exceed a substantial part of the organization's overall activities unless the petition drive directly relates to legislation affecting the function of the organization or the tax-exempt status of said organization.
**Same as above if performed by volunteer services; otherwise, the expenditure test should be used.

	Clergy	501(c)(3)	501(h)	501(c)(4)	PAC
7. Rental of organization's mailing list.	N/A	Y*	Y*	Y*	Y

*If rented at fair market value. Said list could be loaned to a legislative group such as a 501(c)(4) organization since the Federal Election Campaign Act[46] applies only to political campaigns.

Political Campaign Activity

	Clergy	501(c)(3)	501(h)	501(c)(4)	PAC
1. Endorsement of political candidates.	Y[47]	N	N	N	Y
2. Contributions to political campaigns.	Y	N	N	N	Y

---

[46]2 U.S.C. § 431.
[47]See the above section on pastors and representatives of nonprofit organizations.

3. In-kind and independent expenditures for or against political candidates.	Y	N	N	N	Y

4. Fund-raising for candidates.	Y[48]	N	N	N	Y

5. Introduction of political candidates at organization meetings.	Y[49]	Y*	Y*	Y*	Y

*But no endorsement.

6. Political candidates to speak at organization functions.	N/A	Y[50]	Y[51]	Y[52]	Y

---

[48]*Id.*

[49]*Id.*

[50]A political candidate can speak at a meeting hosted by a 501(c)(3) organization so long as the candidate does not overtly campaign; provided, however, that a political candidate may campaign in the context of a candidate forum where other candidates are present to discuss their viewpoints for the purpose of educating the members. Based on REV. RUL. 74–574, 1974–2 C.B. 160, a 501(c)(3) or 501(c)(4) organization may invite political candidates to address its members so long as (1) overt campaigning activities are avoided, (2) the same opportunity is afforded to other qualified candidates, and (3) the attendees are informed before or after the speech that the organization does not endorse any candidate for public office. However, a candidate could certainly preach at a church or address a nonprofit organization without the organization having to invite the candidate's opponent if no endorsements or campaigning activities occurred.

[51]*Id.*

[52]*Id.*

7. Nonpartisan voter registration.	Y	Y	Y	Y	Y
8. Distribution of candidate surveys and incumbent voting records which *do not* contain editorial opinions endorsing or opposing candidates.	Y	Y	Y	Y	Y
9. Distribution of candidate surveys and incumbent voting records which *do* contain editorial opinions endorsing or opposing candidates.	Y	N	N	N	Y
10. Maintaining a nonpartisan bulletin board regarding legislative and political campaign issues.	Y	Y*	Y*	Y*	Y
11. Distribution of political statements and political endorsements in lobbies or parking lots.	Y	Y*	Y*	Y*	Y

*If the organization allows all viewpoints to be presented in a nonpartisan manner without the organization's endorsement.

*If the distribution is not controlled or organized by the organization and distribution is also permitted for opposing viewpoints.

12. Use of the organization's facilities by political candidates.	N/A	Y*	Y*	Y*	Y

*If provided on a nonpartisan basis.[53]

13. Political forum where candidates are invited to discuss political viewpoints.	N/A	Y*	Y*	Y*	Y

*if done on a nonpartisan basis.[54]

14. Nonprofit radio or television media providing reasonable air time equally to all legally qualified candidates without endorsing a particular candidate.	N/A	Y[55]	Y	Y	Y

---

[53]See the above under Political Campaign Activity, example 6.

[54]*Id.*

[55]In 1974, the IRS stated that providing broadcasting facilities to "legally qualified candidates for elected public office furthers the education of the electorate by providing a public forum for the exchange of ideas and the debate of public issues which instructs them on subjects useful to the individual and beneficial to the community." The IRS stated that if the organization makes its facilities equally available to the candidates for public office, then this activity "does not make the expression of political views by the candidates the acts of the broadcasting station within the intendment of section 501(c)(3) of the Code." REV. RUL. 74–574, 1974–2 C.B. 160.

15. Supporting or opposing judicial appointments[56] to state or federal court or to the United States Supreme Court.	Y	Y*	Y*	Y*	Y

*Because such an appointee is not involved in a political campaign, but such activity may be construed as lobbying.

The following two situations, as proposed by the IRS, demonstrate permissible distribution of voter guides by a 501(c)(3), 501(h), or 501(c)(4) organization:

Situation 1

Organization A has been recognized as exempt under section 501(c)(3) of the Code by the Internal Revenue Service. As one of its activities, the organization annually prepares and makes generally available to the public a compilation of voting records of all members of Congress on major legislative issues involving a wide range of subjects. The publication contains no editorial opinion, and its contents and structure do not imply approval or disapproval of any members or their voting records.

The "voter education" activity of Organization A is not prohibited political activity within the meaning of section 501(c)(3) of the Code.

Situation 2

Organization B has been recognized as exempt under section 501(c)(3) of the Code by the Internal Revenue Service. As one of its activities in election years, it sends a questionnaire

---

[56]This only applies to *appointments,* not to *elective* positions.

to all candidates for governor in State M. The questionnaire solicits a brief statement of each candidate's position on a wide variety of issues. All responses are published in a voters' guide that it makes generally available to the public. The issues covered are selected by the organization solely on the basis of their importance and interest to the electorate as a whole. Neither the questionnaire nor the voters' guide, in content or structure, evidences a bias or preference with respect to the views of any candidate or group of candidates.

The "voter education" activity of Organization B is not prohibited political activity within the meaning of section 501(c)(3) of the Code.[57]

The following two situations, as proposed by the IRS, demonstrate improper distribution of voter guides by a 501(c)(3), 501(h), or 501(c)(4) organization:

Situation 3

Organization C has been recognized as exempt under section 501(c)(3) of the Code by the Internal Revenue Service. Organization C undertakes a "voter education" activity patterned after that of Organization B in Situation 2. It sends a questionnaire to candidates for major public offices and uses the responses to prepare a voters' guide which is distributed during an election campaign. Some questions evidence a bias on certain issues. By using a questionnaire structured in this way, Organization C is participating in a political campaign in contravention of the provisions of section 501(c)(3) and is disqualified as exempt under that section.[58]

---

[57]Rev. Rul. 78–248, 1978–1 C.B. 154.
[58]*Id.*

Situation 4

Organization D has been recognized as exempt under section 501(c)(3) of the Code. It is primarily concerned with land conservation matters. The organization publishes a voters' guide for its members and others concerned with land conservation issues. The guide is intended as a compilation of incumbents' voting records on selected land conservation issues of importance to the organization and is factual in nature. It contains no express statements in support of or in opposition to any candidate. The guide is widely distributed among the electorate during an election campaign.

While the guide may provide the voting public with useful information, its emphasis on one area of concern indicates that its purpose is not nonpartisan voter education. By concentrating on a narrow range of issues in the voters' guide and widely distributing it among the electorate during an election campaign, Organization D is participating in a political campaign in contravention of the provisions of section 501(c)(3) and is disqualified as exempt under that section.

Summary

It is important to note the difference between legislative activities and political campaigns. The IRS does not prohibit all involvement in lobbying or legislative activities, but this activity is somewhat restricted depending on the nature of the organization. According to the United States Supreme Court, an organization could divide its activities by incorporating as a 501(c)(3) tax-exempt and tax-deductible organization with certain lobbying limitations, and also by separately incorporating as a 501(c)(4) tax-exempt but not tax-deductible organization which has no lobbying limitations.[59]

There is no lobbying limit on a 501(c)(4) organization, but there are lobbying limits on a 501(c)(3) and a 501(h) organization. Only a handful of organizations have ever lost their tax-exempt status for engaging in too much political activity since the amendments to the Internal Revenue Code in 1934 on lobbying activities and 1954 on political campaign activities. However, no church has ever lost its tax-exempt *status* for engaging in political or lobbying activity.[60]

A 501(c)(3) organization is permitted to engage in certain lobbying activities as long as a substantial part of the organization's overall activities are not devoted to lobbying. A 501(c)(3) organization that makes a 501(h) election is permitted to engage in lobbying activities. The extent to which this type of organization may engage in lobbying activities is more clearly defined because an expenditure test is used. Unreimbursed volunteer services are not considered lobbying activities, and there is no limit upon a 501(h) organization's lobbying activities if it uses volunteers. A 501(c)(4) organization is specifically designed to engage in lobbying, and there are no restrictions on its lobbying activities. The main tax difference of a 501(c)(4), as compared to a 501(c)(3) and a 501(h), is that the former is tax-exempt, but contributions are not tax-deductible, while the latter are tax-exempt, and contributions to these organizations are tax-deductible.

---

[59]*Regan,* 461 U.S. at 540.
[60]Hammer, *Political Activities by Churches,* CHURCH L. & TAX REP., Sept.–Oct. 1992, at 2. Only one church has ever lost its IRS tax-exempt *letter* ruling for endorsing or opposing a political candidate, but even that one church never lost its tax-exempt *status.*

There is a strict prohibition against endorsing or opposing political candidates for public office in a political campaign. This prohibition applies to 501(c)(3), 501(h), and 501(c)(4) organizations. These organizations can still distribute literature designed to educate regarding candidate voting records or viewpoints provided that the voter education guides are nonpartisan and do not endorse or oppose candidates. Voter guides should avoid favorable or unfavorable ratings and be presented in an objective manner. These organizations may also encourage their members to vote and may engage in nonpartisan voter registration drives. Supporting or opposing a person to an *appointed* office is not considered supporting or opposing a candidate. Therefore, nonprofit organizations may support or oppose cabinet or judicial appointments.

Since pastors and representatives of nonprofit organizations are individuals, there are no restrictions regarding the amount of activity they may engage in with regard to legislative or political campaign issues. However, when a pastor or representative endorses a political candidate, it should be clear that the organization is not giving the endorsement.

Finally, Political Action Committees may engage in unrestricted legislative activities or political campaigns with the only limitation being state or federal reporting requirements.

Pastors, churches, nonprofit organizations, and their leaders can be involved in the political process. It is impossible for such people or organizations not to be involved in the political process, because the viewpoints and issues advocated by churches and nonprofit organizations naturally have political consequences. Avoiding the political process limits the effectiveness of churches and nonprofit organizations. The

United States Supreme Court has recognized that "churches frequently take strong positions on public issues including . . . vigorous advocacy of legal or constitutional positions. Of course, churches, as much as secular bodies and private citizens, have that right."[61]

[61]*Walz*, 397 U.S. at 670.

17
RELIGION AND THE FUTURE OF AMERICA

WHEN THE EARLY PIONEERS of this country landed on the shores of what later became known as America, they brought with them a vision. Although certainly not all were Christian, a large portion of the pioneers operated under a Judeo-Christian biblical worldview. This worldview taught them that history is not the monotonous repetitive cycle the Greeks once thought. History had a purpose. While certain events of history may repeat themselves, the Judeo-Christian worldview taught the pioneers that history was moving toward a conclusion. These pioneers were part of this conclusion. The role that many of them played was to bring the gospel of Jesus Christ to a new land. In a real sense, these pioneers were missionaries to America.

It is no wonder that when these missionaries landed, they erected crosses and enshrined monuments, mottos, policies, and laws respecting their Christian faith. It is also no wonder that when they framed their colonial documents, laws, and charters, they expressed the view that their purpose in life was to spread the gospel, that laws should be consistent with the Bible, and that law was derived and based upon the transcendent. Natural law was written on the hearts of every created human being and was capable of being understood. Special law came in the form of direct revelation as revealed in the Holy Scriptures.

In creating the federal government, the early Founders drew from two primary experiences. First, they were familiar with the monarchy from which they had come and did not want to repeat the mistakes of their motherland. Second, they realized human frailty and the inevitable reality that power corrupts, and absolute power corrupts absolutely. Thus, they created a federal government with limited powers, having checks and balances between three branches of government. In setting up this government, many of the founders realized that if God did not build this house of America, those who labored did so in vain.

The Founders recognized the importance of religion in the lives of the governed. With few exceptions they did not schizophrenically separate their religious views from public life. Since the Judeo-Christian ethic was the primary worldview, public schools naturally taught students how to read using biblical verses, and biblical stories often taught points of morality.[1] The average student who did not claim to be

---

[1] The *New England Primer* is a classic example of public education in American for more than two hundred years up through the early 1900s. This book was used as an entry level textbook by everyone entering school for the first hundred years after its publication in 1690 by Benjamin Harris in Boston, and for the next hundred years almost every student read from

Christian probably knew more about the Bible than many of today's youth who regularly attend church. Many of the Founders knew the original languages of the Bible. It was not unusual to study Greek and Latin. Today many students graduating from public schools do not even understand English.

Freedom and autonomy were important to the early Founders. They established the federal government to be a government of certain limited and prescribed powers, primarily banding the colonies together for the purpose of national defense and security. The individual colonies did not want the federal government to intrude into matters of the states, particularly with matters of religion and education. The Founders realized that with increased bureaucracy comes a concomitant decrease in liberties. As the federal government grew, freedom, and specifically religious freedom, would face tension.

Many of the individual states took on different and unique characteristics primarily because they were inhabited by people of different religious faiths or unique ethnic heritage. The individual states were not afraid to develop peculiarities different from their neighbors, and yet they all attempted to coexist and to assist one another where possible. As transportation increased, migration from one state to the next also increased. The federal government continued to increase in size and power, and along with this increase bureaucracy began to mount. Uniformity and political correctness became the unwritten rule of the day.

---

its well-known pages. Religion was a natural component in American public education. For example, when teaching students about the alphabet, the *New England Primer* taught the letter "A" with the following verse: "In Adam's Fall, we sinned all."

Many people have merged into a melting pot with differing religious backgrounds or no religious background. One of our historic mottos describes America as a unified country composed of many divergent backgrounds (E Pluribus Unum—Out of many one). Although America was a melting pot, we shared certain values, morals, and a common religious heritage. Today the emphasis by many is no longer on that which unifies Americans but on that which divides us. Multiculturalism and diversity as promoted today are not American ideals. Focusing on that which makes us different only serves to make us fractured. However, focusing on that which unifies us serves to make us one. One common denominator of American heritage has been our shared values, morals, and religious tradition. Today some people are determined to cause America to splinter and are focused on forcing secularism and amorality in our public schools by means of the courts.

There is a continuing struggle for the heart and soul of America. This struggle involves the Judeo-Christian heritage of this country and religious freedom. A growing bureaucratic federal government is not necessarily compatible with freedom, particularly religious freedom. To some extent this country mirrors the history of Egypt. In Egypt the pharaohs believed that they were gods. As gods, the pharaohs etched their names on monuments throughout the land. Many Egyptian pharaohs chiseled off the previous pharaohs' names and inscribed their own, as though they were the ones who had built the stone relics. Today the same thing is taking place in America. As bureaucracy continues to grow and the trend toward secularism and political correctness continues to mount, there is an increasing clash between a secularistic mind-set and a Judeo-Christian worldview. With the rise of secularism, the god of the state eats away the religious symbols of yesteryear.

As the federal government continues to gain power and as secularism advances, the symbols of our heritage are being removed one by one. For many years the city of St. Cloud, Florida, had a cross erected atop its water tower. Someone objected and filed suit. The cross is now gone. Only a bald water tower top remains. Corpus Christi, a city whose name means "the body of Christ," had for approximately four decades erected Latin crosses to commemorate Easter and the resurrection of Jesus Christ. Now it no longer does so. The crosses are gone. The city officials removed them out of fear of litigation, and the town became a victim of judicial terrorism.

The city of Zion, Illinois, had a Latin cross in its city seal draped with a ribbon that read "God Reigns." The seal was divided into four sections. One section contained the Latin cross, and the other three sections had a dove carrying a branch, a scepter, and a crown. The seal was designed in the early 1900s by the Reverend John Alexander Dowie, the city's founder and founder of the Christian Catholic Church. The city of Zion was established for "the purpose of the extension of the Kingdom of God upon earth." The city was taken to court, and now the seal has been altered. The cross has been removed.[2]

A painting of Jesus was donated to a Michigan school and displayed in the school hallway. Although this painting had hung on the wall for many years, one parent objected and

---

[2]*Harris v. City of Zion,* 927 F.2d 1401 (7th Cir. 1991).

took the school to court. Even though the painting was like similar paintings that depicted great leaders, the court stated that the painting must be removed because Jesus was the founder of the Christian religion. When you walk through this particular school today, the painting is gone. Another victim of judicial activism.

In 1960 the Illinois town of Rolling Meadows adopted a city seal designed for a school art assignment by an eighth-grade student. This seal was shaped like a four-leaf clover. The seal contained pictures of a school, industrial buildings, a church, and a Latin cross. The student designed the Latin cross to depict the many churches in the area. Decades later, after someone objected to this cross, a federal court forced its removal from the seal. The city seal has now been changed and the cross is gone.[3]

In Wicker Memorial Park in Highland, Indiana, once stood a twenty-foot crucifix erected by the Knights of Columbus in 1955 as a memorial to fallen World War II veterans. The figure of Jesus hung from this crucifix for thirty-eight years overlooking the public park. Five residents objected to the crucifix and brought suit in federal court, claiming that the display violated the Constitution. After a long legal battle, the appellate court ruled that the crucifix was unconstitutional. Bringing their cranes to the park, the city officials lowered the cross to the ground—a scene reminiscent of when the real cross and the real Jesus were lowered to the ground after his death. The crucifix is now gone, and the city of Highland became another victim of judicial activism.

---

[3]*Id.*

When I attended public school, I remember that each day was opened with a prayer and the Pledge of Allegiance. Opening class with prayer today is now foreign to public school students. My public school used to have Christmas holidays, but now public school students have winter holidays. Whenever public schools had Christmas concerts, it was natural to sing religious Christmas carols. Now school officials are jittery about putting religious Christmas carols in public school music. I will never forget the day President John F. Kennedy was assassinated. The teachers gathered all of our classes into a big auditorium, and we watched the news on television. We were led by our teachers to pray on behalf of our fallen president. If that event would have taken place today, prayer probably would not be allowed.

In 1990 I traveled to Moscow in the former Soviet Union with a delegation of attorneys to participate in a constitutional conference between the USSR and the USA. The purpose of this interchange was to give ideas to the Soviet Union regarding the adoption and formation of a new constitutional form of government. While in the Kremlin, I was able to visit the church museums with their beautiful gold onion domes. Inside these beautiful structures, the walls, including the ceilings and the enormous pillars, were painted with religious themes. Everywhere the eye could see were pictures of early New Testament events and other great Christian leaders throughout history. I was awed by these massive structures and also somewhat saddened. These churches had actually been thriving centers for religious worship in the very heart of the Kremlin. When the Soviet atheistic government took control, these churches lost their religious worship. Interestingly, the structures remained as relics to a bygone era and were used only as museums. I remember thinking that had those same "church museums" been in America, they would likely be ruled unconstitutional because of their religious heritage. In America I wonder whether we will even have religious relics or continue to push all religious history and memory from existence.

During one of the meetings, a Soviet attorney sitting across the aisle stood up and announced to those assembled how thankful he was to be able to sit in a room with Americans. He expressed that in 1987, America celebrated the two hundredth anniversary of the Constitution, and he congratulated us. He hoped that the Soviet Union could do the same as it was moving through those days of transition. He stated he was so proud and privileged to be able to sit beside an American.

The words of this Soviet attorney have been etched forever in my mind. I am proud to be an American, but it is certainly a different America than what our Founders envisioned. When Alexis de Tocqueville traveled this country in the 1830s, he stated, "The religious aspect of the country was the first thing that struck my attention."[4] If Alexis de Tocqueville returned to America today in the twenty-first century, I wonder what would impress him now? When he visited our public schools, would he be impressed by the religious influence? When the class began, would he hear a prayer? Would he look at an instructional book and see religious influences? When he talked to our representative leaders, on either a state or federal level, would he be impressed

---

[4]Alexis de Tocqueville, 1 DEMOCRACY IN AMERICA 319 (J.P. Mayer, ed., George Lawrence, trans., Doubleday, 1975).

by their desire to serve this country out of a sense of mission? Or, instead, would he be impressed with the rising tide of teenage pregnancy, suicide, abortion, juvenile crime, and indiscriminate killing? Would he feel safe when he entered our nation's capitol, one of the leading crime areas in the world? What would impress Alexis de Tocqueville today? Would it be the religious aspect of this country, or would it be its secularistic trend? Would it be the fact that we are one of the most illiterate countries in the world, that we are removing our nativity scenes from public property, or that we are erasing all of our religious heritage?

Yes, the early Founders did have a vision. This vision was inspired by their Judeo-Christian worldview. They came to this country for a purpose—to advance the gospel. Our country is slowly losing its religious vision, slowly losing the knowledge of its place in history. As the United States begins to melt into a one-world government, we lose our uniqueness which is our contribution to the world. Without a religious cohesiveness and biblical worldview, society will unravel. Virtue will be replaced with vice, compassion with crime, and optimism will fade into cynicism. Having no Judeo-Christian worldview or no religious heritage, a society left with only secularism will disintegrate and destroy itself. Having to answer to no higher power and recognize no other world existence, society left with no absolutes will come unglued at the seams.

The struggle for the heart and soul of this country is real. The contents of this book are not simply theoretical and are not just legal jargon. The issue of religious freedom in the public square is really the battle for the heart and soul of America. If we lose our religious freedom, then we have lost

America. As religion goes, so goes America. The early Founders knew the importance of religion in society, and they were willing to forsake their homes, their comfort, their families and even sacrifice their lives for freedom.

Today we have grown complacent, having graciously inherited the freedom of our forefathers. If we do not catch the vision that they once held, if we let the flame of freedom that they carried die out, if we are not willing to sacrifice and put our lives on the line for freedom in whatever battle we face, then this country, as we now know it, will come to an end. Like an avalanche of snow tumbling down a mountain, it will crumble as surely as world governments have crumbled in the past decades. I love this country too much to sit by and let that happen.

There is hope for America. Despite all the negative things we hear and read, I am encouraged. From my vantage point I see more victories than defeats. The difference between victory and defeat, triumph and tragedy, good and evil is one person standing in the gap, armed with knowledge and called by God's grace. If we whine and moan but fail to show up for battle, then the result is pre-scripted. We lose, plain and simple.

I am optimistic about our future because I encounter scores of people like Morgan Nyman, who, while in second grade, was told she could not distribute her Valentine cards to classmates because they contained religious messages. One of Morgan's cards contained the words, "Jesus loves you—pass it on." Her classmates were allowed to distribute their cards with secular messages from such characters as Harry Potter. Not willing to walk away from this issue, Morgan and her parents contacted Liberty Counsel. The evening we filed suit, Morgan's case received top billing from all the local television media. The stations would describe the story, show the school, and pan to cute little Morgan with her long blonde hair, holding her Valentine card. Then the TV screens were filled with the message of the card, "Jesus loves you—pass it on." The next morning Morgan's story received the top headline on the front page above the fold in the *Milwaukee Journal*. The media was so intense that Morgan's mom asked her the morning after the suit if she wanted to move forward with the case. Morgan responded, "Yep, mom. I prayed three times this morning. I want to stand up for what I believe. I'm ready to go to school!" The national media picked up the story, and we won the case. As a result, we drafted, and the district adopted, a comprehensive school board policy that protects the religious expression of students in a multitude of areas, not just the distribution of Valentine cards.

The following year on Valentine's Day, I was in a Los Angeles federal court fighting for the rights of the Good News Club, sponsored by Child Evangelism Fellowship, to have equal access to school facilities at the end of the school day (a case which we won). On the flight back to Orlando, I thought about Morgan. When I arrived back at the office the next day, there on my desk was a Valentine card from Morgan. I immediately called Morgan's Mom and asked if she distributed her Christian Valentine cards. As expected, she did.

Morgan is a modern-day pioneer. I encounter many of them each week. When one who is called by God's grace takes a principled stand, we usually win, and our liberties are usually preserved. That's why I am encouraged. The mission of Liberty Counsel is to restore the culture one case at a time by advancing religious freedom, the sanctity of human life, and the traditional family. We are passionate about this mission. If we remain faithful, and if we take our liberties seriously, and if we value life and family, we can ensure that America remains a beacon of freedom to the world and an example for all to follow.

APPENDIX

First Amendment Outline

I. Identify the parties.
   A. Governmental actor and
   B. Private actor.
II. Identify the forum.
   A. Traditional public forum.
      1. Streets
      2. Sidewalks or
      3. Parks.
   B. Limited or designated public forum.
      1. Any facility which the government intentionally opens for expressive activity.
      2. Government may open any facility for expressive activity but may also close the facility to preserve the facility for its intended purpose.
   C. Nonpublic forum.
      1. Any government facility which is not intentionally opened for expressive activity.
      2. Examples include airports, transportation facilities, or utility poles.

III. Identify the restriction.
   A. Content-neutral,
   B. Content-based,
   C. Viewpoint-based, or
   D. Prior restraint.

Free Speech Clause

I. Content-Neutral Restriction.
   A. Traditional public forum.
      1. Must be a substantial or significant governmental interest.
      2. Reasonable time, place, and manner restrictions must be narrowly tailored.
      3. Must leave open ample alternative means of expression.
   B. Limited or designated public forum.
      1. Must be a substantial or significant governmental interest.
      2. Reasonable time, place, and manner restrictions must be narrowly tailored.
      3. Must leave open ample alternative means of expression.
   C. Nonpublic forum.
      1. Must be a substantial or significant governmental interest.
      2. Restrictions must be reasonable and rationally related to the governmental interest.
II. Content Restriction.
   A. Traditional public forum.
      1. Must be a compelling governmental interest.

2. Any restriction must be the least restrictive means available.

B. Limited or designated public forum.
   1. Must be a compelling governmental interest.
   2. Any restriction must be the least restrictive means available.

C. Nonpublic forum.
   1. Must be a substantial or significant governmental interest.
   2. Restrictions must be reasonable and rationally related to the governmental interest.

III. Viewpoint Restriction.

A. Traditional public forum.
   1. Prohibited.
   2. Rationale is that government cannot take sides in any debate by allowing one viewpoint to the exclusion of another.

B. Limited or designated public forum.
   1. Prohibited.
   2. Rationale is that government cannot take sides in any debate by allowing one viewpoint to the exclusion of another.

C. Nonpublic forum.
   1. Prohibited.
   2. Rationale is that government cannot take sides in any debate by allowing one viewpoint to the exclusion of another.

IV. Prior Restraint.

A. Presumptively unconstitutional.

B. Must have specific time for granting or refusal to grant permit.

C. Must not permit governmental discretion to grant or deny speech without specific objective standards.

D. Must provide that the government has the burden to file suit to substantiate any denial of speech.

Symbolic Speech

I. Symbolic Speech.

A. The regulation must be within the constitutional power of the government.

B. The regulation must further an important or substantial governmental interest.

C. The governmental interest must be unrelated to the suppression of speech.

D. The incidental restriction must be no greater than essential to the furtherance of that interest.

Injunctions

I. Content-Neutral Injunction.

A. Heightened level of scrutiny stricter than the time, place, and manner test.

B. Must not burden more speech than necessary to achieve its objective.

II. Content-Based Injunction.

A. Presumptively invalid.

B. Must have a compelling governmental interest.

C. Must be the least restrictive means available.

Prisoner Rights

I. Prisoner Rights.
   A. Government must have a legitimate penological interest.
   B. Restriction must be reasonably related to the governmental interest.

Free Exercise Clause

I. Pre-1990 Test.
   A. Sincerely held religious belief negatively impacted or burdened by some governmental rule or regulation.
   B. Must be a compelling governmental interest.
   C. Must be the least restrictive means available to achieve the governmental interest.
II. Post-1990 Test.
   A. Any general law of neutral applicability will be upheld.
   B. Pre-1990 test will be used only in the following circumstances.
      1. If the law specifically targets religion for discriminatory treatment or
      2. The Free Exercise right is combined with some other constitutional right.

Establishment Clause

I. The *Lemon* Test.
   A. Must have a secular purpose.
   B. The governmental action must not primarily promote, endorse, or inhibit religion.

    C. The governmental action must not excessively foster governmental entanglement with religion.

II. Coercion Test.

    A. Whether the governmental action coerces private individuals toward religion.

    B. Coercion may be direct or indirect.

III. The Historical Test.

    A. Review history surrounding the First Amendment.

    B. Determine the original intent of the Amendment.

	TRADITIONAL PUBLIC FORUM (can never close) Street, Sidewalk, Parks	LIMITED OR DESIGNATED PUBLIC FORUM (can close or open) Any Government Facility Intentionally Opened	NONPUBLIC FORUM Airport, Transportation Facility, Utility Poles
Content Neutral	1. Substantial government interest. 2. Reasonable time, place, and manner restrictions must be narrowly tailored. 3. Leave open ample alternative means of expression.	1. Substantial government interest. 2. Reasonable time, place, and manner restrictions must be narrowly tailored. 3. Leave open ample alternative means of expression.	1. Substantial government interest. 2. Reasonable restrictions.
Content Based	1. Compelling government interest. 2. Least restrictive means.	1. Compelling government interest. 2. Least restrictive means.	1. Substantial government interest. 2. Reasonable restrictions.
Viewpoint Based	1. Prohibited *Example: Allow abortion speech but only pro-choice view.*	1. Prohibited *Example: Allow abortion speech but only pro-choice view.*	1. Prohibited *Example: Allow abortion speech but only pro-choice view.*

Symbolic Speech	Prior Restraint	Injunctions

1. Regulation must be within the constitutional power of the government.
2. Must further an important or substantial governmental interest.
3. Government interest must be unrelated to the suppression of speech.
4. The incidental restriction must be no greater than essential to the furtherance of that interest.*
 	
*This four-part test is essentially the same as the time, place, and manner test with content-neutral restriction. (See *Ward v. Rock Against Racism*, 491 U.S. 781 (1989).)
	1. Presumptively invalid.
	2. Valid only if
	  A. Delay is brief.
	  B. Specific time is given for granting or denial of speech.
	  C. Specific guidelines prohibit government discretion by creating neutral objective standards.
	  D. Burden is on the government to file suit to support its denial.
		1. Content Neutral
		  A. Heightened scrutiny above time, place and manner restriction.
		  B. Must not burden more speech than necessary to accomplish the injunction's objective.
		2. Content Based
		  A. Since a content-based injunction is also a prior restraint, it is presumptively invalid, with the burden to prove its validity on the government.
		  B. Compelling governmental interest.
		  C. Least restrictive means.

PRISONS	FREE EXERCISE	ESTABLISHMENT CLAUSE

1. Must have legitimate penological interest.
2. Restriction must be reasonably related to penological interest.
	1. Pre-1990 Test
	  A. Must show sincerely held religious belief is burdened by government.
	  B. Must be compelling governmental interest.
	  C. Must achieve interest in least restrictive means available.
	2. Post-1990 Test
	  A. Any general law of neutral applicability will be upheld.
	  B. Pre-1990 test used only if
	    1. Law targets religion for discriminatory treatment, or
	    2. Free exercise right is combined with another constitutional right.
		1. *Lemon* Test
		  A. Must be a secular purpose.
		  B. Must not primarily promote, endorse, or inhibit religion.
		  C. Must not foster excessive governmental entanglement.
		2. Coercion Test
		  A. Government must not coerce religious beliefs.
		  B. Used sometimes in graduation prayer cases.
		3. Historical Test
		  A. Determine historical meaning and intent of First Amendment.
		  B. Used in legislative prayer cases.

TABLE OF
AUTHORITIES

ABOUT THE AUTHOR

Mathew Staver is an attorney specializing in appellate practice, free speech, and religious liberty constitutional law. He serves as President and General Counsel of Liberty Counsel, Vice President of Law and Policy and member of the Board of Trustees for Liberty University, and Chairman of the Steering Committee of Liberty University School of Law.

Liberty Counsel is a nonprofit litigation, education and policy organization dedicated to advancing religious freedom, the sanctity of human life and the traditional family. Established in 1989, Liberty Counsel is a national organization headquartered in Orlando, Florida, with branch offices in Virginia and hundreds of affiliate attorneys in all 50 states. The Center for Constitutional Litigation and Policy ("Center") operates as one component of Liberty Counsel's training, education, and public policy program. The Center is headquartered on the campus of Liberty University School of Law in Lynchburg, Virginia. The Center trains attorneys, law students, policymakers, legislators, clergy, and world leaders in constitutional principles and government policies.

Staver graduated Summa Cum Laude with a Master's degree in Religion. He was an honorary guest lecturer at the American Society of Oriental Research. He authored *Quest for the Historical Jesus: An Inquiry into the Historicity of the Passion Predictions*. He reads Hebrew, Greek, Aramaic and Syriac. Staver became a pastor and later graduated from the University of Kentucky law school where he was captain of the National Moot Court team.

Staver has argued in numerous state and federal courts across the country. He has appeared on numerous briefs before the United States Supreme Court and has argued before the High Court in the landmark Ten Commandments case of *McCreary County v. ACLU of Kentucky* and the free speech picketing case of *Madsen v. Women's Health Center*. He has authored hundreds of articles and written ten books, including *Same-Sex Marriage: Putting Every Household at Risk*, *Faith and Freedom: A Complete Handbook for Defending Your Religious Rights*, *Take Back America*, *Religious Expression in Public Schools*, *Religion and the Future of America*, *Political Activity of Nonprofit Organizations*, *Union Membership and Its Constitutional Implications*, *Same-Sex Marriage*, and *Judicial Tyranny*. Mr. Staver is considered one of the premier constitutional litigators in the country and conducts hundreds of media interviews each year.

If you are interested in becoming involved in the ministry of Liberty Counsel, please contact:

Liberty Counsel   800-671-1776

P.O. Box 540774   407-875-0770 (Fax)

Orlando, FL 32854   www.lc.org (Web site)

407-875-2100   liberty@lc.org (E-mail)

ABOUT LIBERTY COUNSEL

Liberty Counsel is a nonprofit religious civil liberties education and legal defense organization established to preserve religious freedom. Founded in 1989 by president and general counsel, Mathew D. Staver, Liberty Counsel accomplishes its purpose in a two-fold manner: through education and through legal defense.

Liberty Counsel produces many aids to educate in matters of religious liberty. *Freedom's Call* is a two-minute daily radio program produced by Liberty Counsel providing education in First Amendment religious liberties. *Faith and Freedom* is a fifteen-minute daily radio program dedicated to religious liberty, free speech and pro-family matters.

Liberty Counsel has produced many brochures, booklets and monograms outlining various aspects of religious liberty. Most of the cases in which Liberty Counsel is involved resolve through education, either by a telephone call, informative literature, or letters. Many individuals and public officials are ignorant of the First Amendment. Religious rights are often restricted or lost simply out of this ignorance. Liberty

Counsel also has cassettes covering a variety of religious liberty topics.

Unfortunately, education will not solve all religious liberty issues. Some individuals are hostile and bigoted toward religion. If education does not resolve the issue, Liberty Counsel aggressively fights for religious liberty in the courtroom. Liberty Counsel represents individuals whose religious liberties are infringed, and defends entities against those trying to restrict religious liberty. Liberty Counsel attorneys frequently argue cases throughout the country, including the United States Supreme Court.

Liberty Counsel is a nonprofit tax-exempt corporation dependent upon public financial support. Contributions to Liberty Counsel are tax-deductible. For information about Liberty Counsel, or to make tax-deductible contributions, please write or call:

> Liberty Counsel
> P.O. Box 540774
> Orlando, Florida 32854
> (407) 875-2100
> (800) 671-1776
> (407) 875-0770 (Fax)
> www.lc.org (Web site)
> liberty@lc.org (E-mail)

INDEX

Eternal Vigilance

Index

Index